SOMEBODY'S BROTHER

A History of The Salvation Army Men's Social Service Department

1891—1985

E. H. McKINLEY

Studies in American Religion
Volume 21

The Edwin Mellen Press
Lewiston/Queenston

Library of Congress Cataloging-in-Publication Data

McKinley, Edward H.
  Somebody's brother.

  (Studies in american religion ; v. 21)
  Bibliography: p.
  Includes index.
  1. Salvation Army. Men's Social Service Department--
History. 2. Church work with alcoholics--United States.
3. Church charities--United States. I. Title.
BX9727.3.M34 1986   267'.15   86-8604
ISBN 0-88946-665-3 (alk. paper)

This is volume 21 in the continuing series
Studies in American Religion
Volume 21 ISBN 0-88946-665-3
SAR Series ISBN 0-88946-992-X

Dedicated to My Mother,
With Love and Gratitude

Throw out the lifeline across the
    dark wave,
There is a brother whom someone
    should save;
Somebody's brother! O who then
    will dare
To throw out the lifeline, his
    peril to share?

From Song "Throw Out the Lifeline!"
by Edward S. Ufford, 1884

Table of Contents

Acknowledgements

The research upon which this book was based was carried out over three years, from 1982 through 1985. The number of persons who assisted the author in the work of collecting information and materials for the project is large, and to all of those whose names appear on the following list, he expresses again his warmest thanks. The author anticipated cooperation from many persons before the project began, but the extent of official and personal encouragement, assistance and hospitality which he encountered at every point in what became an extensive and nationwide project so far exceeded expectations as to convert the work of interviewing, study and research into a positive and memorable pleasure.

It is a mistake to select from this list names for special recognition, not because so many do not warrant mention but because the risk of omitting one no less worthy gives pause. Nevertheless, a simple listing of names cannot convey the special thanks which must go to the many persons whose kindness, interest and cooperation not only made the path of research possible, but smoothed it and made it delightful.

Among the very many retired officers who were interviewed for this project, special mention and the author's warmest personal thanks go, with renewed expressions of personal respect, to Brigadier Lawrence Castagna, who freely shared his memories and his large personal collection of Salvation Army historical materials, and who several times made suggestions that opened lines of research that led to important contributions to the finished book, and which would otherwise have passed unnoticed; Lt.-Colonel Peter J. Hofman, who kindly agreed to several interviews, who answered a myriad of questions, who kindly lent or donated many valuable documents and photographs; and Brigadier Cecil Briggs, who likewise placed his enormous personal knowledge of the development of the department and many valuable historical materials at the author's disposal. Brigadier William Jobe and Mr. A. Ernest Agnew kindly provided extensive taped responses to questions. In addition these officers and Mrs. Major Andrew (Annie) Laurie provided invaluable information through lengthy correspondence.

The author conducted extensive research in each of the four territorial headquarters of The Salvation Army. Every officer and employee, on every level of Army administration, was warmly, often enthusiastically helpful, and the author looks back upon the time spent in these headquarters as both profitable and personally pleasurable. Commissioner Will Pratt and Colonel James Osborne (Western THQ) were especially encouraging and helpful; Colonel Willard Evans (Eastern THQ), Colonel Stanley Ditmer (Southern THQ) and Colonel Andrew S. Miller (Central THQ) generously gave of their time, interest and official encouragement. A large part of the research was carried out in the offices of the four men's social service departments, in each of which the secretary and staff were so friendly and helpful as to practically turn the office over to the author. No file was too difficult to locate, no question too obscure or time-consuming, that someone was not just willing but pleased to cooperate. The author wishes especially to offer, again, warm personal thanks and respects to Lt.-Colonel and Mrs. Raymond Howell, to Lt.-Colonel William Hasney, to Lt.-Colonel David Mulbarger and to Major David Allen, who served as guides and hosts in New York, Chicago, Atlanta and Rancho Palos Verdes and who gave the author many hours of valuable time in interviews and in assistance in locating information. In this way they were ably assisted in each case by the general secretary: Brigadier Harold Banta (New York); Major Leonard Caldwell (Chicago), both the general secretary and the assistant men's social service secretary; Major Travis Israel and Major A. S. Peters—an invaluable storehouse of information—in Atlanta; and Major George Baker (Rancho Palos Verdes). The author was especially fortunate at Western THQ to interview Lt.-Colonel Warren C. Johnson as well.

The author visited several adult rehabilitation centers in each Army territory. In each case the administrator and his staff were hospitable, cooperative and full of valuable information, both about current operations and about the development of the program over time. Special notice must go to several administrators who gave the author several days of their time and so arranged the visits to their centers that a visitor could gain as much knowledge as was possible in limited time: Major George Duplain (San Francisco and Pinehurst) and Major Norman V. Nonnweiler (Detroit); Major Nonnweiler also kindly arranged for Brigadier Cecil Briggs to be on hand for the entire visit as well. Major Arthur Ferreira (Jersey City), Captain William Stephens (Newark), Captain Timothy Raines (Manhattan), Brigadier Lawrence Castagna (who in addition to all his other assistance showed the author through the Columbus ARC), Major Glen Winters (Miami), Major Don Watts (Atlanta), Major Israel Velazquez (Chicago Central) and Major Richard Anson (Sacramento) gave much valuable information and were excellent hosts.

The single best source of historical materials for this, or any serious study into the history of The Salvation Army, is the Army's own Archives and Research Center in New York City. Mr. Thomas Wilsted, the archivist-administrator and his able assistant, Judith Johnson, were as always, exceptionally helpful, offering unfailing cooperation in a wide variety of ways over several extensive periods of research.

Much in the way of priceless Army historical material remains in private hands, and the author wishes, again, to pay special tribute both to the care with which several officers have collected and preserved these materials and to the generosity with which they shared these valuable items with the author. The collection of Colonel Paul Seiler (R), Ocean Grove, NJ, is the largest such in the USA and was indispensable for this project. Commissioner Richard E. Holz (R), Neptune, NJ, generously shared many items in the family collection. Brigadier Lawrence Castagna (R) and Major John Busby, Atlanta, also kindly shared their large private collections with the author.

All four territorial Schools for Officers' Training have libraries and museums. The author visited each of these and in each experienced again prompt, cheerful and complete cooperation and warm hospitality. Special thanks are due to Major W. Todd Bassett (Suffern), to Major Raymond Cooper, Margaret Moore and Alfreda Matthews (Atlanta), to Major Donald Arnold (Chicago) and to Lt.-Colonel R. Eugene Rice and Major Glen Gilden in Rancho Palos Verdes. Warm personal thanks, too, to dear old friends who provided the author with the warmth and hospitality of a home during several of the long research trips: Captain and Mrs. James Farrell (Atlanta), Mr. and Mrs. Doug McMahon, Sr. (Ocean Grove) and Mr. and Mrs. Doug McMahon, Jr. (Chicago).

The author wishes to pay special respects to Major Dorothy Breen, the literary secretary for the Eastern Territory and the official liaison and coordinating officer for this project. The major is an officer of commitment, experience and great ability, whose encouragement and guidance, and whose ability to supervise a dozen details at once, have been indispensable. The major entered into an honored and well-deserved retirement as this project neared completion, and will be sorely missed by this author.

Finally, the author wishes to thank Dr. Howard Barnett and the Asbury College Faculty Research and Development Committee, and the College Board of Trustees, who provided a work-leave for one academic quarter during which the author could devote himself entirely to work on the manuscript. This period of concentrated work made it possible to complete the project on schedule.

Acknowledgement of Sources in Alphabetical Order

Aarsen, Peter ◇
Agnew, A. Ernest ◇
Agnew, Mrs. Brig. Fletcher ◆
Allen, Major David ◇ ◆ +
Anderson, Brig. Marie P. ◇
Anson, Major Richard ◆
Arnold, Major Donald +
Baker, B/M Charles ◇
Baker, Major George ◇ ◆ +
Banta, Brig. Harold ◇ ◆ +
Barnett, Dr. Howard +
Barrett, Col. Giles ◆
Bassett, Major W. Todd +
Baxendale, Col. David ◇ +
Bevan, Mrs. Brig. Harold ◆
Blothe, Mrs. Brig. John ◆
Breen, Major Dorothy ◇ +
Briggs. Brig. Cecil ◇ +
Britcher, Major Eric +
Browning, Mrs. Brig. William A. ◇
Burch, Major Lester ◇
Burr, Brig. Howard +
Caldwell, Major Leonard ◆ +
Carr, Ronald ◇
Castagna, Brig. Lawrence ◇ ◆ +
Chamberlain, Mrs. Comm. William E. ◇
Charron, Lt. Col. William ◆
Conrath, Lt. Col. Wallace ◇
Cooper, Major Raymond ◆ +
Craytor, Mrs. Brig. Arthur ◆
Crispell, Charles ◆
Dimond, Major Edward ◇ ◆
Dimond, Mrs. Dorothy Hamley ◇ ◆

Dingman, Frances +
Ditmer, Col. Stanley ◆ +
Duplain, Major George ◊ ◆ +
Dyer, Frank ◊ ◆
Eccleston, Brig. Everett ◆
Edelman, Captain Roy C. ◆
Ellis, Major Houston ◊ +
Evans, Col. Willard ◊ ◆ +
Fahey, Mrs. Brig. John ◊
Farell, Captain and Mrs. James
Ferreira, Major Arthur ◆
Fleming, Lt. Col. Hartwell ◆ +
Frieman, Ray +
Gariepy, Lt. Col. Henry ◆
Gearing, Mrs. Comm. Ray ◊
Genge, Brig, Frank ◆
Gesner, Brig. Eugene ◊
Gilden, Major Glen +
Gilkey, Dorothy +
Gouldron, Orpha Barden +
Greer, Major Duane ◊
Guldenschuh, Col. Frank ◆
Hansen, Brig. Martha ◆ +
Harvey, Mrs. Senior/Major William ◆
Hasney, Lt. Col. William ◊ ◆ +
Hawley, Brig. Royce W. ◆
Hayes, Brig. Ernest A. ◆
Hillis, Brig. William B. ◆
Himes, B/M William ◊
Hofman, Lt. Col. Peter J. ◊ ◆
Hofman, Major Peter ◆
Holmes, Brig. Hubert ◊ ◆
Holz, Comm. Richard E. ◊ ◆
Holz, B/M Dr. Ronald ◊
Howell, Lt. Col. Raymond ◊ ◆ +
Howell, Mrs. Lt. Col. Raymond (Faye) ◊ ◆ +
Irwin, Mrs. Brig. Ronald ◆
Israel, Major Travis ◆ +
Jefferson, Natalie +
Jobe, Brig. William ◊
Johnson, Judith ◊ +
Johnson, Lt. Col. Warren C. ◆
Judge, John ◆
Korn, Arthur H. ◊
Ksanda, Kay ◆
Lane, Aux. Captain Jim ◆

Larsen, Major Ronald ◇ ♦
Laurie, Mrs. Major Andrew (Annie) ◇
Layman, Mrs. Colonel Archibald ◇
Liston, Captain Marcia Jones ◇
Lock, Brig. Albert ♦
Lodge, Damon ◇
McCabe, Thomas ♦
McCormick, Brig. Archibald ♦
McCrea, Major Ruth ◇
McMahon, Mr. and Mrs. Douglas, Sr.
McMahon, Mr. and Mrs. Douglas, Jr.
McMahon, Tom ♦
Marshall, Major Paul ◇
Marshall, Mrs. Major Paul +
Matthes, Major Evelyn ◇
Matthews, Major Alfreda +
Merritt, Major Brian ♦
Miller, Col. Andrew S. ◇ ♦ +
Miller, Kim M. ◇
Moore, Major Daniel +
Moore, Major Margaret ♦ +
Moulton, Lt. Col. David W. ♦
Mulbarger, Lt. Col. David ◇ ♦ +
Nilson, Major Birgitta ◇
Nonnweiler, Captain Norman R. ♦
Nonweiler, Major Norman V. ◇ ♦ +
Oldford, Lt. Col. Roy ◇ +
Oliver, Brig. Esther ♦
Osborne, Col. James ◇ ♦ +
Pack, Brenda +
Paton, Col. John ◇ ♦ +
Pedersen, Major LeRoy +
Pedersen, Rob +
Peters, Major A. S. ◇ ♦ +
Pratt, Comm. William +
Rader, Lt. Col. Lyell ◇
Raines, Capt. Timothy ◇ ♦ +
Riley, Lt. Col. David ◇ ♦ +
Ross, Charles ♦
Rost, Sharon +
Ruthstrom, Brig. Sven ◇
Sacks, Major Lorraine +
Schuerholz, Senior/Major Charles ♦
Scott, Col. Albert ♦ +
Seiler, Col. Paul ♦ +
Seiler, Lt. Col. Paul ◇

Skepper, Captain Corliss +
Smith, Brig. Lloyd ◆
Smith, Brig. Wilbur ◆
Sparks, Brig. Herbert ◆
Squibb, Mrs. Brig. Walter ◆
Stephan, Mrs. Brig. Henry ◆
Stephens, Capt. William ◆ +
Thompson, Capt. June +
Tobin, Major Robert ◊ +
Troutt, Brig. John ◆
Troutt, Mrs. Brig. John (Margaret) ◊
Valdez, Jennie +
Velazquez, Major Israel ◆ +
Vandeville, Mrs. Brig. William ◆
Waiksnoris, B/M Ronald ◊
Watts, Major Donald ◆ +
Wescott, Mrs. Comm. Herbert ◊
Wilsted, Thomas +
Winters, Major Glen ◆ +
Wiseman, Lt. Col. Herbert ◊ ◆ +
Wright, Mrs. Brig. Stanley ◆
Yellis, Mrs. Patty ◊

explanation of symbols:

◆ = interview
◊ = correspondence, tapes
+ = administrative assistance; access to materials; information

CHAPTER I

In Darkest America, 1880–1896

Some of them, a few, killed themselves. The rest died badly enough, but slowly, less dramatically. Most of them were poisoned at last by a ruined liver or kidneys, suffocated by jellied infected lungs, or murdered, perhaps quite casually, out of hand, stabbed or beaten to death for a few cents or a few swallows of wine in a greasy bottle.

These men reached the end by different routes, but the downward process that carried each to his final impotent and despairing end was much the same for them all: a useful and respectable livelihood, followed by less useful and respectable ones; then the kind of work that such men have always done—itinerant painters, circus roustabouts, short-order cooks, dishwashers. Towards the end there was no work at all, no more periods of self-possession and good intentions, nothing but petty crime and panhandling. Life by then was almost unbearable, and would soon become absolutely so; either the body could no longer sustain that feeble spark, or the will could not.

Western civilization has provided few nets for such persons, and these few were tiny and widely separated from each other over time and distance. Still, there were nets, and are. Of those homeless transient alcoholics who over the years have resolved to allow the process of their own dissolution to proceed no further, who gathered their flagging and intermittent courage for one last act of escape, one occasionally found himself, a few days after setting out on that desperate resolve, in surprising circumstances. Not, as he might have pictured himself, drowned or hanged or crushed, but alive, sober, and perched on the seat of a spring-mounted delivery wagon behind an elderly horse whose appearance, no less than the driver's, drew pitying glances from kindly passersby. A familiar sight: a dark green wagon, a patient old horse and a client from the Salvation

Army Industrial Home. A "client"—what hope, what a force to blow upon the feeble but still living embers of manhood is contained in that word—a client! A person, an object of care, official and personal, an agent capable of self-improvement—a client!—a bum no longer, nor so soon to be a corpse as the man himself originally imagined—a Man, a Brother to Somebody, somewhere, at last. Decades will pass, and this scenario, acted out against an infinitely variable background, will be repeated a dozen, a hundred, ten thousand times. The wagons will give way, slowly, after forty years, to motor trucks, green, black, blue, then mostly red. Kitchens, dormitories, chapels, shops, warehouses, stores will proliferate. The story will remain in its basic elements the same.

Had our man stopped off for a last warm meal at the Army hostel before he died; or perhaps had he come for a set of clean underwear, to achieve a kind of final, pathetic respectability in the eyes of the cold indifferent men at the morgue? Had someone at the desk in the Army's front lobby noticed this man more than all the other cold, hungry forlorn applicants that night? Or had it been the officer in charge who noticed? Had the captain or adjutant or major been prompted by a lifetime of experience with men to detect in this one applicant a more than ordinarily desperate expression? Had the man himself been turned from his purpose by the sight of one of the hopeful and sentimental mottos—"Remember Mother's Prayers"— that once adorned the walls of such places? Or had it been a familiar hymn? Was it no more than a kind word, a smile, some little act of courtesy, that drew our man back from the abyss?

It is good to know that such things happened, and happen still. It is perhaps important, and certainly useful, to know why, and how, the Salvation Army Men's Social Service Department arose and became the largest and most successful rehabilitation program for transient alcoholic men in the United States.

The Army began in this country as a straightforward evangelistic crusade. This is true whether one considers the activities of the Shirley family in Philadelphia in October 1878, or those of the first "official" Army delegation led by George Scott Railton in March 1880. Its early and rapid expansion—by 1890 the Army had spread across the country, with 410 corps in 35 states—can be explained almost entirely in terms of its simple orthodoxy and its colorful and attractive means of propagating it.

But the Army was always more than a religious crusade, at least in the sense that its campaign to rescue the lost souls of the world never stopped at broadcasting the truths of the gospel. The Army offered solace to the body as well, and for the same reason that its soldiers marched and preached: Christ commanded it! There were practical reasons that were equally compelling: the desperate material needs of that class of society to which the Army's Founder, William Booth, and early leaders in England and America felt especially drawn.

Pioneer officers attributed the Army's growth to its doctrinal position; God was honoring the efforts of His soldiers who spread abroad the true gospel of redemption in Christ, which, when accepted, led to a life of love for God and man. Many sympathetic contemporaries agreed: the simplicity of the Army's gospel, the direct and unavoidable choice it held out to sinners, had great appeal—but so did the use of religious verses joined to popular melodies, brass bands to carry the happy message over the noise of city traffic, lantern slides, painted umbrellas, flags, "transparencies," the guileless "testimonies" of the recent converts, the clever use of ranks, titles and activities to give new members a sense of importance and purpose. Whatever its doctrinal beliefs, The Salvation Army became as much parade as a movement, deliberately conducted by its leaders and followers alike as a joyful and adventuresome crusade, certain of final triumph.

The Army's appeal, however, while widespread, was not unlimited. Nor did its leaders intend that it should be. From the very beginning of the Movement, its appeal was deliberately—and successfully—aimed at that part of society which Booth and his close advisers were convinced had been overlooked by existing religious activities: the urban and working-class poor. The slums and the tenements of the great cities of the world beckoned to the Army missionaries. The Army, then the church, was called to be the rescuer of the cold-water flat, the fire-escape, the street corner and the saloon—the devil's strong refuges in modern civilization. Ballington Booth, the Founder's second son, who commanded the Army in the United States from 1887 to 1896, spoke for his 1,500 fellow officers when he described himself in 1891 as one "who daily yearns for the salvation of the worst of our great cities."[1]

In particular, the Army's experience as an urban mission led it to espouse the cause of what was in those days called the "temperance movement," a crusade that, ignoring the precise meaning of that word, called for total abstinence from all alcoholic beverages. The Army went further, and forbade its soldiers to be employed in the "drink traffic," which meant not only that they could not drink alcohol, but that they could not work in taverns, saloons, beer halls or distilleries, or even drive a beer wagon. No compromise was tolerable with drink, the curse, the bane, the ruin of the urban poor, the cause of almost all the physical and moral misery that impeded the Army's spiritual endeavors in the slums.

The Salvation Army's first American convert—its first "Trophy of Grace"—was Jimmy Kemp, a Manhattan drunkard known locally as "Ash-Barrel Jimmy" because he was once dragged to police court in a barrel to which, when in a drunken stupor, he had become frozen or snagged. The earliest issues of the Army's weekly publication, *The War Cry*, extolled "God's Power to Save a Drunkard" and contained the testimonies of saved drunkards. An account of a large meeting at the Army's headquarters hall in Brooklyn in 1883 described 1,500 happy converts "praising God for sending The Salvation Army, who were once drunkards, thieves, liars, cutthroats, infidels and proud, empty professors." The Salvation Army existed to bring "poor drunkards and harlots to the Saviour." Throughout the eighties, Salvationists poured out invectives against drink, the great deceiver, deluder, destroyer.[2]

It was inevitable that the Army's theological position and its experience in the "haunts of sin and vice" would combine to prompt its members to perform acts of human compassion on an increasingly organized basis. The Army's version of Christianity, for which its leaders claimed no originality, was based entirely on the doctrinal position of John Wesley, and required but one thing of converts: love—love for Christ, love for the Scriptures as His literal instructions, love for the lost and dying souls of the unsaved, and love for one's fellowmen, especially the worst among them, who in all their misery and shame were beings no less the object of God's love and sacrifice than the proudest soldier in the Army. "Jesus at an Open-Air Meeting: None Too Bad for The Salvation Army!" And certainly the poverty, despair, crime and drunkenness on every hand provided ample opportunity for helping hands.[3]

Official contemporary records of the activities of The Salvation Army in America written in the mid-1880s suggest that the Army had no formal social-welfare activities for the first half-dozen years of its existence. Both George Scott Railton and Commissioner Frank Smith, who served as leader of American forces from 1884–1887, made no reference to social-welfare operations in America in separate accounts written in 1886. Reflecting many years later, Edward J. Parker, a pioneer officer, recalled that when he joined The Salvation Army in 1885 it had no social-work program beyond the drum and the tambourine. Given the Army's own theological position and the fact that it largely confined its evangelical efforts to the "fallen, degraded and forsaken"—and given in particular its emphases on combatting drink and rescuing its victims—social-welfare activities, at least of a rudimentary sort, could not be long delayed.[4]

Indeed, as early as 1884 the American edition of *The War Cry* already carried enthusiastic reports of the Army's fledgling social activities in other countries. The first of these was the "Prison Gate Brigade" in Melbourne, a refuge for released prisoners until they could find honest employment. In 1885, *The War Cry* reported on "Gutter, Garret and Cellar Work" carried on in the slum sections of London, by Evangeline Booth, the General's daughter, then aged 19. In that same year a sympathetic prison chaplain in Hartford, Connecticut, invited the local Army corps to conduct religious services in the jail. This is sometimes cited as the first official Salvation Army social service in America, although it consisted only of an outdoor meeting carried indoors, and nothing permanent was established because of the Hartford meeting. Far more significant was the announcement, in October 1886, that a rescue home for "poor, fallen outcasts" was to be opened in New York City. Often the victims of drink— or drinkers—the unmarried working-class pregnant woman, or converted prostitute who sought to escape from her former associates, had few safe places to go in the hard world of 1886. "The Salvation Army to the Rescue!" proclaimed *The War Cry*![5]

Although there is little in the meager official Army records of the period upon which to draw for proof, Salvationists could not have been wholly unaware of the charitable activities of other organizations at work in American cities in the 1880s, nor indifferent to the success of their efforts. Some of these agencies performed services that were similar to those eventually offered by the Army. For instance, in 1886 Dwight L. Moody established Moody Bible Institute in Chicago, specifically to train persons to minister to the urban poor. The Young Men's Christian Association, large and well-run missions like the Pacific Garden Mission in Chicago and the Water Street Mission in New York, the nationwide Florence Crittenden Mission, the influential Women's Christian Temperance Union, the growing number of activities for the urban poor overseen by the various Charity Organization societies and later joined by the "institutional" churches and settlement houses like Jane Addams' Hull House— all these and many others grew and flourished during the Army's first decade among the urban masses in America.

The effect of these examples on pioneer officers cannot be known; the belief among some of them that they were laboring alone was at least an

effective stimulus to action. It was certainly true that the best efforts of
city mission and charity organization society alike had not touched the
vast majority of desperate people crowded into the slums.

The Army continued to broadcast its evangelism—by the late 1880s
accompanied by the brass bands, drums and tambourines which soon
became and remained the familiar heralds of its ministry—to those whom
its leaders were convinced had been abandoned by the "respectable"
churches: nightly The Salvation Army sang and testified outdoors and
indoors of the simple gospel of grace, forgiveness and love. Commissioner
Frank Smith proclaimed his version of the Army's particular part in the
divine plan in 1886.[6]

> The fact is, deny it who can, the Churches are wedded to
> the wealthy world. Let us of The Salvation Army, from
> this day forth, wed ourselves to the fate and fortunes of
> the so-called dangerous classes. Let us go down to our
> bride in the Boweries of our great cities. God approves the
> union.

Evangelism among the urban poor meant practical activities on their
behalf as well. "Oh, my brother," proclaimed *The War Cry* in 1887, "the
soul savers are after all the truest body savers." Even if William Booth had
not learned the lesson and made it official policy in the days of the
Christian Mission in the 1870s, the Army in America would have been
carried to the same conclusions, based on identical evidence and the same
hypothesis: Christianity is the religion of love, divine and human. Charitable activities continued to multiply throughout the decade. One rescue
home was opened, then others; "prison brigades" visited jails and peniten-
tiaries, held evangelistic meetings and assisted ex-convicts back into society—no easy task in an age when "ex-jailbirds" were largely
unemployable. By 1887 various kinds of social welfare had grown to
sufficient proportions that the new commanders, Marshal and Mrs. Ballington Booth, a clever, attractive pair, revived the Auxiliary League to
attract the "prayer, influence and money" of the general public for the
Army's "great work of reclaiming drunkards, rescuing the fallen, and
saving the lost." The work of reclaiming drunkards was, in fact, on the eve
of a vast multiplication.[7]

On March 31, 1888, as part of the regular weekly column of news about
Army activities around the world, a small notice appeared on a back page

of the American edition of *The War Cry,* announcing the "New Departure Complete." The Salvation Army had officially opened the "night shelter and food depot" in Limehouse, in the slums of East London. There is no contemporary evidence that this information stimulated an immediate response among American Salvationists, whose daily exertions left them but little leisure time in which to contemplate the triumphs of their distant comrades. They are not to be faulted; no one who was not clairvoyant would have perceived in this tiny news item the watershed in the history of The Salvation Army in the United States that it, in fact, contained: the first notice to American soldiers of the beginning of Army work among transient, unemployed men.[8]

The genesis of this aspect of Army work, which in the United States gradually assumed proportions and achieved success beyond the pioneers' powers of imagination, is a familiar and treasured part of Army folklore, impregnated as it is with the most forceful and appealing aspects of the personality of the Founder himself. One evening in late 1887, William Booth returned to London from Army business elsewhere. As his hired coach was conveying him from the railroad station to his house, it crossed the Thames on London Bridge. Booth was startled to notice—apparently for the first time—that poor, homeless men slept under the arches of the bridge at night. He was even more startled to discover that this unhappy fact was common knowledge: his son and chief assistant Bramwell, for instance, knew all about it! The General, never one to linger over a decision, ordered immediate action: something must be done! Bramwell helpfully pointed out that some of these men were unworthy of help, no one could tell the deserving from the undeserving, and in any case the Army could not do *everything.* The distinction between deserving and undeserving freezing, homeless, hungry men seemed a curious one to the General, and as for the practical problems, they were easily solved: obtain a warehouse, clean it up, heat it and provide good cheap food. "But mind, Bramwell—no coddling."[9]

The first Army shelter for homeless men was opened on February 21, 1888 at 21 West India Road, Limehouse. Two others were opened in early 1889, and when these were swamped during a severe dock strike in the summer of the year, the pioneer Army meeting hall in Whitechapel Road was converted into a food and shelter depot as well.

In fact, the speed with which the Army embraced the new activity suggested that the idea did not spring into the General's mind as quite the unbidden inspiration that the traditional story conveys. The General had given considerable thought to the problem of the homeless man in London, which had been confronting him for at least a dozen years. He spent large amounts of time during the next two years bringing together his thoughts on this aspect of the Army's mission, and putting them into systematic form, a task in which he was aided by the eccentric but sympathetic London journalist and reformer William T. Stead. The result of their labors appeared in print in 1890, and did not, unlike its tiny harbinger, pass unnoticed in the United States.

In Darkest England and the Way Out—its title cleverly designed to capture the attention of the English public already stimulated by the appearance in print of Henry Morton Stanley's popular account of the rescue of Emin Pasha called *In Darkest Africa*—was Booth's great work. It is the only book written by a Salvation Army officer to receive widespread attention outside the ranks of the Movement. Its impact on The Salvation Army in America was immediate and—once its message was translated into terms applicable to American conditions—enormous.

William Booth's explanation of the causes of urban poverty, and his suggestion for a cure, reflect his theology and 25 years' experience as an evangelist among the poor and working classes of London. Booth's understanding of theology was heavily influenced by his wife Catherine, the "Army Mother," a highly-intelligent, well-read woman with a powerful personality; but the Booths' great originality lay not in their hypotheses, nor even in the conclusions to which they were led, but in the practical applications of those conclusions. The same was true for their "social theories," their understanding of the nature and cause of poverty, for instance. Booth's genius, and the strength of his Movement as a redemptive force in urban life, lay almost entirely in the realm of the practical.

"Throw Out the Lifeline," written in 1884, was still a new song when *In Darkest England* appeared in print, but the imagery it contained was as old to Booth as time itself. Not alone among Victorian evangelists, the General conceived of the world as an ocean of sin, from which the saved spent their lives rescuing drowning sinners, but to Booth this imagery attained the mystical intensity of a vision. Pioneer officers shared this vision; it mattered nothing to them how people obtained their false notions about religion, or why some people were indifferent to religion altogether: it mattered only that those who became Christians were safe on the Rock of Salvation; the rest were doomed to sink into eternal ruin. Doomed—but not predestined: for if it was the Army's responsibility to throw out the gospel lifeline, it was the sinner's responsibility to grasp it. And once rescued, the new Christian must turn at once to the work of rescuing others. Beyond these simple propositions, theology meant little.

The same direct approach marked all of Booth's solutions to the more worldly problems of the urban poor. The life in Christ required His children to exert themselves to relieve the misery of their fellow beings: it was less important to know how they had become miserable; an explanation of the causes of their poverty would only follow efforts at their relief, so that means might be devised to enable them to make their uplift permanent. Booth expressed this practical approach in the famous "Cab-Horse Charter." The General denounced the fact that the poor in London were not "generally . . . as well cared for as horses." When a cab-horse falls, no one faults the creature for being weary, or careless, or stupid: he is helped to his feet at once, for his own sake and to prevent an obstruction to traffic. And more: once back on his feet, he is given work, fed, kept warm and dry at night. "These then are the two points of the Cab-Horse Charter. When he is down he is helped up, and while he lives he has food, shelter and work."

Once the work of temporary restoration was complete, it became necessary to discover how to prevent a relapse into helplessness and poverty again. To Booth, this was comparatively simple, because like almost all Army officers, in America as well as Britain, the General believed that the "submerged tenth" of modern civilizations, the poor, the honest, as well as those who lived by vice or crime, were the victims of drink.

> Darkest England may be described as consisting broadly of three circles, one within the other. The outer and widest circle is inhabited by the starving and the homeless, but honest, poor. The second by those who live by vice; and the third and innermost region at the center is peopled by those who exist by crime. The whole of the three circles is sodden with drink.

The problem was immense, but there was hope; Booth's book was "no mere lamentation of despair. For Darkest England, as for Darkest Africa, there is a light beyond." The solution was a program on a scale commensurate with the problem and incorporating the "essentials of success:" the program must change the man when his own character or conduct was the cause of his poverty, or change his circumstances if these cause his ruin and are beyond his control; the program must be a permanent one, and—

naturally—immediately practical. Booth, like a growing number of contemporary writers on social welfare, dismissed the lingering distinction
between worthy and unworthy poor as being both impractical and cruel.
To Booth the distinction must be between those who would work and
those who would not. No program of relief should be installed that would
"demoralize" the poor by bestowing "mere charity" upon them: such a
policy would actually injure the people it sought to benefit. Nor was Booth
a revolutionary: no relief program could be allowed to aid one "class" that
"seriously interferes with the interests of another."

   The practical result of these reflections was "The Salvation Army Social
Campaign," also variously called "The Darkest England Scheme," the
"Great Scheme," the "General's Scheme," and other things. There were
to be three parts, only one of which was in even rudimentary operation
when *In Darkest England* appeared in late 1890. The first was the "city
colony," a refuge in the "very center of the ocean of misery." The city
colony consisted of shelters, where the destitute were to be taken in, given
food and shelter and exposed to "moral and religious influences." Access
to the shelters was by payment of a tiny sum, which would be obtained by
work, either in one of several planned Salvation Army enterprises or as a
temporary day laborer sent out by an Army employment service to employers friendly to the scheme. It was intended that most men who passed
through these agencies would be "floated off to permanent employment"
or returned to rejoicing friends and family.

   Those few who remained on the Army's hands would be tested for
health and character and sent to the second part of the Great Scheme, the
"farm colony." Here the beneficial results of a healthy, innocent rural
environment, supplemented by the same "industrial [rather, agricultural]
moral and religious methods" already started in the city colony would no
doubt reform many more men, some of whom would either return to their
former honest employments or would settle in the country as agricultural
laborers. The majority of men reclaimed in the farm colony would, however, be passed by Army authorities onto the third part of the scheme, the
"overseas colony"—that is, they would be assisted to emigrate to proposed Army agricultural communities that were to be established in large,
underpopulated British colonies, such as Canada, Western Australia and
South Africa—the final "home for these destitute multitudes."[10]

   Once the general outline of this plan was safely behind him, General
Booth could dwell in enthusiastic and loving detail on the practical opera-

tion of this great scheme—a "great machine," he called it. *In Darkest England* gave details for the operation of practical Christian social welfare in the context of late 19th century urban civilization that provided both stimulus and guidance to American officers, eager to broaden their own redemptive activities. The concreteness, the minute nature of the detail of the plan made all the more real the golden promise it seemed to hold out that the problem of urban poverty was at last solved. This was particularly true for the "city colony," which proved to be, in England as in America, the only part of the program with a practical future as an agency for the rehabilitation of the urban poor.

Although the first announcements of the "Darkest England" scheme to American Salvationists was crowded to a back page of the American edition of *The War Cry* by the long mournful account of the death and funeral of Catherine Booth, the idea of a new "social campaign" was popular in this country from the start. Ballington Booth was especially enthusiastic: "With what eager eyes," he asked, "would thousands watch this 'new and almost herculean scheme that the General has propounded.' " Army leaders were certain the new project would be a success in England, and that the happy results there would be a "boom" for the Army all around the world.[11]

> Who knows what bearing this long-needed work will have
> upon our American fellow-citizens, thousands of whom,
> alas! denizens of slumdom and garret existence, wait for
> like assistance and mercy.

Copies of the new book were quickly obtained in this country, and widely distributed through commercial bookstores and Army headquarters. More and more column space in *The War Cry* was given over to *verbatim* accounts of favorable reviews of the book and the program that were published in the British and American press. A paperback edition of *In Darkest England* appeared, and was offered as a free gift to new subscribers to *The War Cry*. Officers in the field kept each other informed about local reaction to "the General's Scheme." The Army launched *The Conqueror* in 1892, a glossy new magazine designed to appeal to middle-class readers willing to offer financial support to the Army's increasingly ambitious social relief program; the first issue described the "Darkest England project" as "the greatest scheme in the world." The first shipment of *In Darkest England* was quickly sold or given away, encouraging *The War Cry* to claim that there was a "widespread interest in the General's scheme."[12]

It is ironic that in this country, where the personal influence of the General was considerably weaker than it was in Britain, the lasting impact of his major book was perhaps greater. Writing in 1927 Colonel Edward J. Parker, at that time the foremost American social officer, claimed that the arrival of *In Darkest England* was the "birth of the Army's social service work." The Army confirmed this claim in 1940 when in connection with the 60th anniversary of its work in the United States an official statement declared that the Army's social services in America had lacked any "definite objectives" before Booth's program was proclaimed in 1890. This was especially true in terms of the development of Army operations among homeless unemployed men. Buoyed by the success and popularity of its rescue homes for women and its kindly ministrations to slum families, and to some extent by the rising tide of public concern over the problems of the urban poor, The Salvation Army hovered expectantly in 1890 on the threshold of some new "major attack" on that class of sinner which doctrine, experience and opportunity now embraced.[13]

American officers looked upon the worst parts of their large cities— which even reformers found frightening and discouraging—as the golden door of opportunity for their crusade. They gladly admitted that the General's "Social Scheme" was apparently off to a good start in London and a few other faraway places, but in America the Army would carry the plan to grand fruition. "There are bright and happy days not far away," gloated Ballington in November 1891, "when the General's scheme shall have become fully developed." His optimism was not blind: Ballington's knowledge of the conditions in which homeless unemployed men were forced to live was based on his own midnight forays into the Bowery— suitably disguised in a "shabby appearance"—and on the daily reports of his officers whose evangelical zeal and love for the poor exposed them to desperate scenes.[14]

The Army's leading officers were too well-informed to believe that the world of the homeless man was an entirely virgin field for The Salvation Army in America. Philanthropic and social-welfare projects had developed in several large cities since the Civil War. In New York City one expert estimated that a number of persons equal to one-fifth of the population had received some sort of "help from public charity" in the years 1882–1885. In 1892 Ballington himself stated that 150,000 persons were the "guests of charity" every night in New York City. Contemporary statistics are uncertain, but many of these numbers must have referred to men who were fed and housed at municipal lodging houses and missions. Such facilities, cheap commercial lodging houses and poor houses were found in many large American cities. The problem, so far as The Salvation Army perceived it, lay not in the complete absence of facilities for homeless men, but in their inadequacy. There were far too few of them, and most of those that were open were filthy, overcrowded and overpriced—the more so since many of their clientele were actually penniless. There were but a handful of well-run missions in the country; otherwise no lodging house for the poor made any effort to introduce their clients to kindness, charm, moral instruction or the solace of true religion. Ballington could hardly believe "the inefficiency and discomfort of the lodging houses for out-of-work and homeless men" that he visited on his nocturnal investigations.[15]

The need for a warm, clean and friendly shelter for the homeless unemployed men crowded into the slums and boweries of large cities was unquestionably great, in humanitarian terms alone. Salvationists, of course, were more inclined to see their social-welfare projects only in terms of the command of Christ to love one another, and as a means of steadying a man to the point at which he could absorb the gospel message. Multitudes of desperate men were at hand, crowding past the Army's halls in search of work, food, sleep: respectable working men, some of them too ill or too old to work; immigrants lonely and confused; criminals or ex-convicts, regarded as unreliable for even the most menial employment; touts, grafters, seasoned panhandlers; bankrupts; men ruined by gambling debt; youths drawn to the city in the vain expectation of work, or, less guileless, adventure or vice; other young men who had outgrown their employment as bootblacks, newsboys and telegraph messengers and who had found nothing to do since—a horde who huddled, hungry, sullen and hopeless, in mission halls and Salvation Army barracks until these places were closed for the night, then wandered the dark streets until morning.

Drink was a solace to many such men, glad to disguise their hunger and forget their poverty in bleary fellowship or warm oblivion. Although the Army's first shelters for men were not specifically aimed at drunkards, many of the men who came to them were heavy drinkers, or would have liked to be if only the means could be procured. The Army's campaign against the curse of drink and the saloon had been a part of its evangelism from the beginning of its work, and it continued unabated during the first years of the Army's social work for men. Staff officers fully intended the temperance crusade to form an important part of the influence of the shelters.

The Salvation Army's first "cheap food and shelter establishment in the United States" was opened on December 23, 1891. Taking their cue from the overwhelming popularity among Victorian Christians of nautical rescue imagery, officers proudly launched the new shelter as "Our New York Lighthouse." The shelter could accommodate 36 men, each in his own box bed, all laid together on the floor of a room 24 by 45 feet. There was a "large and well-lighted" room for the men to wash themselves and a restaurant that served a few staple items for pennies.

The Lighthouse occupied the basement of the once-fashionable Berean Baptist Church, which the Commander had noticed but a few weeks before, standing invitingly idle on the corner of Bedford and Downing Streets on New York's lower West Side. The ground floor was used as the New York No. 2 Corps; the operation of the two facilities was officially regarded as complementary, a pattern of mutual support between the evangelical (the ministry of the corps, called then—and now—the "field") and "social" work which obtained for several years, and which obscured from the outset any sharp distinction between these branches of the Army's ministry. The importance of the Lighthouse to the future prospects of the Army may be inferred from the rank and ability of the officers appointed to command it: Staff-Captain and Mrs. John Newton Parker. Before coming to the shelter, the Parkers had commanded major corps, then several corps at once in districts, and finally all Army operations in Oregon and Washington. Parker, who graduated in full uniform from Mount Union College in Ohio in 1887, had been spared none of the excitement of Hallelujah warfare in the West, and came with his wife to New York prepared for action.

The shelter, heralded by two signs lettered "Salvation Army Food and Shelter—The Lighthouse" and displaying a picture of a lighthouse, one sign for each face of the corner, was a success within a few days. The first evening, Wednesday, December 23, 25 suppers were sold and two men came in for the night; on the second day, 59 meals were sold and nine beds occupied; by Saturday 92 meals and 25 beds were taken, and by Sunday night all 36 beds were occupied, "using all the accommodations provided."

The sleeping arrangements were simple enough: 36 box beds placed directly on the floor, each provided with a bare mattress and several sheepskins sewn together with a belt attached, which each client wrapped around himself like an apron. The washroom had new stationary fixtures which 10 men could use at once. The Lighthouse charged seven cents for a bed and a wash. The restaurant was one large room with a counter placed along one side, tables and chairs filling the rest of the space, each table with its own bottle of catsup and Worcestershire sauce. The bill of fare was as straightforward as the sleeping accommodations: soup, coffee or tea were two cents each, bread was two cents more; bread and butter, potatoes, beans, cabbage or rice were two cents per serving; beef or mutton stew, corned beef and cabbage or corned beef hash were four cents, and meat pie was the costliest item at five cents.

Many applicants for these benefits lacked any money at all but this difficulty was easily overcome: work. Men who professed to be penniless were lectured on the "evils of indiscriminate charity" and told, if they came in the evening, that they would be fed and given shelter if they promised to work for the Shelter for two hours in the morning; if they came for assistance during the day they were required to do the work before they were taken in. Men were assigned to one of two tasks: washing dishes or cleaning up the shelter, or—much more commonly—chopping and sawing firewood (which the Army then sold at bargain rates in the neighborhood, where it was used in stoves for cooking and heating). The Army operated from the beginning on the basis of the work-test, for which the woodyard was a common form, which had all but replaced in American philanthropy the outworn distinction between the worthy or unworthy applicant.

In fact, so far as its charitable activity at this early point was concerned, nothing the Army offered to the poor was original. Nor did officers claim originality: the virtue in their program was superiority. The food in the shelter was far better, more wholesome, served in larger portions—and on clean plates—than that offered in cheap hash houses. The shelter was warmer, cleaner, much safer and quieter than neighboring lodging houses. The food was good enough to attract not just transient men but whole families, who were allowed to take away their portions to eat at home. Poor children would beg a penny and spend it on a bowl of Army soup; once five children appeared with one penny and asked for five spoons with their bowl. And the shelter began to attract something like a regular clientele among men who were grateful for a clean and orderly resting place, free of the stink and blasphemous mutterings allowed in other shelters.

In particular, men who were drunk, or had been drinking enough for it to be noticeable, were repelled at the door or, if discovered inside the shelter, were tossed out. Such men, while actively encouraged to attend street-corner meetings, and often welcomed into Army halls to attend evangelistic services, were considered a threat to the "wholesome" atmosphere which officers intended to encourage in the new shelter. The policy was also designed to induce men to give up drinking by rewarding sobriety. And if these competitive advantages were not sufficient to explain the popularity of the shelter, it will be enough to add that the Army's prices were lower, offering for seven cents accommodations that cost 15 or 20 cents in commercial lodging houses.

The inspiration and objective alike of the shelter program was not financial, however, but religious. There were other gospel missions whose ministry was aimed at the homeless man, but none whose leaders were more convinced that "going for the worst," for the most hostile and degraded, was their particular part of the divine plan, or more confident that by multiplying activities across the nation under a single centralized command would it be possible to actually solve the problem of poverty by ending its fundamental cause, the selfishness of sinful man.

The shelter shared the building with the New York No. 2 Corps; the whole structure was quickly named the "Salvation Castle," perhaps in hopeful imitation of the famed Army meeting hall and headquarters in Oakland, California. Although most of the work of evangelism was conducted in the corps hall on the ground floor, the shelter walls were hung with religious mottos: "If you are anxious about your soul, speak to an officer," or a more lasting favorite, "Remember Your Mother's Prayers." Shelter clients were urged to attend the nightly meetings upstairs, where the gospel was offered with joyful abandon.

For if in the realm of the Army's social welfare program, at least in this rudimentary form, it was possible to discuss the degree to which services offered by other agencies were comparable, in religion the Army was absolutely novel. The simple, passionate exhortations from the Bible, the rousing singing, often of Christian texts set to popular beerhall melodies, the happy noise of cornet, banjo, drum and tambourine, and best of all the fervent joy of the testimonies of ex-brothel keepers and drunks sharing their grateful delight in their own fresh rescue from the ocean of sin—all this proved irresistible to many others. Men drawn to the shelter for food and lodging were converted in the corps meeting almost from the day the joint program began. The shelter opened on Wednesday; by Sunday six men had been saved, and these were "satisfactory cases," reported Staff-Captain Parker, "for we've seen their salvation in their lives already."

Evangelism at the "Salvation Castle" proved so effective, in fact, that New York No. 2 Corps became known as the "Shelter Corps" almost at once. It had its own officers, Captain and Mrs. Connett, newly arrived from Canada, but Parker often filled in for Connett and was apparently in overall command of the "Salvation Castle." The Army's national leaders were elated by the great success of the program at such an early point, and predicted great things for it. Within two months, more than 100 men professed conversion. Seventeen of these were enrolled as regular soldiers of the Shelter Corps on January 28, 1892. By then six shelter converts were employed full-time in the Lighthouse, as watchman, cook, waiters and chief helper to the officer—men so poor that Parker had to solicit cast-off clothing for them in the pages of *The War Cry,* but willing and full of promise. Indeed, Parker predicted that the shelter would be "the door through which many men would step into places of usefulness for God and The Salvation Army."

The Salvation Castle glowed in the limelight of official attention, the darling of the Chief Central Division, so full of triumphant Salvationism and so easily reached from headquarters via the Sixth Avenue horse-cars. Ballington presided over several large divisional meetings there, the first as early as New Year's Eve, when a monstrous rally was held to launch 1892 "in true Salvation Army style." A squad of men cadets from the Training Garrison was assigned to the Shelter Corps in order to experience firsthand the joys of salvation warfare, which raged about them.

The local saloon keepers and loungers took understandable alarm at the activities of the Army in their neighborhood. Unlike more respectable temperance movements and uptown philanthropies, The Salvation Army hurled its denunciations in the street, practically on the doorstep, of the dives and saloons it sought to ruin. There were counterattacks—and since argument was futile, violence was used. The Castle windows were broken, shelter cadets were cut on the nose by flying cans, choked, squirted with seltzer water and conked with blacksmiths' tongs. Attacks only encouraged the Army to believe that it was in the right place, and were soon regarded by soldiers as routine, even encouraging in their reliability. In September, a nighttime parade was held to advertise special meetings at the Castle, led by Captain "Trumpeter" Trumble and some of the National

Staff Band and illuminated by red Roman candles. "No special incidents" were reported, except that the bass drum was wrecked and Mrs. J. N. Parker was struck on the head with a rock, bled, and was able to stumble into the meeting only after she had "rallied a bit." Undaunted, seven more converts were enrolled that night as soldiers of the No. 2 Corps.[16]

The Lighthouse Food and Shelter Depot was clearly a success. By some process which the meager contemporary accounts do not explain, the sleeping capacity was increased from 36 to 40 in the same floor space. Soon an "annex" was added for ten more sleepers; apparently more of the unused portion of the basement was converted to this purpose. A "new apparatus" was added to the restaurant which doubled the production of tea and coffee. Coffee with three buns for five cents was added to the menu in order to compete not only with nearby cheap restaurants but also with the free-lunch system in local saloons—an enemy which officers noted was "not met with in England." The woodyard prospered, its produce made attractive by bargain prices and "good measure;" soon coal was added. Men who wanted more permanent employment were added to the shelter staff when vacancies occurred, or were assisted in finding work in the neighborhood. The shelter kept a supply of donated clothing on hand, so men could improve their appearance before looking for work. Although statistics from this period varied in reliability with the enthusiasm of the reporter, surviving figures indicate that the shelter provided assistance to a large number of men. By the end of April 1893, the Army figures for occupancy suggest that the shelter was filled to capacity every night and that 174 were given work in the shelter, 111 found work on the outside and 110 souls were saved. The shelter was certainly becoming well-known: at one point during the winter, Parker had to turn 30 to 40 men away every night.[17]

By February, the Army was already looking for a larger building. Mrs. J. N. Parker declared in March that the day was "not far distant" when there would be not only one Salvation Army shelter in New York, "but a number of them." As spring lengthened into summer the number of applicants at the shelter declined. By early fall the end of seasonal employment in agriculture, resorts and traveling shows and circuses and the approach of cold weather brought redoubled pressure on city missions. Ballington promised five new shelters in the coming year. Sometime in December 1892, the curtain descended on the bright ephemeral career of the "Salvation Castle." The Shelter Corps was left temporarily without a hall, and in January 1893 the food and shelter depot reopened in a rented four-story building at 243 Front Street on the lower East Side of Manhattan. The new Lighthouse was capable of housing 154 men in two- and three-tiered bunks.[18]

The new Lighthouse was a much larger and more expensive operation for The Salvation Army, but it did not represent, except in small ways, a new departure in social welfare procedures. The work-test, and the wood-yard which embodied it in practical—and profitable—form, was absent from the new shelter, but almost certainly because of lack of space. The theory and practice of the work-test remained a fundamental part of Army social work for men. Without the work of sawing, splitting and tying firewood into bundles there were many fewer ways to offer applicants a means of earning the cost of their accommodations. This had two negative effects: it meant that many more penniless applicants would be turned away; and it cast an aura of commercialism over the new shelter. Yet the officers appointed to manage this shelter were fiercely evangelical and believed that soul-saving was the whole purpose of their work. Evangelistic meetings were held nightly, which lodgers were required to attend in order to obtain the coffee and buns which came with their seven-cent beds.

Despite the religious requirement, the new Lighthouse was crowded, at least in the winter. The accommodations were comparatively cheap (seven cents for fourth-floor three-tier "bunks," 12 cents for third-floor two-tier "dormitories") warm, dry and clean. The Army ran an orderly hostelry, with strict rules against excessive noise or blasphemous language. Drunks were strictly excluded, a practice that was still regarded as an essential policy in order to provide comfortable and secure accommodations for the respectable poor man, but the Army felt no less commitment to its traditional crusade to rescue the victims of drink. In the first month at the new location Maud Ballington Booth, wife of the Commander, made an "especial plea for an inebriate ward in the shelter for men." In order to discourage homeless men from drinking, the Army hit upon the idea of selling "shelter tickets" to the public, which kind-hearted citizens could give to panhandlers instead of money.[19]

At least some of the applicants at the Army shelter gained the impression that the operation was animated by a spirit of general helpfulness, even of friendliness. The staff was sympathetic from experience. Sergeant W. "Scotty" Wallace, himself a notorious ex-drunkard converted at the original Lighthouse, was the shelter watchman at night. During the day he labored over a cast-off sewing machine, trying to repair discarded clothing to give to men who helped in the shelter (that, and room and board was their only pay) or who wanted to improve their appearance before searching for employment outside. Certainly no lodger could complain that the Army ran the shelter for profit; despite the fact that each of the two married officer couples had only a single room—one of them so small that "anything bigger than a herring would crowd it"—used a single stove for heating and cooking, and neither officers nor staff expected any salary, the expenses of rent ($1,250 per year), fuel and gas (for lighting) and food exceeded the revenue generated by the Army's low prices in all but the busiest winter months.

In the first dozen years in which The Salvation Army operated in the United States it achieved great success; by the end of 1892 the American branch of the Movement had spread from coast to coast and with 1,500 officers was second in size and importance only to the work in the home country of Britain. Only a handful of these officers were engaged in social programs, and the place of these officers within the Army administrative structure was uncertain. But the importance of explicitly social work in overall Salvation Army operations grew steadily in the early 1890s. Pioneer officers did not accept, did not even acknowledge, that social and religious activities were not perfectly harmonious; both served the great cause of saving souls. From the beginning of its ministry in the United States, the Army had collected funds from that portion of the public which sympathized with its attempts to redeem the worst of the urban poor. The new importance given to the Auxiliary League in 1887 stimulated this tendency, which was given further impetus by the success of the Army's first explicitly social operations. Although identifiable social operations remained a small proportion of Salvation Army activities, that proportion grew, and the publicity attracted to it grew larger still.

At the great "Continental Congress" meetings held in Carnegie Hall in November 1892—the largest public meetings held by the Army in America up to that time—Ballington Booth confirmed the Army's mission for the future would be calling upon the unsaved with a "new attack upon the inebriate classes." Booth praised the work of the New York Shelter in his opening address and a public presentation of the Shelter Brigade formed part of a variety of special messages, musical novelties and announcements during the next evening. Interest in expanding shelter work beyond New York preceded the Congress, however. Two officers, Staff-Captains William Halpin and John Milsaps, had journeyed to the Congress from San Francisco, to propose, as Major William Brewer had recently done with less success for Boston and Major Richard Holz for Buffalo, the opening of shelters in their cities. The Californians, however, had gone much further in their plans: they already had an "admirably suited" building, and easily secured the Commander's permission to proceed with "the second food and shelter depot in this country."[20]

The Californians had more than a building, in fact, and it is just as well that the Commander gave his permission when he did: The Salvation Army in the West had been irrepressible from the start. The Movement had arisen there spontaneously in 1882, when a struggling "holiness" mission, inspired by a stray copy of *The War Cry*, had transformed themselves by unanimous vote into the "Salvation Army" and offered their crusade to the General in London. Booth took it up officially and sent officers to take charge in San Francisco in July 1883. Since then the work on the Pacific Coast had been advanced against great difficulties, especially in San Francisco. Adventurers abounded, and a number of colorful eccentrics were attracted to the ranks. Among these were Captain Joseph ("Joe-the-Turk") Garabed, the "Hallelujah Jailbird" who, by courting arrest over 50 times, freed the Army from municipal restrictions on its open-air evangelism by bringing the offending statutes into public ridicule; another was Captain Joseph R. McFee, former master of the steamship *Great Victoria* and father of the Army's social work on the Pacific Coast.

The cities of the West were new in the 1890s—even the largest of them, San Francisco, had been no more than a hamlet before the Gold Rush— and their municipal and charitable services were still in a rudimentary state. The Salvation Army carried on its evangelism amidst grim scenes of poverty and vice made even more discouraging to their victims by the bright dreams of a golden future that had drawn so many of them. Western Salvationists provided as many little acts of charity as their meager resources allowed, and followed every development of Salvation Army social operations elsewhere with eager and envious eyes. Ballington's visit to San Francisco in June 1891, during which he reported on his recent visit to London where he had discussed with the General the practical prospects of the "Darkest England" scheme for America, was a great encouragement to Western officers. The energizing spirit, however, seems to have been McFee's.

Joseph McFee had begun to drink heavily, and was on the way to ruin when he and his wife, taking an innocent stroll through the Barbary Coast during a few days' shore leave in 1891, encountered an Army meeting at the "San Francisco No. 2 Dive" Corps, where he was soundly converted.

After five months as a soldier, McFee sold his interest in the ship and became an officer in The Salvation Army. A man of energy and full of novel ideas, McFee gave himself at once and completely to developing social operations among the many kinds of poor and desperate men drifting along the Barbary Coast. His first endeavor was a public Christmas dinner for the poor in 1891, which left at least two legacies more enduring than its most enthusiastic sponsors could have imagined. The success of the dinner, which drew more than 1,000 ordinary-looking, decent, hungry poor people convinced many of the city's more fortunate citizens that there was more poverty in the city than they had realized, and that some more systematic means of providing for the poor must be found. The Army drew upon this newly aroused sympathy when it needed money to open a permanent shelter. To finance the first Christmas dinner, McFee employed a device he had seen in Liverpool: a large pot in which to collect change from passersby. The Harbor Commission allowed him to set up a borrowed crabpot on a tripod at the foot of Market Street, where the Oakland ferry landed. The pot bore a sign reading: "Fill the Pot for the Poor—Free Dinner on Christmas Day." The first Salvation Army Christmas kettle—but not the last!

Encouraged by this success, McFee spent the next months in hatching fresh plans to uplift and evangelize the inhabitants of the Barbary Coast. By March 1892, the New York edition of *The War Cry* reported that "plans and proposals" for a food-and-shelter depot in San Francisco had been made to the Commander. In the meantime cast-off clothing and food were collected for poor families who applied for help at provincial headquarters, and regular evangelistic visits were made to the San Francisco city almshouse, the city jail and the California State Prison at nearby San Quentin. Judging from the speed with which they were executed when official permission was secured, McFee's shelter plans were far advanced and prepared in detail when the two emissaries met with Booth in New York in November. A new chief district officer, Major James J. Keppel, arrived on Thanksgiving Day, determined to make "immense strides in Salvation Army warfare." He was soon inspired by the possibilities of a new shelter. On December 10, 1892 the Pacific Coast edition of *The War Cry* announced that the Commander had "sanctioned Major Keppel's proposition to commence the social work on the Pacific coast" and added gratuitously that the work would begin "at once."[21]

Influenced by the nautical imagery already in common use by Salvationists and by his own career, McFee called the new shelter the "Lifeboat." It was located in the building formerly occupied by the San Francisco No. 2 Dive Corps—before that, by the Palace Royal Saloon—on the corner of Sacramento and Kearny Streets. The Lifeboat was "launched" on Christmas Day 1892. There was a free Christmas dinner for the poor at the Lifeboat in the afternoon, at which 1,400 people showed up, coming in such crowds that the cable cars could not pass in the street and the police had to arrange the hungry into neat lines. There was a great "congress meeting" for Salvationists and the public at the headquarters hall in the evening. Connecting the two events in order to herald the enterprise to the public was a torchlight parade, in which transparencies were carried labeled "No More Sleeping in Lumberyards" and "Don't Be A Slave To The Devil!" The highlight, of course, was a huge mock-up lifeboat named *"Salvation"* (built, as *The War Cry* helpfully pointed out, by the same Lieutenant Howell who had built the turkey for the Thanksgiving parade).

The Lifeboat had bunks for 50 men, and three baths; meals could be served to 60 men at a time, with a waiting room for 300 more. It is unclear from remaining accounts when the first overnight lodger was taken in, but these accounts agree that the shelter was filled to capacity on December 28. Bed, bath and one meal cost 10 cents. From December 28 onward men had to be turned away every night. The need for such a shelter was great: San Francisco was crowded during the winter months with men thrown out of work by seasonal fluctuations in such enterprises as agriculture, the Southern Pacific Railroad, maritime shipping, by men drawn by the lingering allure of gold, and by the honest local victims of economic depression.[22]

The San Francisco Lifeboat was intended from the start as a temporary refuge for the unemployed, poor but willing men who with a little temporary assistance would be restored to a useful place in life and who were likely to become converted to Christ in the process. It was true, admitted McFee, that the occasional "bum and tramp" might get in, but that ought not to prevent the Army from helping the great majority of men who were not criminals or panhandlers, penniless and unwilling to work. The Army often drew attention to the respectable men in the Lifeboat Shelter, men whom economic conditions had forced into poverty—the ex-railroad man, the actor, the German immigrant ruined in a mining venture. Some of the men were heavy drinkers, but what of that? The Army claimed a special mission to rescue the victims of drink: the second Lifeboat building in San Francisco had a tin-lined room for drunks to sleep in safety without disturbing other men. This was important work: the best impulses of the human heart, the souls of many men, even the future of civilization was at stake: "With God's guidance and persistent endeavor, we hope to wipe poverty from the face of the earth."

The men who crowded about the Lifeboat in San Francisco were like the shelter clients in New York; they could be divided into two categories—those with the price of a meal or a bed, and those without it. The Army offered benefits to both. The former enjoyed a bargain, which drew many men who actually had jobs but who hoped by living at the Lifeboat to save a portion of their meager pay. Penniless men who were willing to work were kept from begging, crime or starvation. Or they might receive a 10-cent shelter ticket which the Army in San Francisco, like its Eastern counterpart, sold to sympathetic citizens to give in turn to hungry men. In San Francisco this system was far more popular among the wealthy than in New York. One man, Adolf Sutro, a mining entrepreneur and owner of the city's famous indoor public swimming pool, purchased tickets by the thousands, but when his downtown office was swamped with needy applicants he allowed the Army to distribute most of his tickets.[23]

For those who had to work, the San Francisco Lifeboat offered a range of opportunities of literally historic proportions. A woodyard and a labor bureau, for referrals to outside employment, were in place before the formal launching. The woodyard, however, could find little market in a city surrounded by woods and lumber mills. McFee supplemented it almost at once with a range of inventive enterprises which should qualify him as the American pioneer in developing the classic Salvation Army formula for work-therapy: waste materials employed by waste labor in honest and useful production.

McFee began his "workshop" on January 11, 1893, in a large vacant space attached to the San Francisco No. 9 Corps at 210 Grant Street— apparently optimistic pioneer officers rented very large halls. Thirteen shelter men were employed in unravelling old ship's cables and unused rope donated by the Claus Spreckles Sugar Company and then in weaving the component strands into door mats. By February, men were collecting old corks from restaurants, saloons and the city dump to be chopped up and stuffed into ship-fenders and life-preserving pillows; and leftover crumbs were made into upholstery stuffing. Then came "rope dusters" made out of frayed rope, and in May, McFee announced gleefully that the workshop was about to begin a new line of feather dusters (Salvationists were urged to send their turkey and rooster feathers—tail and wing—to headquarters), hammocks, salmon nets and "patent wringers." The results of this enthusiasm were sold in the streets by a uniformed Salvationist named Henry Weickgenannt (who may thereby have secured a tiny niche in history, as the first American Salvationist to push a hand-cart). There were as many as 20 men per day employed in these activities. They were paid in shelter tickets, allowed to take used clothing from a stock called the "Curiosity Shop" and given first chance at better employment opportunities that came into the Army's labor bureau—all this, observed McFee proudly, because of their "willingness to work."[24]

The Lifeboat was certainly "breasting the breakers," as McFee put it, after a few weeks of operation: 400 meals served every day, already a dozen converts. He took the nautical imagery of the crusade seriously, put the "crew"—the staff of six converts—into special "naval uniforms" and spent part of one summer cruising San Francisco Bay in a re-fitted antique launch holding evangelistic services on shipboard and riverbank. Apparently these excesses did not prevent the public from taking the Lifeboat seriously. When unemployment reached critical proportions in San Francisco in the winter of 1893–1894, the Army was asked to administer the municipal soup kitchen set up for the unemployed in a downtown vacant lot. The Army was committed to the work-test even in adversity, however, and McFee arranged for the contractor who swept the city streets to use needy men to do the work instead of his regular horse-drawn machinery. When some men refused to work, the Army asked the police to clear them from the sandlot, a move which the public and civic authorities warmly endorsed.[25]

The San Francisco shelter, like its New York counterpart, in this as well, was soon too small to accommodate the need for its services each winter. The Army gained permission in March to use part of the old City Hall to house 350 homeless men nightly, whom the city had fed and housed in the city prison. The railroads were "extremely kind" and agreed to transport men to their homes or to employment elsewhere if The Salvation Army would certify them as reliable. On October 3, 1894, the Lifeboat moved to a two-storied building which it shared with the No. 10 Corps at 117 Jackson Street. This was an ideal location: 13 of the 20 openings on the same block were saloons. The corps hall, dining room, baths, labor bureau and a cheap barber shop were downstairs. The shelter accommodated 190 men in two large rooms upstairs; one of these was a tin-lined dormitory especially for drunks, presided over by a "patient brother" who prayed for every man.[26]

Sacramento officials soon invited the Army to open a shelter there, but were refused with the assurance that their homeless and unemployed men were on their way to San Francisco anyway. Although the excitement and dangers of regular evangelistic activity, punctuated with Outriders, Charioteers, rock paintings and shootings, dominated most of the Army's attention in the Golden West in the 'nineties, expansion of the shelter work was not forgotten. Seattle opened a temporary shelter on November 30, 1893; according to *The War Cry*, the Army closed the shelter in April when the needs of winter had passed, although the official *Disposition of Forces* lists a food and shelter depot in Seattle from February 1894, onwards. In August the Army announced that part of the Pacific Coast Division's contribution to the worldwide "Jubilee Scheme" (to celebrate the 50th anniversary of the General's conversion) would be an extension of shelter work. In December, the Founder himself visited San Francisco; his major public address on December 17 centered on the "social scheme" and received widespread and enthusiastic public endorsement.[27]

When Ballington Booth announced in January 1893 the opening of the San Francisco shelter, he stated it was the "third" shelter in operation; the second he mistakenly supposed to be in Buffalo. Buffalo was certainly the third, but not for want of effort on the part of the divisional officer, Major Richard E. Holz. A German immigrant, converted in an Army street meeting in Buffalo, Holz had been drawn into joining a rival branch of The Salvation Army in 1884. His role in restoring most of the remaining schismatics to the parent body in 1889 was a triumph for him and for Ballington Booth. Holz proved to be an officer of exceptional zeal and ability; he opened 12 new corps in New York in one year. He understood from experience the needs of a man alone in a large city, and was determined to open a shelter at the first opportunity. News that a shelter was proposed for San Francisco and the Commander's Christmas plea to the Army to do more for "poor *out-of-home* and *out-of-work* creatures" could only have stimulated Holz to search during the winter of 1893 for a suitable building.

Seasonal employment was a particular problem in Buffalo; part of Lake Erie froze in winter, and thousands of men were forced out of work. It was not easy, however, to locate a building that was both large enough for a shelter and cheap enough for the Army to rent. After a false start in January, a food and shelter depot was opened in May 1893. The building, called the "Ark" in the prevailing maritime style, was a former lodging house at 111 Commercial Avenue; it had 150 beds, and a kitchen and cheap restaurant were added within a few weeks. The rent was higher than Holz would have liked; the Army was forced to charge 10, 15 and 25 cents for lodgings in order to clear expenses. The public responded to an appeal for a "subscription" which enabled the Army to lower the cost of the cheapest bed to seven cents, and finally to a nickel. This difficulty was introduced whenever the Army sought to acquire larger, better equipped shelters; officers were forced to charge as much as commercial lodging houses in order to balance their accounts, unless public donations on a regular basis, or the introduction of some profit-making enterprise into the shelter program, provided a reliable subsidy. Otherwise there could be no reduced prices, no way to carry men while they earned money at an outside job, and no opportunity to allow men to earn their lodgings by performing free labor in the shelter: the Army would become either a commercially competitive enterprise, or a "mere" mission—a charity. To avoid both of these alternatives, the Buffalo Ark was dependent upon public subsidy from the beginning. The shelter was filled to capacity through the winter, however, and must be considered a success. The accounts for March 1894 have survived: 642 men employed in the shelter, 18 found jobs outside, "worn clothing" sold to 39, 43 evangelistic meetings and 19 conversions. The rule against unearned charity was apparently enforced: of 9,442 meals served, only 20 were "donated to hungry persons."[28]

Programs designed particularly for the homeless, unemployed man remained only a tiny fractional part of the Army's overall operations—perhaps 10 officers out of 1,500 in 1893 were engaged in this branch of the Movement, and all such operations ran at a financial loss—but enthusiasm was clearly growing for the "Darkest England Scheme," as shelter work was still called. There were several reasons for this rising interest: the need for such facilities in winter was acute, which the Army, called to evangelize the outcast and fallen, could not ignore; the first several shelters were successful, in that men were converted, many more were kept from panhandling or crime in order to survive, and many others were assisted in finding employment; the approval and financial support of the public, hitherto indifferent to the Army or amused by it, began to rise; nor could officers have been indifferent to the impending arrival of the General himself—chief architect of the scheme—who toured the United States from September 1894 to February 1895. Many of his public addresses extolled the wisdom, the victories and the certain final triumph of the "Salvation Army Social Campaign."

A shelter was opened in Portland, Oregon, in January 1894. By February, The Salvation Army's official gazette listed five social programs for men, in New York, San Francisco, Buffalo, Seattle and Waterbury, Connecticut, where only a "woodyard" was listed. Major William Brewer, chief divisional officer of New England (except Connecticut) had been hopeful as early as January 1893, that he could begin a shelter ministry in Boston "on a large scale." The public was solicited in vain for the large sum—$2,000—Brewer required to begin a shelter, and the Army was forced to content itself with a labor bureau, which opened in 1895, sometime before May. The bureau, which operated at chief divisional headquarters, was more than an employment registry, however; needy men were "lodged and fed by different comrades" until they found work. By the end of the summer, International Headquarters observed approvingly that "social operations on the lines of 'In Darkest England'" were being "rapidly extended" in the United States, "and with most gratifying results."[29]

The events of the next several months—alas—were considerably less gratifying. Officers and soldiers alike were caught entirely by surprise by the resignation of the popular Commander and Mrs. Ballington Booth. The divisive controversy that swirled around the Booths for months after the first announcement in March 1896 was particularly confusing to officers engaged in the Army's fledgling social campaign. The Ballington Booths were fervent, talented and effective leaders, tightly strung and sensitive, whose relationship with the Commander's older brother Bramwell, and with his father the General, was complicated by several highly charged elements, in which jealousy, stubbornness and patriotism were prominent. Ballington's public statements, however, failed to touch upon these points, but claimed instead that his resignation (rather than carry out his orders to accept transfer to a position outside the United States) was motivated by important principles—one of which was his reluctance to remain in an organization that favored social work over Christian work!

"Your officers are afraid to speak," Ballington wrote to Bramwell on January 31, 1896, yet there were "a great many who say and feel that the social work is undermining the spiritual and diverting public funds and attention from the Army's first blessed aim and work." It is true that the Commander had commented before the crisis that it was a "little curious" to him that the social campaign "should have attracted an attention from the public out of proportion to the place it holds in the economy of the Army." It is also true, however, that Ballington and his wife had revived the auxiliaries in 1887 and began the *Conqueror* in 1892 in order to channel public financial support into the Army's enterprise to "uplift the fallen;" that he had officially declared that the public should support The Salvation Army because it attacked "vice and sin in their own strongholds"—it combined "effort for the social and physical well-being of men, as well as for their souls;" and finally, because "the Army succeeds." It must also have seemed "curious" to officers that Ballington, who had been in absolute command of the Army in America for nine years, should suddenly have noticed that it was going in the wrong direction. The new movement which Ballington and his wife founded in March 1896, the Volunteers of America, had a distinctly social emphasis.[30]

CHAPTER II

Frederick Booth-Tucker

Whatever the effects of Ballington's departing remarks on the morale of the few American officers engaged in social operations, the arrival of the new national leaders compensated them. Commander Frederick Booth-Tucker and his wife—the General's second daughter, Emma, styled the "Consul"—arrived in April 1896. They faced a delicate situation: there had been no large-scale defections from the ranks yet, but officers and soldiers were shaken and confused, and many influential supporters of the Army were alarmed for the future prospects of the troubled Movement.

Booth-Tucker—a hyphenated name was the price a man paid to marry into the Army's royal family—was the ideal man for the moment. Although a zealous Christian, his deepest interest and his greatest talent were in organization. He moved hardly at all in the realm of the abstract. Good would prevail only if the resources that good people had in unsuspected abundance were developed, organized and marshalled in the proper direction. Trained as a British colonial official, convinced of the redemptive power of the Army's compassionate theology and already well-versed in the intricacies of its military structure, Booth-Tucker was a planner, a labeler, a pigeon-holer for Christ. He was not, however, without a touch of whimsy: he converted the entire text of *The Field Officer's Orders and Regulations,* for instance, into verse ("Now let it well be understood, That every F.O. must be good.") Neither of the Booth-Tuckers was a spellbinder in public, unlike their charming predecessors, but they were gentle, kind-hearted people with an obsessive sense of the mission of The Salvation Army, for which they had already suffered much, and were to suffer more. Booth-Tucker's melting song, "I Cannot Leave the Dear Old Flag," written in 1896 to stem the trickle of defections to Ballington, is often still sung at the annual commissioning of new officers into The Salvation Army.

The Booth-Tuckers arrived in America dazzled by the golden future

31

that surely lay before the Army in such a prosperous and energetic country—once the Army's activities were properly organized. There would be little time, and less inclination, to linger over unhappy memories if the great work of the Army was pushed forward with sufficient vigor. To Booth-Tucker the blueprint for that campaign was already at hand—*In Darkest England*—which he regarded not merely as a general guideline but as an inspiration, the final revelation on social questions. And what was more nearly certain to draw the support of the public and the loyalty of the wavering auxiliaries back to The Salvation Army than a large-scale advance in the social campaign? All was clear to Booth-Tucker: there could be no delay.

Within a few weeks of his arrival, the new Commander, suitably disguised in "slum toggery," made a personal investigation into the living conditions of homeless unemployed men in New York. Ballington had done much the same thing five years before, collected much the same evidence and had come to similar conclusions, but this was forgotten—as the Lighthouse Food and Shelter Depot was itself forgotten: it had apparently failed financially sometime after the winter of 1894. Booth-Tucker found no shortage of clean and comfortable commercial lodging-houses for the poor, but the price (seven cents for a bed was the cheapest he could find), was too high for a destitute man, whose choices were either to sleep outdoors, in some archway, or in an open wagon pulled into an alley or in the county poorhouse, an alternative so dreadful to the poor that Booth-Tucker met a one-legged tramp who claimed he preferred suicide to the poorhouse.

"With regard to America," Booth-Tucker announced after his nocturnal investigations, "our social work is still in its infancy." A special "Social Work Edition of *The War Cry*" revealed how inadequate the effort had been up to 1896: there were but five "rescue homes" for women, 14 "slum posts" (an imprecise term, in that these "posts" were not always regularly staffed), a few visits to prisons. The number of men's shelters had actually declined in the past two years; there were still shelters in San Francisco, Buffalo and Seattle and one for women and children in New York City, but nothing there for men since the Lighthouse had been closed. According to a knowledgeable source, writing in 1905, there were only 11 officers working full-time in all "American social operations" in 1896.[1]

The first major step in the Commander's new social campaign was to transfer a number of officers into social activities. To stimulate and supervise their activities Booth-Tucker appointed for the first time in the American Salvation Army an officer whose sole responsibility was to oversee social-work operations from headquarters. According to his official career sheet Major William Halpin was appointed "national social secretary" on June 24, 1896; the *Disposition of Forces* first lists Major and Mrs. Halpin as "social secretaries" in July 1896. A "Slum and Rescue Division" was listed beneath their names, but no reference to facilities for men appeared until the September number, which listed "food and shelter depots" as part of the Halpins' department. Halpin was English, and had come to America as part of the "Smith Reinforcements" following the schism of 1884. He had commanded some of the Army's most famous and embattled corps, been a divisional officer, and for the last six months before his social appointment, editor of the Pacific Coast edition of *The War Cry.*[2]

Halpin's appointment was announced at an important gathering of the chief divisional officers held in New York City in late June 1896. A great advance of every aspect of Salvation Army activity was proclaimed: corps were to be opened in 100 new cities, a new, more vigorous training regimen for cadets was to be introduced, and the social work was to receive a special share of prayerful attention. Booth-Tucker announced a rapid expansion of rescue homes, shelters, food depots—"together with the introduction of a careful system of self-support"—half-way houses for released prisoners, homes for "waifs and strays," "elevators" (an English term for the workshops attached to the London shelters), and labor bureaus: "Never were the prospects more encouraging."

The money to finance these projects was to come, as usual, from what they could generate in their own operations, but not entirely: outside funds were indispensable for operations on such an optimistic scale. These were to be raised by the "Mercy Box Scheme." Based on "Grace-before-Meals" boxes used by the Army for this purpose in Britain and Canada, the "Mercy Boxes" were decorated with a list of the Army's social activities; they were designed to sit upon the dining tables of Salvationists, friends and auxiliaries to receive from each a penny per week. The Consul launched the mercy-box campaign at a large public meeting at the Army's new national headquarters building on July 23, 1896. She announced that the new campaign was aimed to reach the "criminal, fallen and drunken," the "workless masses" and the "large and hungry class, who border on the above." The meeting hall was decorated with a large—and as it turned out, a historically famous—banner, the joint project of the Army's Property Department and the new Social Department:[3]

OUR SOCIAL MOTTO IS "SOUP SOAP AND SALVATION!"

Booth-Tucker was full of mottos and ideas. The summer of 1896 passed into fall in a paroxysm of activity, most of it in the traditional form of all-night prayer meetings, torchlight parades and street-corner battles for God and the Army. The social program, however, continued to receive "special attention." The Commander praised the Army woodyard in Waterbury and urged the public to buy the wood, slept in disguise in a cheap Chicago lodging house, led a midnight march on the slums of San Francisco's Chinatown, and he and the Consul spoke with all the fervor they could muster to enthusiastic crowds of Salvationists and sympathizers about salvation for the soul and schemes to uplift the "downtrodden masses." Rescue homes and shelters, factories, rules, regulations, schedules, poured forth from the cornucopia of Booth-Tucker's bureaucratic wonderland. The "Knights of Hope" would visit police courts, jails and prisons to evangelize criminals and shelter them upon release in order to nurture them back into respectable society; the "Legion of Love" would do the same for the hapless employees of "streets, dives and brothels."[4]

There was opposition. Ballington was not entirely forgotten: neither the early success of his Volunteers of America, nor the sting of his parting accusations could be ignored. Many officers called for a wholesale return to the Army's first purpose of straightforward evangelism. Army leaders responded that the social and spiritual were but joint and indispensable parts of the great crusade. The Charity Organization Society of New York City protested against the Army's proposed new shelters: such refuges would draw the riff-raff of the country to New York. Booth-Tucker, a few months later, used shelter statistics to demonstrate that "the great majority of the people" frequenting the Army's New York shelter were "regular New Yorkers." When several reformers criticized Booth-Tucker for relying too heavily in his publicity on data compiled in London, he allowed they were correct: the United States *didn't* have a "submerged tenth"—perhaps only a submerged twentieth—perhaps only two or three million of truly poor people in the whole Republic: still "an appalling amount of human woe."[5]

Growth and change were part of the epochal year of 1896. The few programs in existence at the beginning of the year were galvanized into action. Innovations were introduced. By June 1896, the Seattle shelter and woodyard, which had apparently survived in some form since opening in 1894, had a "food and shelter team" to deliver firewood. The firewood Booth-Tucker advertised so energetically on his visit to Waterbury on June 29 was likewise delivered in "the social horse and wagon." Thus the noble horse, soon to become and to remain the mainstay of Salvation Army social work for 40 years, was introduced, delivering firewood. His greatest work for the Movement, however, as a collector of discards, had not begun.[6]

While on sick furlough in London, Major Halpin had written and sent to the American edition of *The War Cry* glowing accounts of the General's social schemes in operation in the mother city. Apparently more than enthusiasm was required, however, for carrying these schemes into practice in America, because Major Halpin was soon replaced as social secretary. As in so many early day developments within the Army, the chronology of this change is unclear. The career sheet of Halpin's successor states that the new appointment began September 1, 1896; however *The War Cry* still listed the Halpins as "social secretaries" at the opening of a new shelter in New York on October 6, and no change appeared in the official *Disposition of Forces* until December. In any case, Colonel Thomas Holland was the new supervisor, listed officially as "national secretary" for "social work"—the new official Salvation Army term for "slum, rescue and shelter work." Holland was English, serving in Canada as chief secretary (second-in-command), to Commander Herbert Booth when the new appointment came. The Army originally wanted Holland to organize a special campaign to evangelize American blacks, but whether because of design or the press of circumstances, "social work" soon occupied all of the energies of the "New Apostle to the Colored Race."[7]

No project, however commendable, was allowed to detract for very long from the wholesale advance of General Booth's great scheme. The Army in the New York metropolitan area threw itself into the briefly exciting work of providing refuge for several hundred Armenian Christian refugees fleeing from terrible persecution under the Turkish Empire. The Army world-wide had championed their cause, and American officers cooperated with the *Christian Herald* and three other agencies to care for those who reached these shores in October. This was recognized by the Army to be merely temporary relief; the "Darkest England Scheme," on the other hand, provided not only a relief from poverty, but its cure. "Ever since the publication of General Booth's *'In Darkest England,'* " wrote Commander Booth-Tucker in that same month, "the entire Salvation Army may be said to have devoted the last six years to the practical working out of the schemes therein embodied." Now it was time for action, for a "social boom" and a "food and shelter hustle" (along with several other kinds of "booms" and "hustles"). Booth-Tucker's enthusiasm was infectious, and many leading officers became loyal supporters of the new emphasis. The ease with which organizational structure came together in Booth-Tucker's hands and his gift for producing an apparently endless stream of novel and popular publicity campaigns propelled the Army's social enterprises into the period of their most widespread and rapid growth in the history of the Movement in the United States.[8]

The first opening, on October 6—the "first installment" in the great "social advance"—was a new men's shelter: the "Dry Dock Hotel," 118 Avenue "D," between Eighth and Ninth Streets, on New York's East Side. The ceremonial opening, conducted by the Booth-Tuckers as part of the regular annual meeting of the auxiliaries, was heralded as the beginning of "a new era in the Army's social work, at least in this city. . . ." The pioneer Lighthouse was apparently forgotten. The "Dry Dock" could accommodate 107 men in three floors of a four-storied building; the street floor was occupied by a wood-veneering business. The building was intended to offer a service, but not to the destitute. Beds were rented for 5 cents, 10 or 15 (the latter two prices advertised for "single beds"), so that a man could work himself up within the social structure of the shelter on what Booth-Tucker helpfully called "the ladder principle." The shelter provided poor workingmen—men with at least a few cents—with a clean, safe place to sleep; an uplifting atmosphere was provided by religious mottos on the walls and by regular evangelistic meetings. There was no provision, however, for a work-test at the Dry Dock Hotel.

A food and shelter depot was also opened in Kansas City in October 1896, and a prison-gate home in Chicago, at 184 North Clark Street. Although not listed as such, the prison-gate home was in fact a shelter for ex-convicts, the first such under Army auspices in the United States. Booth-Tucker opened it personally on October 1, after a parade to the doorstep led by the "Little Girls' Brass Band of the Northwestern Division." Finding that the San Francisco Lifeboat lacked facilities for a ministry among discharged prisoners, Army authorities there opened a prison-gate farm on November 15 in the nearby San Ramon Valley, on 312 acres loaned by George S. Montgomery, a wealthy and zealous supporter of the Army in California. From May to November 1896, three shelters for men and three prison-gate homes were opened, and, in addition, one shelter for women and several rescue homes. Forty thousand Mercy Boxes were distributed. In the fall the Army began a tiny "farm colony"— hopeful model for greater things to come—in Ramsey, New Jersey (originally used, apparently, as refuge for the Armenian refugees) and a national labor bureau and "inquiry department" to trace missing persons through the Army's corps and shelters and by using notices in *The War Cry*. In December the *Disposition of Forces* first listed all of these activities as part of "social work" under Colonel Thomas Holland.[9]

At the end of the year, Booth-Tucker, glowing with excitement, conducted "social congresses" in New York, Boston and Chicago. The social advance in 1896 had been remarkable indeed, as no one who observed the "stereopticon" displays, the "living tableaux" and posters at these meetings would have denied: the number of "social institutions" of all descriptions had increased from nine to 21; accommodations in them had almost tripled, to 1,400. Hearing officers tell of the joys of their work, seeing the rescued tramps and reclaimed prostitutes blinking before cheering crowds as they told of their new lives in Christ, the public should not have been surprised—as Salvationists certainly were not surprised—to learn that the social advances of 1896, which had drawn heavily on The Salvation Army's resources in officers and greatly increased its indebtedness, were but a prelude. In January, the Army announced a "Grand Call to Arms, Rally of the Troops" and "Plan of Campaign for 1897," which promised "some mighty and startling developments" in social work.[10]

In November 1947, The Salvation Army officially celebrated the "Golden Jubilee" of the Men's Social Service Department in the United States, on the supposition—which the meager and inexact surviving records did nothing to challenge—that its industrial rehabilitation program began 50 years before, in the late fall of 1897. This is not precisely true: a kind of industrial program operated in San Francisco in 1893, and even the New York project, from which the Army dates the development of the standard program, began, not in the fall of 1897, but much earlier, perhaps in December 1896, certainly no later than March 1897. Nevertheless, 1897 was the single most important year in the history of Salvation Army social work for men in the United States.[11]

Booth-Tucker's faith in the "Darkest England Scheme" was absolute: it was a "wonderful plan," which was "suited, with slight modification, to every country." He organized a special "Week of War Descriptive of the

Social Work of The Salvation Army," for February 14–22, in which every corps and institution in the country participated. There was "Drunkards' Sunday," "Prisoners' Monday," "Food and Shelter Tuesday," "Rescue Wednesday," etc., all culminating in Washington's Birthday, a "Day of Joy" on which many new projects would be launched or officially dedicated. The Commander was determined to have the entire panoply of the Darkest England Scheme in operation before the next visit of the General to the United States, which, when first announced, was to be later in the year 1897. There was much to be done to supplement rescue homes and shelter depots already in operation and to advance the crusade.

Plans at the beginning of 1897 called for shelter accommodation for an additional 2,000 men and 1,000 women within the year, and 5,000 more cheap meals served per day. A small shelter apparently opened in Salt Lake City in December 1896, and another in Santa Cruz, California, on New Year's Day 1897. The first of the major new openings came in January, when a large new shelter was opened at 21 Bowery, near Chatham Square in New York City. This was significantly called "The Workman's Hotel," a name which soon became the Army's favorite official descriptive term for its shelters. It was housed on the top three floors of a four-storied building loaned to the Army by A. W. Dennett, who had donated $100 toward the project at Booth-Tucker's large "social demonstration" in Carnegie Hall in December.

Likewise in January a new shelter was opened in Chicago, called the "Grotto Food and Shelter," at 1927 Archer Street. Men in the Army's Prison Gate Home did much of the work required to fit out the new shelter, which had 152 iron beds. Another Army shelter, called the "Evangeline," with accommodations for 274 men, opened at 387 South Clark Street on February 1. The "Grotto" was closed in May, and another shelter opened in its place, with beds for 140 lodgers, at 515 South State Street. On February 15 the "Workingmen's Metropole" (one of the General's terms for an Army lodging house) was opened in Philadelphia with accommodations for 110 men. On the "Day of Joy," Washington's Birthday, the "Workingman's Hotel" for 165 men opened its doors in Boston, at 886 Washington Street; the hotel occupied the top two floors of the former Berkeley Temple, which it now shared with divisional headquarters and a corps. Beds were 10 cents. On the same day in San Francisco, shelter operations were transferred to the new "Workingman's Institute," housed in a former athletic club for fashionable gentlemen, on the corner of Howard and New Montgomery Streets. After extensive remodeling, the new facility offered 150 clean beds at 5 cents each, 100 beds with lockers and "extra bed clothes" for 10 cents, 30 single bedrooms with writing tables and washstands for 15 cents, and several "nicely furnished" rooms with bedroom suites at 25 cents per night, or $1.50 weekly. The "ladder principle" was in effect here as well: "Ambition may ring a little tinkle in his ear. A 5-cent man, then a 10-cent man, then a 15-cent man, then—who knows? A graduate."[12]

Shelters opened, in fact, at a rapid pace from mid-1896. "Social institutions are springing up all around us, gloated *The War Cry* in February 1897, "as if at the touch of a magician's wand." Often the location óf these shelters would change after only a few weeks or months, and often several shelters, increasingly officially styled "Workingmen's Hotels," or "Metropoles," would be in operation in the same city. Even at the time, headquarters seems to have fallen behind in recording the correct addresses of all its shelters; because these shelters were almost always in buildings rented on a short-term basis, no description was kept of the properties, or even the addresses, as shelter programs multiplied and wandered. It is not possible, so long after the fact, to reconstruct from existing records an accurate list of Salvation Army shelters during this hectic period. It may be that some programs were not even reported to headquarters. Booth-Tucker's enthusiasm for the great work had become not merely infectious, but epidemic. On March 1, Colonel Edward Higgins, the chief secretary, announced in a special order that "in view of the rapid development of the social work throughout the country, the Commander has decided that no men's shelter, prison-gate home, or other social scheme, is to be promised or commenced without his consent in writing."[13]

Shelters were clearly attractive, not only to ihe Army but to their potential clientele, despite the limits on their effectiveness as agents of social uplift. There was a wide variety of facilities, personnel and program in Salvation Army shelters, but they all had in common the official conviction that unearned charity was humiliating and so degraded the recipient as to at least discourage and perhaps repel him from the path of self-improvement. Some shelters had woodyards and daily labor registries, but none could provide every applicant with the means to earn his food and lodging. For the remainder of the men, Army shelters served as commercial lodging houses. As such, most were clean and safe, and all were comparatively cheap. The "food depots" ran at a great loss to the Army, and provided a bargain to their customers, often neighborhood women and children. Many pioneer shelter officers were sympathetic and self-sacrificing. During the winter the Army's shelters were filled to capacity. Some shelters had regular lodgers from the beginning, and even as cheap hotels for low-paid workingmen the shelter program was a benefit to the poor.

But shelters and cheap restaurants were not, as Booth-Tucker readily admitted, as Ballington Booth had admitted before him, a ministry—or a business—unique to The Salvation Army. In any case General Booth had planned that shelters would form only part of the first step to redemption: "elevators," Salvation Army workshops, were essential to complete the first stage. This in turn led for many only to the second stage, the "farm colonies" about which the General was enthusiastic. Practical considerations as well compelled the addition of new enterprises to the existing shelter program. Factories and farm colonies were, at least in theory, capable of producing net income, and because pioneer officers seldom dallied over the subtle distinctions that separated promise from reality, these new programs had only to be announced to officers for visions of a golden stream to arise to enchant them. Their need for money was great. Shelters and cheap restaurants were expensive to operate; only an astute and efficient manager, running a shelter filled nearly to capacity, could avoid a deficit, and cheap food depots were always run at a loss. None of the Army's other social operations—the rescue homes, crèches, slum brigades and the new Cherry Tree Orphanage in New Jersey (announced on Washington's Birthday as well)—generated any income at all. The sacrifice of the faithful soldiers and officers—many of whom expected no salary or gave away most of the little they could collect—the Mercy-Box collections, and the gifts and loans of a few wealthy friends all taken together were not enough to cover the deficits resulting from the operation of the existing program, let alone pay for the exciting new enterprises which must soon be installed.[14]

The idea of combining some kind of light handcraft industry or commercial enterprise with the Army's shelter program as a means both of providing every applicant with the opportunity to earn his lodging and of generating extra income for the program was not original with Booth-Tucker; nor was the particular plan of collecting household discards for reuse and resale. *In Darkest England* proposed these activities, and explained in detail how they should operate. From 1891 onward, the American edition of *The War Cry* published complete and enthusiastic accounts of the operation of such programs in England. The Army's woodyards, beginning with the first in New York in 1891, were well-known, and studied by other philanthropists contemplating starting woodyards of their own. The fact that the San Francisco Lifeboat manufactured items for sale out of discarded materials was known to the Army nationally. Ballington received a duster from the Lifeboat in January 1893, and had a picture of it displayed in *The War Cry,* although Army authorities in San Francisco stopped the operation of the workshop in 1894 when its output began to compete with the work of local tradesmen. However original the idea may have been with him, the Commander's introduction of salvage operations into the men's program of The Salvation Army as a part of national policy, coming at a time when he had already stimulated intense and widespread interest in social uplift within the ranks of the Movement, represented a turning point in the development of social services in the United States. The salvage program grew rapidly in importance: by 1900 it was "one of the most important branches of this great social work;" and it became, in the end, the foundation upon which all Salvation Army social programs for men were built.[15]

The first "salvage brigade" in the United States was organized almost certainly in March 1897. Booth-Tucker, Colonel Holland and Staff-Captain McFee—recently transferred to New York as part of the national administrative restructuring of social operations—gathered a few unemployed men in the basement of the Dry Dock Hotel at 118 Avenue "D." Each man was given a handcart painted yellow with the words "Salvage Department" lettered in red, and a covering letter from Booth-Tucker addressed to "Friends," which explained that The Salvation Army sought to alleviate the sufferings of the poor without "pauperizing" them or adding to the burdens of philanthropy. This was to be done by means of household waste. It is uncertain where these men operated, what they collected, or what became of the material, but the operation was apparently a success. The amount of refuse that accumulated in the poor sections of large American cities in the 'nineties was enormous. Most cities had no municipal or commercial services to remove trash or clean streets; New York, for instance, had no municipal street-cleaning service before January 1895, when the first operation began under George Waring. There was no shortage of junk for the Army to collect, and it was soon necessary to transfer the salvage operation to a roomier place—in fact, to several roomier places. Sometime in April, the Dry Dock salvage crew was lodged in the six-storied premises of a former box factory in Vanderpool Alley, next door to Hogan's Alley, on the lower East Side. The building stood in a courtyard, facing the back of the alley. *The War Cry* confusingly

listed both Vanderpool and Hogan's Alleys as addresses, while the official
Disposition of Forces for May 1897, lists the New York "Salvage Department" at 26 Cherry Street, under Ensign Johnson. There were two more
salvage brigades by May as well, listed in "flourishing condition:" at 337
Newark Avenue, Jersey City, in an abandoned soap factory, under Captain
McDiarmid as "overseer," and at the corner of Staff and Lorimer Streets
in Brooklyn, in a former church, under William Range.[16]

In early May a salvage brigade was opened in Chicago. Major J. N.
Parker, who arrived on April 30 to take charge of social work in Chicago,
was "forced to close" the "Grotto" shelter almost at once, noting vaguely
that it was "not suitable for our work." He rented a hotel at 515 South
State Street as a shelter, and a separate building at 1337 South State Street
for the salvage department. This building housed the officers' quarters, the
"paper sorting" department—perhaps the first mention of this term in
American Salvation Army literature—and a store. This opening, like the
one in New York, was a boon: it was necessary, apparently sometime
before November, to move the paper-sorting, furniture- and stove-repair-
ing departments to another facility, at 1517 South State Street, leaving only
the store at 1337. The Chicago "social work," which advertised in October for "two strong horses, above the medium size; one single, top
covered wagon" was probably the first to use a team to collect waste
materials. Clearly four salvage brigades in the United States were enough
to demonstrate that "one beauty of the salvage work" was that it could be
"put into operation in every city of the Union." Moreover, announced *The
War Cry*, it was the declared "desideratum" of the Army's "beloved
leaders that brigades should be in operation in every city." The supposedly wealthy readers of the *Conqueror* were asked in June to help the
salvage brigade with donations whenever any of them moved from one
address to another, although at the time of the article only two metropolitan areas in the county had salvage brigades. Colonel Holland predicted great success: early in the year he publicly solicited the donation of
land for salvage brigades in every city with over 10,000 population. In July
he declared the the salvage work would be "one of the strong features of
the social work in the United States."[17]

Booth-Tucker confidently anticipated the rapid expansion of social
operations in 1897 by creating an administrative structure to coordinate
and supervise the programs coming to life. The officers involved received
their appointments from January 20 through April 28; the new apparatus
was almost fully in place by April, and completely so by May 1897. The

national headquarters department was officially called "Men's Social Wing" from February on (*The War Cry* coyly predicting that it would have "many more feathers at the end of 1897 than at the beginning"). In April, the new department directly administered a kind of national labor registry, the Knights of Hope, the reorganized Inquiry Department under Captain Jack Hurlburt, who was also Holland's secretary and ran the "express department," a driver, horse and wagon that ran errands, picked up the mail and delivered orders for the Army's publishing and supplies department. The "social wing" was located on the fifth floor of the new national headquarters building at 120 West 14th Street. Apparently all was not tranquility: a visitor described the office in April as a "hothouse of problems"—problems were "growing there all the time." Directly above it on the sixth floor was the Slum and Rescue Department, which supervised the Army's social efforts on behalf of women. The department was regarded as "practically a branch" of the "social wing," but was not officially attached to it.[18]

To directly supervise the burgeoning social operations in the field, administrative regions were created, each under officers listed in the official gazette as "divisional social superintendents." In April there were three of these districts. The Pacific Coast was under Major William Wallace Winchell, whose office and major program were in San Francisco. Winchell was an extraordinary man, indefatigable, eccentric, stouthearted and full of compassion. Born in Oswego, New York, in 1866, he fell in love with The Salvation Army at first sight, and joined in 1883 during a period of intense and violent persecution. He was variously thrown out by his family, mobbed, arrested and threatened with fire and dynamite: he responded to all with courage and love, and in 1893 described the "essence of Christianity" as self-denial. His long career as an officer—after January 1897 all of it in men's social operations—was one of unparalleled adventure. The Pacific Coast social division included San Francisco's new "Workingmen's Institute," the "Golden Gate Farm" (prison-gate home) and workingmen's hotels in Sacramento (first listed in April 1897), Salt Lake City and a shelter in Santa Cruz.

The Northwest social division was supervised by Major J. N. Parker. His entire responsibility lay in Chicago, where there were the Prison Gate, the Grotto Food and Shelter and two workingmen's hotels. The Greater New York social division consisted of a labor bureau, the Salvage Department and the Dry Dock Hotel, both officially listed at first at 118 Avenue "D," and the Workman's Hotel, 21 Bowery. The social superintendent was

Staff-Captain Joseph McFee, transferred in February from his pioneering labors with the San Francisco "Lifeboat." All remaining social operations were listed as "unattached," and were placed directly under Colonel Holland. These were the "farm colony" at Ramsey, the Waterbury woodyard, shelters in Seattle, Kansas City, Buffalo—the redoutable "Ark" still afloat—the "Metropole" in Philadelphia, the Workingman's Hotel and a woodyard in Boston, and a food and shelter depot listed for North Adams. In May the new "Salvage Departments" were first listed officially, in Manhattan, Brooklyn and Jersey City, and in July a salvage brigade was listed for Chicago. Also in July a new social division appeared, the Northern Pacific, under Ensign F. H. Fowler, who had arrived in Seattle in 1894 "with 25 cents and an old coffee pot and started at once to feed the poor," becoming in the three years since a local hero.[19]

In addition to organized, separate shelter facilities, The Salvation Army provided emergency relief and shelter in its meeting halls to the poor and homeless during the severe winter of 1896–1897. Free Christmas dinners provided by the Army for needy men were becoming increasingly common. Some winter relief programs were extensive; in St. Louis, 200 wooden bunk beds were placed in part of the No. 2 corps hall. Men were given free lodging, supper and breakfast of bread and coffee. Public response to these displays of immediate philanthropy was often enthusiastic, however such charity might have violated the Army's own official policy against mere handouts. Officers on the scene often tried to channel that grateful enthusiasm into organized support for a regular year-round shelter program. In the summer of 1897, Colonel Holland went on a nationwide tour of the largest of such cities, hoping to assist local Army personnel in this endeavor, and in general to give a "lift" to the social wing. At a "Monster Social Meeting" in Chicago's Princess Rink Corps, Holland dedicated the "social staff" of 17 new converts in their "attractive social uniforms." Shelters continued to open through the summer and fall: Pittsburgh; Topeka; Bridgeport, Connecticut; St. Louis. By the end of the year 200 men were listed as "employed" in The Salvation Army's shelters, food depots and salvage brigades, other than the transient applicants for relief who were required to do a few hours of work. The handful of salvage brigades was apparently at least successful in providing employment; of the 200 "employed" men, 70 were listed as at work in the "salvage, or waste materials operations."[20]

At this point a development occurred the significance of which proved to be out of all proportion to the small notice attached to it during the hectic months of late 1897. Booth-Tucker's fervent imagination embraced the whole of the General's great scheme: shelter and salvage brigades now set upon their triumphant course were together only the first stage: farm colonies must follow—and soon: the General's "wonderful plan" required them, and he would soon be on the scene in person, awe-inspiring as ever and ill-prepared, if past experience was any guide to high-ranking officers, to overlook the omission of such a vital part of his great scheme. Therefore the national social secretary must devote his entire attention to producing farm colonies as soon as possible, while another officer would have the responsibility of supervising the "city colony" branch, whose "extraordinary advances" in any case required such a concentration of attention. In October 1897, Lt.-Colonel Richard E. Holz was appointed "national social secretary" for "city colonies." Since during these years Army officers used the term "social work" to refer to social operations for men, precisely the same meaning as they gave to the term "city colony," his colleagues, *The War Cry* and Holz himself referred to his appointment as "national social secretary." Thus Richard Holz became the first officer whose sole responsibility was for all Salvation Army social operations for men in the United States.

Colonel Thomas Holland, meanwhile, became "fully absorbed" in the farm colony scheme. Although he retained the title "national secretary—social wing," he apparently had no authority over Holz's branch. Holland's opportunities to think about shelter and salvage work, let alone to interfere in their operation, soon disappeared, as did the colonel himself, transferred to Colorado and lost to sight in the distant project which came increasingly to occupy, and finally to obsess, Commander and Mrs. Booth-Tucker.[21]

The Salvation Army's farm colonies in the end came to nothing. The hypothesis upon which they were launched—that the urban poor were so corrupted by their environment, overcrowded, full of disease and temptation, that real regeneration, physical and moral, could come to them only in the natural and healthy atmosphere of the countryside—was not unique to The Salvation Army. Many poets, essayists and reformers held similar ideas throughout the nineteenth century; many others believed that a scheme like Booth-Tucker's would alleviate much hardship and increase the use of natural resources, even if it offered little hope as the overall cure for urban poverty. The Army's original farm colony proposal was taken seriously by President William McKinley, Secretary of Agriculture James Wilson, Senators George Hoar and Marcus Hanna, Governor Hazen

Pingree of Michigan, and a host of local officials in western states. For The
Salvation Army, the idea of the farm colony was not false so much as it was
irrelevant: the solution for urban poverty and the cure for sin in the city
had to be found in the city or not at all. It is a testimony to the faith of
Booth-Tucker and his followers that an idea as impractical and as hopeless
as the farm colonies could hold their devotion for so long. These officers
were convinced that it had been given to them to transform the face of the
land, that by employing proven principles of industry and agriculture, The
Salvation Army would cast down merely natural principles forever, and
build a new Jerusalem. God was on their side: salvage brigades, shelters,
farm colonies—one of these schemes, or all of them together, if only
carried forward with sufficient compassion and zeal, would usher in "that
modern Cannan below."

There were three major farm colonies, besides three rural properties
temporarily used by the Army for other purposes. The colony at Fort
Romie, near Soledad, California, was opened in October 1897, even before
the Commander officially launched the scheme at a huge rally in Carnegie
Hall in December. In August 1898, the second colony was officially
opened at Fort Amity in eastern Colorado, which was also the largest of
the three. Colonel Holland and the headquarters of the "National Colonization Department" were transferred directly to the scene of these
promising endeavors, where Holland became both postmaster and chairman of the school board. The Commander opened Fort Herrick in September 1898, on land 20 miles east of Cleveland on the Cleveland and
Painesville Electric Railroad. Colonel Holz was apparently given considerable responsibility for this colony, due to its proximity to national headquarters in New York and its distance from the two western sites. A
considerable body of correspondence between Holz and Booth-Tucker
about Fort Herrick has survived.

The colonies together at the height of their short-lived prosperity
housed 500 people on 3,000 acres. The decline of the project, although
made inevitable by many factors, was delayed by heroic efforts, especially
at Fort Amity, where the Army's investment in money and hope was
greater. In the end, poor soil conditions, lack of farming experience and
proper equipment, and ignorance of local market conditions all played a
part in the ruin of the colony scheme. The departure of Booth-Tucker
himself in 1904, drained by work and grief over the accidental death of the
Consul the year before, removed all that remained of official support for
the project. Romie was sold at a small profit in 1905; Amity at a dead loss

in 1909; Fort Herrick was converted briefly into an Army "inebriates' home" in 1904, then to an Army family camp in 1909; it was carried for many years at a loss on the territorial property account.[22]

In the meantime, the social operations for men that remained undramatically in cities continued to flourish. *The War Cry* for January 1, 1898, displayed on its cover a "mighty structure for the Glory of God," with many blocks, cornices and pillars marked "salvage brigades," "colonization scheme," and maternity work. The General's long-announced third American tour, which finally took place in January-April 1898, gave the expected boost to social activity. Colonel Holz wrote to the departing Founder that the recent visit had given a "mighty impetus" to social work in the United States: thus energized, The Salvation Army would go forward to bring "many despairing ones into a better and brighter life." The year brought important openings. Workingmen's hotels appeared in the Army's official list in March for Los Angeles and Newark. In May, Colonel Holz reported to headquarters that he had located a suitable building in Cleveland and predicted "splendid developments along social lines out here;" the Commander, like other staff officers, was occasionally tempted to view things from 14th Street: in July, he congratulated Holz on how well the new Cleveland shelter was doing, adding that he was certain "these outlying cities will be a source of joy and gratification to us in the future."[23]

The Southern part of the United States was the last region into which the Army's social campaign penetrated. The people of the South—black and white—were located far from the cities in which The Salvation Army was first established and in which it was becoming respected. They had so far responded only languidly to the several Hallelujah crusades sent to win them to God and the Army. There were few large cities in the South in the late 1890s, less overcrowding in them than in cities farther north, much less need for winter relief and shelter. Army leaders were determined to see the flag waving everywhere in the country, but privately were not overly optimistic about their prospects in the South: even after several openings in the region, Colonel Holz wrote that it would "require lots of thrusting and stirring about to make a success of the South." In May, he authorized the chief divisional officer of the Ohio, Kentucky and Southern Province to locate a building for a shelter in Louisville. In July 1898, workingmen's hotels were officially listed in Louisville and Houston, and a new "Southern District" was optimistically created to superintend their affairs. Workingmen's hotels were listed in March 1899, in Atlanta and

Nashville, and sometime later in 1899 a combination hotel, restaurant and "Woodyard for Out-of-Works" was opened in Little Rock. Booth-Tucker called the opening of the Nashville shelter a "marvelous victory," but only it and the Houston shelter survived into the next year.[24]

Despite the advances attributed to it, however, The Salvation Army's "mighty structure to the Glory of God" was not free of difficulties. The practical implications of the new administrative framework were unclear, and with the Commander devoting more and more of his energy to the distant and complicated colonization scheme, Colonel Holz was increasingly left on his own to struggle with the confusion. The fundamental difficulty was that the national social secretary—Holz—did not have direct authority over either the operation of social activities or the personnel appointed to command them. He repeatedly asked Colonel Higgins, the chief secretary, for an official "brief of appointment" that would formally outline his responsibilities in the new position, but, discouragingly, none was produced.

In 1892 the Army in the United States had grown to such proportions that the system of regional oversight based on "districts" (large metropolitan areas, perhaps, or a state) was superseded by one based on chief divisions, which combined several districts. The men in charge of these new areas were called "chief divisional officers," or more commonly, "chief D.O.'s," and were among the Army's most influential leaders. Holz himself had been one of the original eight. Now, however, he took a less sanguine view of their eminence. The chief D.O.'s regarded all social operations in their areas of command as part of that command; without a formal statement of superior authority, Holz was forced not only to cooperate with the chief D.O.'s, but to defer to them. Foreseeing difficulties even in nomenclature, Holz suggested at once that the title for the regional social officers be "social superintendent," not "divisional social secretary," a term which seemed to have convinced several of the new men that their authority was independent of the chief D.O.'s. When Major J. N. Parker arrived in Chicago in April 1897, for instance, he believed that the authority of the social secretary and that of the chief division were about to be separated. The change in title was made—Holz had to remind the chief secretary at least once to use the correct new title—but it solved nothing. Chief divisional officers transferred officers into and out of the social operations within their divisions without consulting Holz, and often without informing him. Chief D.O.'s simply went directly to the Commander for approval for any new arrangement they wanted to make. Holz's appeals, and those of the social superintendents, for more officer person-nel for new social operations were either ignored, or men were offered who lacked ability, or who—as Staff-Captain McFee put it—"were too lazy to make a shadow." Soon Holz's own social superintendents began to act "independently" of him. In the spring of 1898, Holz instructed each superintendent to file a weekly report with social headquarters. By Oc-tober only three had done so with any regularity, two had not responded for four months, and three had never responded at all. Holz had no accurate knowledge of the financial operations of his department.[25]

Finances were—alas—part of the problem. In February 1898, national headquarters issued an official order—called a "minute"—allowing each chief D.O. to draw "25 percent of the profits" of the "social work" in his division. Holz was not only not consulted, he did not receive a copy of the covering letter. The decision was apparently confirmed in the fall of the year. Unhappily for the social officers, "profit" was not defined, so each chief D.O. took what he liked: some took 5 percent of shelter gross, some 10 percent, and one—Colonel William Cozens of Boston—extracted 15 percent, which, with the 5 percent demanded by national headquarters, was "altogether unreasonable." Holz urged a national policy of 5 percent of gross for the chief divisions until the shelter was cleared of debt, then 10 percent. This, along with national's 5 percent, would be 15 percent of gross, which he contended would be "about the limit the shelters can stand all the year around." But the chief D.O.'s were not only skimming the shelters, they were taking large sums of the money raised for the annual Christmas Dinner Appeal (theoretically a responsibility of the social wing) and using the money for other purposes within the division. And worse still, in August, responsibility for Mercy-Box collections was transferred to the chief divisions, which were to retain two-thirds of the funds collected to spend at the chief D.O.'s discretion on social work in the division, the remaining one-third going to national headquarters. To add insult to injury, in two divisions the chief D.O. added the duty of actually collecting the Mercy-Box funds to those of the local social super-intendent![26]

Holz informed Higgins and Booth-Tucker not once but several times that his position was "very unpleasant;" he used the term "anomalous" to describe his position in writing both to Booth-Tucker and to subordinates. The Commander was largely responsible for the confusion. He insisted that there was no distinction between the Army's evangelistic and social activities—his entire campaign to increase the Army's social work, in fact, was based on that insistence: the Army's special part of the divine plan was to uplift and redeem the poor, by whatever means the Army could find, or invent. An administrative division would have been symbolically false. Then, too, Booth-Tucker's genuine enthusiasm for social work did not prevent him from believing—which he candidly admitted to Colonel Holz—that the Army's field work was more demanding than the social department, so that the chief D.O.'s inclination to transfer men with poor records to the social branch had at least the Commander's tacit blessing. "After all," he wrote to Holz in January 1899, "the work of a corps officer is far more difficult in many respects than that of the management of a social institution;" the latter required honesty, a capacity for detail "and thirdly, spirituality;" many men possessed such qualities who had not been "particularly successful in the field," or whose health had been ruined by their "excellent service" there. This in fact was part of the beauty of the scheme in Booth-Tucker's eyes: when the social work was in the experimental stage, and for the major administrative positions now, officers of experience and ability were needed—men like J. N. Parker, Holland and Holz himself—but once the great machinery of social redemption was operating, it should generate its own staff from those whom it rescued—men whose sole qualification would be zeal and a willingness to learn. Staff-Captain Parker had predicted in 1892 that shelter staffs would arise from converts. The Commander cheerfully assured Holz that he would certainly support the secretary in rejecting any really "useless" men from the social branch.[27]

The Booth-Tuckers, and Colonel Higgins, were wholly committed to the success of the Army's social campaigns, and did all they could within the system they had created to accommodate Holz and his staff. The Consul held a series of "little social gatherings" in her home for the national staff. Holz was appointed to the national finance and property councils, which administered among other holdings all Army social properties (all of which, incidentally, were either rented or heavily mortgaged). The national leaders wrote often to Holz during his years as national social secretary, soothing and encouraging him, praising him for the "magnificent advances" made by the "city social" and predicting an even more wonderful future for the work. Their boundless enthusiasm must have been infectious; the Consul wrote to Holz in April 1899:[28]

> God is indeed with us in our schemings for the poor and
> needy, and if only we can mix in an abundance of spiritual

No. 1- Chicago Central "Center Chorus" with Sr.-Captain William Beuton, c. 1959. [Courtesy of Lt.-Col. Hasney, MSSD-C.]

No. 2- 1914 Commerce truck from the Los Angeles Industrial Home.
This is often cited as the first truck used by The Salvation Army.
It apparently is the oldest surviving photograph of a Salvation Army truck.
[Photograph by Paul Parker, courtesy of SAA.]

No. 3- Chicago Central Men's Social Service Center in 1950s showing old-style dormitory with lockers and imprinted bedspreads. [Photograph by D. Ottaway, courtesy of Lt.-Col. William Hasney, MSSD-C.]

No. 4- **First Group Regional Directors of "Service-to-Man" program in Eastern Territory, 1945.**
From left (standing): Herbert Sparks and Frank Guldenschuh;
(seated) Harry Sparks, Peter G...ld, H. F.....A......, Bid...d.....l. A.........H.....

No. 5- The Philadelphia Men's Social Band, 1925.
[Courtesy of SFOT-E.]

No. 6- A dining room scene at the New York No. 1 Industrial Home (c. 1912-15).

Yourself and friends are cordially invited to be present at a select gathering to meet

Lieut.-Col. Richard E. Holz,

of New York,

(NATIONAL SECRETARY FOR SALVATION ARMY SOCIAL WORK.)

Thursday, December 1, 1898,

eight o'clock p. m.

Fourth Avenue Presbyterian Church Chapel,

Fourth and Kentucky.

Rev. J. Kinsey Smith will preside

No. 7- A printed invitation sent out for people to meet Lt.-Colonel Richard E. Holz on the occasion of his being appointed National Secretary for Salvation Army Social Work in New York. [Courtesy of SFOT-E.]

No. 8- The Paterson, N.J., Men's Social Service Center yard.

light and love with all our work I believe we shall see *mighty accomplishments* in this country. I should not wonder if we do not alter the whole face of society in the big cities.

The social officers were often a source of encouragement to Holz as well. Adjutant Wilbur Gale, Holz's "aide-de-camp" at headquarters, was delighted with his new appointment, calling the social "this special field." Staff-Captain McFee, sent as social superintendent to Chicago in January 1898, began almost at once to quarrel with the Northwestern Chief D.O., Lt.-Colonel George French, about finances and personnel. Still, whenever he was tempted to resign, he wrote to Holz that "the human wrecks" that came to him for help always made him "turn back to their aid." Relations between Colonel French and McFee were admittedly discouraging, but Holz found other "sectional officers" more cooperative. He continued to travel widely, scouting cities for social openings and encouraging local staff. In October 1899, when Holz was transferred back to the field as a chief divisional officer himself—for the enormous Ohio and Southern Chief Division—he looked upon his years in the social as a "bright spiritual experience."[29]

Holz presided—more or less—over important developments in the Army's social work for men. The administration of shelters continued to be difficult. Measures introduced to reduce operating costs were often counterproductive; Holz reported to Booth-Tucker in March 1899, that the Buffalo "Ark" suffered a prolonged "set-back" when it discontinued serving free coffee and rolls to lodgers. Even though shelters continued to open, Holz and many other officers were convinced that salvage operations should become the mainstay of Salvation Army social work for men. They believed this not only because Booth-Tucker and the General believed it but for more immediately practical reasons as well. Army principles still required a work-test wherever it was possible to employ one. Woodyards, while still much in use, could not be operated profitably in many places because of the cost of purchasing raw wood and competition from cheap machine-cut firewood. Army shelters joined with salvage operations, on the other hand, would become self-supporting, well-run hostels for needy men willing to work, and—theoretically at least—could be expanded to accommodate every applicant: the public would recognize the Army as the final solution to the problem of the homeless poor, and give it unstinting support.

If only we can supplement our shelters with some sort of
industrial work, we will be able to get a great deal of
public support, and gradually get hold of most of the relief
work in our big cities.

At the same time, the practice of placing a shelter and a corps in the
same facility was breaking down. The "shelter corps," such a noteworthy
adjunct to the earliest food and shelter depots, tended to attract as regular
attenders the same sort of people who joined The Salvation Army in every
corps: working class families, respectable immigrants, children, converts
who were anxious to shun the temptations and embarrassment of old
associations. Shelter converts were more sympathetic to the clients, but
even they were often as uncomfortable as the regular corps people were
with any prolonged contact with the shelter's seedy, unsociable and often
drunken clientele. At an important series of national and chief divisional
staff officers' councils in May 1899, these matters were fully discussed: it
was widely noted that if a large building was rented for a corps, it could be
used as a shelter as well, whereupon—hopefully—income from the shelter
could be applied to the rent for the whole. At the same time the councils
declared that shelter and corps must be kept "entirely distinct" from each
other, and it was to be a "rule" that there should be a "separate entrance"
for hall and shelter. Yet the conversion of the men in the shelter was the
uppermost objective of the entire operation. Every shelter was festooned
with mottos that proclaimed evangelism as its purpose.[30]

Clearly, the ideal institution would be one that combined clean and
respectable housing for homeless men with an industrial program to serve
as work-test and a means of restoring self-respect to the man and as a
source of income, and in which evangelistic activity was carried on by the
officer manager and his staff as a regular part of the operation of the
facility. The Salvation Army Industrial Home was the result. The first use
of the term, apparently, appeared sometime before September 1899, a list
compiled at the end of that month for publication contains "Industrial
Home for Men" as the name of the Army's facility for men in New
Brunswick, New Jersey. Before the end of December 1899, a new "Industrial Home for Men" was listed for Newark. Other, similar descriptive
terms began to appear in Army directories: "Industrial Salvage Brigades
for Homeless Men" in Denver and Cleveland, "Industrial Salvage Depots
for Homeless Men" in Boston and Jersey City (at 137 Newark Avenue; a
half-century later this was believed in long retrospect to have been the

first-named Industrial Home in America). The salvage operation in Chicago, by the end of 1899 the "most extensive and successful" in the United States, was still listed as the "Salvage Warehouse" at 411 Harrison Street. It is not certain which of these programs, or if any of them, was the first to combine housing, collection and reclamation of salvage and evangelistic activity in one program, nor is it certain what sort of materials were collected, nor how these were disposed of for profit. An official list in late 1899 shows "Junk Store for Sale of Goods to the Poor" in Chicago and Boston. The transition to institutions of the new pattern was slow and uncertain. The official *Disposition of Forces* first employed the term "Industrial Home" in June 1900, listing five of them; but the *Disposition* for that month still listed 12 "salvage brigades," 69 hotels and shelter depots and 23 food depots and restaurants. The terms "industrial home" and "salvage brigade" were used interchangeably in headquarters accounts in June 1901. However it was defined, industrial or salvage work was not an extensive part of The Salvation Army's social operations at the end of the century: in late 1899 there were 49 shelters for men, accommodating 5,311, and 14 salvage brigades and woodyards, with housing for 213. The successful combination had been found nonetheless: the future of the Army's social work for men lay with the industrial home.[31]

CHAPTER III
The Industrial Homes, 1900–1920

Ideal patterns, the perfect solutions that eclipsed all false solutions, escaped recognition for years. Many different kinds of programs were in operation at once, sometimes duplicating or competing with each other. The industrial home gained but slowly on the shelters, woodyards and farm colonies. In 1907, fully 10 years after the official introduction of salvage operations into Salvation Army social work, 83 percent of the Army's 9,700 accommodations for men were still in workingmen's hotels. National headquarters was no more clairvoyant in selecting an efficient bureaucratic structure to administer its social operations.[1]

Colonel Richard Holz's complaints to the Commander and chief secretary that the national social secretary should have definite authority over personnel and operations apparently brought belated results sometime shortly after he returned to the ranks of chief divisional officers in October 1899. Briefs issued to divisional—now called "provincial"—social officers in 1901 gave them authority over the selection and transfer of officers in their institutions, general management of program and the leasing or purchase of new property. Such authority was subject only to the final approval of the national social secretary, and, in the case of property matters, the national finance board. The relationship between the provincial social superintendents and the men in the industrial homes and shelters in each region was clarified, at least in theory. In practice many early day institutional officers were zealous eccentrics, more concerned with rescuing sinners than following, or even reading, directives or filing reports. The relationship between the provincial social officer and national headquarters, however, was clear in theory.

After Holz's departure, Colonel Thomas Holland remained in nominal command of all Salvation Army social programs, as he had before. He remained at Ft. Amity, where his duties as national colonization secretary and farm manager occupied his time. A "general secretary"—at first Major Howells, then Brigadier Thomas W. Scott (later Lt.-Colonel)—was appointed as assistant secretary or "prime minister," a kind of deputy in charge of city social operations nationwide. Until January 1, 1900, the assistant secretary served as superintendent of the Metropolitan [Greater New York] Province as well, but these duties proved too great a burden for one man; on January 1, 1900, the two functions were separated when Staff-Captain Sam Wood was made superintendent of the province. Born in Canada—billed as the "Saved Canuck"—Wood had moved to California as a child, where he became a boy drunkard on fermented cherries and pursued a life of crime after reading several dubious novels. Happily he was converted in The Salvation Army and later joined some of the Army's wildest pioneer adventures in California. Wood began his long and eventful career as a social officer in 1898, as divisional superintendent in New England. On August 1, 1901 he was replaced in command of Greater New York, the "home province," by Major Walter F. Jenkins, an English officer with wide experience in British and American posts, and former chief divisional officer in Michigan. Outside of New York, however, considerable authority over social operations somehow remained with chief divisional officers, and even corps officers could still begin "social work" on their own, simply by renting an old hotel for a shelter. The cloudy division between farm colonies and the "city social department" at national headquarters, moreover, continued until July 1902, when the "national social department" was officially designated, but, alas, not for long. In July 1903, another administrative change was introduced, and in October, still another.[2]

Commander Booth-Tucker, having responded in part to Colonel Holz's request for more independence, at least for the provincial social superintendents, seemed, after the colonel's transfer, to withdraw close attention from the details of the administration of the city social program on the national level. His faith in the General's scheme was unflagging, but even his energy could not stretch to cover his pet farm colonies, the Army's burgeoning evangelistic crusade and the variety of social activities he and the Consul had so enthusiastically launched. Progress was made on the ground despite the uncertain state of the national administrative machinery during the last years of the Booth-Tucker administration.

Most of the gains in men's social operations were in shelters. As cities expanded into their suburbs and populations shifted, commercial properties in once-respectable neighborhoods came on the market at bargain prices. Medium-sized hotels were, of course, the most attractive to Army leaders, but church buildings, theaters, athletic clubs and gymnasiums, public lecture halls and office buildings were also rented or purchased. Officers were convinced that cheap, clean and well-run hotels for the working poor, or for any homeless man who could come up with a dime, were a great social service. Despite the fact that many shelters were not able to provide the applicant with a means of earning the price of admission, having neither woodyard nor employment bureau, that some did not offer regular religious services, and that all hotels, regardless of size, equipment or location, were difficult to operate on a profitable basis year round, the Army continued to operate these facilities and to open new, ever-larger ones. This was because the need for such shelters, especially seasonally, continued to be very great, and because, in theory anyway, shelters were supposed to operate in connection with the "elevators"—the industrial homes—which were being opened during these same years.

Shelters varied widely. The "Dry Dock Hotel," 118 Avenue "D" in New York, opened with such enthusiasm in 1896 as "the first installment" of Booth-Tucker's new social campaign, sank slowly into seedy neglect. By the turn of the century only the "lowest and toughest element" frequented it, and the Army officially described it in 1902 as "a rather dirty and poorly equipped house." Boston had three shelters, the "Hub," which housed 63 double-decked beds of "japanned iron piping, absolutely indestructible and hygienic," all in one large room, the auditorium of a former theater; the "Central" on the second floor of the Army's provincial headquarters; and the "Unity" in north Boston, supervised by Adjutant William I. Day, the once-famous "Happy Bill" of California, who wrote that a social officer should be, in order, "zealous for souls, kind-hearted, clean and neat, a good business operator, and economical." In 1904, Chicago had six hotels for poor and unemployed men, and one small one for women, with a total bed capacity of 1,000. The "Metropole" in Philadelphia, one of the city's two shelters for men in 1902, was clean and warm, but had no bathing facilities, so the Army fell back on the use of a public bathhouse, whose generous owner gave the Metropole officer free tickets to distribute to "worthy bathers." By April 1903, the Army nationwide had 80 hotels and shelters of all sizes and descriptions, four of them for women.[3]

Some of these facilities were very large, surprisingly so by the standards of a later day. The "Lighthouse" shelter on the corner of Ninth and Market Streets in St. Louis was the largest Salvation Army operation in the

United States in early 1902; it offered 420 beds at 5 cents each. It was superseded in eminence later in the year, however, when the Army purchased and refitted its "model high-grade hotel," the "Braveman," 18 Chatham Square, New York. The Braveman had 10 floors, elevators, steam heat, electric lighting and modern showers. Its 505 beds were intended not so much for the penniless as for underpaid workers on a tight budget—men the Army called "mechanics and clerks." The Braveman was officially opened by the Consul in January 1903, with a large crowd of Army dignitaries and a brass band in attendance. In 1906, another large Salvation Army lodging house "deluxe" opened its doors: the famous Boston Peoples' Palace, accommodating 288 guests. With an indoor swimming pool and its nicest outside rooms renting for $2.50 weekly, the "Palace" served lodgers that were not among the desperately poor. A writer for the *Boston Transcript* visited the Palace a year after it opened and was surprised to find that the renters were decent, well-dressed workingmen and many students.[4]

Industrial homes remained, of course, an indispensable part of the same great plan that generated shelters. If a man who lacked a dime applied to an Army shelter, he was to be sent to an industrial home, where he could obtain room and board in exchange for his labor in the home while he searched for permanent employment. Booth-Tucker urged the public to support these institutions, where "human wastage" was employed "in collecting, sorting, repairing and selling the material waste." The difficulty in opening more of these places of useful enterprise was financial: "Our industrial homes are filling a great need," declared Commander Booth-Tucker in 1902, "but we are terribly handicapped for want of suitable buildings. High rentals and poor accommodations," he lamented, were "the rule rather than the exception." The rental or purchase of facilities suitable for the Army's industrial operations, and remodeling them and purchasing equipment was much more expensive than providing the same number of accommodations in a shelter, and, unlike a shelter, an industrial home did not generate income from the first day of its operation. The Army obtained a contract in Chicago in 1899 to clean all the refuse from the streets and alleys of several wards. In Boston, the Army placed 500 baskets in the homes of sympathetic householders; later Army wagons called "regularly" to collect the deposits, which were then sifted and sold in a salvage store. The "one difficulty" in the path of "extending this interesting and suitable method for dealing with the unemployed," wrote

Booth-Tucker in late 1899, was that "considerable expense" was "connected with the purchase of teams and baskets."[5]

Despite the financial difficulties, successful programs had become established in several cities in the three years of the new century, and existing operations moved to larger, better quarters. In October 1900, an industrial home opened in Paterson, New Jersey. Its operation, and the Army's growing reputation in this field, attracted favorable attention. In November 1901, the board of directors of the Paterson Rescue Mission at 42 Mill Street voted to invite an equal number of Salvation Army officers onto their board and to turn the operation of the mission over to the Army, which gladly accepted, converting the mission into an industrial home at once. The mission, first opened in 1895 for the "honest poor and homeless," retained its original name for another 50 years. Another important opening in 1901 was a new location for New York's pioneer salvage operation in a new industrial home on West 30th Street near 10th Avenue, opened with places for 20 men. Within a year it had outgrown the facilities; the stables had to be moved to make room for more paper sorting, and the second-floor retail store moved to a nearby location to increase sleeping accommodations. It was during this year as well that the Commander, always interested in better ways to advertise the industrial work to the public, issued instructions for new signs for these facilities. The regulation, dated August 1901, called for white lettering on a dark-blue background and the wording: "The Salvation Army Industrial Home for Men." By the end of 1902, by Booth-Tucker's own count, there were 53 Salvation Army "industrial homes, woodyards and second-hand stores for the unemployed" with total accommodations for 650.[6]

Progress through 1902 had been encouraging, but only when compared to nothing, which was the official status of industrial work when Commander Booth-Tucker came to America. The Army provided accommodations for a few hundred, when tens of thousands were in need: more must be done. In June 1903, The Salvation Army launched an elaborate financial scheme to raise quickly the sums necessary to purchase and outfit new industrial operations on a large scale. The Salvation Army Industrial Homes Company was incorporated on June 17, 1903. The stated purpose of the company was to acquire property for, and to carry on, the operations of industrial work, shelters, hotels and restaurants. The means of acquiring the cash for the purposes of the corporation was the sale of $500,000 worth of capital stock, in 50,000 shares of 10 dollars each, 25,000 shares of common stock and 25,000 shares of preferred, which paid a six percent annual dividend. To preserve complete control of all operations in the hands of The Salvation Army, only the preferred stock was offered to the public. All but a few shares of common stock were transferred to The Salvation Army Corporation (the General had agreed, belatedly and reluctantly, to the incorporation of The Salvation Army in New York in 1899; his refusal to do so in 1884 had caused the first of the Army's two major schisms); the few remaining common shares, plus a few preferred shares, were assigned to the various members of the board of directors, chaired by Booth-Tucker and made up entirely of national headquarters staff officers. The Salvation Army controlled 25,321 shares before sales were opened to the public, and thus retained complete control.

This scheme did in fact generate capital. Stock valued at $220,000 had been sold by 1911 when the enterprise was abandoned. Some of the stock had previously been offered to officers who had loyally bought shares on the market. There were difficulties connected with the Industrial Homes Company from the start, which proved in the end to be overwhelming. Firstly, as directors of a corporation, the national staff officers had to supervise every detail of the financial administration of every industrial home, since these were now part of the assets of a corporation for which they were legally responsible. Horses, for instance, were part of capital investment. In December 1904, The Salvation Army Industrial Homes Company owned 277 of these useful creatures; the directors' minutes through these years were filled with requests such as one to "sell bucking horse," or, rather touchingly, one from Baltimore for $100 for the horse renewal fund—"In place of 'Ginger,' who died." Secondly, and more alarmingly, the Army's social operations had garnered criticism from several influential professionals in the field of organized philanthropy, and even some friends, who disapproved of the fact that The Salvation Army had become a financial corporation. The most prominent of these critics was Edward Solenberger of the Massachusetts Charity Organization Society, who publicly condemned the Army in 1906 for being a profitable business that could afford to pay huge dividends to its investors. Thirdly, and more serious still—although it must remain largely a mystery because of incomplete documentation—was the fact that something seemed to have gone seriously wrong between several high-ranking officers and The Salvation Army after the stock scheme was started. At least one of them, J. Ransom Caygill, threatened to use the stock he had been allotted as a director, along with other shares he had purchased on the market, to do something vaguely unpleasant. Sad to relate, Booth-Tucker was also involved. His relationship with his former in-laws, the Army's international leaders, deteriorated badly after the death of Emma in 1903 and his transfer back to London early the next year. He kept his industrial home shares, and private correspondence in 1911 shows that American Army leaders distrusted his motives and were anxious to buy him out. And if these difficulties were not enough to finish the Industrial Homes Company, it was revealed as early as 1905 that while capital funds were being generated by the scheme, the payment of dividends on outstanding stock caused an annual deficit in the operating budget.[7]

In 1903, however, there was a lasting improvement in the affairs of the Army's industrial homes. Enthusiasm for the stock scheme was at first very great; officers felt a new start had been made, and several major new facilities were acquired with down payments made up from initial stock sales. There were further changes in the national administration, one of which brought to the men's social branch of The Salvation Army in America an officer who became perhaps its most influential and successful leader, Brigadier Edward Justus Parker, then aged 34 years. Born in Elgin, Illinois, in 1869, Parker became an officer at age 16, and a district officer at 22; before coming into social work he had been in the national Trade Department for almost five years, the last two as secretary of the department.

Parker was an officer of exceptional ability. A veteran of the Army's earliest days, when officers were sent penniless, fearless and full of joy into one adventure after another—he had 12 appointments in his first three-and-a-half years as an officer—Parker never lost his courage or his passion for souls. Time and experience revealed, moreover, that Parker was a talented administrator. He had a natural talent for bringing order out of chaos and found pleasure in even the most routine details of office work. Like Booth-Tucker, Parker had a taste for categories, plans, and projections, but Parker was steadier, less whimsical than the Commander. He was not dull, however; he was fascinated with mechanical marvels, which he felt certain could be utilized to great effect as weapons in the great salvation war; the Trade Department under Parker's leadership sold a vast array of cameras, stereopticons and phonographs. He himself was a skillful amateur photographer, who produced and showed the lantern slides that accompanied the Consul's popular lecture series. Her death in a train wreck just four weeks after his new appointment was a severe blow to Parker, and so preoccupied Booth-Tucker with grief that the new administrative structure was left to function on its own for months.

Parker's appointment was part of a reorganization of the "social wing" that was announced in two parts, in July and October 1903, but which seems to have occupied headquarters for most of the year. Farm colonies to one side, the rest of the social wing, still under Holland and Scott, was divided into three parts: first, the "National Social Department" remained directly under the two leaders. Second, a "Central Social Department" with headquarters at the Braveman Hotel was created under Brigadier Ashley Pebbles. Another veteran of the Army's California pioneer days, Pebbles was converted at an Army street meeting in Sacramento in 1884 and spent four years as Rocky Mountain Chief Divisional Officer before joining the social staff. Apparently the Central Social Department was a regional distribution of direct responsibility for shelters and hotels. The third part was a "National Industrial Department" under Walter F. Jenkins. This arrangement was short-lived and probably never functioned. In October, all social work for men outside of farm colonies was more logically divided into two distinct branches: The "National Industrial Department," responsible for industrial homes, under Lt.-Colonel Thomas W. Scott, and the "National Metropole and Relief Department" under Brigadier Edward J. Parker.[8]

The National Metropole and Relief Department over which Parker now presided included hotels and shelters for men, and a few for women, cheap restaurants, labor bureaus, two homes for Scandinavian sailors in New York, cheap coal and ice for the poor, prison work, missing persons and the team and wagon of the express department. The major responsibility of the new department was, of course, the "metropole" program, but of these, even as to their exact number, Parker knew little. He discovered that there were no national standards or guidelines for the Army's hotels, except the 10-cent nightly charge. By the time Brigadier Parker took charge of the Army's hotels, a pattern in their operation had begun to emerge, which the passage of time only clarified. Although the Army continued for many years to acquire hotel properties—culminating in terms of size in 1913 with the purchase of the enormous Booth Memorial Hotel at 225 Bowery, which had 610 rooms—these facilities increasingly served simply as cheap hotels for "decent fellows" who wanted a safe, clean, quiet place to sleep. Religious services ceased to be mandatory for lodgers, and in many hotels the only evangelism was that offered to a man who asked a religious question of the officer in charge. Critics openly disputed the Army's claims that its hotels had any charitable or evangelical function. After the turn of the century there was a steady decline in the use of wood as household fuel, and the Army's shelter woodyards, which had experienced competitive difficulties in the best of times, gradually disappeared. Penniless applicants either were sent to the nearest industrial home, or a lucky few were allowed to do chores around the hotel. The rest were sent away. Salvation Army leadership regarded the management of a hotel, except for the largest ones, as less demanding than that of an industrial home. Social officers themselves came to look upon an appointment to an average-sized Army hotel as lacking in prestige.[9]

The industrial homes, on the other hand, gained every year in importance and effectiveness. Parker's first years in the department were a period of transition for the Army's industrial work. There, too, woodyards were abandoned, to be replaced in most places by the collection and resale of wastepaper. Even in San Francisco, where wood continued to be used in stoves and household furnaces, income from paper matched that from wood by the end of 1904. The handcart quickly went the way of the woodyard. When Parker came to headquarters in 1903, collections in Manhattan were still made in pushcarts. Each morning the men who pushed the carts lined them up on 14th Street, and ran off with them in all directions when an officer blew a whistle. The volume of collections, especially the increasing amounts of bulk materials like wastepaper and clothing, quickly made the cart obsolete. The horse-drawn wagon, first used in Chicago for this purpose in the fall of 1897, became by 1905 the Army's standard means of collecting discards. Among the first wagons obtained by headquarters were 10 light vans purchased from the Red Cross for $25.00 each; although these represented a great improvement over pushcarts, they were too light for hauling heavy loads of paper and rags—"a ton was an overload"—and were soon replaced. There was at that time no departmental guideline as to the quality and value of draft animals. The prices paid for horses in one center over five years, for instance, varied from $15.00—for a horse which hopefully could still walk—to $85.00 for a strong, healthy animal.[10]

The administration of Frederick Booth-Tucker came to an end in November 1904. His departure, made inevitable by the strain of overwork and grief and by the fact that he had been in the American command, a premier appointment, for eight years (a long time by contemporary standards), was nevertheless unsettling to American social officers, for whom

Booth-Tucker had been a kind of "zany" Moses. The record of the Army's achievements in social welfare during Booth-Tucker's years in command were indeed startling: accommodations for the poor had increased from 600 to 10,000, and the total of all social institutions from 30 to 209. These increases, he proudly reminded field officers in March, placed "social work in America ahead of even England in point of numbers," and gave to American forces the "leading position" in the Salvation Army world. The Commander's departure was made even more unsettling by the fact that his successor, Evangeline Booth, the General's daughter, who arrived in December, was not to inherit his powers intact: there was to be a major change in the geographic structure of The Salvation Army in the United States. The administration of social operations, still adjusting to its recent changes, was swept into a fresh vortex.[11]

Evangeline Booth held the rank of commissioner and retained the title of commander, but a kind of deputy commander, Lt.-Commissioner George Kilbey, was appointed to directly administer Army affairs in a new Department of the West. All operations in Illinois, part of Indiana and all states west of the Mississippi River were included in the new department. Kilbey was subordinate to the Commander, but also responsible in his own right to the General in London. Other than the Commander, no officer any longer had responsibility for any operations on a national scale. In January 1905, when the new arrangement became official, Brigadier Parker briefly became "private secretary to the chief secretary for social work." Confusingly enough, despite what sounded like a national appointment, Parker's responsibilities were confined to metropoles in the Department of the East. The division between industrial and shelter work was in any case eliminated almost at once as unworkable, since many men employed in industrial homes slept and ate in nearby Army hotels, and all authority over social facilities which remained in provincial commanders' hands— confined as it was to a number of shelters—was transferred to the social secretary. Lt.-Colonel T. W. Scott was placed in charge of the social work in all of the new departments of the East, with the exception of a new Department of the Metropolis which was created and given to Parker. This included responsibility for all social relief activities operated out of the headquarters building on 14th Street, and direct administration of all men's institutions in greater New York and New Jersey. In September 1905 Brigadier Emil Marcussen, recently transferred from his native Denmark, became secretary for the Midwestern Social Province—Colonel Scott's former region—with headquarters in Cleveland. This division of regional responsibility within the eastern department of regional responsibility remained more or less intact until 1920, but in 1908 Parker became social secretary for the East with direct responsibility for his own eastern region and overall responsibility for the department. Brigadier Ashley Pebbles became social secretary for the new Department of the West, with headquarters at 365 State Street in Chicago.[12]

In 1905, Brigadier Parker, now in charge not only of metropoles but also of industrial homes, resolved at once to seek information about the details of their operations, which he already understood in principle from the two years he had spent administering the Army's shelters, which operated in some cities in conjunction with the homes. The best place for information was the officers themselves. So that Parker could meet the men in charge of the Army's industrial work in the new Department of the Metropolis, an historic banquet was arranged in the dining room of the Braveman hotel early in 1905, formally to welcome the Parkers into industrial work. It was Parker's first official contact with the officers whose work he would not simply supervise, but guide and develop, for more than 20 years.[13]

The manager of the Braveman since 1903 was Adjutant Charles C. Welte, a Swiss immigrant born in 1875, reared on New York's lower East Side, and an officer since 1896. Management of the Army's premier institution was officially looked upon as an exception to the Army's otherwise cavalier opinion of shelter officers. Welte was regarded as a man of ability, and his successful operation of the Braveman, a difficult appointment, was well known to Parker from headquarters accounts. Now that he met Welte on the spot, as it were, Parker was even more impressed, and resolved to use the young officer in more important ways. Parker arranged for the adjutant to become his private secretary. When Parker became territorial men's social secretary in July 1908, Welte became the assistant secretary, his trusted right-hand man. Parker was a good judge of men; and he found Welte to be highly efficient, industrious, discreet—that rare man who was able, and willing, to put the goals of an organization above his own ambition, and who could serve as an assistant with touching loyalty for 22 years.[14]

Industrial homes continued to open, and existing programs moved into better facilities, even as Parker began to introduce nationwide guidelines for their operation. The industrial work in Newark expanded from one pushcart in 1900 to a large two-horse dray to carry paper and a dozen one-horse wagons to collect discards in 1904, when it moved into large new facilities; all outside signs and the helpful mottos inside were painted by a grateful sign painter once helped by the home. In Pittsburgh, the Army converted a former German Turnerhall at Home and Plummer Streets into an industrial home, under Staff-Captain John Sprake. As German-American populations moved out from city centers, their large concert-hall/gymnasiums became available to the Army; several of these buildings were used as industrial homes. In Minneapolis, the industrial department obtained the former city hall. New facilities were purchased in Syracuse, Cleveland, Evansville and in Los Angeles, which opened in May 1906; a shelter and an industrial home dormitory shared different floors of the same three-storied building in Los Angeles, still a common arrangement at that time. In Chicago, the industrial home at 167 Aberdeen and its warehouse at 411 W. Harrison supplied merchandise to 10 stores. The major project of these years, however, was in New York City. In 1906, The Salvation Army built, and in July 1907 occupied, the "largest and most completely equipped industrial home in the world," the five-storied New York No. 1 Industrial Home at 533–537 W. 48th Street. Built as a kind of national model institution under strong pressure from now Lt.-Colonel Parker, the "New York No. 1" was complete: stables in the basement, wagons carried to the roof for storage, and the chapel, shops, paper baler and dormitories for 150 men on the five floors between. Staff-Captain Sam Wood, who had managed the home at the former location on W. 30th Street, was placed in charge of the new operation.[15]

On the other end of the scale were the many small homes, which together formed the large majority of the Army's industrial institutions. In 1910 the average capacity in an industrial home was 23. Many were much smaller. One cause of the high turnover among clients in the small home was that the men could not take a bath: the officer's wife objected to using the same tub. In 1906 Adjutant John O'Neill purchased intact a social operation of sorts from the local Army corps in Grand Rapids. It consisted of two former laundry wagons, a horse ("Bob—with a limp"), a rundown rummage store and two employees, who promptly quit when O'Neill asked them to collect materials in a systematic manner.[16]

System was not, however, unknown in industrial work: uniform mailing cards, designed to solicit discards from householders, were introduced in 1905; a regulation was issued that "industrious and sober" workers were to receive a standard "premium" of 25 cents per week after five or six successful weeks on the job; and the industrial home board ordered portraits of the General placed in "selected" institutions in 1907. There were many successes, many "trophies of grace," during these years, most of them anonymous men whose contact with The Salvation Army was brief; once "washed in the Blood of the Lamb," they passed on through obscure lives into the bliss of the redeemed. Some were more famous: the poet Vachel Lindsay was sheltered by the Army in Atlanta in April 1906 and in Newark in May 1908, and left as a grateful tribute his most famous poem: "General William Booth Enters Into Heaven." John Allan, first American-born Salvation Army officer to become international Chief of the Staff, was converted in the Paterson Rescue Mission-Industrial Home which his father managed, and entered officers' training from there in 1906.[17]

The Army's commitment to uniformity, which only became more pronounced with each passing year, did not dampen its enthusiasm for new ideas. In July 1903, the Toledo Industrial Home displayed its own five-piece brass band, "the only Social Band in the United States"—not however, the first: 10 years had passed since the San Francisco "Lifeboat" crew had sallied forth with two snare drums and a fife. Parker himself was fond of mechanical innovations: in 1908, he produced a traveling lecture entitled "Problems of the Poor," illustrated by a "Combination Electrical Dissolving Stereopticon and Cameragraph under the skillful direction of Ensign Raymond Starbard." He also convinced the industrial homes board in 1909 to install a telephone in his home, as the home managers often used public telephones to call him there at night on the telephone of his long-suffering next-door neighbor. Less innovative, or less efficient, rivals began to fall by the wayside. In 1905 the Volunteers of America in Worcester and the American Salvation Army in Philadelphia (the last forlorn remnant of the "Moore Split" of 1884), sold to the Army the stock and facilities of failed industrial programs in those cities.[18]

In July 1908, the administrative structure for social programs was changed again, and, except for an interlude in the Department of the West from 1909 to 1913, placed on the basis it has retained until the present day; the creation of three territorial commands in 1920 and a fourth in 1927, multiplied but did not alter this hierarchy. Lt.-Colonel Edward J. Parker was made Eastern Territorial Social Secretary. He had territorial responsibility for all programs, and immediate responsibility for all institutions in the seaboard states; Lt.-Colonel Thomas Stanyon was made "Midwestern Social Secretary," subordinate to Parker, with immediate responsibility for institutions in the rest of the territory. Brigadier Emil Marcussen went to Chicago as social superintendent of the Department of the West. In 1909, however, that department was divided into three independent regions: the Western Social Department, with headquarters in Chicago, under Lt.-Colonel John Addie; the Pacific Coast Social Department under Brigadier Marcussen who was transferred to Oakland in September 1909, to take charge; and the Central Social Department, the smallest in responsibility, created with headquarters in Denver. Its first superintendent was not appointed, however, until 1910: Colonel Thomas Holland had never fully recovered from the effects of the train wreck which killed the Consul in 1903; the Denver appointment was seen by headquarters as a kind of rest cure for Holland, but to no avail: he died in June 1911. In August 1913, this threefold division of the social Department of the West was abandoned, and Marcussen was restored to Chicago as social secretary for the undivided Department of the West. Parker's direct access to the national chief secretary, Colonel William Peart, his membership on the industrial homes board and his direct authority over the all Army social operations for men in the populous eastern United States gave him great influence. The instructions he prepared in increasingly minute detail had the force of law for institutions east of the Mississippi, and were accepted as the standard everywhere in the country.[19]

Earlier in 1908 Parker convinced the industrial homes board that all purchasing of supplies and equipment for the institutions of the eastern department should be placed in his hands. Separate "Minutes" by the chief secretary, dated June 1, 1908, established a uniform system of six kinds of record books for every industrial home—five for hotels (which required, of course, a register, but no stock or store books), regulated the transfer of furniture or equipment from institutions without permission, placed control over all wastepaper sales contracts in the hands of headquarters, and forbade managers to take home food supplies from the institutional pantry. Parker's "Minutes" went much further. The first 29 of these were issued together on December 1, 1910; others were added from time to time until after World War I. These orders laid down uniform standards for every aspect of the operation of industrial homes and hotels: the men were to bathe upon coming into the home for the first time, and at least once per week thereafter; menus were suggested (breakfast: cornmeal mush; dinner: potato soup; supper: mutton stew); wagons were to be dark green with red gear and trim. The longest order, No. 17, dealt with the purchase and care of horses; it ran to ten 8½″ by 11″ typed pages. Order No. 21, explaining the 13 grades of paper stock sold by the Army, ran to five pages. When Parker joined the department in 1905 he visited an industrial home in which the dining room walls were loyally painted in wide parallel bands in the Army's colors of yellow, red and blue. No more! Order No. 23 stipulated ivory ceilings, tan walls and red baseboards.[20]

The difficulty with these helpful instructions, of course, was that only the largest institutions could implement them. But commitment to a common goal and experience with common problems created unity among social officers in other ways. In every regional division social officers met together in councils to read papers and share experiences. Colonel Scott conducted industrial councils in Chicago in November 1904; Brigadier Marcussen held a similar annual gathering for officers in the Midwestern Social Department. The social and industrial officers of the metropolitan New York area met weekly for "spiritual and social encouragement." Social officers from the entire territory met annually at the beautiful New York No. 1 building on W. 48th Street, in meetings presided over by Commander Evangeline Booth herself. The problem discussed at these gatherings were much the same year after year—paper and rag sales on a fluctuating market, feeding the men, feeding the horses, keeping books, increasing store sales, preventing pilfering of items and petty cash (euphemistically referred to as "leakage")—and so, more encouragingly, were the stories of rescue and redemption which gave purpose to the whole enterprise: "last but not least," announced one catalogue of discussion topics, "men." Industrial home officers used these councils to affirm that there was "no such thing as waste material, human or otherwise."[21]

There certainly were problems in these years before World War I, but not, apparently, with money. The years 1904–1914 were a period of great advance in numbers of institutions, accommodations, rolling stocks and in the numbers of new soldiers and officers brought into The Salvation Army from the industrial department. This advance, which laid the foundation upon which the Army's men's social services rested until after World War II, was paid for by paper. Prices for paper were not especially high. During this period the Army never received more than 45 cents per hundredweight for "mixed" (all grades of clean paper scraps), 60 cents for "news" (clean, dry, neatly folded newspapers) and $1.00 for "book" paper (book pages, bound and unbound, and such things as ledgers, blank books and school exercise books). Indeed, in 1911 paper prices collapsed when the Federal Government brought pressure on the monopolistic practices of the "paper trust," causing a few months of "considerable difficulties" for the Army. The Army's steadily high income from paper came not from high prices but high volume, and from the competitive advantage of the "Salvation Army pack," which the Army modestly offered as "the cleanest packed paper stock in the market." There was an enormous increase in paper tonnage shipped by the Eastern Territory: from 1904 to 1912 the total increased from 21,088 tons to 34,650 tons; in the 10 years following 1909, the department shipped 350,000 tons of wastepaper. The Army's retail stores during these years, while also a source of income, were regarded by most offcicers as a service to poor families.[22]

These were boom years for the Army's industrial programs. The year 1910, described as "the very best in the history of this department from every standpoint," witnessed the acquisition of five new major properties in Atlantic City, Boston, New Haven, Brooklyn (on the corner of Raymond and Tillary Avenue) and Jersey City. The previous home in Jersey City—shortsightedly housed in a former saltpeter factory—had been consumed in 1908 by a spectacular fire from which the inhabitants barely escaped. The Salvation Army built a new building to its own specifications at 248 Erie Street and placed in charge the irrepressible and ever-more-famous Major W. W. Winchell. The neighbors were not at first encouraging: throughout the neighborhood children pelted the officers with stones, and frequently hurled stones and insults through the windows of the new structure. The Winchells lavished "very pretty picture cards," fruit and lead pencils on the assailants, held special children's meetings and outings for them, and finally won them over. In New York City, the Army, not content with the largest industrial home in the world, made it larger, adding two more floors to the New York No. 1 on West 48th Street. An Army newspaper just for social officers, called *The Social News,* was launched in 1911—not, as Commander Booth assured them, that their work needed any introduction. Industrial officers developed a sense of *esprit de corps* that was radiant, calling themselves "socialists" and exchanging many winks and knowing glances when in the company of their comrades from the field. One social officer, Staff-Captain James Simons, went so far as to originate the "socialist yell." There were many reasons for encouragement in 1913: since 1904 the Army's social institutions had more than doubled, increasing from 195 to 415. In 1911 there were 107 industrial homes in the United States, with beds for 2,421; in 1912 there were 118, and in 1913 there were 124 homes with accommodations for 3,139. In terms of the total capacity of the Army's facilities for men, industrial homes increased from 24 percent of the total in 1911 to 29 percent in 1913. Hotel officers need hardly have despaired, however; although the total number of hotels declined by one in 1913—because the Braveman and another in New York City were sold—a still more daring experiment in hotel management began in that year, when the Booth Memorial Hotel opened at 225 Bowery. It had 610 rooms. Besides the national headquarters building itself, social officers could now proudly point out that they operated the two largest and most expensive (and heavily mortgaged) Salvation Army buildings in the United States—New York No. 1 Industrial Home and the Booth Memorial Hotel.[23]

So far the advance was borne by the noble horse, the object of considerable official solicitude and genuine affection. Staff-Captain Welte displayed an industrial home team to a visitor in 1907 as if they were pets, "for pets they are." Social Order No. 17 carefully instructed industrial home managers to hire stablemen who would be "kind and interested in the welfare of the animals under their care." Industrial-home horses were not to be used by the manager for Sunday driving: "The horse that has worked faithfully six days of the week deserves a rest on Sunday and holidays." Favorite animals were coddled, given light work, entered in work-horse shows and parades, and groomed to a hair. One officer—admittedly an immigrant from England—seriously proposed in 1912 that the Army should revive the farm-colony scheme in order to provide a retirement pasture for the Army's faithful "worn-out horses, who have labored for us so willingly day after day, and some for many years." For many years the official letterhead of the social department portrayed an industrial-home horse and wagon. But change was in the air.[24]

Considering their expense and the sense of novelty that still attached to motor vehicles in these years, and The Salvation Army's special fondness for publicity, it seems incredible that no clear record remains of when and where the Army obtained its first motor vehicle. The Army in America had used borrowed motor vehicles as early as 1908 for special children's excursions, but it is almost certain that the first motor vehicle actually purchased by The Salvation Army was an industrial-home truck. Writing long after the fact, Parker recalled that he had had difficulty in persuading the official board at headquarters that was responsible for social operations to purchase a truck, which he recalled was a "Kohler," and which he believed was the Army's first truck. (In fact, no such motor vehicle name as "Kohler" existed, but Koehler trucks were manufactured in New Jersey from 1913 to 1923.) This impression is confirmed in Parker's statement written in 1916, much nearer to the time in question, that "the first automobile for the industrial," to which the board agreed after long hesitation, was purchased to carry the heavy loads of paper being shipped from New York No. 1 Home. A pamphlet, published in 1916 by the New

York No. 1 Home, indicates that an electric vehicle was used there for hauling rags and paper; a photograph printed in the pamphlet shows a vehicle, but it is too indistinct to make a positive identification: it may be a Koehler model 1913–1915. Koehler did not manufacture electric vehicles.

In any case, a better claim for the honor of purchasing the Army's first truck is found elsewhere. Adjutant Ray Starbard, appointed to the Worcester, Massachusetts, Industrial Home in 1912, apparently purchased a Koehler chain-drive truck for the home in 1913. Starbard's son recalled that the purchase was made in 1912 or 1913, certainly before he—the son—went to London in 1914 as a young member of the corps band, which participated in a great Army congress in that year. The enterprising Starbard even arranged for a local Salvationist businessman, Albert Ridyard, to secure the Koehler agency so that the Army could obtain a truck for the home at the dealer's discount. Brigadier Lawrence Castagna recalled that when he and his parents, Adjutant and Mrs. John Castagna, arrived at Worcester in October 1921, they found an "old one-lung Kohler [sic] left in the yard as it did not operate." Adjutant Castagna had Ridyard remove the old truck. The driver of the Worcester truck was Percy Hamley, a newly arrived bandsman from England. According to his daughter, Mrs. Major Ed Dimond, driving the truck was probably his first job in America, but if it was the Army's first truck the young Mr. Hamley did not realize it at the time. The Providence Industrial Home purchased a Koehler from Ridyard shortly afterwards. The oldest existing photograph of an Army vehicle in the official records shows a 1914 Commerce truck, a kind of vehicle manufactured in Michigan and later in Ohio from 1911 to 1932; the truck in the photograph had 1914 California license plates and bore the address of the Los Angeles Industrial Home. This photo is often used to represent the Army's first social truck, as no earlier picture of one has been found. In the spring of 1915 the Philadelphia No. 1 Industrial Home purchased a motor truck, an event which the manager, Staff-Captain John McGee, who was "mighty pleased," considered noteworthy enough to report to *The Social News*. By July 1916, motor vehicles were more commonplace: New York No. 1 had four of them, and there were 17 in the Eastern Territory.[25]

Rapid expansion and mechanical marvels notwithstanding, these years were not unblemished by difficulties. In 1912, the Army's Founder, General William Booth, died, and so, finally, did the industrial home stock scheme, which was formally dissolved in January 1912. The remaining stockholders received gold bonds that paid the same interest, secured by a mortgage on properties the Army owned outright. The company's board of directors had not functioned effectively since 1908, when Edward J. Parker and Emil Marcussen became full-fledged territorial social secretaries. The Army's industrial ministry inspired competition during these years, mostly from unsavory persons who liked the idea of collecting things for free and selling them later for money. Masquerading under a variety of military-sounding titles, appearing on street corners and on doorsteps in uniforms which only an expert could distinguish from those worn by Salvationists, these fraudulent collectors inspired the Army to conduct several careful advertising campaigns to alert the public: "Beware of Imposters!" stormed Staff-Captain Myles Pickering in Brooklyn. The Army finally had to resort to lawsuits to eliminate the worst offenders.[26]

The courts were not always so accommodating. From time to time The Salvation Army had been subject to criticism from officials of municipal and private charitable organizations, centering on its industrial work, which these professionals regarded as a profitable enterprise in disguise as a charity. The most serious of these incidents occurred in Philadelphia in May 1906, when Edwin D. Solenberger of the Massachusetts Charity Organizations Society publicly condemned the Army at the annual convention of the National Conference of Charities and Corrections. In February 1914, an assistant district attorney in Buffalo investigated the industrial home there, as part of a general investigation of the city's missions. The Army readily admitted that it did not give away all the goods donated to it, but that this was clear from the language of its solicitation literature, and from the Army's well-known commitment to self-help. More serious was a case in Los Angeles, where in 1913 the city council created a Municipal Charities Commission and empowered it to grant licenses for charities to operate within the city limits on two conditions: that all funds collected be under the control of persons who were local residents, and that all funds be spent locally. The Salvation Army agreed to these conditions readily enough, but the president of the charities commission, Dr. Milbank Johnson, denied an operating license to the Army's industrial home on the grounds that the territorial and national assessments on its income violated the new ordinance. Two visits by the territorial commander, Commissioner Thomas Estill, in December 1913, and April 1914, were of no avail. In September, the charities commission withdrew even the Army's temporary permit. Three storekeepers were arrested for selling donated goods without a license. On January 26, 1915, the industrial officer, Major William J. Dart, reopened the store, was promptly arrested and jailed when he refused to pay the fine. The police treated Major Dart courteously, and he became the unofficial prison chaplain. Public opinion turned strongly in favor of the Army, which resolved to fight the case in the courts at whatever cost. On February 3, 1916 the California Supreme Court unanimously struck down the offending statute on constitutional grounds.[27]

As accommodations in industrial homes grew in number and the program prospered by the introduction of such time- and labor-saving devices as the telephone, steam-powered baling machine and the occasional motor truck, the Army did not abandon its ancient crusade against alcohol. Although the largest institutions declared as part of their advertising material that the purpose of the home was to "provide employment for homeless and workless men," the "unfortunate man" who lost his job because of the closing of a shop or old age formed one group of men in many of the homes. However, the great majority of men living and working in the Salvation Army industrial homes were heavy drinkers, men who had lost their place in society and could find no other because of drink. At a great social congress in London in 1911, William Booth proclaimed that the distinction between Army industrial homes for the unemployed and "homes for inebriates" or "drunkards" had never existed in the United States. One experienced manager estimated in 1912 that 80 percent of the men who came to the Army industrial homes were "victims to some extent of the drink appetite."

Many managers took it upon themselves to direct special religious appeals to the heavy drinkers in their institutions. Officers counseled those working with drunkards to show kindness, patience and understanding in explaining religion to them, and advised that those who became converts and tried to renounce the "foam of death" required more kindness and patience still. Special meetings were held to encourage new converts by the example of saved drunkards who had persevered. Industrial officers enthusiastically participated in the annual "Boozers' Parade" in Manhattan, which began in 1909 and continued until Prohibition became law. The most exuberant warrior in the war against the "Moloch of Drink" was Major W. W. Winchell, who organized the "Drunkards' Brigade" in the Jersey City Industrial Home in 1911. Winchell, his assistant and five or six converts from the home, roamed the streets well into early morning, collecting drunken men and carrying them back to the home in an industrial wagon (the "ambulance"). There they were sobered up with hot coffee or the major's famous "cocktail"—Worcestershire sauce, a raw egg and Epsom salts—given solid food and lodgings, and, hopefully,

No. 9-   The New York No. 1 Industrial Home.
[Courtesy of SFOT-E.]

No. 10-   Classes held at the Gold Dust Lodge, NYC,
during the Depression.
[Courtesy of Annie Laurie (Mrs. Major Andrew C.)]

No. 11- Men's Social Service Handbook Committee. Denver, Nov. 20, 1957.

From left: Captain George Duplain (San Francisco, Calif.), Brigadier Wm. Jobe (Kansas City, Mo.), Sr.-Major Ernest Agnew (New York), Major Wm. Browning (Washington, D.C.), and Brigadier Peter Hofman (Cleveland, Ohio).

[Courtesy of Lt.-Colonel P.J. Hofman.]

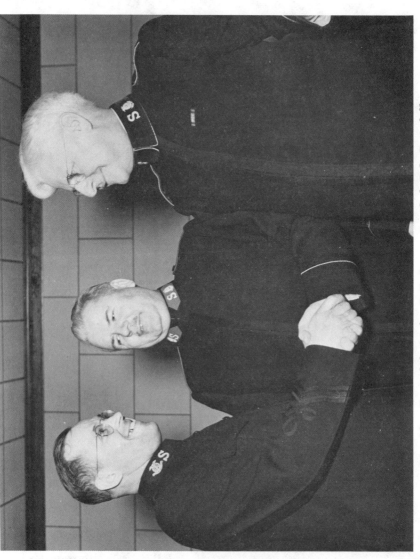

No. 12- From left: Major R.E. Baggs, Lt.-Col. J.O. Dowdell, and Comm. Alexander Damon in Philadelphia, 1940. [Courtesy of Mrs. Patty Yellis.]

No. 13- Commissioner Richard Holz enrolls a dozen adherents,
September 9, 1979, at the Fresno A.R.C. private chapel service on Dedication Sunday.
He admonished them to be true to their commitments to the Lord and The Salvation Army, remembering always the privilege of being among the twelve chosen to be enrolled on this very first Sunday in the new chapel.
[Courtesy of MSSD-W.]

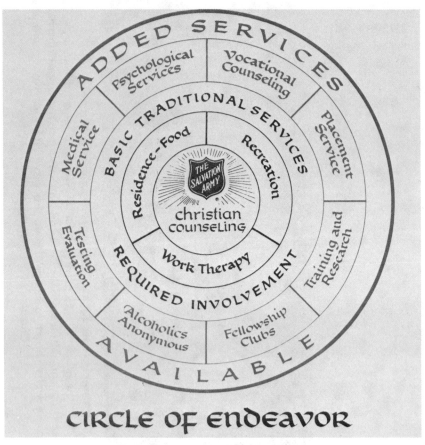

CIRCLE OF ENDEAVOR

No. 14- The Circle of Endeavor
showing elements in the rehabilitation of the total person,
The Salvation Army's ultimate goal.
[Courtesy of MSSD-W.]

No. 15-   The Dry Dock Hotel in New York City.
[Courtesy of Brig. Lawrence Castagna (also available from SAA).]

No. 16-   The transition from the horse-and-wagon team
to the truck at Washington, D.C., Men's Social Service Center, 1935.
[Courtesy of MSSD-S.]

converted. Despite this colorful approach, Winchell had a well-planned program of follow-up for the men he rescued, and his methods won many notable converts. In 1912, The Salvation Army established an organized program for drunkards in every industrial institution. The "Climbers' League," founded September 1, 1912, was open to any "employee" over 18—that is, any man who worked in any part of an industrial home program and was not a paying lodger in a shelter. The object of the league was "to cultivate good feelings, kind deeds and brotherly love" among its members, who had to pledge never to "touch, taste or handle intoxicating liquors or baneful drugs of any kind" and to persuade others to take the same pledge. In New York No. 1 the members of the league had a newspaper of their own, called *The Climber,* and put on concerts and shows for the other men. By 1915 the Climbers' league was described as "a powerful factor for the regeneration of the men," and a branch existed in "nearly every" industrial home in the United States.[28]

The men at work in a Salvation Army industrial home in those years could well have used "good feelings, kind deeds and brotherly love." The most difficult job, and the most prestigious, was that of wagon driver. Managers complained steadily that there were not enough steady and honest men in their homes to cover all the wagon routes. Captain Thomas Seaver of Hartford Industrial Home declared in 1912 that finding "suitable drivers" was "one of the liveliest, burning questions" in the Army. The reason, of course, was that the driver on the Army wagon represented the organization to the world. Only a few wagons (although *all* motor vehicles) were sent out to collect items from persons who contacted the home and offered the material in advance (which was usually done in those days not by telephone but by penny postcard); the large majority of the wagons followed a regular prescribed route every day, soliciting door-to-door for discards and emptying baskets or boxes kept on hand for that purpose by the sympathetic householder. This meant that drivers were in a position of trust: they had access to homes, often without close supervision, and all donated materials passed into their hands first.

Temptations abounded in the path of the driver, who might be newly converted, if at all, with no accurate knowledge of The Salvation Army, its purposes or operation. In principle, men went in pairs: an experienced, trusted man as driver, a new man as helper; in fact drivers were often alone, or were no more seasoned than their helpers. The day began early, and was long: nine hours on the road was the rule for horses. The drivers worked longer hours; they had to maneuver the animal into the shafts, connect the traces and chains to the harness at 6:30 in the morning and disconnect them all at noon and again at supper. (In large cities many routes allowed the wagons to return to the home for lunch; otherwise a supply of food for the horse had to be carried on the route. In any case the animal had to be watered at regular intervals throughout the day.)

Driving a horse in traffic required skill and experience which many unemployed applicants only pretended to have. Even honest ones faced the difficulty of maneuvering wagons, which were unstable when over-loaded and top-heavy when empty, over trolley tracks, around curbings, past dogs, while avoiding faster teams and nasty boys who teased the horses. Once on the route the horse would more or less take over, plodding through the familiar routine without guidance, but ruination beckoned the driver on every hand. The helper might run off, bored, thirsty, anxious to sell something pilfered from the wagon. The new driver was now alone, in an unfamiliar job. A servant—perhaps two in a row—would slam the door in his face, causing him to abandon his door-to-door solicitation at new addresses, and he did not yet know where things were kept in the houses that were regular stops. Even when he found the right house he might take a trunk, or a pile of books, that the owner did not intend to donate. Discouragement. Noontime arrived, and there he sat, alone on the wagon seat, with a bologna sandwich kindly provided by the home. The horse waited to be watered and fed, and in the meantime gnawed the bark from a convenient curbside tree. Across the street flamed the music, the cama-raderie, the refreshment of the saloon—which, let it be remembered, provided a free lunch to every purchaser of a 5-cent beer. And 5 cents, or several times that amount, was not difficult to obtain for a man sitting on a wagon full of merchandise: rag peddlers were everywhere, always eager to buy a bundle of old clothes from an enterprising driver. And these dis-couragements and temptations were faced by the hardest-working and most-reliable men.

Other important jobs, requiring skill and regular hours, included that of dock foreman, who distributed materials from the wagons as they returned laden, despite temptations, each afternoon. Clothing had to be divided into rags or clothing for resale or for distribution to the needy men; furniture had to be instantly appraised and sent either for resale, repair or to be chopped into kindling for the coal furnaces that warmed the building—the fate of most donated furniture. Paper, which provided the largest amount of employment for the men—traditionally, the baling room employed brand-new men, men who were too old or ill to lift bundles onto a wagon, or who were considered too unreliable to be allowed out-of-doors on their own—had to be constantly collected and shifted in neat piles and sorted for grade. The stableman was responsible for the care of the horses when they were not working; the stableman daily carried out Parker's 10 pages of detailed instructions on horses and 10 more pages on harness and wagons. There were no spare animals: a sick or injured horse meant an idle wagon and idle men. And for all the men, food was a crucial factor in determining the quality—and stability—of life in the institution. Although there were rudimentary attempts in the largest institutions at recreational activities, an industrial home was made attractive to reliable workers by its cleanliness, the friendliness of the officer and the interest he showed in them, and the food. When Adjutant O'Neill in Grand Rapids had a promising young assistant who quarreled with the cook, the latter coolly informed O'Neill, "The woods are full of assistants, but cooks are hard to get."[29]

The industrial home was clearly intended to be something more than a shelter for transients, just as its salvage program was intended to be something more than a profitable enterprise. Describing a large meeting for converted drunkards held in New York in 1914, *The War Cry* declared approvingly that "the rehabilitating process goes quietly on. . . ." *The Climber* described New York No. 1 in 1911 as follows: "The men remain in the home for various periods. Entertainment, library facilities and spiritual training are supplied." The Minneapolis Industrial Home had its own nine-piece brass band in 1914, and New York No. 1 had its locally famous "48th Street Choir." The next year the home in Portland, Oregon, had an orchestra of its own, with two violins, two banjos, a guitar and cornet.[30]

In 1912 a burial fund was established into which each man in a home would be required to contribute 5 cents per week, so that men who died while in a home could have a respectable 50 dollar funeral. A few years later, in 1915, the Army introduced a central registration file for all men in the homes, in order to assist the Army's Missing Persons Department to provide guidance to searching relatives, and to coordinate employment opportunities and those needing work on a national scale. The Central Registration Bureau (invariably referred to in Army circles as the "C.R.B.") also made the old-time system of "blocking" an undesirable man from all Army institutions much more effective: the "very small minority" of men who were "incorrigibly bad or lazy" would now be kept out of *every* Army institution, once a "census board of experienced officers," including the manager, had expelled them from any one home.

This would make room for other men more likely to respond to the Army's efforts to rescue them. The burial fund met a great need in the homes and generated large surpluses besides: by 1917 it had a balance of $17,192, and the Army decided to extend the benefits to include medical and hospital treatment for the men in the homes.[31]

New facilities continued to open: in Pittsburgh, Chicago, and in Louisville, which was nicely fitted out in the former University of Louisville School of Dentistry where a small hotel and industrial home, separated by a wall, shared the same building. Confidence in the possibilities of the industrial program was extended to youth: the once-famous Salvation Army orphanage at Lytton Springs, California, was converted into an industrial home for boys. The official optimism seemed to require new expression. A new departmental newsletter called the *Octogram,* was launched in 1915, but this was not enough, for the buildings themselves must bear the mark of change: although the transformation in nomenclature proceeded slowly through another 15 years, the official description of the new institution dedicated by Evangeline Booth in Philadelphia in June 1916, was a harbinger of things to come. Known as the Philadelphia "Industrial and Social Service Center" it had 72 beds, 30 teams of horses, and two trucks. The *Disposition of Forces,* however, less imaginative than *The War Cry,* continued to list Philadelphia as an industrial home.[32]

America's entry into World War I in April 1917, had several effects on the Army's industrial homes, all of them serious. While the United States was still neutral, Major Winchell had enjoyed himself in Belgium administering the Army's relief program for war refugees. The German occupation authorities had ejected British Salvationists from the work, and were dubious about the whole organization. Winchell's way into their trust was smoothed by a curious character named Dr. Maximo Asenjo, the "saved Nicaraguan revolutionist." A medical doctor trained in Germany, Asenjo had been governor of the Province of Leon in Nicaragua. He staged an unsuccessful coup, escaped, and ended his wanderings as a penniless exile in Jersey City in 1911, where Winchell gathered him up and cared for him in the industrial home. Asenjo favored the German cause in the war and in 1916 he became the editor of a Spanish-language newspaper aimed at building support for Germany in Spain and Spanish America. Naturally the German officers in Belgium trusted Asenjo, and he easily convinced them of the value of The Salvation Army's work. Winchell returned home before America entered the war.[33]

A number of industrial home officers were taken, or volunteered, for The Salvation Army's war work in France. Among them was Ensign Harry Kline of the Omaha Industrial Home, who was the first Salvation Army officer to become an official military chaplain. Adjutant Ray Starbard, prepared no doubt by his pioneering experience with the Koehler automobile, was placed in charge of The Salvation Army's automobile and transportation department in France. Major J. E. Atkins, a hut worker and unofficial chaplain to the infantry regiment commanded by Theodore Roosevelt's son, came to France from the Kansas City Industrial Home. Adjutant J. O. Dowdell was assigned to the war from the tiny Covington, Kentucky, Industrial Home. Even Colonel Parker himself served in France, to supervise Salvation Army work there, from July to November 1918; he later served in an advisory capacity to the U.S. Government during the demobilization of the U.S. Army, and was appointed to the Graves Registration Committee.

The temporary loss of officer personnel would have caused difficulties in the administration of the Army's industrial home program had it not been that the war sharply curtailed their activities as well. The needs of the armed forces and of the war-related industries that boomed in 1917–1918 drained off many men from the Army's institutions. The first to go, as volunteers or draftees, or war workers, were the steady men, the converts and regular employees who formed a reliable production network in each home. The new men, transients and steady drinkers, men not yet uplifted by their experience in the industrial home, were the next to go, some of them into the service, more of them into well-paying jobs left behind by the departing soldiers, opened now for the first time to men who had been unable to find steady and respectable work for years. To attract men into industrial home production, the Army for the first time paid the competitive wage scale which had—alas—increased by 30 percent between 1915 and 1917. Even by bearing such expense, the Army could not fill its homes. Twenty-five small industrial homes were closed in the East and South, and five more in the Central states. Even those that remained open could not attract men, suffering a 25 percent decline in annual residency. Worse was to come: paper production fell by about 35 percent. All railroad freight lines were congested by troop movements and war shipments; occasionally civilian shipments were simply embargoed altogether. In addition, the government urged the population to conserve waste materials, including paper, as a patriotic gesture, and thousands of small agencies and new firms rushed to compete with The Salvation Army for the now valuable paper market. The Army closed its interstate labor registry in 1918 because of the "heavy shortage of labor." These pressures proved to be too much for the heavily mortgaged flagship of the industrial home fleet: in April 1918, the seven-storied building formerly occupied by New York No. 1 Industrial Home was offered for lease on the real estate market.[34]

Nor could anyone predict what the effect on Salvation Army social services for men would be when the Eighteenth Amendment to the Constitution was finally ratified and enforced. The Salvation Army endorsed the prohibition amendment throughout its existence, but if it worked as its sponsors enthusiastically predicted, it would end drunkenness by eliminating drink. It was uncertain whether the industrial home program could find a group of men as large as its present clientele that would be in need of its service. Only the Army's cheap hotels rode out the storm with their futures not only secure but considerably brightened. The wartime migration of young men to cities to join the armed forces or to find war work, and soldiers on leave, had filled the workingmen's hotels to capacity. As the influx of population seemed permanent, because of the added pressure on lodgings caused by the demobilization of the armed forces after the war, and because, after a bumpy start, prosperity seemed assured for years to come, the Army opened many new hotels, and later added a requirement that required hotel "sections" should be included in every new building acquired as an industrial home. For instance, the new headquarters for all social activities in Boston, which the Army opened in 1917, and which housed the No. 5 Corps as well, centered on a hotel for workingmen.[35]

CHAPTER IV

Men's Social Service, 1920–1940

In October 1920, The Salvation Army in the United States was divided into three separate territorial commands: the Eastern, under Commissioner Thomas Estill, who since 1908 had commanded the now defunct Department of the West; the Central, under Commissioner William Peart, who, for 15 years, had been the national chief secretary; and the Western, with headquarters in San Francisco, under Lt.-Commissioner Adam Gifford, a respected pioneer officer who, since 1908, had been New England Provincial Commander. Men's social service activities within these territories were directed by Colonel E. J. Parker in the East, Lt.-Colonel David Miller in the Central, and Lt.-Colonel Emil Marcussen, who had been social secretary in Chicago from 1908–1909 and, then in the new Western Territory, from 1913 to 1920. The regional subdivisions in the former Department of the West ceased to apply in 1913, and all three territories adopted the system of district officers already in use in the East as a means of regional coordination of men's social service activities.

Hotels continued to prosper in the early years of the new era. Divisional headquarters and even corps found that the migrations of men stimulated by the war and demobilization made shelters both useful and profitable. In some cases attempts were made to continue as commercial enterprises the shelters built or purchased as servicemen's hostels during the war; one of these, for black soldiers, was operated in Washington, D.C., until 1922. Despite the Army's delight in recording statistics, many of these small shelters were open only briefly, and no accurate record remains as to how many there actually were, nor what accommodations they offered. In 1924, headquarters, at least in the East, tried to bring some order out of the confusion when a plan was announced to bring all shelters with at least 25 beds under the control of the men's social services secretary. A new class of medium-sized hotels was opened, designed not specifically as shelters or missions, but as respectable commercial lodging houses for employed single men. In honor of the recent Armistice and because so many of the clientele of these hotels wcre expected to be ex-soldiers, the new class of institution was named "Argonne Hotel" for a part of France where the U.S. Army had won a great victory in the fall of 1918. It was intended at first that these hotels should have only single and double rooms. From the fact that the regulations called for each room to contain six sheets and pillow cases and a dozen face and bath towels, it seems that the Army hoped to attract a regular clientele of weekly renters.[1]

Territorial social service departments continued to administer a range of small programs, including the missing persons and prison departments; the former drew heavily on the national network of institutions. The Salvation Army ministry of social uplift may be said to have started in the Hartford jail in 1885, and the prison department remained the most highly developed in the Eastern Territory, still the largest of the three territories and the scene of the Army's beginnings in the United States. The Army's first regulation prison camps, with prisoner-soldiers, began in San Quentin Prison in California in 1894, but the idea was warmly espoused by both Ballington and Booth-Tucker and spread nationwide. The largest and most remarkable of these prison corps was formed in 1920 as a result of a prison-yard Salvation Army service in the Indiana State Reformatory in Jeffersonville. Only the San Quentin Corps proved durable, however, and the bulk of the Army's work among prisoners was done in two other ways. Salvation Army field and social officers visited prisons, conducted religious services in them—the first official Prison Sunday was in 1916—and encouraged converts to remain in contact with the Army's spiritual and socially redemptive influences by joining the "Brighter Day League." This had been formed in 1904 by Ensign Thomas Anderson, who had himself been converted in jail through the Army's ministry. He later formed the "Lifers' Club" in 1915 for the same purpose, for men who could not hope for the "brighter day" of their release. Most converts, of course, were not life-termers, and were eventually released. For those who volunteered, or were paroled to it, the Army provided in its industrial homes a half-way house back into society. In 1919, Captain Stanley "Red" Sheppard joined the prison bureau in New York City and remained there, active and effective, for another 32 years. In 1924 the Eastern Territorial Prison Department was separated from the men's social service department; the first prison secretary was Brigadier Thomas Cowan, who instituted the observance of Prison Sunday and offered a novel Bible correspondence course for prisoners.[2]

The Army's various programs to assist released convicts, its missing persons bureau, the interstate labor registry, even much of the work of the Naval and Military League, set up in 1896 as a mission to Civil War veterans, a "hive of industry" during the world war but now settled back into peacetime tranquility under Ensign Ernest Holz, all rested for success on the nationwide chain of industrial homes. The new decade opened with a roar for the industrial department. In the fall of 1919 the market for paper, freed from wartime restrictions, soared to record heights; by September 1920, paper prices were stratospherical: mixed, $2.30; news, $2.90; bookstock, $4.75 per hundredweight. Part of this heady increase was caused not by industry demand but by speculation, and the boom collapsed early in 1921. The department, which drew 75% of total income from paper sales, made a killing while the good times rolled. The low point in the price cycle came and passed in April 1921, after which prices rallied and remained fairly steady at encouraging levels until the Stock Market Crash of 1929 which briefly generated large piles of high-grade printed certificates for the good work of The Salvation Army. (It is an ill wind that blows no good.)[3]

These prosperous times seemed to call for growth, indeed, to demand it. It was a decade of expansion, of innovation, of consumer confidence, and the Army shared the general optimism. A number of new buildings were purchased or constructed. Several "model" institutions with all the latest improvements were part of the expansion: Atlanta, opened in 1919 at 272 Luckie Street, and Washington, D.C., at 102–116 "B" Street N.W., opened in 1923. However, a more generally benign climate—the fact that population centers were smaller and more dispersed than in the northeast and upper midwest, and that The Salvation Army's evangelical ministry had not prospered there—made it more difficult to operate social institutions successfully in the South. Still, some of the homes there had charm: an antebellum mansion in Richmond, an elegant old hostelry in New Orleans with louvered doors and wrought-iron balconies, and the Memphis Bethel Mission. Elsewhere in the country new facilities opened—or reopened, following wartime reductions—every year. In 1923, after several, fortunately unsuccessful, attempts to lease or sell the building, the New York No. 1 Industrial Home was reopened, under Adjutant Joseph Ogden Dowdell, from Punxsutawney, Pennsylvania, at 43 years of

age an experienced social officer and another hero of the war work in
France. From 1920 to 1924 the number of men's social service institutions
in the United States increased from 87 to 102, the officers in them from 118
to 149, and their total accommodations from 4,059 to 4,262.[4]

The Prohibition Amendment, which The Salvation Army continued to
officially and warmly support, went into effect on January 16, 1920. It
apparently did not hamper the successful operation of the Army's industrial homes, but the Army changed the official appeal of these institutions
for part of the decade. The law effectively interfered with public drinking,
and partly eliminated the cheap beer and wine upon which the unemployed or low-paid working-class drinker depended. People with the financial means to obtain costly distilled liquor, which was imported illegally,
were less affected by the law, but men of this class had never been the
mainstay of the Army's ministry. The Army now publicly declared in its
appeal for support—and to secure a supply of applicants to its homes—
that the mission of the Salvation Army industrial home was to provide a
shelter and a better life for the unemployed homeless man who was willing
to work. The appeal was to men who had lost their employment because of
injury, sickness, lack of skill or the closing of a factory. The evangelistic
element in the program was still emphasized, but no mention was made of
rescuing men from the curse of drink. There were still many unemployed
men in the 1920s, many of them for the very causes listed by the Army in
its new official invitation, and, in any case, the Army had acquired the
habit during the war of paying competitive wages to obtain workers in its
industrial homes. Where the first appeal failed, the second might fill the
home work force. The combination proved successful: in 1923 the 51
industrial institutions in the Eastern Territory generated a net profit of
$365,000 against total operating expenses of $1,278,000; almost half the
net—$175,000—was budgeted for property extension.[5]

In 1921 General Bramwell Booth presided over the Army's second
international social council in London. Colonel Edward Parker led the
American delegation of 20 officers. He returned "effervescent with the
inspirational and practical benefits." In February 1922, Parker organized
the first social district officers' councils, in Atlantic City. The first official
decision of the first session called for a "Handbook for Social Service
Officers." This, of course, was music to the ears of Colonel Parker, whose
love for uniformity, planning and minute instructions was by now legend-
ary. He and his staff worked on the project through the year, and the new
handbook was distributed to the second annual social district officers'

councils, held at the new Washington center in 1923. The new "handbook" consisted of 61 of Parker's "special orders"—many of them unchanged since 1910—fastened together between 6½ by 10¼-inch hard gray canvas covers. This set of 1922 orders, to which 10 more were added in August 1923, became standard equipment in most Salvation Army men's social institutions in the United States, and remained the official guide for their operation until after World War II. The official *Orders and Regulations for Social Officers (Men)* issued by International Headquarters in 1915 was ignored by American officers in the homes, most of whom never saw a copy, and were aware of its existence only when a headquarters officer quoted from it as to the primacy of soul-saving in Army industrial work or made reference from it to some other general principle.[6]

By 1923, the operation of the institution had come to center on the men who lived and worked there, and something like a modern program had emerged in large centers. The official change in appeal had no effect on this important development. The Central Registration Bureau (C.R.B.) in New York City now recorded every man who was admitted, or readmitted, to an institution in the East and South. The bureau's centralized records made it possible for managers to know of a man's past record as a recipient of the benefits of any industrial home in the territory, all recorded on cards loyally coded in the Army's colors: blue "acceptance cards" (forwarded from the C.R.B.), salmon-pink "departure cards" (returned to the C.R.B.), and yellow "reference cards" for men who stayed in an institution more than three months. This system was not perfectly enforced, and depended entirely upon the efficiency of the U.S. Mail for its speed of operation, but it represented a continued commitment to the important principle of central registration of records for the benefit of the men. Entertainment provided for the men in the evening included musical solos, vaudeville acts of varying degrees of professionalism, and rented motion pictures. Parker, his enthusiasm for the latest thing undimmed by the years, urged managers to buy radio sets for the homes—"an ideal form of entertainment for the men in our institutions." The Army still frowned on card-playing; the only table-games allowed in the homes were dominoes and checkers. When the men washed, they were to have clean regulation towels, and they fell asleep under regulation white-and-blue bedspreads, each bearing the Salvation Army shield. For those who slept to rise no more there was the regulation funeral (now valued at $85.00) with a "hardwood square-cut flat-top casket with white silk lining (no handles)." The homes were no longer new, and some men had grown old in them:

such men were to be cared for in a kind of retirement home for industrial-home beneficiaries. In 1920, the Industrial Department took over a former rescue home for fallen women at Tappan, New York. The Eventide had space for 15 men, and was operated for years for a handful of elderly men by the kindly Major and Mrs. P. Royce Hawley. With all this came a renewed committment to the Army's first purpose: the salvation of the lost! Every institution held two compulsory religious meetings per week, and even the weekly business meeting was supposed to have a "spiritual talk by the commanding officer." Holidays, birthday parties, special out-ings were all to be so conducted as to be "helpful to the encouragement of our men as well as a moral uplift." Of the thousands of men who passed through The Salvation Army's industrial institutions during the 1920s, the department officially estimated that perhaps 10 percent "claimed for-giveness of sin." The Army's men's social work, according to Parker, was "the world's most glorious enterprise."[7]

Clearly these institutions were more than mere "industrial homes"—more than a combination of a shelter and a salvage operation. They offered an encouraging range of social and spiritual activities. Their official name should convey this to the world. In October 1922, officers were instructed to list their institutions in the local telephone directory as "The S.A. Social Service Dept.," or "The S.A. Industrial Home for Men." The detailed instructions for color and lettering on trucks and wagons spec-ified, however, that the words "Social Service" should appear—along with the new red shield, first introduced in 1916 as a symbol of the Army's war work with the British Army and a familiar device to every returned American war veteran. In a special edition of the Eastern version of *The War Cry*, dated November 1923, and dedicated to men's social service work, the institutions were called "Salvation Army Industrial Homes or Social Service Centers." The change came slowly over the next few years. "Social Service Center" was increasingly used in official minutes, pro-grams and on stationery from 1924 to 1927. Contemporary photographs show that both kinds of signs still appeared on buildings from 1923 through the early 1930s: the Ft. Wayne center at 1408 South Calhoun St. had a sign in 1931 which carried both names. In the new Southern Territory's *Disposition of Forces*, first issued in February 1927, every institution in the territory was called an "industrial home," except the one in Washington, which was called a "social service center." The official change appeared in the other three territorial gazettes in 1931 and 1932. Officers continued to use both terms interchangeably for many more years; social and field officers had jocularly referred to the Men's Social Service Department as the "Dusty"—an abbreviation of "industrial" with a double-meaning—and continued to do so throughout the 1930s.[8]

Production, of course, was still important. There was no source of income for these centers other than what they generated by their own activities. The Salvation Army headquarters provided no funds for any part of the regular operating budgets for local institutions; their only relief came in 1911, 1912, and 1922 in the form of special orders from headquarters, forbidding nearby corps to collect rummage or hold sales of donated materials in competition with the center's operation. Business acumen was an important factor in official evaluations of a social officer: in the 1923 Handbook (Social Order No. 19), the "ability to secure business efficiency from men" was placed in order of importance above "spiritual results in dealing with men," and an official "Brief for a Social District Officer" made the same point in 1929. As to the best means of achieving profitable production, however, opinions varied. The 1920s display a curious, almost whimsical, amalgam of the old and the new in Salvation Army social work for men. The old-time shelter tickets, distributed to friends of the Army to hand in turn to panhandlers, were revived in 1922 as "relief introductory cards." When young Captain Ernest Hayes went to Atlanta in 1925, he found the men still using handcarts. Paterson still operated a woodyard in the 1920s, but the wood was chopped by a steam press. The old method of door-to-door solicitation was supplemented through the decade by the telephone call or postal card from a housewife asking for a wagon to call for materials. In 1927 Brigadier Sam Wood referred to these calls as the "dependable financial backbone of the institutions." Paper and rags remained the mainstay of income, but these fluctuated disconcertingly, especially over the short-term. Officers in the West were apparently the first to use modern equipment, such as compressed-air painting and large cleaning vats and woodworking machinery, in order to clean and repair furniture for resale.[9]

Store sales, in fact, continued to grow in importance across the country throughout the 1920s. Items of clothing formerly sold in bulk as rags were separated out and placed in stores for sale. Headquarters hopefully prescribed standardized racks and bins to display clothing in the Army's stores. Parker made a special point of praising the "very pleasing up-to-date appearance" of the occasional store in which he found clothing stock displayed on hangers. To improve the prestige and effectiveness of "official storekeepers"—later called managers—headquarters decreed that only Salvationists could be hired for the position, prepared a regulation "Brief of Appointment" for storekeepers and held regular regional storekeepers' councils for them. Officers who spoke at these meetings emphasized the sale of old pictures, lamps, vases, household items that were known as "bric-a-brac," and especially of furniture. These items cost a little more to collect than paper and clothing, yet they brought in many times as much money per sale. The Army ran its own bookstore in New York City. Special folders were distributed to the public urging them to "Shop at the Sign of the Red Shield," which they apparently did: by 1929 store income from operations east of the Mississippi had surpassed paper as a source of income, providing "approximately half the annual budget."[10]

To collect the material for production, the Army continued to rely heavily on horses. The lengthy special order issued in 1922 and covering their purchase and care was almost identical to the 1910 version; the faithful horse was still to have his day of rest on Sunday. The horse still provided certain advantages. Many managers preferred horses, which were ideal for door-to-door solicitation and route collecting in congested urban areas. A horse and wagon were easier for an inexperienced man to handle than the trucks of those years, which had mechanical transmissions, unreliable lever brakes and often lacked a self-starter. Accidents with horse-drawn vehicles, while surprisingly frequent, were much less serious than those involving motor trucks, and horses were cheaper to operate. They were also much cheaper to acquire, which, more motorminded officers suggested, was because modern companies were switching to trucks, and thus crowding the market with cheap used horses. The Army was certainly willing to take advantage of these bargains: sometimes horses that were purchased were so elderly that their pathetic appearance in the shafts of the Army's wagons brought complaints from animal lovers. Not all the second-hand horses were second-rate, however: in the mid-1920s, when the fire departments of America finished the long transition to motor trucks, many fire horses came on the market. These were fine animals, quick and strong—and cheap: the single defect, from the Army's point of view, was that they dashed off, social service wagon and all, at every fire bell and siren. Still, it was a major factor with budgetminded managers that a horse and wagon—even a young horse and a brand-new wagon—cost less than a used truck, and several times less than a new one, yet could compete with a truck in production on compact downtown routes. There were other advantages: the experienced horse knew the way home; if a driver abandoned his rig, or fell into a drunken stupor in the back, the sympathetic passerby or householder had only to untie the horse and pat him on the rump. Horses were living things, sentient beings, pets—almost friends. The public liked to see the Army horse and wagon. In 1923, the Eastern Men's Social Service Department had 112 trucks and 280 wagons and many centers still used only horses.

In 1927, the Philadelphia Men's Social Service Center placed an entry in the annual Workhorse Parade; "Charlie" and his veteran driver, John McMillan, won first prize in the delivery wagon division. The spotless Charlie and the glossy dark green and red wagon were applauded all down the line. In 1928, the Army entry took only second prize—"a younger horse got ahead of him this time"—and a second again in 1929, although McMillan and Charlie received a special silver medal for participating in three parades. The Pittsburgh No. 2 Center, not to be outdone, put its "Bessie" into the Western Pennsylvania Humane Society's Workhorse Parade and won a red ribbon in 1927 and a white one in 1928, although her newly repainted wagon made a "very good showing." Commandant John Castagna, an experienced manager, was not only disinclined to replace horses with trucks, even as renewal, but actually reversed the trend: in 1928 he replaced a truck in New Haven with two new horse-and-wagon teams.[11]

The truck had its advocates as well, and in the end, of course, these triumphed. Horses, even double teams, could not compete with trucks for heavy loads—such as carrying bales of paper or rags to a mill or depot— nor on long trips to outlying districts. As time passed, more and more men came to centers who could operate motor trucks, even the Ford, the most common kind in the department throughout the 1920s. This was no easy task, considering that the transmission in a Model T truck consisted of planetary fiberboard bands operated by foot pedals, the engine was advanced by using both a spark and a gas lever on the steering column, the brakes were weak on the level and useless on grades, and the motor had to be started by turning it over by a hand crank, a difficult and unreliable process. The 1923 department handbook for the first time provided instructions on truck maintenance. The regulation color for trucks was the same as that for wagons: dark green, red trim, with the Army's red shield for identification. Among the growing number of managers who accepted the comparative benefits of trucks were a few who were too zealous to hasten the transition from horses. Captain Roy "Soupy" Smith, balked in his request to replace the horses at Hartford, ordered all the teams out on their routes during rush-hour traffic, causing—to no avail—a traffic jam. Other officers were content to master technical details about operations and costs and to prove the superiority of trucks by using them profitably. Brigadier Sam Wood, metropolitan district manager, was especially fond of the durable and efficient Brockway truck, a brand manufactured from 1912 to 1977 in Cortland, New York. After 1926, when the New York No. 2 Center moved into its new-built facility at 4109 Park Avenue, the Bronx, Wood arranged a series of "then and now" publicity photographs that were widely circulated in Army circles: the pictures show a push cart, a horse-and-wagon and a 1928 Brockway truck side by side; the triumph of the motor age was too obvious for words. By the end of the decade the balance in equipment had shifted to trucks: in 1931 there were 258 trucks and 182 wagons in use.[12]

There was another, and final, administrative change for The Salvation Army in the decade. In 1927 the Southern Territory was created out of parts of the Eastern and Central Territories. The new headquarters were in Atlanta, under the colorful and energetic leadership of Lt.-Commissioner William McIntyre. Commander Evangeline Booth formally installed the new staff at the Wesley Memorial Church in Atlanta on April 10, 1927. There were 20 industrial homes and 18 hotels in the new territory; four of the centers were in the "Chesapeake District" under the direction of Brigadier Myles Pickering; the rest were unattached. The prospects for the new department were not rosy. With the single exception of the Washington, D.C. Social Service Center, every one of the Southern institutions ran a yearly deficit. They received but little public support and suffered from inadequate program. According to Lt.-Colonel Gilbert Decker who was stationed as a young captain at the Richmond Industrial Home when the territory was created, the new Men's Social Service Department was a "major economic problem to the territory." Apparently, the Army did not regard the task of administering these few struggling institutions as a full-time job: Lt.-Colonel A. W. Baillie, the first territorial men's social services secretary, was also the property secretary and the supplies and purchasing secretary.[13]

An administrative change of importance to managers, not only in the East but nationwide, was the transfer of Colonel Edward J. Parker out of the men's social service department. On March 22, 1927, Parker was made chief secretary for the Eastern Territory, and two days later, Lt.-Colonel Charles C. Welte, his loyal assistant for 22 years, was appointed to succeed him. Few staff appointments have been more popular with the rank and file: wrote one manager to Welte, "Elisha has succeeded Elijah."[14]

Despite the admittedly languid state of affairs in the South, these were times of expansion and excitement in men's social service work throughout the country, which social officers were anxious to share within the Army. This was not always easy. In the minds of many officers in other kinds of work, a gray aura of grime and failure seemed to hover over the men's social services department; its "dusty" image clung to it still. Some officers felt, as Booth-Tucker had, that social work was less demanding, required less energy—even less ability—than the more important field work. The expanding needs of social operations for personnel meant that officers were frequently appointed to it—often directly from the training colleges—with no experience and no inclination for the work. These men often felt, at least at first, as if they had been demoted, or even insulted. Field officers who actually applied for a transfer to men's social service work were often discouraged, or simply refused, by their divisional commanders. To correct some of these deficiencies, the social district officers' councils in 1923 proposed a three-tiered program of on-the-job training for new lieutenants appointed to industrial homes. By 1924, a ten-week course of morning lectures and afternoon practical experience was in place. Parker urged managers to watch for promising men in the homes who could be encouraged to become social officers, thus raising the number of officers so that only men who wanted such work would be assigned to it. And many men did want it; many of the very officers who were appointed to the social without regard to, or in opposition to, their preference came to cherish the work and to rejoice in the great ministry of rescue. Salvation Army leaders wished to insure cooperation, not rivalry between industrial homes and corps activities. This had been the motive for the long-established policy that converts from an institution who wished to join the Army as soldiers should be enrolled at the nearest corps. High-ranking officers spoke frequently of the unity of the Army, the single great purpose shared by all its departments. Field officers were reminded as well that the general public drew none of the distinctions that loomed so large to them. Colonel Richard Holz, writing in 1924, declared that the public looked upon "the social work as being as much a part of the Army as the open-air meeting."[15]

Music continued to play a major role in the life of the Army's social institutions. In 1923, the tradition of institutional bands lived again in the

Lytton Springs "Young People's Industrial Home and Farm Band," and, again, in 1925, when the Philadelphia Men's Social Service Center formed a band, led by Brigadier Allan Neill, the district officer. In 1927 it was called a "splendid orchestra," and was "much sought after." Neill taught the young men in the center to play instruments, and, like many other men's social officers, was heavily involved in Salvation Army musical activities. Parker himself and the faithful Welte had played second trombone and bass drum in the National Staff Band at the turn of the century. Staff-Captain George Darby, a social officer for the first 16 years of his career (until 1924) led the band for years. Ensign George Granger, in charge of centralized paper sales at social headquarters, was bandmaster of the famous New York No. 1 Corps Band. His musical abilities and his zeal for bands were not so easily contained, however. In 1929 he organized a band made up entirely of men's social service officers and employees in the metropolitan area to play for the opening of the new center in Newark. The "Men's Social Service Staff Band" appeared for the ceremony in "cooks' white uniforms" and made a "decided impression."[16]

The Model A Ford arrived in 1928, a relatively cheap and efficient truck with the new standard three-speed clutch transmission. It quickly became the most popular vehicle in all four territorial departments. Programs, profits and building plans continued to multiply. When Parker retired, he could count 13 new centers built for the Army during his administration and 19 other purchased and remodeled. By 1928 only eight centers in the East were still housed in rented properties. In the South, Commissioner McIntyre, already famous for his lifelong commitment to house the Army in modern facilities, ordered the construction of new social service centers in Dallas, Baltimore and Louisville and a new Argonne Hotel in Nashville, all between 1927 and 1930; in those years the real estate value of men's social service properties in the South increased by 40%, to $1,471,004. By the end of the decade most of the country's 106 social centers were in "splendid permanent properties" built for the Army. The building boom of the 1920s culminated in the social service center opened in Newark on April 21, 1929; it was "the closing signature of all the model plants erected in the last few years." With five floors and beds for 400 men—200 of them in a separate shelter section to be used for referrals from other Army relief agencies—the Newark center included every modern and progressive idea for production, transportation, relaxation and recreation. It had, of course, both garage and stables; it even had a real log fireplace and leather armchairs. Three bands played at the opening, including Ensign Granger's

Men's Social Service Staff Band. The program handed to each of the 750 guests contained a paraphrased quotation from Jeremiah 9:2.[17]

> Oh that we had a place in the wilderness for
> wayfaring men.

The great stock market crash of October 1929, while it did not pass unnoticed in men's social service circles, was not at first regarded by officers as especially alarming. The first few months after the crash passed routinely, although fluctuations in the waste-material market were troublesome. In 1930 the department enthusiastically participated in the nationwide celebration by Salvationists of the Army's 50th year in the United States. A special social services band, composed of employees and officers from New York and New Jersey, was again formed, this time for the congress festivities. Led by Adjutant Andrew C. Laurie for the period of the congress, the band was made up of a number of men who also played in the New York No. 1 Corps Band. In 1933, Adjutant George Granger revived the Men's Social Service Band, which played for several years in the metropolitan area. Several of the players went on to careers of great distinction in the department, and two of them, Edward Carey (who played in the Jubilee Band) and William Chamberlain, became national commanders.[18]

The worsening effects of the economic depression, however, were soon felt in the Men's Social Service Department. The years from 1930–1935 were probably the most difficult ones in the history of the department nationwide. The number of applicants increased rapidly, while income from every traditional source declined; budgets were exhausted within a few weeks of the beginning of the fiscal year 1930–1931. Officers of widely varying backgrounds and abilities were transferred to social work for the duration of the emergency, while, at the same time, many experienced social officers were forced to divert increasing amounts of their time from the operation of their own spiritual and productive activities in order to administer the ever-swelling volume of temporary emergency programs. The result of all this, of course, was severe disruption of regular men's social service activities for several years, indebtedness of many centers, and emotional and physical exhaustion for many officers. The repeal of the Prohibition Amendment, upon which the Army had placed such high hopes, was another unwelcome development. Veteran social officers looked back on the Depression, even many years later, as a prolonged "nightmare."

The most pressing problem was simply to accommodate, let alone provide any employment or moral uplift for, the thousands of unemployed men who came to The Salvation Army for help. Contemporary departmental records and the Army's official publicity material both suggest that every men's social center in the country provided emergency transient relief—soup kitchens, food depots, overnight shelters—during the worst of the Depression. The Army's industrial homes were never intended to serve in this capacity; unearned charity violated the fundamental principle of self-help upon which the Army's social services for men were based. Many centers, especially in the West, revived the woodyard and many others imposed some brief work-test on applicants—perhaps an hour's labor around the building—but the sheer numbers of applicants made this increasingly difficult anywhere, and most homes never attempted it. Brigadier W. W. Winchell, who managed the Memorial Hotel during the crisis, estimated that as many as 400,000 unemployed men had drifted into the Bowery by 1930, where there were accommodations for perhaps 16,000 in cheap lodging houses and missions. In every major city in the country, the public—including many of the transients, especially those in the large majority who were new to the life of the homeless unemployed—looked to The Salvation Army to provide relief. The Army was "acknowledged to be the one big agency for the homeless man, the migrant and the mendicant." Commissioner McIntyre cited a national survey taken in 1933 which showed that the Army housed and fed 40,000 transient men in March of that year—fully one-fifth of the entire population of such men in the country.[19]

In New York City, The Salvation Army opened large food depots and transient shelters. The largest of the food depots, located at 455 Tenth Avenue, was financed by Mr. Edward F. Hutton, the chairman of the board of General Foods, and his wife. At one point in 1931 the Army's 14 kitchens served 48,000 meals daily. The Army provided shelter for stranded seamen on the *SS Broadway,* an old coastal steamer loaned to the Army by her owners, the Dimon Line. The *Broadway* was moored at Pier 15, Stapleton, Staten Island. The Army had always been especially alert to the needs of seamen, friendless and alone amidst the temptations of a big city. Many of these men were Scandinavian, and of special interest to the active Scandinavian branch of The Salvation Army in New York. The Army estimated that there were as many as 22,000 unemployed mariners in New York alone in 1930. The *Broadway* was intended to help some of them, without offending their pride. She had a nightly capacity of 500, but men were encouraged to remain until they found employment (which—amazingly—98 percent of them did). During the life of this project, from December 1930 to April 1931, 1,720 different men registered aboard. To avoid the stigma of charity, which respectable seamen despised, the *Broadway* kept to a regular schedule of four-hour "watches" in which every man was expected to take part, as well as in daily maintenance duties to keep up the ship.[20]

It was far more difficult to avoid the stigma of charity in the Gold Dust Lodge, the largest Army shelter in the country. The manager, Adjutant Andrew C. Laurie and his wife, Annie, were nevertheless determined to do so, insisting that the lodgers were "guests." The lodge was named for the flour company that loaned the six-storied building to the Army; it faced on Corlears Park in Manhattan, and housed 2,200 men nightly. It was filled every night during the winter, half-filled during the summer: it provided two meals per day, showers, free laundry and barber shop facilities and a "mighty moral and spiritual clinic" for the more than 75,000 different men who stayed there in the nearly seven years the lodge was open (December 1931 to August 1937). The Lauries, a talented and kindly couple, assisted by young Captain William Chamberlain and former Colonel Thomas Stanyon, who served as chaplain, refused to operate a mere "flophouse": they arranged for professional men among the lodgers to conduct night classes for the others, for a series of concerts and "entertainments" (often featuring the Men's Social Staff Band) and for a long succession of famous guests, including in 1935, Eleanor Roosevelt. The Cheer Lodge on East Sixth Street provided food and daytime shelter for another 750 men while they searched for work. In Chicago, the Wrigley Shelter was operated by the Army in a building first loaned, then given in 1930 by William Wrigley, the chewing gum magnate. From 1930 to 1933, the shelter, located at 509 North Union Street, had a capacity of 2,382 men, but averaged 1,807 per night. The program was supervised by the veteran Brigadier Sam Wood, and sheltered a clientele similar to that of the more famous Gold Dust Lodge. In New York and Akron, shelters for black homeless unemployed men were opened during the worst months of the Depression, but these "colored men's shelters" did not survive the economic crisis. The few "colored transients" who wished to participate in other aspects of men's social activities were apparently allowed to do so in most places outside the South, but little remains of a documentary nature on this aspect of the history of the department in the 1930s.[21]

The vast nationwide apparatus of emergency relief that men's social officers operated during the Depression from a variety of loaned or rented facilities did not replace the regular religious and productive activities in the regular centers, nor such regional services as the C.R.B. and the Transient Service Bureau, both in New York. The Transient Service Bureau was opened in 1927 in the palmy days of prosperity to handle referrals from other social agencies and courts in the city. Emergency relief was simply added on to regular activities, and in many cases managers were expected to provide Thanksgiving and Christmas dinners for needy families and relief for the victims of natural disasters, which, as bad luck would have it, came with discouraging frequency during the 1930s. Money was needed for all of these special activities, as well as the regular men's social programs of the centers. The occasional special appeal—like the Army-Navy Game played in 1930 for The Salvation Army's benefit— were helpful, but the responsibility for balancing budgets remained within the department. Nor was the financial crisis looming over the department confined merely to the large cities of the northeast and the midwest: in the Western Territory so many hungry homeless men besieged The Salvation Army in 1934 that it looked "like the aftermath of a war, or a major disaster," while the Southern Territorial edition of *The War Cry* pleaded with any unemployed northern readers who happened to find a copy to abandon all hope of coming south to look for work: there was no work, and transients would "simply become dependent upon charity, and a burden upon the community." The Army in the South, certainly, could bear no more.[22]

The Depression, hardly welcome anywhere, was felt with special force in the centers of the South. The institutions there had always been weak, despite the best efforts of many officers. The single exception continued to be the Washington D.C. Men's Social Service Center. Men's social work had attracted dedicated and able officers to the national capital since Staff-Captain Jesse Gearing opened the industrial home there in 1903. The new center, opened in 1923 at 102-116 "B" Street N.W., earned the honorific Social Service Center designation from the start, while every other territorial center bore the less toney label of industrial home. In 1931–1932 Washington was the only center in the South to show a credit balance. Only by closing centers outright, or transferring their operations to the local corps, and by enforcing "the most stringent economies" on the large centers that survived, could the territorial department reduce its annual deficit. A number of historic centers were closed or transferred— Charleston, Galveston, Little Rock, Nashville—one of the first places in the South with a men's program—Norfolk, Wheeling. In the fiscal year 1933–34 the total departmental income sank to the historic low point of $263,858.43, but the stringencies reduced the actual deficit for that year to a tolerable $9,755.68.[23]

The burdens of emergency and disaster relief and a sagging paper market were not the only burdens on the nation's centers in the 1930s. It became much more difficult to collect materials, either for the rag and paper market or for store sales. Householders, faced with reduced income, or no income at all, discarded fewer items, wore clothes longer, and did not replace the icebox with a refrigerator quite yet. And worse was to come: the well-meaning President Roosevelt announced on February 10, 1934, that he had asked the Boy Scouts to conduct a nationwide campaign to collect secondhand clothing and "household waste of every description" to give free to the needy. The Salvation Army gamely cooperated, lending its trucks and warehouses for collections and helping to distribute the material through its regular family welfare and corps relief outlets. The Army was allowed to keep any "surplus" for its own institutions, and that promise alone was enough to make cooperation attractive: by 1934, so little clothing was coming into the Army's centers "in the regular way" that it had become almost impossible to provide clothing even for the men working in the centers. Even if material had been available for the Army's stores, however, the demand from the Army's traditional working-class and poor customers had declined with their income.

The solution, clearly, was the one proposed in the Eastern Territorial Social Officers' Councils conducted by Colonel Welte in 1932; the officers vowed "to curtail operating expenses to the limit, at the same time, endeavor to increase the income." Certainly operating expenses had administrative implications as well. At the territorial level, top leadership positions were combined. In the West, in 1931, Brigadier Arch Layman, a distinguished Canadian officer and former divisional commander was appointed men's social service secretary, to which duties of property secretary were added the next year. In Atlanta, in 1932, where men's social service, property and trade departments were already administered by one officer, Ensign A. E. Baldwin was made only "assistant men's social service secretary;" when Lt.-Colonel Baillie was transferred to Chicago, no one was appointed to the property or trade secretary positions until 1933, when Baldwin became trade secretary as well. In Chicago, meanwhile, Lt.-Colonel Baillie served as Chicago district officer and for the first year was also departmental secretary. Baldwin was a finance officer, and no doubt was appointed to the men's social service department to balance the departmental books, but he brought a touch of music into the social as well: he was the bandmaster of the Southern Territorial Staff Band from 1927 until it was disbanded in 1946. Economies continued in the southern department after Baldwin: when Major William Range was made men's social service secretary in 1935 he was expected to manage the Atlanta Men's Social Service Center as well.

In the East, the beloved Colonel Welte died unexpectedly in December 1932, as he was preparing the annual Christmas letter to the managers. To replace him, after a brief interim appointment, territorial headquarters did not select another officer who, like Welte, had risen from the social ranks; instead an officer with keen business abilities was chosen for the duration of the crisis: Lt.-Colonel Vernon R. Post, the former property secretary.

Retrenchment was not confined to the territorial administration. The position of district social officer, which dated in substance from 1897, was abolished in two territories in 1931 and 1933; in the East, where the system had been most fully developed, the decree abolishing the position came in July 1933. One district was spared: because of the extensive social and emergency relief activities in the New York metropolitan area, the Manhattan and Bronx District was kept in place, under Major J. O. Dowdell. In the Central Territory, seven districts were progressively reduced to three in 1933, and finally to two—Detroit and Minneapolis—in February 1935. Districts continued to function in the West until 1940.[24]

Balancing the books in the individual centers, which were not lavishly operated in the best of times, required close attention to detail during the 1930s. Old clothes too dirty to sell, broken shoes, books and furniture that was past repair were burned as fuel instead of coal. Some managers had the drivers pick up vegetables in rural routes, and canned the produce for use in the winter. Managers also displayed great ingenuity in devising new ways to employ needy men besides repairing furniture or bailing waste materials. Roy Barber in Boston made children's furniture out of wood taken from furniture too battered for resale, Dayton made songsters' uniforms and Christmas bell-ringers' capes, Scranton renovated old porch rockers, and young Captain Peter Hofman in Springfield produced smoking stands, stools, lawn chairs, and flowerpot stands "with octagon tops" all made out of the tops of tables and bureaus too scratched to sell. Colonel Post knew little of social operations, and had great admiration for men who knew more; he encouraged officers to report their advances to

No. 17. The chapel at the Tampa Industrial Home for Men, 1926. [Courtesy of MSSD-S.]

No. 18- A dormitory at the Tampa Industrial Home for Men, 1926, showing imprinted bedspreads

No. 19. Paper baling, a major source of income for the industrial homes for many years
Fort Worth, Texas, 1940.
[Courtesy of MSSD-S.]

No. 20- A line of new Chevrolet open-body trucks for the Dallas, Texas, Men's Social Service Center, 1939. [Photograph by Frank Rogers, courtesy of MSSD-S.]

No. 21- The era of the Model 'A' Ford truck, Los Angeles Men's Social Service Center, 1929. [Photograph by Ron Carr, dir. of public relations, courtesy of Santa Ana ARC.]

No. 22- Colonel Winchell's "Drunkards Brigade," Jersey City.
[Courtesy of SAA, 35-2118.]

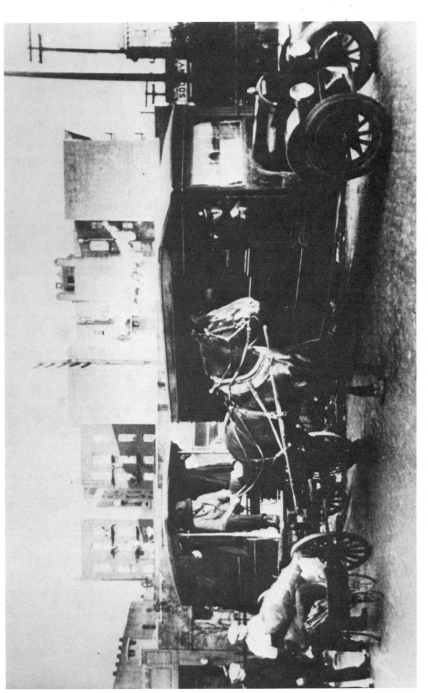

No. 23- Two old methods of Army pick-up, side-by-side, New York No. 2 MSSC, Bronx, N.Y., 1928.

No. 24- Adjutant John O. Neal (second from left) and Sam Woodgate, his assistant (third from left), before going to training, at the Grand Rapids, Mich., Industrial Home, c. 1907. [Courtesy of Brig. Cecil Briggs.]

each other at officers' councils, in order to stimulate profitable competition.[25]

The financial exigencies of the Depression breathed new vigor into the debate, which had continued for 10 years between managers who kept horses for some routes and those who advocated completely motorized fleets. This argument was a frequent topic of discussion in officers' councils in the 1930s. The position of those who favored the horse was further strengthened by the fact that many senior managers, among them the most eloquent and respected officers in the service, like John Castagna, John O'Neill, Horace Dodd and Henry Newby, advocated its continued use on short routes where heavy tonnage was not involved. The advantage offered by the horse-drawn vehicle was its comparatively low cost to acquire and operate: this was especially so through the early 1930s, when almost all remaining horse-drawn commercial enterprises switched to motor vehicles, placing large numbers of still-useful animals and vehicles on an already depressed market. Charles Schuerholz in Brockton found that farmers would give draft horses to the Army, simply to save the cost of keeping them through the winter. Conditions varied widely between centers, but in general the low replacement and operating cost (the purchase price of a truck was about twice that of a good horse and a new wagon, and the truck cost about four times as much per year to operate, including replacement) was not offset by the fact that trucks produced a much higher annual gross income—at least twice as much—as a wagon. In 1933, Brigadier John O'Neill cited figures gathered from his own highly successful Philadelphia center and four others to demonstrate that wagons generated about $275 more in net profit every year than trucks. Old arguments reappeared as well—the horses knew the route, they required only one man per wagon instead of two for a truck (which was used for furniture pickups), accidents involving trucks were more frequent and much more expensive, and many officers still believed that the contributing public was still sentimental about the Army horse and wagon. And what was to happen to the horses themselves, if the Army, practically the last agency in the country still using them, were to trade them off for trucks? Major Henry Newby of Brooklyn was forced to remind his comrades in 1936 that the horse had served The Salvation Army "faithfully and well for nearly 40 years without a murmur."

The horse actually gained ground in the Eastern Territory from 1931 to 1933, and the number of motor vehicles declined. This reversal occasioned some awkward moments for new city-bred managers who knew little about the animals they now had to acquire. Adjutant Frank Guldenschuh purchased three horses for Akron in 1933: one was "Dot," a likely-looking bay mare who, as it happened, was pregnant—with a mule colt, which she delivered in a month; Guldenschuh cleverly listed it as "an unexpected addition to our equipment." He was less fortunate with the other two: one dropped dead before she was even hitched up, and the other hanged herself in her harness after nine months. In September 1935, Brigadier J. O. Dowdell became men's social service secretary in New York, after Colonel Post. Dowdell was a highly successful manager, a hearty, friendly man, and the first center manager to become head of the department in the East. Dowdell knew the field thoroughly, and had definite ideas about everything, including horses, which he favored. It is not quite true, as some managers remembered it later, that Dowdell ordered officers to replace trucks with horses, but he refused for several years to allow managers to replace horses with trucks, on the perfectly sensible grounds that every center that had done so had gone into the red. Where stable facilities, equipment, feed and experienced drivers were available, horses continued to be useful for soliciting on compact downtown routes. At the end of 1936, there were 140 horses in the Eastern Territory Men's Social Service Department, and they were still in regular use in 12 centers in the East in 1940, and in at least two centers in the South—Washington and Louisville. The last Army horses in the Central Territory had been retired from Indianapolis in 1933 and from Chicago Central in 1934–1935, and from the Western Territory long before that.[26]

The ultimate victor in the contest—the truck—was not without its drawbacks. For one thing, they were not all the same—or even nearly the same—color. The dark green color for wagons was widely adopted across the country; a few wagons were dark blue or black. No such standard was imposed for trucks: despite departmental orders, trucks were not all dark green, even in the same territory, and there was no national standard color. A common color scheme in every territory for vehicles was dark green or blue body and black fenders, but all-black trucks were also common; most trucks had red shield and white lettering. Trucks purchased second- or third-hand were often not repainted. The East began to use red trucks in 1933—after ascertaining that the New York Fire Department had no objections!—but this color was not widely adopted in the territory in these years, and was not used in other territories until many years later. Another, far more serious difficulty with trucks—which the horse faction never tired of pointing out—was their accident rate, which was incredibly high in the 1930s. The annual accident rate for the East, for instance, was 75 accidents per 100 trucks in 1935, and 73 per 100 in 1938—rates so high that the Army had to change insurance companies frequently, either because the companies dropped the Army, or because the rates were raised to ruinous levels. Then, too, managers had to be warned to remove the Army's shields from trucks as they were sold or traded in, lest they fall into the hands of unscrupulous junk dealers. On the other hand, they were also warned not to remove too *much* from trade-ins because truck dealers were complaining that Army trucks came in stripped of every loose part and tool, including the spare tire.[27]

By 1935 the worst of the Depression was past for many Salvation Army men's social service centers. Federal policies had brought relief to the Army in several ways. In September 1933, President Roosevelt created the Federal Emergency Relief Administration (F.E.R.A.) and placed Harry Hopkins in charge. The F.E.R.A. assumed a minimal responsibility for all homeless transients—resident transients (a curious term) were not included—in 200 concentration centers around the country. Following a meeting between Hopkins and Colonels Parker and Post and representatives of the Central and Southern Territorial Headquarters, the government agreed that private charities would be used as feeder hostels for these large government centers, and would be compensated at the rate of 50 cents per day for three meals and a clean bed. When this cooperation actually began in November, the rates were less—30 cents, then 40 cents per day—but still a welcome source of regular income, which increased steadily until 1935 when the program was ended. Alert officers such as Captain Peter Hofman in Springfield, Massachusetts, bid for government contracts to house and feed men drawn to large cities such as Boston, to work on reforestation and public works projects. In 1934 the federal government gave out surplus foodstuffs to charitable agencies, including the Salvation Army men's social service centers. The Army cooperated with the National Industrial Recovery Act from the beginning; men's social service units—wagons or trucks—and corps bands often marched in the bumptious "We Do Our Part" parades of the early months of NRA. The Army was therefore naturally pleased when General Hugh Johnson, head of the NRA, announced in August 1934, that he was issuing industry-wide guidelines to end the "ruinously competitive" marketing policies in the wastepaper industry. The new government prices—$6.50 per ton for mixed, $8.50 for folded news—were welcome news to center managers, who had continued to collect paper at a loss as a means of employing as many men as possible. In a number of cities the Army cooperated with municipal relief administrators both to educate the public about the Army's need for discards in order to provide temporary employment for destitute men, and to supply emergency food and shelter to the homeless in the streets. Financial compensation for these services, a gradual decline in emergency applicants, an increase in paper prices and store sales, brought relief. By mid-1934 gross revenue in all parts of men's social operations in the East had grown by six percent faster than expenses. The record for all departments for the year, while far below the annual totals for the years 1925–1931, were encouraging when compared to 1932 and 1933.[28]

Major new institutions were opened in the second half of the decade. The social service center opened in Mount Vernon, New York, on November 17, 1935, was the largest in the country at that time; it housed 150 men—and still had stables. The expansion of the National Capitol Building in 1936 occasioned the relocation of the men's social service center in Washington. The new center was a utilitarian building on the corner of First and "F" Streets, N.W. 1937 was the first year more than a single southern center showed a profit—a "new day" for the territory; in the East, Brigadier Dowdell called 1937 "a splendid and victorious year"— almost too good to be true: only two institutions did not balance accounts. In Kansas City, Captain Cecil Briggs supervised the building of the first new center in the Central Territory since the Depression; it opened in 1938 at 518 Broadway. The Army's Mount Vernon, N.Y. property remained the country's largest center only until December 1937, when a facility twice as large was opened in a purchased property in Philadelphia; with 120,000 square feet of floorspace and beds for 250 men, it was not only the nation's but the "world's largest" Salvation Army facility. Dowdell and the territorial commander, Commissioner Alexander Damon, were kept busy· officiating at the openings of new or expanded facilities in the late 1930s. Some of these openings had been arranged only after great difficulty: finding and securing facilities that were suitable for the Army's residential and salvage programs, where the program did not warrant the cost of new construction, remained a problem in large northeastern cities. For instance, when the Army lost the social service center at Ashland Place in Brooklyn to a federal housing project it was difficult to find a suitable new location. The federal claim to the property was laid in April 1940; after officers looked at 25 or 30 unsuitable properties, they asked the government to extend the deadline for vacating the existing center, and were finally able to relocate in September 1941. In every territory there were still small programs as well, struggling in inadequate buildings. For instance, the social center on West and Mickle Streets in Camden, New Jersey, consisted in 1941 of a storefront so small that furniture had to be displayed on the sidewalk, rags were tossed out a second-floor window to be pressed by hand in the yard below, and the same room served the men as lounge, smoking room, recreation area and chapel. Still, managers and men long remembered the place as uniquely warm and friendly.[29]

The traditional connection between the Men's Social Service Department and bands, far more strongly developed in the East than in the other territories (despite Major Baldwin's long tenure as Southern Staff Bandmaster, or the fact that Major William Broughton was assistant secretary of the department in Chicago from 1931–1932), came to fruition from 1935 to 1940. The Men's Social Service Staff Band led by the baton of Adjutant George Granger played at the annual social picnic at Tappan 1933–1935, put on concerts, played at officers' welcome and farewell meetings, serenaded sick comrades and welcomed General-Elect Evangeline Booth when the *Leviathan* docked in New York in September 1934. In 1935, Adjutant Granger became New York Staff Bandmaster, but the social band did not at once disappear. In 1936 a "Men's Social Service Metropolitan District Band," made up of officers and men from the Manhattan and Bronx Districts, was formed. Adjutant William Slater served as bandmaster; the group disbanded in May for the summer, but was revived in November for a concert at the Gold Dust Lodge, enlivened by a "gag solo" by Captain Fletcher Agnew and a more serious one on the cornet by Envoy Fred Farrar.

Many centers had brass bands as well. In 1935 Adjutant John Phillips, himself an excellent E^b horn player, organized a "Men's Social Service Institutional Band" at New York No. 1 Social Service Center on W. 48th Street; it consisted of Envoy Farrar on cornet, Phillips and three other officers and a soldier, Walter Southwood, on bass, and functioned regularly until 1939. The Boston Men's Social Service Center under Captain Roy Barber had a 20-piece band, under the leadership of Major Thomas Malpass, from 1934 to 1939. The players were described in 1938 as all "associated in one way or another, with the institution," but it is unlikely they were clients, as the same report declared that 15 of the band were second- or third-generation Salvationists, and some of the men in the Men's Social Service Center Band also played in the Boston Palace Corps

Band. The "Boston Men's Social Service Center Silver Band" wore donated green uniforms and played often for local Army benefits. Newark had a "social band" and songsters; in 1935 the faithful Captain Albert Lock led the band which accompanied the center managers, Major and Mrs. Robert Klepzig, on their many engagements as special speakers at nearby corps. There was a 15-piece band at the Philadelphia Center in the last half of the decade; for part of that time the bandmaster was Ray Leivense, whom the men in the center elected president of their Bible class. There was a "Westchester County Men's Social Service Band" in Mount Vernon, and a social band at Pittsburgh No. 1 Center, both in 1936–1937. Captain Peter Hofman had a social service band in Springfield in 1936, which may well have become the "Springfield Instrumental Radio Sextet" listed early the next year. Cincinnati had an "orchestra" for part of the time while Brigadier Allan Neill was manager from 1933 to 1935. There was also an orchestra at the Syracuse Center. Colonel Post was "surprised to be greeted by music from an eight-piece orchestra" when he visited Major John Castagna in Providence in 1934. Major Frank Smith in Cleveland was so enthusiastic about these reports that in 1937 he talked some center converts into buying second-hand band instruments, and practicing "every spare moment" in order to form a band of their own. The men in Dayton contented themselves with harmonicas, and—rather anticlimactically—all Post could muster at headquarters was "the historic quartet" the members of which were, Major John Harbour (Memorial Hotel), Brigadier Dowdell, Adjutant Alfred Jackson and himself.[30]

Historic quartets were not alone in the forefront during the decade. Across the country a promising list of young lieutenants, captains and adjutants were maturing in the service as managers and assistants who would preside over the department's development in the critical years after World War II, which even now loomed as an ominous threat in their future. To the discerning eye their number was encouragingly large, and came from every territory: one selects almost at random from the contemporary documents such names as Tefler, Carl or Stillwell in the West; Briggs, Jobe, Youngman from the Central; Hofman, Baggs, Guldenschuh, Barber in the East; and in the South, Strandberg, Holmes, Needham, Ruthstrom, Gesner. There was enough for them all to do, and more. The gradual passing of the worst of the Depression left men's social service centers with traditional programs strengthened, even in the South, where by the end of fiscal year 1938–1939 the financial condition of the department had improved to the point where it supported a guarded optimism. The status of territorial leadership remained clouded for a year, however, when Adjutant A. E. Baldwin was made only "acting" territorial men's social services secretary, when he was brought in after two years as manager in Washington to replace Lt.-Colonel Range, who, with his wife, was killed in June 1938, in a train accident en route to a conference in Seattle. Elsewhere in the country, production and occupancy figures rose encouragingly through the last five years of the decade.[31]

In every territory in these years, store sales gained steadily on paper and rags as a proportion of departmental income. Store sales offered important advantages to a manager: they were not as dependent on a fluctuating and unpredictable market as paper and rags, and store sales generated much more net income per unit of variable production expense—that is, the cost of labor and vehicle operation. Both Post and Dowdell pushed store sales vigorously; the latter regarded an institution that derived at least "half if not more" of total income from stores as "healthy," and he insisted on careful monthly records of waste and store sales from each center. Colonel Post, trained in property matters, had been appalled at the ramshackle appearance of most of the stores he saw on his first official tour of the department in 1933. This convinced him that the Army knew only "as little about merchandising as possible" in order to survive. The situation, however, improved steadily through the decade. From 1933 to 1938, 23 different papers on stores and store sales were read at the Eastern Territory's Men's Social Service Officers' Councils. Adjutant Richard E. Baggs extolled the advantage of salesmanship at his successful stores in the Bronx—"the compelling psychology of forcefulness." Other officers pointed to the advantages of good locations for the stores, of hanging clothes on racks, neatness, clearly pricing items, not reducing potentially valuable furniture to kindling or covering it with mud-colored paint, selling large items such as used pianos by means of classified advertisements, and keeping an eye out for anything that was, or looked like, an antique. Large institutions like New York No. 1 and Philadelphia, which derived more than 75 percent of their income from store sales in 1935, deliberately attracted antique dealers and collectors by placing potentially valuable items together in one section of the store. In Boston, Roy Barber more democratically unloaded hundreds of old chairs by piling them in a store window with a sign marked "59¢ each while they last!" This store, incidentally, was apparently the first Salvation Army store to have air-conditioning; such luxury was not officially authorized, but Barber had rented the store without knowing of the feature, which came on automatically and pleasantly on the first hot day in June 1937. One enterprising manager converted discarded top hats into "modernistic lampshades," and another suggested to Dowdell that what with the live alligators, goats, pigs, white mice and rabbits that came in to the department, the Army ought to open a "pet shop."[32]

Other more practical innovations were introduced into the production process. Adjutant Ernest Hayes was the first manager to use the telephone for soliciting donations. In 1936, Hayes made a card for every number in the Dayton telephone directory, and arranged the cards by street and district. He then used two telephones—the "dial type," he helpfully suggested—to solicit, with one truck for each phone to collect the donations. This wonderful procedure continued for eight weeks, doubled the trucks' daily tonnage and brought in 958 pieces of furniture. One manager traded the loan of office furniture to a local radio station for two free advertisements over the air, and for one week in 1937 the Syracuse Telephone Company played a short message for "the Army wagon" whenever a person called for the correct time of day. In several cities department stores held "trade-in sales," accepting pieces of used furniture as trade-ins on new ones and giving the old pieces to The Salvation Army. Most managers, however, continued to rely upon traditional door-to-door solicitation, enlivened perhaps by the generous distribution of the new line of small pamphlets introduced by Major J. J. Stimson of the Eastern Territorial Printing Department in 1934: among the most popular of these were *Hidden Treasure in Your Trunk; Spring! Just Around the Corner: House-Cleaning Time;* and the best-known of all, *If A Poor Man Could Eat Paper, Would You Burn It?* Managers widely used this last motto in newspaper and poster advertisements as well. The pamphlets were in fact quite effective, and had a demonstrable effect on production in the centers that used them.

In February 1935, a centralized rag bureau was opened at the New York No. 1 Center, headed by the widow of Field-Major Fred Miller—the second wife of one of the hardest-working managers of the industrial home era, often moved, seldom thanked—and Lieutenant Harold Southwood. The plan, which went well at first, was to collect and grade all rags from nearby institutions, then sell them in sorted bulk on the highest market, working only with large dealers for the best price. The "Rag Sorting Department" paid each center at the prevailing local market rate plus a 50 cent per hundredweight premium for delivery to New York. As was the case with its paper bales, the "standard S.A. pack" for rags was competitively attractive, as it contained a high percentage of valuable woolens and clean wipers, and a few cheap "roofers," useful only for filler in roofing material. The rag sorting department, however, was an idea whose time had not yet come: by 1940 the combined effects of a fluctuating market, the expenses of the sorting process—which employed 24 people—and the needs of centers for clothing to be sold in the stores had killed the "Central Textile Bureau," as it was known at the end. Several territorial headquarters continued from time to time to advocate centralized rag sales.[33]

Headquarters continued to monitor sales figures, to encourage innovations and to shower forms and memos down upon managers. In 1937 Colonel Dowdell announced that henceforth officers were to collect and preserve his instructions to them, as these together would form a new manual for the department, replacing the "previous handbook"—Parker's 1923 book of "minutes" which was now officially declared obsolete. Probably the best advice Dowdell gave, however, was when he put his principles for the successful operation of a center into a few lines which he sent to Captain Lawrence Castagna in 1935 when he appointed him to manage the Pittsburgh No. 2 Center. Dowdell was refreshingly frank in these letters: Pittsburgh No. 2 was a loser financially; if Castagna couldn't make it pay, Dowdell would return him to "an assistant's position and try someone else." Dowdell's advice was simple: production must cover expenses, so increase income by better marketing, and decrease expenses by buying, or using, exactly what and how much you need; never buy spares and remember when hiring that the Army cannot help everybody in the world. This concern for economy caused Dowdell to give hearty endorsement and widespread publicity to a plan introduced at the Bronx Center by Adjutant R. E. Baggs in 1937: the "Order of Merit" for drivers who went one year without an accident. Dowdell called Baggs "energetic and enterprising" for his idea, which quickly spread to other centers, as Dowdell had hoped. A healthy competition sprang up between centers until Adjutant Schuerholz ended it by submitting the name of a driver with 10 accident-free years—the best record in the territory.[34]

It was the men, after all, who mattered. These years saw an increasing awareness among men's social service officers that rescuing men from sin and wasted lives was still the first purpose of their work. The Founder, dead for a quarter of a century by 1937, was remembered by few officers and fewer men, and then only because his fading portrait still hung in many center chapels. One by one the old pioneers, the last living links to the days when the shelters and the salvage brigades had battled their way out onto the dark sea of sin to haul in the lost, died. Now, however, in the last years before the war, William Booth's vision came alive for many in a new generation of Salvationists, in many places in every territory. Captain Walter Cruikshanks looked upon his efficient new center at Mount Vernon no differently from the way his predecessors had looked upon their gas-lit upstairs shelters; both were refuges for the lost in the wilderness. So Cruikshanks and his assistant went out in one of the new dark green trucks into a blizzard in January 1935, to spend the night collecting homeless men and bringing them into the center for food and warmth. This small act, recorded only by chance, and a hundred or a thousand like it now lost to all recollection—officers who called their men "Mister," who trusted a man with a little sum of money, who explained a new job twice or three times when once should have done, who perhaps only smiled; all such little things that change men's lives forever—stand beside the volumes of memos, forms and production figures which were but ephemeral and long-forgotten means to the end that at least some in the world would believe that Christ died to show that every man is somebody's brother.[35]

Evangelism, the remaking of men physically, socially and spiritually, had been the official purpose of the Movement from the beginning. In this work the closest cooperation between social and corps activities was advocated, and practiced, despite anomalies in two territories. In the South the practice of incorporating small shelter and salvage programs into corps, survived the Depression, which gave them birth. In the East there were activities in one or two centers that were traditionally regarded as proper only for corps—Cleveland, for instance, started its own home league in 1935, made up mostly of women employees, but its records were kept at the nearby corps—and in Dayton an entire corps was operated within the social center from 1935 to 1939; when it was transferred back to divisional supervision it was the last "social corps" in the United States. It was clear by the 1930s that as valuable as official cooperation between the social and field certainly was, the greatest part of the uplifting work among social-center residents would be done in the center itself. Colonel Parker had said that *"To save the whole man for Christ"* was "the ultimate object of our men's industrial homes." The pressure of the Depression and the emphasis on production had never crowded that object aside completely, and in the 1930s new, more modern, efficient means of helping men were introduced.[36]

As early as 1931, the Central Registration Bureau in New York began to employ an "intensive case-work treatment" for the purpose of the "rehabilitation" of the homeless transients who came to the Army. The program called for careful and complete individual records for each man, so that officers would know how best to plan for his immediate physical reconstruction and his more permanent social and spiritual restoration. The overwhelming numbers of applicants in the Depression forced the C.R.B. in 1933 to confine its permanent records to the employees in the Army centers, but two historic papers were delivered in that year to the social officers' councils, which explained in some detail how "case-work" methods could be employed in individual centers. Adjutant Chester Brown suggested that no actual "technical training" was required; social officers had long experience with the homeless poor, which, coupled with "friendly interest" in the individual man and some sort of network between centers designed to pass information on a man from place to place so a useful complete record was built up, should be enough to "develop very materially" an ability to help at least some of the men. Captain A. Ernest Agnew's paper, read in Newark in May 1933, went further. Agnew, commissioned in 1928, had a degree from the University of Chicago School of Social Service Administration, and was at the time of the paper the director of the Army's family social service bureau in Newark. As one of the few academically trained officers in the country, Agnew's interest in introducing professional standards into the operation of the Army's largest and most visible social welfare branch—the Men's Social Service Department—was understandably great. Agnew was little known in the department in 1933, but his influence, and the effect of his work, became important as the years passed. In 1933, he argued that "modern social case work" would enable men's social institutions to more effectively carry out the original purpose of the Movement, the "rehabilitation" of men, "body, mind and soul." He suggested that a typical "case" would require a careful interview, complete record of findings, including the results of attempts made to find the man's relatives and letters sent to former employers to confirm the man's own story about his past work experience—all of this information designed to help the man recover. Agnew also suggested that rather than indiscriminately placing men into work assignments, the center staff should put the man whose record reveals a history of shiftless behavior onto a wagon with a reliable man, hold out the promise to the new man that he will be taught a valuable skill like upholstering if he is faithful on the wagon, interview him from time to time, have friendly chats, and look for ways to influence him spiritually.

The next year, 1934, Nels Anderson, a nationally recognized expert on the problem of the homeless man, noted that while The Salvation Army was "not generally a case-working organization," he was encouraged by the receptive attitude of some officers, and felt that the Army was going in the right "direction." Major Andrew Laurie claimed in 1935 that the Army was committed to an "individual approach to the lives and problems of its many converts" and that officers learned something each day that bids them "hope for better days and better results" in "rehabilitating men [who are] out of work and almost out of mind." In 1932, there was a "Salvation Army Session" at the National Conference of Social Work; in 1933 officers from all four territories attended the conference in Detroit. In 1936 the Army participated fully in the conference as an official "associate group." By the end of the decade officers were stressing the importance of the "initial interview with the client," the need for a "personal officer" to supervise the introduction of the man into the center and analyze the record of each man for careful follow-up and counseling. The manager, especially in the large centers, was often too busy to check the men in or to do extensive counseling. When a new men's social service center was dedicated in Paterson (on the site of the old Rescue Mission), its purpose was officially declared to be "the rehabilitation of wasted manhood."[37]

The Salvation Army officially recognized that to blow new life into the "dying embers of their manhood," as Colonel Dowdell put it in a paper at the National Council of Social Work in 1939, required some knowledge of the individual man and his problems. The worst of these problems—at least the most common—was still, as it had always been, the "curse of drink." Even while Prohibition was the law and many centers were crowded with sober men who had been thrown out of work by the Depression, a systematic analysis of the Army's centers in New York City in 1931 stated, "Alcoholism is so frequent a characteristic that it is rarely entered in the record. It is the most frustrating influence with which the Army must contend." The Salvation Army had always regarded alcohol as its particular enemy; in the 1930s the old conviction that the Army had a special, divine calling to rescue the drunkard was combined, here and there around the country, with a new spirit of professionalism, which recognized that alcoholism is caused by special factors, physical perhaps, certainly mental and emotional, and that understanding these things will help officers to guide the drinking man to a permanent solution. Despite the energetic sincerity of the greathearts of the Boozers' Parades—and not gainsaying the real conversions from these efforts—some officers had come to the conclusion in the 1930's that simply sobering a man up with prayer or strange concoctions did not ordinarily cure him of what was in some cases an addiction. Other agencies increasingly recognized the Army as having a large investment in solving the problem of alcoholism. In 1937 Adjutant Roy Barber was appointed to a special committee comprised of leading social agencies in Boston to study the problem of the homeless alcoholic. The Army was the only private agency represented. Programs specifically designed to deal with alcoholism in a thorough manner were formed within the Army. In 1939 the Detroit Harbor Light Corps opened its doors; it was the first Salvation Army facility specifically designed for the treatment of drunkards, as opposed to simply exhorting them or sobering them up for brief periods. There was also a small, family alcoholic program in the Army corps in Holland, Michigan. In that same year, 1939, in Philadelphia, Major R. E. Baggs started the first Alcoholics Anonymous group in any Salvation Army center in the country.[38]

The Army was interested in the welfare of men, but it was not alone in that regard. In September 1933, the Commander signed a "certificate of compliance" with the NRA—the great blue eagle streamed gallantly in front of national headquarters—which placed limits around the working conditions of those who were clearly employees of the Army: 40 hours work per week with extra hourly pay for hours worked beyond 40, and $15.00 per week minimum wage. Compliance with the NRA's myriad of codes was voluntary, which was probably a good thing (considering that $15.00 per week was the salary of a married adjutant) but the Army made a genuine effort to comply, especially regarding the number of working hours. State workmen's compensation laws, however, were not voluntary. In the 1930s several cases involving Salvation Army centers came before state authorities—in Connecticut in 1934; in Ohio in 1938. Headquarters emphasized in official instructions to the managers that a "responsible officer" must see to it that each new applicant at a center sign an "admittance card" stating that he agreed to provide labor in exchange for the benefits of the residential program of The Salvation Army, for which he was voluntarily applying because of his own needs. Officers were warned not to mention such words as "job" or "employment" in speaking to new men. Along with workmen's compensation officials came others who enforced building and health codes. These officials became attentive and zealous in the reform-minded 1930s. Booth-Tucker had complained in *The War Cry* almost 40 years before about government regulations, but with considerably less reason, considering the casual manner in which lackadaisical officials enforced building and health codes against the Army in the 1890s. The days were but a happy memory when an inspector from the public health department or the fire department would wink at violations of the codes because he sympathized with The Salvation Army, or felt sorry for the officer, or simply because nobody downtown cared much what happened in the run-down and crowded neighborhoods in which the Army centers were located. The conviction that government agencies had a large responsibility for the poor and helpless had become popular in the 1930s; it was, in fact, part of the public support for the Roosevelt administration, and many state governments as well, especially in the elections of 1936.[39]

In June 1938, the U.S. Congress passed and the President signed the Fair Labor Standards Act. Because the Act was a political compromise, coming after long and bitter debate, it left much to the discretion of an appointed administrator. One thing in the new Act was clear from the beginning, however: all employees engaged in "commerce or the production of goods for commerce" were granted a minimum wage of 25 cents an hour for the first year, 30 cents for the next six years and 40 cents an hour thereafter, and a maximum work week of 40 hours. More hours required a higher rate of pay. The Salvation Army was not at first alarmed by this legislation; the Army did not regard its men's social service centers as commercial operations but as places where homeless needy men were cared for without having to suffer the stigma of unearned charity. The fact that many of these centers, by the sale of goods collected, repaired, baled or sorted by labor, generated a sum of money greater than the cost of producing them, however, appeared in an ominous light, especially as high-ranking officers had encouraged, and even insisted upon, such surpluses. Department heads were quick to correct these false impressions. Colonel Dowdell warned his managers in April 1939, to "be very careful" what they said about their centers: "make the words 'self-help project' stick in your vocabulary when expressing the function of the home."

The new Act provided for exemptions for the employment of handicapped workers, who could be paid a lower wage. The administrator was authorized by the Act to establish a sheltered workshop advisory committee. The Salvation Army and several other charitable "industries" joined this committee, on the understanding, which all the agencies understood in common, that its main function was to help the government uncover false charities that exploited their workers. The government saw the committee as serving in a somewhat more practical way, however; the government also considered the charitable agencies on the committee as covered by the provision of the new Act, and set about collecting data to prove its case. In August 1939, the U.S. Department of Labor, Wages and Hours Division, sent to the Army's National Headquarters, now presided over by Commissioner Edward Parker as "national secretary," a "circular" stating the broad coverage of the Fair Labor Standards Act and enclosing for circulation to all men's social service centers a "most comprehensive questionnaire." Parker informed the territorial commanders in September that these two documents together were "the most sweeping thing the government had ever sprung upon us in connection with our social work." He contacted the directors of Goodwill Industries about making a joint presentation of their common cause in Washington. The chairman of the sheltered workshop advisory committee turned out to be, by happy chance, Colonel John N. Smith, Jr., an old friend of Parker's from the NRA, when the Army had so agreeably signed one of the voluntary compliance codes. These two men had a "very satisfactory interview" in Washington, and Commissioner Parker was appointed to the sheltered workshop advisory committee on December 8, 1939.

From this vantage point, Parker could more easily defend the Army's official contention that it was not covered under the Fair Labor Standards Act, with or without sheltered workshop exemptions, because it was not engaged in commerce. The Army's position became much more detailed as time passed, especially regarding the religious nature of its claims for exemption and its explanation of surplus income, but it never varied on the basic principle. In January 1940, Parker informed the commissioners that it was "pretty well finalized" that The Salvation Army was exempt from the Act. In February, however, the Labor Department sent applications for sheltered workshop certificates directly to several men's social service center managers. Parker telegraphed the territorial headquarters at once: "Please Instruct Take No Action This Matter Writing." Apparently a few managers, not knowing proper procedures, filed applications. Parker instructed the Labor Department to disregard these. On March 1, 1940, The Salvation Army officially filed for a "blanket application" for a certificate covering every institution, including as an official part of the application the reservation—which was typed directly onto the printed regulation form—that the Army was exempt from the provisions of the Fair Labor Standards Act. The territorial commanders agreed to await the decision of the advisory committee on the Army's contentions, which were at first shared by the other agencies on the committee as well. In July 1941, the counsel for the Labor Department gave his opinion that the Army was engaged in a commercial activity that was covered by the FLSA. The Army and the other agencies agreed to cooperate to the extent of answering financial questionnaires, which had been sent to individual institutions by the government administrator. In the course of time the other agencies relented, and one by one applied for, and were granted, sheltered workshop certificates, which allowed them to pay reduced wages but which placed them by their own voluntary admission entirely within the purview of the Fair Labor Standards Act. The Salvation Army was adamant in refusing to take this step. In December an important conference was held in New York, attended by Parker, Dowdell, Major A. E. Baldwin and Lt.-Colonel Frank Genge, the men's social service secretary from Chicago. The consensus of the Army conferees was that if the Army's centers came under the Act, the Movement "would be practically ruined."[40]

Certainly The Salvation Army and the U.S. Government had other things to worry about in December 1941, than the relevance of the Fair Labor Standards Act. The issue was a vital one, however, and even the pressures of the war that now came upon Americans could not prevent, but only postpone, its final resolution. The last full year of peace had been a mixed one for The Salvation Army anyway. It had started well: the old Memorial Hotel, the only non-commercial lodging house in the Bowery, had been brought at last out of the red—the "meritorious achievement" of Envoy Thomas Stanyon, whose efficiency and kindness made the hotel popular. In June 1940, Commissioner Alexander Damon opened the Lowenstein Cafeteria at the 48th Street Center in New York. Subsidized by a fund endowed by a wealthy leather merchant, the cafeteria seated 500 at a time and served 5-cent meals all day.

The year ended sadly for the Army. In October, the month after Adjutant Roy Barber took command in Pittsburgh, the cook became confused by the identical color of pancake flour and rat poison, with the result that 12 men died and 40 became seriously ill. *LIFE* magazine ran a full-page photograph of the funeral, the 5-cent funeral fund having provided a row of identical coffins for eight of the transient men who were unclaimed.[41]

CHAPTER V

The Years of Crisis: Service to Man, 1940–1960

World War II came over the Men's Social Service Department with a forcefulness many times greater than that of the 1917–1918 war. The combined effect of the many shortages and restrictions inflicted on the Army's social centers, however, was a change in program that had an impact that was at once so far reaching and long lasting as to be, if not in conception, then certainly in its result, a revolution. Although alert managers in every territory recognized and acted upon the new principles, the officers in the Eastern Territory took the leadership in the new movement and publicized it; from them it spread quickly among kindred spirits nationwide.

As far as the Salvation Army Men's Social Services were concerned, World War II lasted from 1940, when the economy began to mobilize to supply the war needs of the western democracies already fighting, until the release from active duty of the bulk of American servicemen in late 1945. In that six-year period, the Army faced a severe shortage in manpower. The rapid increase in the number of well-paid jobs in war-related industries drew many men from Army centers. The Selective Service Act, which went into effect in September 1940, drew off many more men. When World War II ended in August 1945, there were more than 12 million Americans under arms; that was three times as many, in terms of percentage of the total population, as were in the armed forces in 1918. The majority of men in Salvation Army centers before 1940 were over 40, past the age for active military duty, but a large minority were of draft age. In addition, the heavy drain of young men from the economy opened the way for older men in the centers to obtain attractive outside jobs for the first time in years.

There were other shortages. Gasoline was rationed, and many kinds of staple food items, wire for baling, and new motor vehicles for civilian use could not be obtained after early 1942. There were severe restrictions on the use of freight and transshipment facilities for civilian use. Certain buyers with war contracts to fill had official priority; these companies were supplied first, while low-priority buyers were delayed in obtaining needed supplies, or even failed altogether to obtain them, even though the item was not rationed. Buyers with priorities had first claim on almost any product they chose, so that they could divert raw materials needed by one firm, and the finished product of another, at the expense of regular customers, disrupting sales and delivery networks upon which the producer ordinarily depended. The Salvation Army social service operation was caught in all of these squeezes, and others: as consumer durables became rationed, they became irreplaceable. Fewer were given to The Salvation Army, which soon ran out of, among other things, radios, clocks, lamps, vacuum cleaners and all major household appliances, such as refrigerators and stoves. Periodic paper and scrap collections, carried on with religious efficiency as a patriotic endeavor by the housewives and schoolchildren of America, further threatened Army programs. Almost every center curtailed some aspect of the production process; some centers—like Omaha—became mere hotels during the war, while others were transferred to corps operation as shelters and rummage stores. The reduction in men's social service operations nationwide made it possible for the Army to transfer many social officers for the duration of the war into the newly formed United Services Organizations (USO), which the Army helped to organize in 1941. The international Salvation Army also appropriated the red shield which, in America, was the symbol of the men's social services, and was used to designate its clubs and canteens for service personnel; these clubs drew heavily on men's social officers as well. Many other social officers were transferred to the field for corps or headquarters work.[1]

The fact that the Army's men's social services were not much more severely hampered by these restrictions and losses—the fact that the department survived—was due to several factors. The Army participated in many of the community salvage drives, lending to the war effort the experience of managers and men and the Army's knowledge of the salvage business. The chairman of the Bureau of Industrial Conservation officially praised The Salvation Army in 1942 for its help in the national salvage campaign. For its own production the Army employed advertising that explained to the public that, in addition to helping needy men back onto their feet, donations to the men's social services were a "help in home defense," a kind of "practical patriotism." The famous Salvation Army "drop-box" was a child of this necessity: in 1942 Captain Cecil Briggs used collection boxes in Kansas City when there were no longer enough men to cover all the routes; in December of that year Captain Roy Edwards in Omaha placed piano crates on busy street corners in order to collect license plates, which expired at the end of the year. The territorial commander, Commissioner John Allan, expressed approval of this innovation, and the drop-box was widely adopted. The Army's cooperation with wartime salvage drives, both community-sponsored and the Army's own, its association with the USO and the Red Shield Clubs, the visits of Army lassies to the wounded in veterans' hospitals and the Army's canteens and a vast array of friendly and helpful services among military men at the front—all these activities caused The Salvation Army to be trusted and popular among the American public, so that donations in money to other branches of the Movement partly offset the decline of material donated to the men's social, and evidence at least suggests that many citizens made sacrificial contributions of items partly for patriotic reasons but chose the Army as the agency for their gesture out of sympathy for its programs.[2]

The shortage of trucks worked less hardship in the East than in the other territories: the New York headquarters had operated a centralized purchase plan since 1936. Trucks were traded in every two years for centers that kept up their $20 per truck monthly payment to the central truck fund, which meant that almost all the trucks in the territory were less than a year old when the war came—a fleet of equipment that one manager described as "priceless" by 1943. The appeal of the Ford had declined in all four departments as the all-popular Model A trucks were replaced. By the war years, the dominant name in social garages was Chevrolet (whose light and powerful trucks were economical to operate), International and REO. And there was gasoline for them, in every territory. After the first months of stringency, the Army's "practical patriotism" displayed in salvage work brought official approval in a practical and welcome form: "C" ration stickers for the front windshields of the Army trucks. A severe shortage of rubber for tires, hoses, belts and seals, and of copper for electrical writing, continued throughout the war, however; vehicles had to be used as efficiently as possible even when fuel was available. Spare parts were difficult, and new tires impossible, to obtain. Fortunately for The Salvation Army the little kits of small square patches and glue for repairing punctured inner tubes by the roadside, which were standard equipment in the cars and trucks of the day, remained available through the war years. As it was, the decline in materials and men kept trucks idle some of the time in every center; in some centers trucks were idle more than half the time.[3]

One unsung casualty of World War II was the Salvation Army horse. Gone for years in the West and Central, the faithful quadruped labored into the war years in Louisville in the South, and in Atlantic City, Paterson and Jersey City in the East. All accounts agree that the Southern social horse lasted the longest in Louisville, but there is some small question as to how long that was. When Lieutenant Eugene Gesner served as assistant in Louisville in 1940–1941 he found no horses; but when young Captain A. S. Peters went there as manager in February 1945, he found, if not a horse, at least the fresh farewell droppings of one, which the previous manager, Major Harry Purdum, had sold only shortly before Peters arrived. The case seems clearer in the East. Between August and September 1945, Atlantic City's horse and wagon disappeared from official accounts; Paterson still had two horses and three wagons and Jersey City had five horses and nine wagons. In October 1945, the Army changed the form of the regulation center ledger sheet at departmental headquarters: "Horses: Renewal and Hire" was replaced by "Religious Rehabilitation"—which, one hastens to add, had appeared in another way on the old form. Until February 22, 1946, however, someone neatly inked out "Religious Rehabilitation" on the Jersey City page in the ledger at headquarters and inked in "Horses: Renewal and Hire" and entered there the small monthly amount for feed which the manager, Brigadier James Bovill, continued to spend. The page for March 29, 1946, does not contain the alteration, nor does it ever appear again. Thus the last of a long line of "Bessies," "Dots" and "Charlies" passed into the shadows. "And what about the horse?" Major Newby had asked 10 years before. Had he not "served The Salvation Army faithfully and well for nearly 40 years without a murmur?"[4]

The difficulty with horses was not, oddly enough, that they were uneconomical to operate: quite the contrary, even in 1945. The problem was in finding drivers. Men who knew how to handle a horse in harness were naturally fewer, and the few steady men who remained in the Army's centers after the attractions of war-time employment and the draft had worked upon them preferred to drive trucks, which paid better, was easier work (more time driving, less time walking and loading) and gave a man useful experience if he wanted to find work outside. Major Lawrence

Castagna kept horses in Paterson until 1945, and gave them up only when the men refused to use them any longer.

Horses were expendable; men were not. The shortage in men was the one shortage which could not be overcome. The percentage of occupancy in the 44 Eastern centers fell drastically as the war progressed; 87 percent in 1941, 74 percent in 1942, 57 percent in 1943 and the low of 47 percent in 1944. A few well-placed managers were able to operate centers profitably by using for part-time work, men who came to the city for war work and needed a place to eat and sleep until they received their first pay check (or after they had squandered it). Officers like Cecil Briggs in Kansas City and Peter Hofman in Cleveland provided a valuable service to such men, and were among the few managers in their territories to operate their centers "in the green"—the department traditionally used green ink to indicate a credit balance. Other centers had fewer men than in 1940, often too few to operate a program, and the few they had were elderly, infirm or chronic alcoholics. Captain A. E. Agnew conducted an official survey of Eastern centers during the first two years of the war; he found many conscientious managers, but none with an effective intake policy: every applicant, old or new, was accepted—or as Agnew put it in referring to the New York No. 2 Center in the Bronx, which he visited in December 1942, readmissions seemed to be "on a pretty liberal basis."[5]

At the same time that the dwindling number of men in the centers made it impossible for most managers to emphasize anything but production— to the dismay of many of them—the emphasis on "casework" and individual treatment that had arisen in a few places before the war was not forgotten. The outstanding example of effective casework during these years was the Philadelphia Men's Social Service Center in Roxborough, under Major Richard E. "Eddie" Baggs. On March 10, 1940, Commissioner Damon and Colonel Dowdell presided over the dedication of the new "Jubilee Chapel" built by the men themselves. Dowdell reported officially of Philadelphia that "an extensive casework program" was carried out there for the men "who come to us for rehabilitation," and that many of these had been "greatly helped in reestablishing themselves." Baggs and several other managers were in frequent communication during the war years, exchanging experiences and ideas about the limited improvements that wartime restrictions allowed. These officers were aware of another factor. The war had eclipsed the Fair Labor Standards Act. The Wages and Hours Division did not test its contention during the war that the Army was a sheltered workshop under the Act, but the agency regularly sent questionnaires to center managers. In 1943 the Commissioners' Conference stated officially that The Salvation Army would answer the questionnaires, and would make every effort to pay the minimum wage to its employees, but that the Army was not covered by the Act and would not apply for certificates as a sheltered workshop. Alert social officers reflected on what sort of program they should have in place that would justify the Army's contention that it was not a commercial enterprise, that would utilize new techniques to effectively help men in the centers when the inevitable day of victory came and the wartime shortages of men and material ended.[6]

The Philadelphia Center served as a model to these officers. In early 1941 Adjutant A. E. Agnew, the social welfare secretary, in charge of the Army's family welfare program, in Philadelphia, visited and analyzed the center. He prepared an extensive report on the casework carried out there, which since 1939 had been done by a full-time employee, Robert Matthews. Agnew defined casework as treatment tailored to the individual needs of the man, a "particular effort" for each which was added to the "generalized" religious, hospitable and uplifting influences that were exerted on everyone in the center. He stated that the Philadelphia program was based on adequate information on each man, recorded on a face sheet, which was filled in with the answers to questions about the man's background, abilities, problems, which he would answer after he was relaxed and comfortable in the center; this was contained in a chronological case file. This was to be the standard casework program which the department later adopted. Agnew found that the men in Philadelphia had been roughly classified on the basis of the liability to reform and the economic productivity of each, and that between one-fourth and one-third of the men were "on the way to a satisfactory adjustment." Colonel Dowdell, already impressed by Baggs' success as a manager, found "much good" in Agnew's report, and distributed copies of it to every manager in the territory. He added a warning, however, that the report was not a new procedure, and that officers should not take all Agnew's recommendations "too literally." Dowdell was a bluff, hearty man of demonstrated ability, whose long, hard experience as a manager had left him unsympathetic to any merely bookish or theoretical suggestions for the proper working of a center: he noted in his covering letter for the Philadelphia report that "the professional social worker" had a "weakness for linguistic inventiveness."[7]

Dowdell was committed to improvement in the department, however,

and not blind to Agnew's abilities. He arranged with the divisionial commander, Brigadier Samuel Hepburn, for the adjutant to be released from
his duties at divisional headquarters for six months in order to conduct
studies of a number of centers in the territory, along the lines suggested by
the Philadelphia study. From October 1942, through April 1943, Agnew
visited 13 centers. Returning to Philadelphia, he worked closely with
Major Baggs in preparing a "survey" with proposals for the "proposed
institution of a modernized social program." It was Baggs who contributed the name for the new program, a phrase which soon became famous,
and in the end, official: "Service to Man." Agnew was quick to give Baggs
and a few other progressive managers much credit; in fact, in the individual "studies" of the centers he noted, over and over, that much of what he
proposed was already in operation: Major Baggs had made Philadelphia
into a model center; Adjutant Peter Hofman in Cleveland had a full-time
intake worker since 1941 and worked closely with the local Alcoholics
Anonymous (A.A.) to find help for his men; he and his center loomed "as
leaders in this forward movement." Major Frank Guldenschuh had instituted "case work studies" at New York No. 1, and Major Herbert Sparks
gave "unusually careful attention to the social side" of his work in Pittsburgh, supervising intakes, working with other agencies to find the best
care for the men. Agnew also noted that many other managers were
sincere, kind-hearted, eager to try anything that would help the men—he
particularly noted Major Henry Stephan in Boston—but who were
swamped by wartime pressures. Based on the success of the more progressive examples, by his close association with Baggs, Hofman and
others, Agnew, in his commitment to the theory of modern social work
practice, proposed a program that was based on the best of the old
approach combined with "individual" casework and serious efforts at
alcoholic rehabilitation which centered on the principles of self-help and
mutual support of A.A., whose "Twelve Traditions" were themselves still
in the process of final formulation during these years.[8]

     Although they were phrased only in general terms, the proposals of
Agnew and Baggs represented an important development in the history of
the department. Agnew's visits to centers had revealed that "with few
exceptions" the needs of the men were subordinated to the needs of the
institution. Even if the officers were progressive-minded and kind-hearted,
the intake process was often in the hands of production foremen, who
chose men on the basis of what they could contribute to production. This
must end: the work itself was not useless or degrading, and most managers

were scrupulously honest in their financial dealings with the men, but production must no longer be the end of the Army's program, but only a means to that end, which was rehabilitation. Each man should be admitted to the center on the basis of what help the Army could provide him, and assigned to work that would best meet his needs. Outside of work hours, the center should provide worthwhile social and recreational activities, and should be clean, well-equipped and homey, so that the men felt that the Army cared for them as persons—even as friends, brothers. Agnew pointed out that this encouraging environment had little to do with the age of the building: Boston and Pittsburgh, for instance, were old buildings, but friendly, homey centers, while New York No. 2, a modern facility, was "decidedly bleak." Careful casework files should be kept, where anything likely to aid in permanently helping the man should be recorded. The Army's regular religious program must, of course, be maintained. But there must be a wholly new, far more extensive effort to rehabilitate the alcoholics in the centers. The pattern had shifted and blurred over 50 years, but its outline was still clear: "alcohol forms the one big and ever present problem in all the social services centers." In the ideal, completed program there would be the "whirlpool" of work, recreation, snack bar— Baggs had installed the first one in an Army center, in 1941—physical comforts, medical care, an educational or retraining program, which carried the willing client into the "vortex" of the program: individual casework, spiritual activity and Alcoholics Anonymous.

The advocates of this program did not call for immediate adoption, because the pressures of the war and the fact that no one in the department was trained to install or administer such a program would render it impossible. For the present the good developments already at work in various centers should be encouraged, and a series of regional meetings held around the territory, at which the outline of the new Service-to-Man program could be explained to all the managers. Agnew had found in his travels "a highly encouraging proportion of men who can be counted on to form the nucleus around which a service-to-man program might be built.[9]

Colonel Dowdell received this report with mixed feelings. He had been a social officer since 1909 and was proud of what the department had accomplished so far; in his personal copy of Agnew's final report Dowdell wrote "GOOD" in the margin and underlined all the parts that praised the existing program. He was, in fact, tiring of Adjutant Agnew, for reasons which are only partly clear after 40 years. Dowdell discounted criticism of the department from an officer whose experience of it was limited to six

No. 25- Depression relief at the Detroit MSSC.
[Courtesy of Detroit ARC.]

No. 26- Detroit MSSC store, 1940 (store addition dedicated 1936).

No. 27- The Cleveland Industrial Home provides employment sorting cast-off clothing, thus helping men help themselves, 1928. [Courtesy of Lt.-Col. P.J. Hofman.]

No. 28-   Major George Granger helping a needy client.
[Courtesy of SAA, 4-200.]

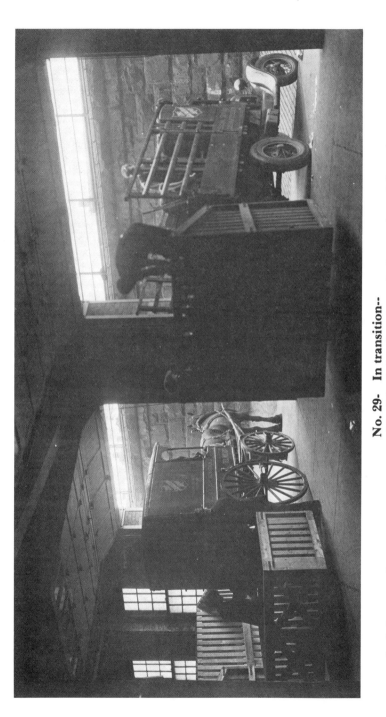

No. 29-   In transition--
both horse and motor power were used by The Salvation Army in its men's social service program
in collection of contributed household goods and other items.
[Photograph by Paul Parker, courtesy of The Salvation Army National Information Service.]

No. 30- **The historic meeting of E.J. Parker with the managers of New York No. 1 Center at the Braveman Hotel in 1905.**
[Courtesy of SAA, 35-1789.]

No. 31- Colonel E.J. Parker.
[Courtesy of SAA.]

No. 32- Colonel E.J. Parker
during his active years as the men's social service secretary.
[Courtesy of SAA.]

months and who emphasized theory and professional phraseology, which Dowdell found irritating and irrelevant. On the other hand, the colonel was genuinely committed to improvements, accepted Agnew's suggestions for ways to enhance and improve the strengths of the existing program with much better grace than his criticism of it, and shared Agnew's high regard for Baggs, Hofman, Guldenschuh, Sparks and the others upon whom Agnew drew for material and guidance. In any case, Dowdell accepted the formal recommendations contained in Agnew's report, which he received in April 1943. Shortly after that he informed Commissioner Ernest Pugmire, the new territorial commander, that the Men's Social Service Department was about to launch a "million-dollar idea" on the Army world, and secured his permission to appoint a "Postwar Planning Committee" to be chaired by R. E. Baggs.

Dowdell's high hopes for this committee were only partially realized. All the managers on the committee were certain that the new program would transform the department into an important agency to rehabilitate men, increase production, win souls—and bring a new sense of professionalism and pride to its officers, who naturally rejected the second-class status which some of their comrades on the field had unfairly thrust upon them. Less encouraging to Dowdell, however, was the fact that many of these managers looked upon the Postwar Planning Committee as a means to set up a network with themselves as "regional directors" to instruct other officers in the new program and supervise its development. In the course of these meetings several officers seemed to have suggested that Colonel Dowdell was too committed to the old ways to be a reliable leader into a future so bright with promise, and too committed to the traditionally centralized, autocratic structure of the department to welcome the imposition of a layer of authority between himself and the managers in the centers. Reports of these sessions, which were apparently conducted on occasion in a spirit of disarming and jocular candor, naturally reached Dowdell, who interpreted some of what was said as a direct attack on headquarters in general and himself in particular. Disappointed and angry, Dowdell dismissed the Postwar Planning Committee on May 11, 1943. This action, and some of the colonel's comments—Dowdell was never subtle—convinced some of the reformers that the secretary opposed the whole Service-to-Man program. Other managers disagreed, and continued to look upon Dowdell with respect and affection. Contemporary private correspondence and official reports support the loyalists' interpretation: Colonel Dowdell supported the new program, which he could clearly see would be a great benefit for the men in the centers, but his relationships with a few leading officers became temporarily strained.[10]

Despite this little setback, the plans for a new rehabilitation program went forward. The administrative heads of the territory, the territorial commander, Commissioner Ernest Pugmire and the chief secretary, Colonel Norman S. Marshall, had become enthusiastic about the program, still waiting expectantly for Dowdell's "million-dollar idea." Colonel Marshall was Dowdell's immediate superior in the Army hierarchy, and as such had kept himself informed of developments in the department. He was well aware of Agnew's study, his final report, the hopes of the reforming managers, and of Dowdell's pride in the long record of slow, steady efforts to help men and finance the department built up over the long years by many faithful social officers. He knew of the problems caused by the war, which bore down more heavily on this department than on any other in the Army. Marshall never compromised Dowdell's position within the department, and did nothing officially regarding the department except in response to recommendations from the colonel, but his knowledge of the men in the centers, his sympathy with the reformers and his patient mediation were of great—perhaps incalculably great—value in reconciling Dowdell with the ex-Postwar Planning Committee men. Marshall arranged several important meetings at headquarters in which the commissioner, he, Dowdell, Agnew and the men who were almost certain to inaugurate the new program were present. In May 1943, Dowdell approved the provision of a "caseworker" as an official employee in every center that could afford one, and in June he requested Agnew to submit an outline of the "proposed rehabilitation program," which he received in July, in the form of 11 typed pages, much of which appeared again in 1948 in the Army's first official manual for the new program. The program was based on pleasant living accommodations, good working conditions, "general activities" and "most important" of all—casework, that is, "activities aimed at the specific needs and problems of the individual man." Managers must have "an intense—we might almost say, compassionate—interest in the man and his welfare," and recognize that the center is not a shelter, a career or a profitable enterprise; it exists for no other purpose than the "permanent rehabilitation" of the man.

> This goes [further] than a new start, or self-respect gained
> through self-support. It includes new work habits and

skills, new moral habits, new spiritual patterns. It includes all that The Salvation Army stands for, applied in a thoroughly thoughtful, organized, and constructive manner, focused on the individual man, according to his individual needs.

The Salvation Army's commitment to this interpretation of the purpose of the men's social centers both motivated and justified its refusal to accept the applicability of the Fair Labor Standards Act to their operation: the Army was not engaged in commerce, profitable or otherwise: its purpose was rehabilitation, and the work the men performed was part of the therapy. The Commissioners' Conference confirmed its position again in November 1943.[11]

The inspiration for a new approach to men's social operations did not come solely from Agnew's proposals. Dowdell considered Agnew's outline to be too vague to provide guidance in the practical operation of a center, and requested that a more concrete "educational program" be drawn up, but many officers had been drawn to some of the same conclusions before Service to Man was first discussed. Major Albert Ramsdale, a family social and public relations officer in Chicago, told the Army's delegation to the National Conference of Social Work in 1938 that they should remember that the program in the men's social service department was for the man, not vice versa. Of much greater significance in the development of men's social programs were the proposals of Peter Hofman. A Dutch immigrant and a social officer since becoming an officer in 1929, Hofman was a man of great and original intelligence, but he found his own best inspiration for his fresh approach to social work in the long-forgotten classics of the founding of the department. It was General Booth's *In Darkest England* that confirmed for Hofman his own observation that alcoholism is a disease, requiring treatment, rather than merely a sinful disposition that could be changed by an act of the unaided willpower, however sincere. An ancient copy of *Orders and Regulations for Social Officers (Men's)*, originally issued in London in 1915 and almost unknown in American circles, appeared one day in a bin of old discards, and provided fresh inspiration. As irrelevant as much of it was, the tattered red-bound book provided a better theoretical explanation of the purpose for which men's work was started than Hofman had even seen before in a department whose only official guidelines were a few official "minutes" and what of value an officer could still find in E. J. Parker's "social orders" of 1922. In Springfield, Massachusetts, and Central Falls, Rhode Island, Hofman became adept at production, at maintaining a clean, friendly and comfortable center, and at experimenting with ways to nurse the men back to moral life. In 1941 Adjutant Hofman was transferred to the Cleveland Men's Social Service Center, where he brought his ideas to maturity. Much of Hofman's thinking influenced Agnew, Baggs and other managers, and found its way into print in the Service-to-Man materials of 1943–1944. Other managers were moving independently in the new direction: when Colonel Marshall visited Paterson in the early 1940s he congratulated Adjutant Lawrence Castagna on the success of his Service-to-Man program, a term which the startled Castagna had never heard.[12]

In other territories as well, there were officers who realized that the war and the shortage of clients would end eventually, that the issue raised by the Fair Labor Standards Act would one day have to be faced, and most importantly of all, that the Salvation Army Men's Social Service Department existed to help men, or it had no valid reason to exist at all. There were managers in every territory who discovered when Service to Man was officially publicized that they had been doing many of the same things for years. Major A. E. Baldwin, the men's social service secretary for the South, was one of the leaders of the new thinking in the South. He put together a short, unofficial "manual" for the guidance of his managers, which placed the man at the center of all men's social operations, and which came to the favorable attention of the Commissioners' Conference. In the West, Colonel Arch Layman, who had supervised a pioneer program for men in Hawaii when he was divisional commander there in 1929, took an alert and well-informed interest in center activities and laid the foundation for a full-fledged rehabilitation program during his long tenure as men's social service secretary, 1931–1945. In 1942 a "survey course" in "social welfare work" was developed, and later revised, by officers in the Southern, Western and Central Territories who were "recognized specialists" in social work, including Major Gilbert Decker and Mrs. Adjutant Loyd (Anita) Robb. The course was designed both for training college and correspondence courses, and included extensive explanations of interviewing, proper casework procedures and counseling. By February 1945, the course was in use in some form in every territory. In November 1943, the Commissioners' Conference authorized an annual conference of the four territorial men's social service secretaries, and appointed Colonel Layman as chairman and Major Baldwin as official liaison for transmitting recommendations to the national commander. The first meeting of the new conference was delayed, however, for a year, and met only once during the war.[13]

Service to Man continued to develop in the East. Colonel Marshall informed Dowdell in September 1943 that the commissioner was "anxious to launch this new plan immediately and set the wheels in motion" before the upcoming men's social service officers' councils. Major Agnew prepared a more practical version of the "orientation course" in outline form. Colonel Dowdell may have had lingering doubts about the establishment of the "regional directors" to implement the program; in addition, his relations with Major Agnew were by now badly frayed. Agnew was not an officer in Dowdell's department, and could—and did—communicate his proposals and suggestions directly to the chief secretary. Marshall, a gentleman, was alert to preserve Dowdell's prestige—and his feelings—but Dowdell could hardly have been pleased that all of the materials Agnew prepared for distribution to the managers was marked "Issued by the Authority of the Territorial Commander" with no mention of the head of the department. The regional directors were selected in September, staff and divisional commanders were informed—any who mistakenly looked upon the new appointment as having administrative authority were set straight by Dowdell in his characteristically direct style—and announced to the whole department in November 1943. Despite the reputation for opposition to the program that still clings to Dowdell's memory, he did much to get it well launched: he appointed to the new positions the leaders of the movement, and gave them great latitude in setting up and conducting the regional meetings that were announced to begin in January 1944. The first regional directors were Major R. E. Baggs (Philadelphia), Adjutant Peter Hofman (Ohio Region), Major Frank Guldenschuh (Metropolitan New York), Major Herbert Sparks (Pittsburgh), and Major Peter Crispell (the manager of the Albany Center, for the New York State Region).[14]

Dowdell prepared a formal "Memorandum of Instruction" for each regional director, and distributed it in February. The regional directors were to "enthusiastically" guide, and abet "each officer . . . in the successful development of this rehabilitation program." They were to preside over monthly meetings (called "institutes") for all the managers in the district, to be conducted by Major Agnew. The regional directors had no administrative responsibility, and were responsible directly to the men's social service secretary. The directors were to visit each center in the region at least once every three months, and to report to headquarters the names of any managers who were not cooperating with the new program.

The institutes were held monthly in each region through 1944. Although Colonel Dowdell continued to support the general proposition of preparing the centers for postwar changes, his dislike for Agnew had grown so intense that it colored his appraisal of the institutes. He suspected that Agnew was stirring up complaints against his administration of the department, and he said so, apparently in public at a regional meeting in Scranton, certainly in a series of letters to the territorial commander. When Dowdell learned in May that Agnew had, in turn, made complaints to Marshall about the secretary's "lack of support" for Service to Man, he was outraged: he demanded that Agnew be removed as a disloyal incompetent. He went further, and began openly to suspect that the regional directors were too friendly with Agnew; this could only mean that they were not really interested in a new program of rehabilitation as much as they wanted position and power. When the commissioner and the chief secretary became alarmed that these unfortunate developments might impair the success of the new program and asked Dowdell to arrange for the regional directors to send in reports on the progress of the institutes so far, Dowdell made his suspicions of the directors official, but he grudgingly agreed to collect the appraisals from them.

The reports of the regional directors were full of gratitude and praise: Major Guldenschuh called the "institutes" an "answer to many sincere prayers" and the "greatest single step" he had seen thus far in his career. The other reports were similarly enthusiastic. Dowdell was apparently mollified by these reports, passed them on to Marshall and began to place encouraging remarks on the progress of Service to Man in the weekly departmental newsletter, "News of the Moment," which Dowdell wrote personally. Pugmire and Marshall were hopeful again. Then—alas— Dowdell's suspicions overcame him once more, and in October he denounced the institutes as a "dismal failure," and proposed that the sessions be discontinued. Dowdell's attitude was obvious to managers who saw him often; it may have encouraged managers in the New York area, who regarded Dowdell as a close personal friend, to dawdle in, even to resist, attending the institute in that region. At least Major Guldenschuh suspected this, and complained to Dowdell; he even requested that these officers be transferred to other centers, out of the region. Dowdell rejected Guldenschuh's complaint as groundless supposition. Colonel Marshall responded masterfully to this unhappy situation. He expressed official surprise at Dowdell's fluctuating enthusiasm for Service to Man. He agreed with Dowdell that Guldenschuh's accusations against the managers in his region could be dismissed; still, these officers had been mentioned in an unfavorable way in an official letter, and Marshall thought it only fair to them to allow them to express themselves directly to the chief secretary at a personal conference. Marshall pointed out that by now—October 1944—the institutes had generated territorial and national attention, and that the regional directors and the managers of the large centers must display "some measure of enthusiasm" for Service to Man as an example to the territory, "and for that matter, for the rest of the country."

The cloud passed. Dowdell had never personally liked or understood Agnew, and some of what was said at the first few "institutes" hurt him; he was defensive of the real accomplishments of the traditional program and perhaps did not fully understand how every part of the proposed new program was really novel or important. But Dowdell never wavered in his commitment to improving the program. No officer was more aware than he of the problems facing the department during the war, and those looming before it in the future. He was, for instance, one of the first officers to grasp the implications of the Fair Labor Standards Act, and he accepted the need for caseworkers in each center long before Service to Man was publicized. He supported the ideas contained in the institutes, and he was determined to keep the regional director system in place, on a modified basis, to direct the implementation of those ideas. Before the social officers' councils in 1944, a number of regional directors, the men whom Dowdell respected most in the department, took him out for an elegant supper in New York, to show good faith and to win him over to continue the new program. Dowdell, hardly naive after 35 years in the men's social service department, enjoyed the expensive meal, innocently inquired of the men if they had something they might want to talk about, and benignly agreed to most of what they proposed, as he had planned to do from the start. An important formal conference was held between Dowdell and the regional directors on November 27, 1944, at New York No. 1 Center. There Dowdell announced that the institutes would be discontinued, but that the regional directors would not only be retained, but would be given "added responsibilities:" to directly supervise the development of the new rehabilitation program in each center, and to assist each manager in working out both an immediate and a long-term plan for his center. The regional directors were to meet quarterly for a "clinic" or "workshop," presided over by the men's social service secretary, or his assistant, the general secretary. Each regional director was to visit each center monthly, and hold a conference for all his managers quarterly, which the secretary or general secretary would attend "whenever possible." Finally Dowdell, all congeniality, asked Peter Hofman to prepare a review of all that had been accomplished during the 1944 institutes.[15]

The institutes, in fact, had been a triumph. The new program revitalized the department, not only in the East, but, as ideas spread to energetic officers, the three other territories were powerfully affected as well. Service to Man represents a major contribution to the history of The Salvation Army in the United States, for which A. E. Agnew and the reforming managers deserve great and lasting credit. The institutes promoted the idea that the purpose of the men's social service center was the rehabilitation of men, socially, physically and spiritually. The physical background of such a program was related to its success: centers should be clean, well-lighted, nicely decorated—farewell to the uniform buff-and-ivory color scheme of Parker's day—with comfortable furniture and convenient bath and shower facilities. The men should eat at small tables, covered with "tastefully chosen linoleum," rather than at long tables, and the sandwich for lunch, universally detested by the men, at the center or in the truck, should be banished forever. There should be table games, good reading material, movies, and radios. Proper medical care, eyeglasses, dental work should be provided for the men. The idea of the "scientific method" of social work was explained: careful observation and recording of facts, objective analysis of facts leading to scientific laws and predictability, a rejection of false previous ideas and freedom from mere traditionalism and prejudice. The evangelical service should be made attractive and relevant, even the mottos on the walls should display modern techniques of color and design, and should be used sparingly: "Remember Mother's Prayers!" was to join the buff walls and the sandwich in obscurity. There should be a major new emphasis on alcoholic rehabilitation, and in particular, the institutes called for the introduction of the techniques of Alcoholics Anonymous into all centers.

The Army's first few contacts with Alcoholics Anonymous were almost uniformly unfortunate. Some members of A.A., almost all of the middle-class and professional persons, rebuffed inquiries from Army managers who invited A.A. speakers or counselors into the center, or if they came, they frequently patronized the center as a skid-row mission and the men as low-lifes and panhandlers. A number of officers distrusted A.A., but others felt that if A.A. members understood the Army's program they could make an invaluable contribution to the men in the center. Since it was formed in 1935, the A.A. movement, based on unity, self-help and a combination of willpower, divine aid and mutual support, had enjoyed great success in helping alcoholics to escape from the habit. Officers like Baggs and Hofman who persevered in bringing A.A. into their centers were enthusiastic about its potential for helping men. In 1944, Hofman formed the Cedar Group of A.A. in the Cleveland Center, which became a model for the successful operation of A.A. within Salvation Army centers. Interest in understanding alcoholism and finding modern, professional help for its victims, to supplement the traditional religious approach, grew steadily among officers during the 1940s. In 1942, George Purdum, divisional welfare officer in Philadelphia, joined the Research Council on Problems of Alcohol, part of the American Association for the Advancement of Science. The first issue of its *Bulletin,* two years later, noted that Brigadier Chester Brown, head of the Army's social welfare department in New York City, chaired a discussion in that city in June 1944 on "The Church and the Alcoholic," part of a national symposium on alcoholism. At the second symposium held in Cleveland later in the same year, Major Peter Hofman contributed to a discussion on group aids in therapy. The association that allowed the largest number of officers to develop an understanding of alcoholism and its treatment was with the Summer School of Alcoholic Studies of the Yale University Laboratory of Applied Biodynamics, which began in 1943 under the leadership of Dr. E. M. Jellinek. The famous "Yale School" was a major influence on the developing alcoholic rehabilitation program within The Salvation Army. The director drew upon the experience and facilities of Major John Kirkman and the New Haven Social Service Center. The experiences of 12 officers who attended the first three Yale Schools, the success in rehabilitating alcoholics displayed by men like Baggs and Hofman, and the institutes of 1944 led the commissioners to agree in September 1944, to recommend that any center large enough to have a program that could "effectively use such a service" should hire a full-time "personnel director" to conduct casework with alcoholics in the center. In the fall of 1945, The Salvation Army established a national committee for the study of a rehabilitation program for alcoholics. Two years later this committee, now styled a "commission," recommended that territorial commissions be formed as well, but only the Central Territory acted upon the recommendation, due to the influence of Brigadier A. E. Baldwin, who was chairman of the national commission and men's social service secretary in Chicago. On April 7, 1948, the first "Salvation Army Institute on the Problems of Alcoholism" was held in Chicago.[16]

The experience of Brigadier James Bovill, the veteran manager of the Jersey City Center, was typical—and touching. Bovill was an experienced, compassionate and successful manager in the old tradition: his center was the last to give up the use of a horse-and-wagon team. Bovill attended the Yale School in the summer of 1945. He had never before thought of alcoholism as anything more than a sinful weakness. He had preached "deliverance" in all good faith. If a man drank while living and working in the center, Bovill routinely threw him out. It had never occurred to Bovill, for whom it came as a kind of heartbreaking revelation, that alcoholics were not just sinful but "really sick persons as well." Bovill now declared that most officers had no knowledge of how complicated the problem of alcoholism was, so they could find no means to apply the correct solution, even when they had it in the power of God and in the facilities and program of the center. The Yale School transformed Bovill, and he resolved to put what he learned to good use in Jersey City, hoping to repeat "the accomplishments of officers like Major Baggs of Philadelphia and Major Hoffman [sic] of Cleveland since they attended the School." Hofman, however, had not confined his work to the center; he and converts from the center held meetings in Cleveland's "skid-row" area in 1945, in which the converted men told of their own rehabilitation from alcohol. Soon centers in Cincinnati, Columbus and later Philadelphia were holding similar meetings.[17]

It was natural, then, that these officers should spend a large part of the 1944 institutes on a discussion of alcoholism, and that not just these but all the sessions should seem like important events to those who promoted the concept of Service to Man. Major Hofman solicited letters from all the managers who had participated in the institutes in 1944 in order to prepare the report which Colonel Dowdell had requested at the meeting with the regional directors in November 1944. The letters revealed "a spontaneous enthusiasm for the course, the program and the meetings" expressed with an "unanimity hardly equaled among us." The managers agreed that the institutes had raised their material efficiency as well, by allowing them to share their problems and solutions with each other, and had given them a better understanding of the new Service-to-Man program, boosted their morale, enhanced their sense of comradeship and group loyalty, and provided good spiritual blessings as well. The reformers were touched to see how many of the "old-timers" became enthusiastic about the new program, once they saw that "salvation of the soul" was still central to the new plan. There were a few skeptics, a few managers who supported the plan but whose circumstances during the war were so desperate that they could not put any part of it into operation, and a few managers who simply could not understand what was being proposed.[18]

World War II, of course, remained the unchanging context in which all these welcome developments began to unfold, in many places cramped and tentative in the midst of the ongoing pressures of labor shortages, rival wastepaper drives, rationing of food and materials and the unrelieved tension of wartime. These restrictions could not, however, prevent the laying down of at least the groundwork for the new program: a new "case-record folder" was introduced to the centers, and papers on proper admittance and interviewing procedures were read at the first regional meetings. Despite the pressure of the war, the new emphasis on rehabilitation was discussed and encouraged in the other territories. In September 1944, the Commissioners' Conference recommended that information on the Service-to-Man program be distributed to the Southern and Central Territories, and that an officer from these territories be sent to confer with Major Agnew on the orientation course. No formal action was taken on these proposals, but considerable informal cross-fertilization of ideas had already started between territories. Major A. E. Baldwin, men's social service secretary in the South until 1946, then in the Central; Cecil Briggs and Warren Johnson in the Central; Colonel Arch Layman and his successor Lt.-Colonel Sydney Cooke in the West, were among many officers who had been thinking and working towards better ways to accomplish permanent improvement in the lives of their men. These officers readily made, and encouraged others to make, contact with the leaders of the new movement in the East during the last year of the war.[19]

The end of the war in May and August 1945, did not immediately affect the Army's social service centers: some kinds of rationing, and wage and price controls lasted through 1946. The 12,123,455 members of the armed forces on active duty on June 30, 1945, were not released overnight. Within a few months, however, the Salvation Army Men's Social Service Centers were in the midst of an economic boom: income from waste paper remained high as industry retooled for peace, discards of inviting merchandise began literally to pile up as war-weary consumers and returning veterans tossed out used appliances and furniture, sometimes by the houseful, to purchase new. Manpower came back to the centers. Nine million persons were discharged from military service by June 1946. Marginal war workers could not make the transition to a more selective civilian job market, and in any case the dislocation of the economy caused by the Armistice caused severe regional unemployment for all kinds of workers. One new source of men in the centers, however, was veterans who found the transition to civilian life difficult, or who refused to begin life again on its old terms and needed temporary help in relocating themselves to a new place—usually a large city. One major study of returning veterans, made in 1944, concluded that veterans would be the "major social problem of the next few years." In 1946, 37 percent of the active case load in the Cleveland center were veterans. The U.S. Office of Price Administration still controlled building materials, and gave priority to building projects for veterans; Major Hofman was given permission to build a new addition on the center within 24 hours after he secured a letter from the local director of veterans' affairs "certifying" that the Salvation Army center was a facility for veterans! The percentages varied regionally—and some centers had not started keeping careful intake records—but in every territory returning veterans ended the Army's manpower problems.[20]

Peace brought reorganization to two territories, and a final clarification of the status of regional directors in the third. In the Central Territory the position of district officer had never entirely lapsed—two districts, Detroit and Minneapolis, had survived the curtailments of the Depression years. These were given new life and energy in 1944 when Major William Jobe was returned to men's social services, after 18 months in U.S.O., as district officer and manager in Minneapolis. Brigadier Earl Crawford at Chicago Central and Brigadier Fred Reinking in Detroit were given similar positions. The prestige and authority of these positions were enhanced partially to assist in coordinating centers while conserving gasoline and experienced personnel (who could, in fact, run several centers at once) and were retained in peace as the new emphasis on rehabilitation and the postwar boom stimulated the department. In the South, two district offices were created on August 31, 1946; there the motive was three-fold: gas rationing and continuing restrictions on air travel made effective supervision of distant centers difficult, these two new positions were to oversee the "spiritual and social welfare of the center," and more pragmatically—to enable the commissioner to promote to the rank of brigadier two successful and respected officers. Brigadier Harold Gesner, manager of the Dallas Center, became Southwest Social District Officer, and Brigadier Arne Lekson, manager in Washington, became Washington Social District Officer. The Washington District included centers as distant as Memphis and Louisville, gas rationing apparently not the major consideration in this appointment.

The position of district officer was not, in fact, indispensable. The Salvation Army has never been top-heavy in administration, but the Men's Social Service Department was streamlined even by the Army's lean standard: the secretary and a second-in-command, and the managers in the centers. District officers provided little significant assistance to the former, or guidance to the latter, and required considerable, and, in the end, needless, duplication of correspondence and supervision. In both the Central and Southern Territories, these positions were allowed to lapse when their incumbents retired or were transferred to other positions.

The situation of the regional directors in the East was quite different: these six officers inspired and supervised a program of genuine value. But the problem of the bare administrative structure of the department was the same there as everywhere else. There was simply no place for an aggressive and successful manager who welcomed the recognition and responsibility of promotion to go except to become secretary of the department. This position, to which several dozen men might reasonably aspire at once, came open only at long intervals, and was often filled by an officer from outside the department. Many social officers preferred the challenge and independence of managing their own centers, whose successful operation required a rare combination of business skill, social psychology and zeal for lost souls; nevertheless, ambition was not unknown, even in the Men's Social Service Department. This was particularly the case in the matter of rank, which in a military hierarchy brings prestige and recognition both of which have charms even for the officer who sincerely desires to remain in direct contact with the men in the center. For men animated by either kind of ambition the position of regional director glowed invitingly, somewhere part-way "up" on the scaffolding of power.

In March 1946, several regional directors' meetings proposed certain kinds of reinforcement for their position: that they meet as a group monthly instead of quarterly, and that their titles be "recognized" by appearing officially in the *Disposition of Forces,* the Army's gazette of ranks and appointments. Colonel Dowdell agreed to these proposals, but when they reached the new chief secretary, Colonel Bertram Rodda, he and his staff had no knowledge of what exactly regional directors *did*, other than organizing A.A. meetings in each institution. The regional directors were disappointed at this little oversight on the part of top leadership, and grumbled about it at their June meeting. Worse was to follow. Colonel Joseph Dowdell retired in October 1946; gruff and candid as he may have been, Dowdell was an experienced social officer who well understood his officers and their problems. His replacement as secretary was Lt.-Colonel Harold Smith, formerly head of the Eastern Territorial Evangeline Department, responsible for administering women's residences, to which the Naval and Military Department and the fresh-air camping programs had been added because of the shortage of headquarters personnel during the war. Smith was an earnest, kindly man, fondly remembered by officers who worked closely with him at headquarters, and he made a determined effort to acquaint himself with his new department, but he knew little of all that had taken place within its ranks over the past critical 10 years. Smith committed himself at once to Service to Man and announced that he planned to retain the system of regional directors. He took the regional directors at face value, however, as no more than developers of the new rehabilitation plan, an activity which, as he told them in February 1947, he "heartily" endorsed: he would, for instance, gladly renew Colonel Dowdell's attempt to secure recognition for the directors in the *Disposition of Forces*. Beyond that, he preferred the simple old-fashioned way of administering the department, did not plan to create district officers as other territories had done, and in fact did not look upon an appointment as a regional director as a promotion at all. Nevertheless, no officer who was not successful and respected was ever appointed to one of these positions. Smith met with these officers three times per year and gave them major responsibilities in formulating policy as part of Service to Man, and an appointment as a regional director continued to be regarded, if not by Smith then by everyone else, as a promotion.[21]

These matters, of course, had no effect on the tide of good fortune that carried the department along. These were golden years in the Southern Territory; even before the war, Commissioner William Arnold had been determined to provide proper facilities in which to conduct a modern men's social service program. He reduced the territorial assessment of men's social income to one percent, and ordered any excess into property renewal funds. The first new center to result from the program was opened in 1944 in Ft. Worth. After the war, Major Gilbert Decker, the men's social service secretary, resolved to spend the new revenues entirely on capital improvements; these revenues were supplemented in 1946 by the sale of two bankrupt reminders of the post-World War I hotel boom, the San Antonio Palms Hotel and the Army-Navy Club in Norfolk. After the privations of the war years, the department planned to refurbish old centers and to open new ones. In Birmingham, Major Hubert Holmes, appointed in January 1946, from the U.S.O., abandoned an embarrassing old social building, purchased a better facility and developed the men's social service center into a program that other agencies came to regard as respectable and worthwhile. The Army optimistically purchased an enormous building in Houston, a former factory so large that the men's social operation only occupied one small corner. When Major Decker first visited the Houston Center in 1946, he had the momentary impression that the building was only "temporarily occupied," but after wholesale renovations carried out by Adjutant Walter Needham, Houston came to be regarded as a model program. Decker looked upon the Houston Center under Senior-Captain Sven Ruthstrom as the best spiritual and rehabilitation program in the territory, and recommended it as the official training center for new officers appointed to the department. Ruthstrom had the "only real social-casework program" in the South, established by Senior-Major Hilda Woodall, who introduced A.A. into the center program.

The men's social occupied the promising city of Miami in two easy stages. The city command there had operated a shelter and salvage program as an adjunct to the corps—an arrangement more common in the Southern Territory than in any other—which had begun as a private self-help philanthropy in 1939, and which occupied three unattractive buildings, one of them 20 blocks from the others. In 1946, the city commander asked the Men's Social Service Department to include this languishing program in its expansive schemes, but to operate it under the official auspices of the corps. The department, eager to begin work in the largest Southern city still closed to it, gladly agreed. The arrangement was not successful, however, as neither the first several social officers nor the city command staff could agree on operations. In 1948, Senior-Captain Eugene Gesner, who was committed to a modern program for men, was sent to the Miami center. He convinced his colleagues in the field branch that the shelter should be closed, along with a few stores, so that Gesner could concentrate on properly housing the men for real rehabilitation and proper merchandising to pay for it. Later in the year the center was transferred to the men's social service department for operation in the regular manner. A sum equal to the original cost to the city command of the facilities was placed in trust in order to build an adequate modern shelter for transients who did not wish to begin the regimen of rehabilitation at the center. There were plenty of men to go around: Miami attracted large numbers of wanderers and job hunters. The program flourished under Gesner, income was quadrupled, which more than supported a full line of rehabilitative and religious activities. Interestingly enough, Miami was one of the first centers in the territory to rely almost entirely on store sales for its support; postwar paper sales were only seven percent of income, and there were almost no rag sales: almost all clothing donated to the center was resold as used clothing, rather than baled as rags. Miami's downtown store had the highest income of any store in the territory after 1948.

Centers in Little Rock and Charleston, which were operated by the department for awhile under the auspices of field commands that had taken them on during the lean times in the past, were transferred back to departmental control. Introducing adequate housing and rehabilitation in place of shelter, a basic principle of the reform movement, continued: in Nashville, where the men's social had been forced to close during the war, the Argonne Hotel was closed in 1950 and a proper men's social center opened. Within five years after the war, six facilities had been refurbished and enlarged in the South, and bed capacity was doubled.[22]

A new feeling of camaraderie and professionalism spread among Southern managers. In Atlanta in 1946, Major Decker conducted his first territorial men's social officers' councils. The talk was all on spiritual themes—the officers specifically asked for Bible teaching, and Lt.-Colonel Wesley Bouterse was secured to give scriptural instruction at two subsequent councils—and on the new "social welfare" aspects of the program. Southern officers were proud of the zealous evangelism that marked the work of such officers as Major George Strandberg in Ft. Worth, or Senior-Captain William Browning in Oklahoma City, where, in 1950, a revival among the men led them to hold street meetings in their old haunts. In the Western Territory, men's social work was spread to two new cities: Bakersfield in 1946 and Santa Monica in 1947, and a large new facility was opened in San Francisco, at 1500 Valencia Street. Probationary-Captain George Duplain was appointed to Fresno in 1947 and began shortly to attempt to combine successful production techniques with means of improving the lives of the men on a long-term basis; he soon became a leading—and successful—proponent of the Service-to-Man program in the West. In fact, the new program and new ideas were much in the air in every territory. In 1947, The Salvation Army sent the largest delegation in its history—100 delegates—to the National Conference of Social Work in San Francisco.[23]

1947 was a banner year for the Men's Social Service Department: it had been 50 years since a few homeless men had collected bottles and rags in handcarts and carried them back to the pioneer salvage brigade in an alley at the rear of 26 Cherry Street on New York's lower east side. Those 50 years had carried Booth-Tucker and most of the pioneer social officers into happy memory; a few survived in honored retirement. But the idea of using waste labor to convert waste material into something useful, and in so doing saving souls and rebuilding ruined lives, had only grown more successful, more popular, more triumphant throughout the years. Now, in 1947, the department seemed to have climbed to the edge of a glittering plateau, on which its centers could continue their beneficial work forever, buoyed up by prosperity and scientific rehabilitation. Here indeed was something to celebrate! The national commander declared November 2, 1947, as "Golden Jubilee Sunday" for the Men's Social Service Department. Every territory held celebrations in every center, but the most elaborate and exuberant were in the East, where men's social work had started. Lt.-Colonel Smith officially requested one of the metropolitan social officers—like many social officers, a talented musician—to write a commemorative band march for the occasion. Major Milton Kippax, manager of the Staten Island Center and a euphonium player in the New York Staff Band, wrote "Golden Jubilee" march, which became and remains a favorite of Army bands. On Friday, November 7, 1947, the first "Men's Social Night" was held at New York's Centennial Memorial Temple, as part of the long-standing "Friday Evening at the Temple" series. It was a memorable evening: Commissioner Parker shared reminiscences, the staff band premiered "Golden Jubilee," four center converts gave witness to their conversions, Major Walter Cruikshanks—who once spent a night in Mount Vernon rescuing homeless men from a snowstorm—delivered the sermon, and Colonel Dowdell—who had but 18 months more to live—brought the last prayer of the night.[24]

The Eastern Territory remained by far the largest of the four, in terms of men's social activities. In 1949 there were 105 social service centers in the United States, with accommodations for 5,309 men; of these 43, or 41 percent, were in the East, with 2,641 beds, or half the total national capacity. In the East the great increase in departmental income had gone largely into program. From 1941 to 1950 income from all centers had increased by 194 percent (to $6,084,092), but expenses had increased by

194 percent (to $5,668,241); in 1948 and 1949, in fact, the department had a deficit in the midst of plenty. The largest component in these increased expenses were those marked "direct to clientele," and equipment for program. For instance, of 425 trucks in the department in September 1950, 377 had been purchased new within three years. The Central showed a pattern during these years similar to that of the East, and markedly unlike that of the South, and to a certain extent, the West, where large portions of the new income were spent in refurbishing and purchasing buildings. None of the new buildings acquired by the South was built for the Army; all were purchased intact and adapted to the Army's needs, a procedure that was generally much less costly in terms of service area acquired than paying for new construction. In fact the Washington, D.C. Men's Social Service Center, built in 1936, was the only center in the entire Southern Territory that was housed in a building designed and built by the Army since the territory was erected in 1927. The results of the decision of the East to concentrate on program rather than new buildings, with the deficit that resulted, could not have been foreseen, and this was made sadder by the fact that the motive to heap the Army's new riches back into service for the men was so entirely commendable. After the war, other territories as well steadily improved the interior arrangements of centers: year by year the 2'6" cots were replaced with three-foot-wide beds, lockers gave way to drawers, automatic washers replaced wringers and tubs, rooms for three to seven men took the place of the old-style large dormitories with their "sea of beds."[25]

That The Salvation Army's motivation was commendable was not, strange to say, universally admitted. The administrator of the Fair Labor Standards Act (FLSA), for instance, did not admit it; rather, he looked upon the Army's motivations as irrelevant to the applicability of the Act to the Army's operations. The Wages and Hours Division waited patiently through the war years for The Salvation Army to apply for sheltered workshop certificates for its men's social service centers, as every other similar charitable organization had, one by one, agreed to do. The Army remained a member of the sheltered workshop advisory committee, but from 1942 on, the Army representative was accompanied by Mr. Robert E. Lee, of the law firm of Cadwalader, Wickersham and Taft, the Army's general counsel, who reminded the FLSA administrator from time to time that the Army's cooperation with him was voluntary. In October 1945, the Commissioners' Conference reaffirmed the Army's position that it was not covered by the Act, that applying for sheltered workshop certificates would be an admission that the law was applicable, and that the Army was not going to make any such application. The Commissioners' Conference was resolute: the Army would cooperate with the Wages and Hours Division on a friendly, voluntary basis, but if the government should attempt to compel the Army to accept the Act's applicability, the Eastern Territorial Headquarters would challenge the government's contention in court, and the other three territories would support New York.

By 1946, The Salvation Army was in an uncomfortable position: it was the last large charitable organization that continued to refuse to admit that FLSA covered its activities, the only agency represented on the Sheltered Workshop Advisory Committee that had not applied for the supposedly required certificates. And as almost nothing in life is an unmixed blessing, the fact that the Army was enjoying record income from its waste materials and stores sales did not strengthen its position with the Department of Labor. The government's contention was not, on the face of it, unreasonable: there were even a few officers who believed from the start that FLSA applied to The Salvation Army. The Act was intended to cover "employees"—persons who were "suffered or permitted to work"—and commercial enterprises—those "engaged in commerce or the production of goods for commerce." Although there was no express exemption for religious or charitable organizations under FLSA, federal law did provide for the issuance of sheltered workshop certificates for the employment by non-profit organizations of disabled or handicapped workers at a lower rate of pay than the minimum.

So long as other major organizations claimed exemption from this law on a variety of grounds, the Army's own position, which was in the process of development during these years, was relatively secure. But by the end of the war, the Army stood alone among large organizations in claiming exemption, so that the grounds upon which the claim rested had to be clarified and strengthened. The Salvation Army's contention that its men's social service centers were not covered by FLSA was by 1946 based on two assumptions: the first was that the Army was not a commercial enterprise, for profit or otherwise; it was a religious institution whose sole purpose was the rehabilitation of men, the operation of which only "secondarily and incidentally" had a "commercial aspect;" the second was that the man being cared for in the center was not an employee: he was a beneficiary, being assisted in his rehabilitation, which had as its goal his restoration to a useful place in society and, as often as possible, his acceptance of salvation in Christ. His handicap was not permanent; most of the men in the Army's centers were alcoholics, or had other emotional or spiritual problems, but the center program was designed to assist the willing man to overcome these deficiencies. It was true the man was "suffered or permitted to work," but that did not in itself make him an employee, any more than children who did housework for their parents were necessarily employees. The beneficiary had not contracted to "perform services for compensation:" compensation in any real sense would, in fact, defeat the purpose of the program, by enabling a new man to return to his former drunken ways before he could receive permanent help for his problem. Officers on every level were glad to note that the Army's sincere commitment to the new Service-to-Man program greatly strengthened the force of its official contentions regarding the nature and purpose of its men's social service program.

In January 1946, officials from the Wages and Hours Division visited the Minneapolis Social Service Center to investigate its "sheltered workshop" status. The district officer, Major W. B. Jobe, was appalled: he informed headquarters that he had given his life to evangelism and all this "dickering" with the government distressed him; if the Army looked like a commercial enterprise to "government representatives and others," that fact should "arouse" officers to "take personal inventory and 'set our house in order.'" Jobe was one of several officers in the Central Territory who were working to introduce aspects of a Service-to-Man program into the department. Territorial headquarters, uncomfortably aware of the Army's new status as the last holdout, urged a cautious approach, suggesting that officers be flexible on unimportant points. Regional directors' meetings in the East were spent in discussions on the applicability of the Fair Labor Standards Act to the Army, and none too soon: in May the Department of Labor conducted labor surveys in the Philadelphia Center and in all the centers in the New England Region, and issued sheltered workshop certificates to those institutions. The Salvation Army refused to accept these certificates. Colonel Dowdell alerted his fellow secretaries in the other territories. National Headquarters issued an official warning to the commissioners in June: the Department of Labor was "certificating" Army centers in the face of the Army's continued contention that it was exempt. In December, the Commissioners' Conference agreed to accept certification on an "approved basis," but this was only intended as a kind of courtesy, since the conference reaffirmed that the Army did not come within the scope of FLSA. The men's social service secretaries were ordered to meet together at once to prepare a plan of "uniformity of action" for accepting certificates on the new basis.

The spirit of voluntary cooperation carried well into the next year; in May 1947, the commissioners congratulated themselves that "no serious difficulty had developed to date." They noted that there was "some difference of opinion as to the ultimate remedy," but all agreed that a "friendly, cooperative spirit" should be continued. The sense of impending threat receded still further: Brigadier Decker devoted part of the men's social officers' councils in New Orleans to the Fair Labor Standards Act, but a few days later he allowed himself to be quoted in *The War Cry*, by way of explaining to the public what the men's social service center did, that the men in them were "paid for the work they do." In February 1948, the Commissioners' Conference seemed willing to accept that "total exemption" from the Act was only a "rather remote" possibility; the Army could function well enough if there were some "modification" of the government's position on the relationship of a charitable organization to its beneficiaries. At their next meeting in June, the commissioners postponed further discussion of the now-routine sheltered workshop question.

In fact, 1948 saw the culmination of something which seemed at the time to be of much greater immediate importance to the department: the first handbook for national use in 25 years. Late in the war the commissioners had ordered the distribution of copies of the *1944 Institutes* as an intermediate step in the direction of introducing Service-to-Man programs in every territory. They also arranged for committees, made up of social officers, to be formed in every territory under the chairmanship of the departmental secretary, to submit suggestions for a new national handbook, then to review the collected results, which would be put into final form by the research and publicity staff of National Headquarters. Produced by those in every territory who were most sympathetic to the ideals of Service to Man, and written against the background of the long-standing, if recently more leisurely, discussion of the Fair Labor Standards Act, the new handbook proved to be of enormous value in officially introducing the new program into every center—and in providing the Army with an effective defense when its contention of exemption from the labor law was suddenly challenged again.

The Salvation Army Social Service for Men: Standards and Practices drew heavily in its formulation of basic principles upon *In Darkest En-*

gland (1890) and *Orders and Regulations for Social Officers (Men)* (1915), demonstrating the extent to which the reformers thought of themselves as using new methods to achieve the Army's historic first purposes: "The alleviation of the condition of the poor and outcast, and their permanent deliverance" through salvation. "The primary function of the men's social service center" was described as "the rehabilitation of men mentally, morally, physically, socially and spiritually." The "primary means" to accomplish this goal was an industrial work-program, which would have social value to the man and economic value to the institution; the work program, then, had a "dual nature" that would have to be balanced, but the rehabilitative aspect of it was clearly the more important. Everything was subordinated to the "primary function" of rehabilitation. Any aspect of institutional operation, however venerable in Salvation Army practice— such as renting bed space in a "shelter" section, or operating an employment service—that had no permanently beneficial effect on the client should be dropped from the center program. Since permanent rehabilitation implied the capacity for improvement in the man's condition, men should be taken into the center on the basis of "treatability," who admitted their need for help, and who were "reasonably" able and willing to work.

The bulk of the new handbook, which officers came to refer to as the "gray book" (because of its gray paper covers) during its few years in official use, was devoted to the particular means to the "paramount" end of rehabilitation: intake, proper social work procedure (the use of fully qualified professionals was still only a distant hope), interviewing, psychological testing, physical rehabilitation, counseling, and the use of community resources—especially Alcoholics Anonymous. A range of spiritual activities was suggested, but none was required except the Sunday morning chapel service. The industrial program should give the man a sense of usefulness and self-respect, training—or retraining—him in good work habits, giving him valuable industrial skills like upholstering, shoe repairing, furniture refinishing, etc. The officer must be ever vigilant so that once a man had progressed sufficiently in the restorative process, he should be discharged from the institution or made into a regular employee who received pay for what he produced. The new manual still provided for seven grades of wastepaper, five of junk metal, and three of rags. The function of sales in the great scheme was carefully and frankly explained: on the one hand, sales were used to generate maximum income for the center (baled paper and rags, and the occasional sale in a store of a valuable antique or unusual piece of bric-a-brac) and on the other hand, sales provided a service to those who had "limited resources" and could not afford to purchase the new articles they needed for a respectable life, such as clothing, ordinary furniture and household goods.[26]

Many officers in every territory felt a sense of accomplishment when the gray book was distributed: admittedly it was tentative in some of its phraseology—even in its mimeographed format—but it was an official, nationwide confirmation that the new program had been accepted as Salvation Army policy. That year saw other proof that men's social officers believed in the new program: in Cleveland, Major Hofman's Cedar Group began to hold evangelistic services on their own on Tuesday nights in the Cleveland Citadel Corps, hoping to appeal to other alcoholics; the divisional commander, Brigadier Edward Carey, and Hofman, jointly expanded these meetings into a full-fledged "Bowery Corps"—a Harbor Light Corps—which opened in 1949. These developments came at the right time: no sooner had the new emphasis on rehabilitation been visibly confirmed than Congress amended the Fair Labor Standards Act to increase the minimum wage from 40 to 75 cents per hour. Moreover, the Wages and Hours Division showed every sign that its period of "friendly cooperation" with The Salvation Army regarding enforcement of the Fair Labor Standards Act was about to end.

Mr. Robert Lee and Mr. William J. Moss who joined the case in 1949 represented the Army's general counsel. They were aware that the applicability of FLSA to the Army's operations, while the pivotal issue, was not the only one: if the Fair Labor Standards Act could be made to apply, it would only be because the Army's twin contentions—that it was not a commercial enterprise and its clients were not employees—had been overturned. If that were so, then a legion of other laws and regulations could be interpreted as applying to the Army as well: Social Security taxes, workmen's compensation laws, the imposition of collecting federal income tax and state disability benefit payments, a possible liability for such taxes not withheld in the past, a possible weakening of the Army's exemption from local property taxes (and later, the Unrelated Business Tax, passed in 1950). The Army's counsel repeatedly pointed out that the financial burden alone of paying the clients in the centers even the reduced minimum wage allowed to certified sheltered workshops would bring financial ruin to the Men's Social Service Department, without adding the costs of the other potentially applicable laws. In the face of these chilling revelations, The Salvation Army decided upon a resolute new course of action: the Army would demonstrate its continuing willingness, even eagerness, to cooperate with the government in all ways short of actual compliance—resignation from the sheltered workshop advisory committee, for instance, was rejected as needlessly provocative—while at the same time finding means to strengthen its contentions that the centers were not commercial enterprises and their clients not employees. The attorneys were authorized to make a careful analysis of the operation of an Army center; headquarters selected Major Baggs' model institution at Philadelphia for this purpose. The lawyers studied every aspect of the Philadelphia program through December. On January 18, 1950, after consultations with social officers on every level, Cadwalader, Wickersham and Taft submitted to the national commander a detailed, 17-page set of proposals which "affected the form but not the substance of the operation of the center." These included changes in accounting procedures and suggested that each beneficiary be assigned a "primary handicap" which the center program was designed to relieve, that men be allowed to remain as beneficiaries no longer than one year, and that centers take steps to avoid becoming permanent homes for the elderly. These proposals were discussed and refined by headquarters over the next few weeks and prepared for official implementation.

A critical meeting took place on March 14–16, 1950, at National Headquarters. The Commissioners' Conference, chaired by the national commander, the four territorial financial secretaries, the four men's social service secretaries (Decker, Smith, Lt.-Colonel John C. Marshall from Chicago and Lt.-Colonel Sydney Cooke from the West), met together with Lee and Moss. The attorneys contended that the changes recommended in their January proposal would support the argument that the beneficiaries of Salvation Army men's social service centers were not covered by the Fair Labor Standards Act. The commissioners reaffirmed the Army's position: the Army was prepared to accept any compromise other than application for certificates or admission that FLSA covered the Army. If the administrator insisted upon his position, The Salvation Army was prepared to ask him to join its lawyers to test his contention in the courts. Meanwhile the Army would remain on the sheltered workshop committee and would implement the proposed changes in center operation.

On June 20, 1950, the administrator of the Wages and Hours Division informed the Army's counsel in writing that the beneficiaries of The Salvation Army were employees within the meaning of the law, because their labor produced income for the organization. Therefore, the Army

No. 33- Commander Frederick Booth-Tucker.
[Courtesy of SAA.]

No. 35-   Colonel Richard E. Holz, Sr.
          [Courtesy of SAA.]

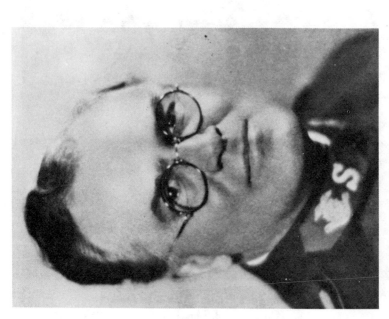

No. 34-   Lt.-Colonel William Wallace Winchell.
          [Courtesy of SAA.]

No. 36- Newark Men's Social Service Center,
65 Pennington St., on the corner of New Jersey Railroad Ave., in 1929.
[Courtesy of SAA.]

**No. 37- The famous New York No. 1 Industrial Home
at 533-537 W. 48th St.
[Courtesy of SAA.]**

No. 38- Newark Industrial Home,
65 Pennington St., on the corner of New Jersey Railroad Ave.
[Courtesy of SAA.]

No. 39- An illustration which appeared in *The Conqueror* (February 1892, p.73) of the New York Lighthouse, the first men's shelter in the United States, which opened December 1891.
[Courtesy of SAA.]

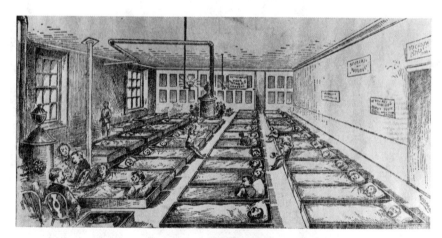

No. 40- The shelter bunks, costing seven cents per night, at the New York Lighthouse. This illustration is a woodcut and appeared in *The War Cry* (February 6, 1892).
[Courtesy of SAA.]

No. 41- A center resident repairs old furniture at the Newark Industrial Home in 1905.
[Courtesy of SAA, 82-26.]

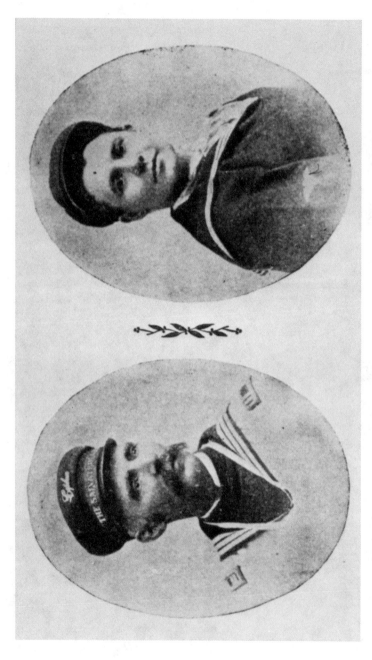

No. 42- Staff-Captain Joseph McFee while he was in command of the San Francisco Lifeboat. This appeared in *The Conqueror* (October 1893, p.375).
[Courtesy of SAA.]

was covered by the Fair Labor Standards Act. He refused, however, to submit the question to the courts. Government agents did investigate a number of centers for "violations" of FLSA, and on October 19, 1950, Commissioner Pugmire was removed from the sheltered workshop advisory committee. The Army moved quickly and efficiently to establish the new operational guidelines in all four territories. National Headquarters requested confirmation by November from all four territories that such guidelines were in place and being followed. In February and April 1951, further modifications in procedure were announced; the most important of these, involving the accounting procedures used to record donations of materials to the Army, went into effect on October 1, 1951. Every part of the new system was completely in place and working smoothly nationwide at the end of 1952. Despite the delays and grumbling from many managers (who were forced to adopt, among other things, an entirely new system of accounting) the changes accomplished their purpose: the Army's contention that it was not a commercial enterprise and its clients not employees could now be factually demonstrated. The prospect that the government would find facts suitable for an effective attack on the Army's position in court had been reduced, if not to invisibility, at least to a place of comfortable remoteness.

The new system, accepted by the Commissioners' Conference in January and March 1950, and supplemented again in February and April 1951, required a complete change, not so much in the operation of the program of a center as in the way in which that program was recorded. It was, in fact, a new system of bookkeeping, dovetailing perfectly with the new Service-to-Man program. The second of the Army's two major contentions—that its clients were not employees—was the easier to demonstrate. Two distinctions were established: the employee was "a person hired for a specific task at a predetermined rate of pay, usually in a key or staff position." He received wages; in fact, he received at least the minimum wage, and was paid overtime for anything over 40 hours, exactly as the law required for employees. The client—the old name "inmate" was officially expunged, although it had not been in common use for many years—was a person making voluntary application for aid, and for whom the institution was designed, "this upon his full acceptance of all rules pertaining thereto." He was "paid" nothing, because he was not admitted into the center for any good he could do for the center but because he needed the good the center could do for him. He was given food and lodging and a small "gratuity" for treats and his few personal expenses, and while this

small sum might be increased in response to the man's progress in rehabilitation, it was in no way related to increased production: it was a gift. The
old system of paying truck helpers—clients—a commission on production
was ended. The accounting procedure of listing "wages and gratuities"
together in a single column was abandoned, as was the compulsory deduction for the venerable funeral fund, since an enforced deduction from a
gratuity was inconsistent with its nature as an unearned gift. Applicants
were required to sign a "Beneficiary's Admission Statement" that demonstrated that he understood and accepted this relationship in principle. To
further protect the distinction between employee and client, the Army
determined that certain jobs within the center required more dependabil-
ity, skill or experience than a man requiring rehabilitation could be expected to possess and still be accepted by an objective observer as a
legitimate beneficiary. Such positions must be reserved for employees,
who received wages. The most important of these, besides key staff
positions like intake supervisor, bookkeeper or dock foreman, was truck
driver. In addition, the amount of the highest gratuity should not approach
the amount of the lowest wage. The Army's position, which the widespead
adoption of the Service-to-Man program greatly strengthened, was that
the Army and the client shared the same objective: physical, social and
spiritual rehabilitation of the client. Laws like the Fair Labor Standards
Act which were designed to protect employees from exploitation by employers whose interests were different from, and often in conflict with,
those of the employees did not apply to The Salvation Army.

To demonstrate the first of the Army's vital contentions, that it was not a
commercial enterprise, was more difficult. A high ratio of clients to employees—general counsel suggested the ratio of two-to-one as a minimum—would lessen the appearance of the center as a commercial
enterprise. Headquarters instructed officers, both staff and managers, to
minimize the success of commercial operations, and instead to emphasize
their pride and delight in progress in the rehabilitation of the men. But,
ironically, the difficulty of the surpluses remained. An unsympathetic
observer—which as general counsel never tired of reminding the Army
was the kind it would have to satisfy—might look upon the surplus of
income over expense generated by the department as a whole, and suggest
that this income was produced in large part by the labor of the men in the
center, whom the Army ought to be willing to compensate at least at the
lowest rate the law allowed. To refute this charge the Army adopted an
entirely new accounting procedure to record and deduct from income the

value of "donations in the hands of the donor," better known as "dona-tions-in-kind" and universally abbreviated by officers and bookkeepers to "D.I.K."

The Salvation Army argued that anyone who believed that the centers produced a large financial surplus due entirely to the labor of the men in them took what Mr. Moss called a "rather superficial" view of the Army's operation. To assume that a center's income from sales depended entirely on the labor of the men working in the center ignored two salient facts: first, The Salvation Army contributed something towards the final sales value of the goods by its investment in trucks, operating costs, repair materials and everything else supported by the center; and second, the materials donated to Salvation Army centers had value even before any-thing was done to prepare them for resale. The men in the center, however valuable their labor might seem to the administrator of the Fair Labor Standards Act, were not capable of the miraculous: they could not make something out of nothing. These goods, moreover, were given by the public to support the charitable activities of The Salvation Army; they were not donated to the men in the center as individuals; they were probably not even donated to the particular branch of The Salvation Army known as the Men's Social Service Department—the public knew little of the division of responsibility within the Army, and would have cared little had such a distinction been explained to them. The value of these dona-tions-in-kind represented a contribution to The Salvation Army no dif-ferent from a donation in cash. To accurately report the income realized from the operation of the center, the original value of the donated material should be subtracted from total receipts before the final figures were entered. Colonel Llewellyn W. Cowan, Eastern Territorial Financial Secre-tary, and his staff, were largely responsible for adapting the new proposals to center operations, and deserve considerable credit for the success of the new program. As Cowan explained in April 1951, the value of dona-tions should not be set against the operating expense of the center—at least not "in the sense of the ordinary business statement of operation." The contribution of the clients to the income of the center was thus seen in a new, much dimmer light. In fact, they made no contribution to the Army at all. The Salvation Army provided much more to the men than it received from their labor. Colonel Cowan even explained that the Army could enjoy much larger surpluses—"real" surpluses—if it had no beneficiaries at all, but simply passed the materials from donors to buyers. Sales might de-cline, but expenses would decline much more. Clearly the Army did not need the beneficiary's labor; rather, he needed to work, to regain his sense of self-respect and learn steady habits and a useful skill. These contentions were clear, once the Army's contributions to the center operation—i.e., center operating expense and the original value of donations-in-kind—were subtracted from sales income generated by the center.

Some means would have to be found to establish the value of the donated materials. It would be impossible to appraise each item as it arrived on the unloading dock, so the Army arranged for an established and respected firm of professional appraisers to evaluate a large sample of donated goods received at centers of various sizes in all four territories over a period of time, and to prepare from this a general appraisal in terms of a percentage of the final selling price of the goods in a Salvation Army store. The American Appraisal Company was engaged for this purpose. The initial appraisal suggested that the value of goods donated was at least one-third of the final store sales price of those goods; for convenience, the Commissioners' Conference decided upon a nationally uniform amount of 30 percent. Therefore, when the new accounting system went into effect in all territories in the fiscal year 1951–1952 (which began on October 1, 1951) 30 percent of center income would be deducted and remitted to the territorial department fund, where it would be used to cover the "true operating deficit"—i.e., to purchase new centers (a kind of building re-newal fund), to support the officers' retirement fund, to pay a share of the cost of operating the entire territorial headquarters, and to provide the fund with "interest" on the moneys so far invested in men's social service properties. This new remittance would of course replace the three former remittances—the ten percent "supervision," the intra-Army "rentals," and the surplus—and would involve no actual increase in cash flow to-wards headquarters—facts that officers were advised to share with local supporters of the Army's work, who might resist the idea that so much "money" was being funneled away from their communities to support programs in other places.

The new accounting procedure would eliminate the problem of large surpluses, which the Army's lawyers regarded as a nearly fatal weakness in the defense of the Army's contention that it was noncommercial. The typical center would now operate with a deficit, so that the new means of determining whether or not a center was a financial success would not be a large surplus but a small deficit. This idea took a little getting used to for officers who had thought in terms of a simple balance sheet. The new statistical forms were confusing; officers began to look fondly on the large red cash book, the voucher book and the check book (with cancelled checks simply pasted back in), which were now to disappear forever. These bookkeeping novelties were coming with unpleasant frequency: first, a comparative statistical and financial annual report form was introduced in 1948, and now, in 1951, an entirely new way not simply of reporting income, but even in thinking about it. To compound the inconvenience, in the Southern Territory centers ran out of the old forms before the new ones arrived. Several years later Lt.-Colonel Frank Guldenschuh, secretary of the department, recalled nostalgically "the good old days when we were either in the red or green." Nevertheless, by the end of 1952, all four territories reported that the new system was functioning. The valuation for donations-in-kind, however, varied with each territory. Only the Western Department actually used 33 percent, and in no territory was the percentage actually remitted to headquarters nearly as large as the one originally specified. During the second year of operation, 1952–1953, the value of donations-in-kind and the percentage actually remitted to the central fund varied widely from territory to territory: Eastern, 25 percent value and 14 percent remitted; Central, 28 percent and 21 percent; Southern, 31 percent and 19 percent, and Western, 33 percent and 18 percent. This was to be expected, as the actual sums sent to headquarters were not increased by the new accounting system, and had never been as large as 30 percent of income. The donations-in-kind system was designed to demonstrate that beneficiaries received more from the operation of a center than they contributed towards it; the actual percentage that departmental headquarters expected from centers was much less.[27]

Still, the constant fact of a margin between the ideal and actual in these figures suggests that none of The Salvation Army's new procedures was launched into a vacuum. The boom in salvage prices continued into the 1950s with prices for paper and rags fluctuating wildly upward in 1951— paper in the Eastern market went from $13.30 to $30.30 per ton, and rags from $94.47 to $148.89 within the year, settling again in 1953 at $14.57 for paper and $106.41 for rags. Federal price controls forced a rollback in 1951 and market conditions did the rest. Many centers lacked adequate store outlets and were almost wholly dependent on a high paper market, over which their managers had no control, to operate their programs. Inflation and the higher minimum wage for regular employees affected departmental budgets by raising expenses. The Korean War caused a decline in occupancy in the Army's centers, but more troublesome than that was the high turnover rate, as men were again drawn into defense industries. This time, however, the Army's official commitment to rehabilitation made it impossible to offer men who were classed as clients anything more than a small gratuity since commissions for truck helpers or any sort of incentive for clients that smacked of commercialism were forbidden in the new system. Priority rationing for some materials was imposed. "If it wasn't one thing, it was another," Sr.-Major Herbert Sparks declared to his colleagues at the Eastern Social Officers' Councils in April 1951: few managers present had ever known "normal times" in their active lifetime. It was "Boom and Bust, Depression, Recession, World War II, Reconstruction, Cold War, Hot War and Inflation." It was "about time," as far as Sparks was concerned, to give up on "normal times" and "make the best of the situation as we find it from day to day." Fortunately the impositions of the Korean War on The Salvation Army program were briefer than in World War II, and in many ways less onerous: the Army's attorney even advised officers to avoid using the priority rating [classed as DO-97] to which they were entitled because there were inconvenient quantity quotas attached to it, and most things the centers needed were available without priority ratings anyway.[28]

"The re-emphasis of the Service-to-Man program, beginning with the 1944 institutes, has now become the basic philosophy of our service," declared Lt.-Colonel Smith in 1951. Officers were increasingly interpreting the new program of rehabilitation as a revival of the compassion for men, body and soul, that drove the Founder and the pioneers of the Movement, but whether a new idea or an old one, Service to Man moved across the country. Lieutenant George Duplain, in Seattle since 1949, was joined in the West by Captain Warren C. Johnson, who was transferred to the territory in 1952; Duplain went as manager to the San Francisco Center in 1955, and Johnson to Los Angeles in 1956. Both centers became models for the new program. Both officers emphasized the use of a professional counseling staff, which their exceptional skill in increasing production made financially practical. Young Lieutenant David Allen first carried Service to Man ideas to Honolulu in 1957, where he was sent to revive men's social services. Captain Lairon White brought a "new day" to the run-down center in Tulsa when he became manager in 1952. In every territory energetic younger men were joining seasoned managers in reaffirming in principle and demonstrating to the men by daily action that, as Lt.-Colonel Arne Lekson told them when he retired from Washington in 1953, they were brothers.[29]

The decade of the 1950s saw recognition and honor come to many experienced and respected managers. Field officers in leadership positions might continue to resist the transfer of young officers of ability into the Men's Social Service Department, but their motive was no more than a natural desire to retain promising people for their own branch: no longer could anyone seriously regard men's social services as inferior or subordinate to the field. Other social-work and professional agencies began to make referrals to the Army centers, and the most prestigious national commissions on alcoholism included Salvation Army representatives. The development of new production techniques, the widespread introduction of power baling machinery and forklifts, and the opening of new markets meant not only that centers could afford more complete and effective rehabilitation programs—especially, the ability to employ more professional staff and to greatly improve residential facilities in every territory— but also that the Men's Social Service Department was able to provide more and more financial support for the whole range of territorial headquarters programs. None of this was lost on Salvation Army leadership. Experienced managers became men's social service secretaries in two territories: Brigadier Harry B. Stillwell in San Francisco, followed in 1958 by Brigadier Peter Hofman, veteran manager of the showplace Cleveland Center; and Lt.-Colonel Earl Crawford in Chicago in 1955. So long as a semblance of the old "district officer" system survived, a few managers who held that title could attain the rank of Lt.-Colonel: Lt.-Colonel W. W. Winchell, for instance (1927); and Lt.-Colonel Arne Lekson, Washington, D.C. (1950); and Fred Reinking, Detroit (1950). General secretaries were routinely promoted to that rank in the East (Alfred Jackson, John Phillips), and the men's social service secretary could be made a full colonel in the East (Colonel Harold Smith), and in the Central (Colonel John Marshall)—both promoted in 1952. The newly invigorated department was honored with a distinctive symbol all of its own: the Salvation Army red shield, which had been displayed in connection with the men's social work since World War I, became, in 1951, the official nationwide symbol of the department, by official decree of the Commissioners' Conference.[30]

For the men in the centers, recognition came in more practical form. Canteens, where the men could congregate for a cup of coffee and buy a few small personal items, first used in Philadelphia in 1941, became popular. Television was not mentioned in *Standards and Practices* in 1948, but by 1951 it had become "the best attended daily entertainment," eclipsing forever the movie projector and the rented film. One manager reported that television had such a drastic effect in keeping men in his center that he suddenly found it hard to recall how the department had survived without it. (Television was, of course, useful for publicity as well: in 1954 Sr.-Major and Mrs. Ronald E. Irwin arranged for their annual Thanksgiving dinner for the men in Scranton to be televised—an historic first!) Few centers still had brass bands, but choirs, quartets and "amateur nights" flourished. In Worcester, Sr.-Major Charles Schuerholz, a skilled stage magician, put on one-man shows for the men and built up a loyal following of fans in several centers.[31]

The rehabilitation of old buildings for use as centers was still more common than building new ones: men's social captured the old municipal streetcar barn in Indianapolis in 1954 and, still more satisfying, a former winery in Scranton in 1956. This procedure was always more economical in the short term, and occasionally facilities newly built as men's social service centers were less satisfying than those obtained by renovating existing buildings. It was especially difficult to design adequate small centers, in which rooms had to serve a double or triple purpose. In 1953 Colonel Decker pronounced the new little New Orleans Center to be "ridiculous": the clients could reach their sleeping quarters only by going through the thrift store or the dining room, or by climbing the fire escape, and the space for parking and unloading trucks was so small that the officer could not run enough trucks to break even. The new center in Houston, opened in 1954, was much more suitable. The decade saw 12 new locations in the East, five in the West and nine in the Central.[32]

The new center in Kansas City was especially promising. Officially dedicated in March 1952, at 1310 E. 10th Street, the new center occupied the spacious facilities of the former Unity Christian School. There was an elegant chapel—the dignity of which the Army solemnly promised to uphold—kitchens, dormitory facilities, classrooms and large spaces perfectly suited to production activities. It had more. In November 1952, the manager, Major Byam G. Youngman, opened the first medical clinic for the treatment of alcoholics in any Salvation Army facility in the country. There was a small six-bed infirmary under a licensed staff physician, Dr. Robert Hodgson, where severe cases spent four days in clinical treatment for the effects of alcoholism and four days in "recovery" before they were admitted to the center's regular six-month program of rehabilitation. Youngman was also one of several pioneers in the Central Territory who used non-medical therapeutic techniques for the treatment of alcoholism; he helpfully explained to a reporter that the Army's program was "virtually the same as that of Alcoholics Anonymous except for the terminology."[33]

The new manual, *Standards and Practices,* had predicted in 1948 that
The Salvation Army's Men's Social Service Center would become a "laboratory of social research in the field of the unattached man," a group
which had so far been "very much neglected" in the field of social,
sociological, psychological or clinical inquiry. From October 1952,
through August 1953, Mr. John B. Brantner, clinical director of the Minneapolis Center, conducted a pioneering study of men in the center to
determine the incidence among them of tuberculosis. The rate of active
cases was 55.5 times as great as the general rate for Minneapolis in the
same year, leading the center staff to the conclusion that homeless transients were "quite probably a primary source of reinfection for tuberculosis in the United States." Again, in 1958, Brantner supervised a
survey of the clients in Minneapolis, this time to categorize their social
attitudes—which turned out to be, not surprisingly, none too good: in
terms of the high degree of social maladjustment among the center clients,
they did not differ to any statistically significant degree from men in the
same age groups who were prisoners in the state penitentiary.[34]

The Salvation Army officers in charge of the Minneapolis Center during
these surveys—Cecil Briggs for the first one, John Troutt for the second—
were already aware that most of the men who applied to the center were
badly worn down and susceptible to disease, and that many of them were
bitter, self-pitying and deceitful. These were, of course, the reasons that
The Salvation Army was operating the Men's Social Service Department.
Healthy, well-adjusted men with regular employment—even alcoholics
who still had jobs and who could count on the love and support of family
and friends—did not require the services of The Salvation Army, and did
not apply. Many who came did so without deliberate choice, in the sense
that they were referred or sent to The Salvation Army, which they accepted only because it was preferable to them to their next best alternative. Referrals from other social-welfare agencies, paroled prisoners and
"provisional discharges" from state mental institutions made up an increasing, but still relatively small, percentage of the Army's clients. Those
who came voluntarily, however, were almost always in the same situation:
The Salvation Army was the only alternative to something worse, like
freezing or starving, or dying of neglect, hidden in an alley or a culvert,
drunken and forgotten. Many of these men were frankly surprised to
discover that the Army had a plan for their rehabilitation.

The minimal program was prescribed in *Standard Procedures for Rehabilitation Program in All Centers,* issued in 1952. The first step was the
admissions process, which included the all-important intake interview,

which should be of "primary concern," conducted by the officer or the
"personnel worker." The "most important" part of the interview was
explaining the program to the new man, who might have "a hazy understanding" of the services available at the center. The man should be
screened to determine his "ability and willingness to profit by the center's
program." The man would then sign an "admission statement" and be
sent off for whatever he needed most: a shower, clean clothes, food. Then
personal data would be filed on a master card-folder. In the South, this was
done on a $5'' \times 8''$ card, which was sent to the Central Registration Bureau
in Atlanta, to be kept in a central filing system; no other territory employed a centralized system in the 1950s. The man would be assigned to a
bed, a time to be examined by a physician during his first week, and given
a work assignment. Almost invariably the first assignment was the least
demanding in terms of effort, skill or attentiveness, and also the least
desirable: the baling room. Store sales increased steadily in importance
throughout the decade in every territory, and waste materials correspond-
ingly became less important; as a result, more and more new men were
assigned as truck helpers and unloaders. Men could progress to more
interesting work that required skills that they already possessed or could
be taught.

In a few days the client was interviewed, asked about his progress, any
misunderstandings were discussed, and the man was guided to recognize
the nature of his problem and assisted in working out "his own plan for his
rehabilitation." Other interviews were held as needed. A careful record of
these interviews, of clothing requisitions, changes in work assignments,
weekend passes, and infractions of rules, etc., was added to the official
"chronological record" that was kept for each man. Evangelistic services
and spiritual counseling were a major part of the official program. In a few
centers professional counseling, group discussions and an Alcoholics
Anonymous group were available—in Cleveland, Brigadier Peter Hofman
conducted "sobriety award" ceremonies—and in every center a determined effort was made to provide adequate recreation and leisure-time
activities. The most popular of these in the 1950s was television, followed
by quiet table games (checkers), pool and billiards, and reading. In most
centers the manager's wife made some effort to lend a "homey" touch to
the dining hall, and to arrange birthday and holiday parties for the men.
Mrs. Sr.-Major Richard E. Baggs even organized an entire "women's
auxiliary" in Philadelphia in February 1951. Made up of local volunteers,
the auxiliary put on monthly entertainments and arranged an annual

picnic for the men. Despite some interest in official Army circles, however, this idea did not spread. In the Southern Territory, a continuing shortage of officer personnel in the department required most officers' wives to accept "almost full-time activity" in the centers. During his stay in the center, the client would be helped to the extent of the abilities of the center personnel and the facilities at their disposal. At the end of that period, he would be "graduated" to employee status (most likely as a truck driver, office worker or store helper) or separated from the center.[35]

Rehabilitation programs, beyond the minimum optimistically prescribed for every center, varied according to personnel and facility, but every program had in common the need for money. "Regardless of its altruistic character," observed the 1948 handbook, "no enterprise can be conducted long without involving the expenditure of money." To support and expand the new Service-to-Man program after 1950 required the development of retail store sales. The market for rags, while unstable, was still profitable, but materials, sorted out and sold as used clothing, even for a few cents per article, were much more profitable. The bulk paper market, however, not only fluctuated, it fluctuated in a discouragingly downward direction. Traditionally the only means available to an officer who wished to stay afloat, though faced with falling prices, was to increase tonnage, but this could not be done to any great extent with available equipment and personnel; once prices fell below a certain point, the cost of collecting and processing wastepaper was greater than the return, and increasing tonnage only compounded and hastened the ruin of a center's finances. Once the salvage boom of the postwar years, golden but brief, had passed, The Salvation Army could no longer rely on paper sales as even a reliable secondary source of financing its center programs. There were exceptional areas—National Gypsum opened a wallboard plant in Pryor, Oklahoma, and stimulated the wastepaper market in Oklahoma and Arkansas in the early 1950s—but in every territory, although there was no official policy to discontinue paper collection in any territory before 1958—knowledgeable officers at headquarters and in many centers discouraged the collection of paper and magazines, except as a courtesy when people donated other things at the same time, or left a bundle of papers at a center. One difficulty that Major Eugene Gesner encountered in Baltimore and Dallas in the 1950s was having to explain to the public that there was no longer a market for paper and cardboard, so that any that was donated to the Army had to be carried to the dump. The East and Central continued to collect paper on a reduced scale, but paper collections were ended in the West in 1958 when Brigadier Peter Hofman, a strong advocate of store sales, became secretary.[36]

Store sales offered multiple advantages: they supplied a market that was not subject to wild and unpredictable fluctuations, and one which, with energy and ingenuity, could be greatly expanded. Captain Ray Howell suggested in 1959 that drivers should be encouraged to collect high-value materials, not simply to work for high tonnage, noting that as a rule more valuable items came in from telephone calls than from scheduled routes. Headquarters in New York and Chicago did not abandon waste materials but agreed that production should be geared to store sales: in the 1950s the open, stake-body style trucks, useful for bulk materials like paper and rags, were replaced in wholesale lots by trucks with closed bodies, preferable for furniture and clothing. (The color, however, continued to vary, even within a single territory: trucks in the East were red, those in the Central changed from black to red in the late 1950s; but the West insisted that special "climatic conditions" there required light-colored trucks, to which the Commissioners' Conference agreed—first sand-colored trucks and then—oddly enough—dark blue; in the South several colors predominated in the 1950s—the old dark green and black and the new red). Production rules became standard procedure. Bundles of donated clothing should be carefully sorted by experienced persons so as to maximize the number of garments available for retail sale. Furniture should be handled carefully on the truck and during unloading. Paint should be applied sparingly; many hardwood pieces required only cleaning, not a coat of light green paint. Books might be more profitably sold instead of piled together as wastepaper bookstock. Officers must be especially careful to detect valuable antiques or unusual items of bric-a-brac, which even without repair had unexpected value. There was, after all, no telling what people would buy, promised Mrs. Frank Guldenschuh in 1951, alluding to the "musical toilet tissue holder" and the bisque doll with no head that had been snapped up in Mount Vernon, New York. In the Central Territory some centers sent storekeepers to take special courses on recognizing and pricing antiques, and centers in the East gave workers time off to attend public lectures on such subjects.

The appearance and layout of Salvation Army stores became matters of serious, official attention in every territory in the 1950s. Although officially designated "social service stores" in 1942, "family service stores" in 1951 and "red shield stores" in 1958, some stores had no proper identification at all in the 1950s. When Major Cecil Briggs went to Chicago Central as manager in 1956, the center ran five stores, but only two had Salvation Army signs; one was called "Famous Novelty," one was "Sam's Tailor" and the last had no markings whatsoever! Old-fashioned high bins and glass cases were replaced by convenient low bins and display tables. Clothes were taken from bins and placed on hangers, wider aisles were opened, proper lighting was installed. For the first time in many stores, window displays were simplified, and changed regularly. When a local reporter joked to Captain George Duplain in 1957 that the Army's new store in Petaluma was "too fancy," Duplain devised a sign that captured a new store-consciousness and became famous: "A Place Where Good Neighbors May Shop With Dignity." While stationed in Dayton, 1957–1959, Sr.-Major Clarence Simmons designed the "Captain Says" posters to stimulate production backstage. The new emphasis on merchandising benefited the Service-to-Man clients in other ways than producing extra income for the program: jobs relating to sorting, categorizing, repairing, and pricing were more pleasant and satisfying, and more useful in preparing to return to outside employment, than baling waste materials. By the end of the decade the Men's Social Service Department in every territory relied on store sales for the largest portion of their support; in every territory the amount of store sales income was greater than that produced by paper, rags, surplus and junk combined.[37]

It is natural to expect that the Salvation Army Men's Social Service Department, enjoying a new prosperity and offering its clients a demonstrably more helpful and redemptive program, would experience a period of warm cooperation with the Army's other branches—in particular, the field, or corps department of the Movement. For the most part this was true in the 1950s. Almost all managers cooperated to some degree with the divisional headquarters and with local corps; many managers were warmhearted supporters of corps programs, participating in them as faithful soldiers and arranging activities at the center so they did not conflict with important meetings on the corps schedule. Some managers encouraged converted men in their centers to enroll as soldiers in the local corps. For their part, divisions and corps often provided concerts and special speakers at nearby centers. Corps bandsmen and soldiers often voluntarily went to considerable lengths to provide transportation between center and corps for men who wished to attend. There were, however, persistent difficulties in the relationship as well. In a few places the regular corps people felt awkward around the men from the nearby center, an uneasiness which the men naturally interpreted as snobbishness or unfriendliness.

Other matters were more serious: the fact that the men's social service center was "self-supporting" (in the sense that it did not solicit cash donations from the public; donations-in-kind accounting caused most centers to operate with a bookkeeping "deficit") kept the center out of the local Community Chest, a distinction which confused potential donors. Community Chest officials resisted the gradual absorption of corps salvage into the Men's Social Service Department, which progressed through the decade in every territory. The public often donated materials, old clothing and furniture to corps in areas where men's social centers operated; corps officers were supposed to turn these materials over to the men's social, but a few succumbed to the temptation to hold corps rummage sales instead. Headquarters repeatedly issued warnings against this, reminding officers of the time-honored rule, still in effect, that centers accepted goods as donations and corps accepted money.[38]

A certain confusion lingered in three territories on other matters as well. The revived district officers' positions were allowed to lapse in the Central and Southern territories as the men who held these positions retired or were promoted (Harold Gesner in 1949, Arne Lekson in 1953, Earl Crawford, William Jobe and Fred Reinking all in 1955). This left the "regional directors" in the East in an ambiguous position: officers new to the department were uncertain about the authority attached to these positions, and Colonel Smith could not settle upon a distribution of responsibility to these officers that entirely satisfied him. His successor, Lt.-Colonel Ernest A. Marshall, who took over in 1954, made several changes in personnel in the regions, reduced their visits to each center to twice annually, and attempted to breathe new life into the office by defining the regional director's role as "counseling, guiding, advising and inspiring" managers about Service to Man, not to "inspect or boss but to help." The regional directors met on that basis in the years that followed, often making suggestions to headquarters that resulted in more precise and helpful guidelines for the program. The arrangement was not, however, equally satisfactory to everyone. Brigadier Richard Baggs recommended that the regional directors either be upgraded to district officers or abolished: the position at present was no more than a "subterfuge," with no real authority, and no prospects for promotion. A manager with no duties beyond the center would not be considered a department head; the highest rank to which he could aspire would be that of brigadier, which came automatically after 30 years' service, and which, by a quirk in Army terminology, was inferior to that of lt.-colonel, which was reserved for department heads—or, in the all-too-recent, happy past, to district officers. Marshall replied that such a thing was beyond his authority, but he would bring it to the attention of the territorial commander. When Marshall filed this correspondence, however, he added a reminder to himself to discuss with the commissioner whether or not it was advisable to continue the position of regional director.[39]

Three developments converged at mid-point in the decade: the continued uneasiness about the relationship of the Fair Labor Standards Act to The Salvation Army, which became acute in 1955 when the Act was amended again to increase the minimum wage from 75 cents to $1.00 per hour; the increasingly obvious success of Service to Man both as a means of helping men and as a stimulus to profitable production; and the growing pressure from many managers for a formal manual of operations, to provide guidance and unity for Service-to-Man programs on a national scale. On October 3–5, 1956, the men's social service secretaries met in conference in New York City, chaired by the national chief secretary, Colonel L. W. Cowan, and attended by the national commander, territorial staff officers, two divisional commanders and three center managers—Sr.-Captain Warren Johnson (Los Angeles), Sr.-Captain William Albert Browning (Washington, D.C.) and Sr.-Major William Charron (Pittsburgh). The conference, which dealt with two of these matters, was one of the most important in the history of men's social services in the United States.

The period 1949–1952, in which the administrator of the Wages and Hours Division had been active in pressing the government's claim that the Fair Labor Standards Act applied to The Salvation Army, had passed without serious incident. The test of this contention in court for which the Army's general counsel had pressed did not come. Managers were officially warned, however, to be vigilant in their application of the new Service-to-Man standards. Brigadier J. C. Kelly, general secretary, informed men's social officers in the Central Territory in July 1954, that headquarters regarded it as "most important" that they not be "lulled into a false sense of well-being" on the asssumption that the government had become indifferent to the Army's refusal to submit to the labor act. Officers were not lulled for long. In 1955 the Fair Labor Standards Act was amended again, increasing the minimum wage. More ominous clouds began to gather. The Army's attorneys had conducted reviews of territorial financial statements since the new program and related accounting procedures were introduced in 1951. The statements for 1954–1955 (which were reviewed in early 1956) revealed that the department had prospered materially to an extent which no one had anticipated. This happy news, ironically, exposed the centers to the danger of coverage by the Fair Labor Standards Act, by undermining the Army's contention that these institutions were operated at a deficit for the benefit of the men; 34 of the Army's 112 centers had done so well, in fact, that they still showed surpluses *after* the donations-in-kind deduction was taken.

General counsel suggested to national headquarters in April that action be taken to remedy this situation, which was not only embarrassing but potentially ruinous. The attorneys arranged to obtain current data; a new set of questionnaires was sent to every center. In the meantime, the Army arranged for an updated—and hopefully higher—appraisal of donated materials, in order to raise the donations-in-kind deduction; for different accounting procedures to more accurately reflect center expenses; and more importantly of all, for an increase in expense on the rehabilitation program. Colonel William G. Harris, chief secretary in Chicago, expressed the official concern to Lt.-Colonel Earl Crawford in May: the officers in the Men's Social Service Department had somehow failed to grasp the "very definite need" not only to fully understand the Service-to-Man program but to put it into "realistic operation in the various centers." The territorial financial secretaries met in May to discuss various proposals to improve the accuracy of center accounts, and to widen the distinction between employees and beneficiaries by excluding any of the latter from coverage by workmen's compensation laws. The commissioners decided in July to arrange a full-dress conference in October in New York, at which the Fair Labor Standards Act and its unhappy implications would be the solitary topic of discussion.[40]

The conference dealt in turn with the grounds of The Salvation Army's refusal to accept the applicability of FLSA, the summarized results of the fresh questionnaires (which revealed another, even more alarming increase in the number of centers with surpluses after donations-in-kind), and detailed procedural and accounting changes designed to both demonstrate and strengthen the Army's twin contentions, which had not varied: that its men's social service centers were not commercial enterprises, and that its clients were not employees. William Moss explained that the good reputation of The Salvation Army, the theories upon which it based its social services for men, or even the intentions of its officers, were not at question: the applicability of the law would be determined by the appearance of the center operation to the "disinterested, possibly unsympathetic, outsider." And Moss reminded the officers that if the Fair Labor Standards Act could be made to apply to the Army, then "any law which would treat the beneficiary as an employee . . . or the center as a commercial enterprise with profit as its principal motive" could be made to apply as well. The result, in terms of "unnecessary regulation and burdensome taxation" would be, as the attorneys had contended with grim determination since 1938, the financial ruin of men's social service.

The national chief secretary, Colonel L. W. Cowan, accurately predicted in his welcoming remarks that "nothing really new" would be expounded at the historic conference. The main work of the conference, and its lasting importance in the history of the department, was in confirming the preeminence of Service to Man over commercialism, both in principle and by a series of practical procedures.

"Employee" was carefully defined, and those "covered" by the Act were specifically listed; in general, responsible, skilled jobs related to "production" (collecting and sorting of materials), and office work related to this function, were "covered" categories. Other employees, such as the caseworkers, kitchen staff or store personnel were not covered. Covered employees were to be paid according to FLSA and provided with all the benefits of workmen's compensation laws. Many were graduated beneficiaries who lived in the centers; a sliding scale of room and board charges acceptable to the government as part of the minimum salary scale was proposed.

Beneficiaries were still defined as men who admitted their need for help and who voluntarily entered the center for rehabilitation. Since rehabilitation implied some improvement in the man's condition, only men with handicaps that the Army was able to remove—called "primary" handicaps—should be admitted, rather than men whose handicaps—"secondary" ones such as mental retardation, physical disability, old age—could not be overcome within the program. The most common primary handicap listed for beneficiaries was, as always, alcoholism. Men should not remain, as a general rule, too long in a center as clients, or it became questionable as to how much lasting improvement was being brought to the man: a year's stay was taken as a reasonable maximum.

Beneficiaries were to be distinguished from employees in several ways, but the two most crucial were in compensation and in the ratio between them: employees were to be compensated for labor; beneficiaries were to be aided in their progress in rehabilitation by small sums given as gifts that were entirely unrelated to productivity. The highest gratuity should, as before, be below the lowest wage: overlap would suggest to the ever-present "unsympathetic" observer that beneficiaries were difficult to distinguish from employees. The ratio between them should be large, so the rehabilitative and charitable nature of the operation would be manifest. Two beneficiaries to every one employee was adopted as the general rule—very general: in 1956 only 68 centers out of 111 could muster the two-to-one ratio, and one center—in the West—had no beneficiaries at all. The attorneys further recommended that no beneficiary be assigned the same task as an employee. The East did not assign beneficiaries as truck drivers, but this rule was not closely enforced in the other three territories in 1956; 28 centers used beneficiaries as truck drivers.

To reduce the current unwelcome spate of surpluses, the conference agreed to recommend as national policy a three-part program: first, increase the expenditures on rehabilitation programs by spending more in "direct to clientele expense;" second, increase the donations-in-kind deduction by using the latest appraisal figures from the American Appraisal Company—which, as bad luck would have it, fell in all four territories after the company's new surveys were completed. "The conference then discussed the feasibility of refining the appraisal procedures", but no better system could be devised; and, third, increase the amount and type of expenditure that could be charged directly to center operating accounts, rather than to the departmental fund. One way, for instance, was to reduce to ten years the life expectancy of equipment for replacement purposes, thus requiring a larger annual deduction for renewal. Unfortunately, it was discovered that in the South, Central and West, current operating accounts "seemed to exceed the provisions of the suggested plan."

The conference opened in a spirit of commitment to the Service-to-Man program, not simply as a means of escaping from the obligations of an expensive law, but primarily because the Men's Social Service Department had found, again, its wellspring and its purpose, which was the conversion and rehabilitation of that class of mankind that was most despised, even by itself, and therefore the most helpless: the homeless, transient alcoholic. Every turn in the conference deliberations, every new revelation from survey and questionnaires, led the delegates back again to the starting point: the only effective, reliable and justifiable solution to the dilemma of the surpluses, and the only one consonant with their commitment as Salvation Army officers, was to broaden the program for men. The conference recommended that territorial headquarters "encourage the addition of new services and facilities for the rehabilitation of the beneficiary, particularly at centers which have shown large or recurring surpluses," and further, that the men's social secretaries consult with their departments and prepare for submission to territorial and national headquarters, "a list of the services and facilities considered to be basic to the rehabilitation program and those considered to be desirable, whether now offered by any center or not." This was to lead to an analysis of the proposals by national headquarters, "an exchange of ideas between the territories" and the development of a "priority schedule for the increase in . . . services and facilities" in Salvation Army men's social centers. The Commissioners' Conference, meeting just three weeks later, accepted every recommendation that the men's social conference laid before it.[41]

For years before the historic 1956 conference, officers had recognized the need for a thorough-going handbook of center procedures. Colonel Parker's "special orders" were still remembered fondly by older managers, who had long since ceased to use them for more than nostalgic reflection. Brigadier J. O. Dowdell began in September 1937 to issue a series of department orders that were to be filed together in each center as a "manual." Major A. E. Baldwin prepared a kind of "manual of procedure" for Southern centers in 1942, but it was regarded as no more than a series of "suggestions" and had only limited circulation. When he became secretary in Chicago in 1946, Baldwin issued the first of a series of departmental orders, which he, like Dowdell, intended to become an official manual for each center. The wartime reemphasis on rehabilitation, the new Service-to-Man program and the operational and accounting procedures required by the Fair Labor Standards Act made a new handbook, with national application, an absolute necessity. *Standards and Practices,* the 1948 "gray book," contained few program details and nothing on the new accounting system. Colonel Cowan suggested that because the commissioners had enacted as policy all the recommendations of the 1956 Men's Social Service Conference, the minutes of that conference "could be used as a handbook." Copies of these minutes, bound together in red paper covers with 25 pages of Eastern departmental orders and standard forms, were distributed nationwide. It served as a general guide while a new, more extensive volume was being prepared.[42]

The national commander—the same Commissioner Norman S. Marshall who had so advocated Service to Man while chief secretary in the East—appointed a special committee in 1957 to prepare a new handbook. Brigadier Peter Hofman of Cleveland, Brigadier William Jobe of Kansas City, Major William Browning of Washington, D.C. and Captain George

Duplain of San Francisco each prepared sections, which were brought together at regular meetings of three days each, held three times per year at different centers around the country from November 1957 to April 1960. The format of these meetings followed a general pattern: on the first day the committee reviewed what each member had prepared, the second day the officers toured the host facility to analyze how their proposals would work in practice, and the third day they concentrated on brainstorming and editorial work. These meetings were chaired by Sr.-Major A. E. Agnew, who also had the responsibility of rewriting the material into a common style once the four officers had agreed upon it. The minutes of their deliberations were forwarded to each territorial headquarters, allowing the Commissioners' Conference to supervise the process closely. The members of the committee were all respected and successful managers, whose experiences were widely different, and whose recommendations, especially as to the details of procedure, differed. These men, however, were united in their commitment to rehabilitation as the first purpose of the department, and all were zealously evangelical; their sense of a broad common purpose carried the proceedings along with remarkably few serious hitches—not, however, fast enough to avoid one prod from the Commissioners' Conference, which officially hoped in the fall of 1959 that the new handbook could be "expedited" and ready "at an early date." The final product was presented to the Commissioners' Conference and approved by them in October 1960. The new handbook was supposed to be ready for distribution by the end of March, but was delayed in production until May 1961. The new handbook, in both looseleaf and hardbound editions, was "received with joy" by the men's social service conference. While they were center managers, three of the secretaries had been actively in favor of Service to Man: Hofman, Crawford and Frank Guldenschuh. The secretaries recommended, and the commissioners approved, that every officer should have a copy at once, and be required to submit a detailed review of its contents; that the book should be the sole subject of discussion at the upcoming territorial men's social officers' councils; and that each territorial training college should develop a new social-work course based entirely on the new handbook. Every official effort was to be made to "make the material immediately effective in our general program."[43]

The approval and publication of *The Salvation Army Men's Social Service Handbook of Standards, Principles and Policies,* known at once and ever since as the "green book," was a significant event in the history of men's social services. The handbook was the first officially endorsed national manual of principles and procedures for the department. It embodied in the sections on theory and on detailed program the principle for what the Service-to-Man reformers, and the best of the generations of managers who had preceded them, had so long contended, that the primary function of the center was "the rehabilitation and/or the spiritual regeneration of unattached and homeless men." It was a monument to high principle, but its practical value was attested by the fact that it remained, with few revisions, the standard manual of operations for the department until the mid-1980s.

The handbook was divided into eight sections; room for expansion was provided by non-consecutive numbering, and—in the copies intended for use in the centers—looseleaf construction. The original sections were: *Origins, Goals, Purposes* (the fundamental principles upon which the service was offered); *Officer Personnel* (the role of the manager, his assistant and his wife in both "Service Program" and "Business Administration"); *Employee Personnel* (the function of the employee, the distinction between employees and beneficiaries, with special sections on truck drivers and professional social service workers—the use of which, the authors noted, was a "comparatively new and, in many instances, untried practice"); *Service Program: Philosophy* (definition and description of the "typical" beneficiary, alcoholism, intake policy—that is, the careful admission of men for whom the program was designed, namely homeless unattached adult males with identifiable and treatable handicaps, the use of the gratuity as a "therapeutic tool," and a firm commitment to the fundamental evangelical "goal of all Salvation Army endeavor"—not just rehabilitation but "regeneration" through salvation in Christ); *Service Program: Treatment* (by far the largest and most detailed section, outlining the goals of the program, intake procedures, casework, counseling, the use of fellowship clubs, and Alcoholics Anonymous—which the handbook endorsed as "one of the most useful helps toward a frontal attack" on alcoholism, which was the primary handicap of perhaps 70 percent of the men. The handbook suggested A.A. sobriety anniversaries—such as Hofman had used with great success in Cleveland—innovations such as group therapy and even professional psychotherapy where possible, and included guidelines for leisure activities, medical treatment, and termination. Helpful patterns for casework, A.A. and clinical treatment were included, and "criteria for realistic progress"); *Physical Appointment* (design and outfitting of the facilities); *Principles of Administration and*

Support (housekeeping, discipline and schedules, proper business office procedure, another explanation of the donation-in-kind accounting system, truck deployment and maintenance—the social work enthusiasts even recommended a "case record" for trucks, and the efficient direction of salvage operations); and, last, *Community Relations.*

One of the most useful sections in the handbook was devoted to "criteria of realistic progress," designed to show the "alert men's social service officer or program staff member" when it was appropriate to send the beneficiary out from the center to find employment or "graduate" him to employee status within the center. The length of time required for this beneficial process to unfold would vary, generally, from three to 18 months. Officers were counseled not to rely upon two of the criteria for "graduation" from client to employee upon which Victorian social officers relied almost without exception: a religious profession by the man, or a need for the man's services in an activity "properly filled by an employee." A much better indication of progress would be for an alcoholic to avoid drinking for a considerable period of time, but even in such a case, merely to "dry a man up" was not sufficient. Other "evidences of improvement must accompany his sobriety:" better work habits, increased reliability, honesty, a recognition of past wrongs and some attempt to make restitution, a willingness to encourage new men in the center and to help them to benefit from its program, and—at least—a "sincere interest" in the Christian religion based not on mere profession but in consistent daily life and work within the center. The primary means to accomplish this restoration of damaged lives was "work therapy," which gave the man a sense of self-respect, occupied his mind and most of his time "on an organized and useful basis," and taught him in many cases a valuable skill. The results of this work provided part of the financial support of the center, and enabled it to supplement the work with other kinds of social, physical and religious therapy.[44]

The end of the decade brought forth another official volume as well, less monumental than the handbook, but still welcome. Men's social officers had clamored for years for a songbook written especially for use in the centers. Several officers expressed this hope during the "institutes" in 1944. Institutional bands, like horses who knew their way home without a driver and the good old days of red/green bookkeeping, were the stuff of memory; while there were occasionally instrumentalists—almost all of them string players—in a few centers, even these centers, like all the others, had to rely almost entirely on vocal music for their religious services. The difficulty with the standard Salvation Army *Songbook* was—and is—that it contained no music, only words, and these were closely printed on the page. This quaint arrangement enabled the song leader in a corps meeting to employ any one of a variety of tunes he liked for each song, so long as the meter fit, and the tiny type allowed a maximum number of songs in a medium-sized book. These books were not easy to use, however, in a men's center. Many of the men had some religious background and were used to hymn books with musical notation printed with the words. Some of the older men had trouble reading the small type. An additional problem was that the keys in which the piano accompaniments to the regulation Army *Songbook* were written were often too high for male voices to sing comfortably. These difficulties were not, of course, insurmountable—for instance, Chicago Central formed a fine men's chorus in 1959—but they were sufficiently daunting to the average man in a center that by the late 1950s, managers were receiving a growing number of requests for songbooks with music and larger type.

The Commissioners' Conference in February 1960, authorized the publication of a new songbook for the men's social service department. The responsibility for the production was given to Major Richard E. Holz, head of the Eastern Territorial Music Department—and grandson/namesake of the pioneer social officer who had presided over the birth of a separate men's social service department 63 years before. There were unexpected delays in arranging the final engraving of the music—Holz candidly admitted that he had never prepared a songbook with *notes* before—but there were happy moments in the preparation of the new songbook as well. Erik Leidzen, one of the Army's best-known composers and arrangers, put all the songs into a comfortable range for men's voices, and added 14 lovely arrangements for full male chorus. Most familiar gospel songs and hymns—like "Throw Out the Lifeline!"—were included; the Rodeheaver Company, owner of the copyrights on many of America's most familiar Christian songs, generously allowed the Army to use 16 of them for the new book. A handful of the Army's own gems found their way into the book as well. The Salvation Army *Songs for Men* finally appeared in 1962 and overnight became the standard songbook in the nation's social centers.[45]

CHAPTER VI
1960–1985

The Salvation Army Mens Social Service Department entered the 1960s in an exuberant mood. Service to Man was official policy on a national scale. The days were long past when the social officer's work for God and the betterment of man was regarded by anyone within the Army as inferior to that of staff and corps officers. Although the trend was more marked in the Western and Southern Territories, in every territory an increased reliance on store sales brought not only increased income, but income that was more reliable than that from waste materials. When General Wilfred Kitching retired in 1963, the territorial commanders were asked to list all the "important extensions" of Army work that had taken place in each territory since he had become General in 1954. The report from the men's social service departments revealed many advances—new, professional personnel and therapeutic techniques, the new handbook, the new songbook, special courses in the schools for officers' training, new buildings, renovations in many older ones—all carried forward on a golden stream of prosperity: more trucks, more stores, more income.[1]

In 1961 the Vocational Rehabilitation Administration of the U.S. Department of Health, Education and Welfare financed a pioneering study of the effectiveness of two Salvation Army men's social service centers in rehabilitating chronic alcoholics, and to ascertain the effects on rehabilitation in the Army added two "specialized services," psychotherapy and vocational rehabilitation counseling. The study was carried on by Dr. Lawrence Katz in the San Francisco Center and in Lytton Springs, a former Army boys' home now used as a kind of rural annex to the San Francisco program. The officer in charge of both centers was Major George Duplain, one of the Western Territory's most successful officers. Duplain looked upon Katz's proposal to use the two institutions for the

171

five-year pilot project as an opportunity to gain hard data about the effectiveness of the existing program and of new therapeutic tools as well.

Katz's project revealed a number of things about the Army's program for homeless, alcoholic men, both nationwide and in San Francisco. For one thing, the Army's work among alcoholics had become very large, surprisingly so even to officers who, working with a few hundred men in a single center, might have lost sight of the magnitude of The Salvation Army's total program. In 1961 there were 124 men's social service centers in the United States, with a bed capacity of 10,388. In the course of the year, more than 57,000 different men passed through these centers— compared to the 20,000 to 30,000 men with drinking problems who were treated in all outpatient clinics in the country in 1959. The Salvation Army Men's Social Service Department had become the largest alcoholic rehabilitation facility in the United States! Yet, strange to say, these centers were little known outside the ranks of their clients. "Despite their significant role in the care and treatment of the alcoholic," Katz observed, "relatively little has been written in professional journals about these centers." The reasons for this, he surmised, were two: the Army was self-sufficient and asked for no public funds for these centers, and the Army employed few trained professional social workers who could reach a large professional audience. The picture was improving as Katz began his study. He sent questionnaires to all Army centers in the country, of which 119 replied. These results were encouraging considering how short a period had passed since Service to Man had become official policy. In 1947 the Central Territorial Commission on Alcoholism sent questionnaires to centers in every territory but the West: 69 responded, and 43 of these claimed to have "a specific program in operation . . . in behalf of the drinker." These programs were generously defined in the questionnaire, however, and included any sort of counseling, planned recreation and snack bars (regarded as a deterrent to drinking) along with intake interviews and A.A. groups. By the 1947 standard, 100% of the centers that responded to Katz 14 years later had "specific programs." A growing, but still small number of centers in 1961 had group therapy (34), psychological testing (24) and professional social workers (15).

The San Francisco center, which was the subject of Katz's particular interest, was one of the most advanced in the country when the project began in 1961: clients were given several psychological tests which were professionally interpreted, and had at their disposal the complete clinical and laboratory facilities of St. Luke's Hospital, conveniently located across the street, with which Duplain had established a beneficial relationship early in his career at the center. Group psychotherapy, individual psychological and vocational counseling and assistance in finding a job were provided for some men, all under the guidance of the first chaplain/ clinical director, Rev. William Lindsay-Stewart. When vocational rehabilitation was added, first in the form of counseling, then in 1963 by referrals to the California Division of Vocational Rehabilitation, the percentage of men who were helped in substantially demonstrable ways increased. Almost 2,000 men participated in the five-year study. Of these, 400 men were followed up six months after they left the program: about 50 percent had improved in abstinence, and half of these "showed great improvement;" 43 percent had improved in work patterns, and again, half showed "significant improvement," and half had improved only "moderately." The San Francisco Center was the first in the country to employ vocational rehabilitation counselors.[2]

As the project began to unfold, Major Duplain sought a simple, graphic means of describing the Army's total men's social program, not only for Katz or for the many social work and therapeutic interns who increasingly used the San Francisco Center for supervised field training, but for the use of other officers and men in the department as well for training and publicity purposes. He produced a simple design, which was adopted nationwide: the "circle of endeavor." The design was executed by Wesley Dawe, a Salvationist engineer who led the band at the San Francisco Citadel Corps where Duplain attended. The "circle of endeavor" consisted of two concentric circles. The inner circle, labeled "basic traditional services: required involvement," showed the standard Army program as laid out in the new handbook: residence, "leisure-time" (or "recreation") and "work-therapy." At the center of the inner circle was "spiritual counseling" and showed a large red Army shield. The second, larger circle was called "added services available" and showed psychological services, vocational counseling and placement services, testing, medical services, Alcoholics Anonymous, fellowship clubs, and training and research.[3]

Increasingly during the 1960s, officers were determined to concentrate on an effective, long-term treatment program for alcoholism, which continued to be the "handicap" of a high percentage—the handbook said 70 percent, the Katz study suggested "over 80 percent"—of the men who came to the Army for help. Several studies of the homeless unemployed man conducted during the 1950s and 1960s provided Army officers with valuable guidance by producing a composite picture of the "typical" homeless chronic drinker: he was in his 40s, unmarried, separated or divorced, poorly educated, reasonably able and willing to work, but beyond the occasional welcome exception, possessed no skills except for those of the still-traditional occupations of the transient man—seasonal farm worker, cook or housepainter. The typical heavy drinker who habituated skid rows and Army centers preferred wine because it was the cheapest beverage per unit of ethyl alcohol. The most interesting result of the recent research, however, was that the typical homeless habitual inebriate was not addicted to alcohol! He drank, not from an "uncontrollable drive to become intoxicated" but because he was "under-socialized"—that is, he had failed to adjust to the "life patterns of the normal individual," experienced few of the positive or negative sanctions of normal society, knew little of trust, affection, security, self-respect or prestige; in drinking he found companionship, purpose and escape. It was for this "drastically under-socialized" man that the Salvation Army program of protected residential care, leisure, work and religion was designed, and men from this group provided the Army with most of its clients and its triumphs of grace and patience.

But there were difficulties with this explanation of chronic drunkenness. For one thing, officers knew that the man who consciously chose to drink for the effect, or because he had no useful or happy way to spend his time, was less likely to recognize that he was in trouble than the man who felt trapped by an addiction that he recognized to be the cause of his ruin. The success of the program of rehabilitation in a Salvation Army center was based on two conditions: that the client have an identifiable and treatable handicap, and that he recognize his need for help. Experts like Peter Hofman and Second Lieutenant Charles Smith of the Cleveland Corps, and later the Detroit Harbor Light Corps, regarded the client's willingness to admit his need for help as absolutely essential to his rehabilitation. The handbook declared that the "most challenging aspect to the person dealing with these homeless problem drinkers" was that "most of these men do not seem to feel that they have a drinking problem." The value of group therapy and individual counseling during the program was to enlarge and clarify the recognition of that need and to guide the man as he found his way to a solution.[4]

The other difficulty with an interpretation of chronic drunkenness that emphasized its voluntary motivation was that it did not explain why some men became physically addicted to alcohol—or for that matter why some men, with the same kinds of personal problems in life as others, and who might even drink as much as these others did, did not become chronic drunkards. Apparently there was a sense in which alcoholism, or some form of it, was a disease. Although the idea gained widespread circulation among officials and agencies in the 1950s and 1960s, it was not new. Peter Hofman and a few other Salvation Army officers who were sympathetic to the disease concept in the 1940s, because it seemed to offer a broader range of therapeutic activity, had been delighted to discover that General William Booth had declared in his book *In Darkest England* in 1890 that drunkenness in some cases "must be accounted a disease." The standard list of medical nomenclature first issued in 1933 with the approval of the American Medical Association, the American Psychiatric Association and many other professional organizations, listed "alcoholic addiction" as a disease. One of the leading advocates of the concept, and probably the expert who most influenced Army officers, was Dr. E. M. Jellinek, a founder of the Yale School of Alcoholic Studies. His lectures on the "phases of alcohol addiction" reached many officer delegates. Jellinek distinguished between "habitual symptomatic excessive drinkers" and "alcohol addicts;" the latter had lost control "over the intake of alcohol," which loss of control was a "disease condition per se." Jellinek did not claim to know whether this loss of control was caused by psychological or psychical pathology, nor whether it originated in a "predisposing factor" or was acquired as a result of prolonged drinking. Jellinek confirmed that the majority of excessive drinkers did not experience this loss of control. In 1956 a board of the American Medical Association formally requested hospitals to admit patients diagnosed as having alcoholism "equally with patients brought in for admission under other diagnostic labels." Ten years later there were landmark decisions by two U.S. District Courts that held that because alcoholism was recognized as a disease, a homeless alcoholic could not avoid being drunk in public, and therefore could not be punished for it. In 1967 the U.S. Crime Commission and two other major authoritative commissions declared that the criminal law was an ineffective and inhumane device for the prevention and control of alcoholism, and urged a public health approach be substituted for arrest and incarceration. In 1968 Congress passed the Alcoholic Rehabilitation Act, the first federal law covering the treatment of alcoholics, and in 1970 the Comprehensive Alcohol Abuse and Alcoholism Prevention, Treatment and Rehabilitation Act, which provided a legal framework within which the states could approach alcoholism with public health rather than criminal law proceedings.

Not all officers were willing to accept this definition of alcoholism.

Brigadier A. E. Baldwin, the chairman of the Army's National Commission on the Problems of Alcoholism, wrote his own "minority report" in 1948, distancing himself from the commission's official recommendations on this point: Baldwin regarded the disease theory as misleading because it tended to "minimize the moral responsibility involved" in the decision to begin drinking in the first place. This reservation, that treating alcoholism as a disease ignored its sinful motive, was shared by other evangelical Christians and continued to be held by a sizable number of Salvationists. One leading authority on alcoholism found when he surveyed the field in 1968, however, that most Salvation Army social officers took the "enlightened view" of alcoholism as a disease. Certainly many officers were anxious to employ the latest medical techniques in their efforts to effect a cure of the drinking problems of the men in their centers.[5]

Several pioneer projects were launched in the Central Territory. Captain William W. Hasney, who joined the department in 1960 after three years as a corps officer, became interested in finding a medical treatment for alcoholism while stationed at the men's social service center in Springfield, Illinois. He began a 90-day "detoxification" program in 1964–1965, but was able to launch a full-scale "detox" clinic only after taking command of the much larger Chicago Central Men's Social Service Center in 1967. Assisted by a $30,000 grant from headquarters, Hasney opened the first detoxification clinic in The Salvation Army in 1969. Hasney was supported by the center's "alcoholic counselor," John J. Judge, a recovered alcoholic who had wandered into the center by chance in 1960 and became a product of the classic Service-to-Man program, guided to recovery by the kindly Major William Benton. Together Hasney and Judge created an innovative program for the Chicago center, which combined an elaborate medical treatment for withdrawal, such as tranquilizers, antinauseants, magnesium salts to prevent delirium tremens, with various traditional and novel means to break down the client's defensive claim that his problems were beyond his own control. Once the period of withdrawal was safely past, the remainder of the new program was based on the traditional Army position that "recovery from alcoholism is largely a mentalistic phenomenon." The most important parts of the Chicago program were the detox clinic and the "program committee," which was a "nuclear group" of sober men who understood their own problems and were sincerely working to find solutions. Members of the nuclear group welcomed new men into the center and sought to inspire in them the conviction that everyone was, after all, somebody's brother. In 1971, Judge wrote a formal description of the new program for the prestigious *Quarterly Journal of Studies on Alcohol* in which he could not resist noting that Katz's observation in 1964 that "relatively little" about The Salvation Army had appeared in professional journals was "changing appreciably." The Western Territorial Men's Social Service Officers' Councils in 1969 held a workshop on detoxification programs based on the Chicago model; in May 1971, the men's social service secretaries conference proposed that John Judge be sent to social officers' councils in all four territories to present a program on the training of "alcoholism therapists."[6]

Once the medical approach to alcoholism gained judicial sanction in 1966, the problem of how to control public drunkenness became acute. Because not all public drunkenness was caused by alcoholism, the requirement that such offenders be given medical treatment, while more humane than the useless "revolving door" process of arrest and temporary incarceration, might overburden the nation's health services. In May 1971, Major Norman V. Nonnweiler, new manager of the Salvation Army Men's Social Service Center in Kansas City, accepted funds from the Northwest Missouri Law Enforcement Assistance Council and the Kansas City Model Cities Department of the U.S. Department of Housing and Urban Development to open a pilot project for a "non-medical, non-penal sobering-up facility with concommitant counseling and referral services." The new facility, called "Sober House" was housed in the Salvation Army men's social service center. Men picked up by the police for drunkenness were allowed to choose between arrest or voluntarily going to Sober House. If he chose the latter, he was allowed to sober up on his own, under supervision; those who showed any signs of complication were sent to a nearby hospital. Once the man was ambulatory he was transferred to a dormitory and could voluntarily attend lectures and counseling sessions. After a few days he was referred by his own consent to some other agency or resource, or allowed to return to his home if he had one. Fifty-seven percent of the men who completed "self-detoxification" accepted referral for further help—and 60 percent of these went into the host Salvation Army program.[7]

Although Sober House successfully adopted a non-medical approach to alcoholism, many leading managers endorsed detox programs as one means of helping the man who seemed most helpless. Captain Hasney's detox clinic was closed only when city hospitals began to offer the same service. Brigadier Cecil Briggs, who opened the world's largest men's social service center in Detroit in 1971, added a detox clinic almost at once, operated by men who had taken a two-months' intensive course on alcoholism given at Wayne State University. Major Nonnweiler, while giving full support to the voluntary, non-medical nature of the activities at Sober House, took a more physiological approach in his own center's program. In particular, Nonnweiler was one of the first managers to use the drug Antabuse as a means of keeping men sober, and he quickly became its leading advocate among Army officers. It was first discovered in a clinic in the Netherlands in 1948 that the chemical disulfiram had a sensitizing effect to ethyl alcohol; if the chemical is present in the body even in very small amounts the person cannot ingest alcoholic beverages without feeling distinctly unpleasant. Under careful supervision severe reactions were rare. The substance was apparently otherwise harmless, and had no discernable lasting effects. For a few years it seemed to alcohol therapists like a panacea but the vogue quickly passed.

The largest problem with Antabuse was not physical, but emotional: most chronic drinkers were not compulsive or addictive; they drank for the tranquilizing effect of the liquor. Many of these were lonely, insecure, afraid of failure; Antabuse closed the door of escape to them. Many men preferred to withdraw from a rehabilitation program rather than accept the use of Antabuse. A more reasoned appraisal of the value of Antabuse was not that it was the universal cure, but that it could be a helpful adjunct to other kinds of personal therapy, because Antabuse did force men to avoid taking the unplanned, impulsive drink. Nonnweiler introduced the use of the drug in Kansas City in 1971 and continued its mandatory application when he took over the large Detroit Center in 1977. No national pattern of reaction by officers to the use of the drug as a therapeutic tool emerged. A few officers in every territory introduced Antabuse, mostly on a voluntary basis. Major David Mulbarger found in the early 1970's that compulsory use of Antabuse in the Miami center only succeeded in forcing men to use marijuana in order to experience the escape into fearless euphoria that alcohol would otherwise have provided them.[8]

The Salvation Army's official position paper on alcoholism, approved by the Commissioners' Conference in November 1971, took a balanced position, emphasizing the traditional evangelical approach to alcoholism, but embracing the full range of scientific therapies as well:[9]

> The Salvation Army believes that every individual who is
> addicted to alcohol may find deliverance from its bondage

through submission of the total personality to the Lord-
ship of Jesus Christ.

The Salvation Army also recognizes the value of medical,
social and psychiatric treatment for alcoholics and makes
extensive use of these services at its centers.

Dr. Katz observed in 1964 that the "nature of any specific program will
be limited by each center's financial productivity"—which in The Salvation Army now meant store sales, which blossomed invitingly in recession
and inflation, boom and bust alike. The era of dependence on waste
material sales was over, even in the Central and Eastern departments,
which had large returns in these columns and still maintained centralized
sales of waste materials; in the West and South bulk sales of waste paper
and rags were little more than a trifle. In every territory, store sales carried
the program; in 1965, 74 percent of departmental income nationwide came
from stores. The day of the million-dollar center had arrived: the first was
in the West—the Los Angeles Center in 1964, under Major Warren
Johnson; the second was in the Central—Brigadier Cecil Briggs' enormous Detroit Center; the third was in the East—the Brooklyn Center
under Major Raymond E. Howell. The first center in the South to gross
one million dollars in income for one year was Miami, during the administration of Major David Mulbarger, who had proved to be a quick learner:
he went to Miami in 1969 after only four years in the department and 18
years in corps work.

Production and sales techniques occupied considerable attention during
the 1960s, and many innovations, introduced by enterprising officers, later
became territorial, then national policy, and have remained standard procedure. Some techniques, on the other hand, remained only the personal
preference of the individual manager. Managers often debated the value of
soliciting for materials, rather than relying upon what was spontaneously
donated. Many managers advocated an aggressive approach, based on the
long-recognized fact that the items that came in as a result of special
solicitation were, as a rule, more valuable—i.e., they could more easily be
resold in a store—than items that were simply donated. The competition
was sometimes fierce: Major Lloyd Smith in Columbus informed Colonel
Guldenschuh in 1961 that a local rag dealer was offering trading stamps to
housewives who gave him their old clothes! Telephone solicitation, first-
class mailers with third-class return cards, old-fashioned door-to-door
solicitation were all used to canvass specially promising neighborhoods.

Large paper bags were left invitingly on the doorstep, and an amazing variety of handbills, newspaper advertisements and publicity materials were advocated.

Clothes were the largest single source of income for every center, and in most they brought in more than all the other types of merchandise combined. The best means of quickly and accurately sorting the daily avalanche of donated clothes into rags and merchandise for resale, and the latter into various price categories, was clearly of the first importance. Major Johnson installed a double-belt system in the Los Angeles center for this purpose, to which he was much attached—and apparently with good reason: at the 1964 social officers' councils in the West, Brigadier Andrew Telfer, the respected general secretary, presided over a long discussion between those who advocated belts and those who favored bins for sorting, which came to the conclusion that belts did, in fact, increase the volume of production. The bin-loyalists were unbowed, however: bins allowed for more leisurely sorting and therefore more accurate—and profitable—results. There was more agreement, in every territory, on the value of the drop-box. The first models, like those used in Detroit in 1961, were almost always made of plywood. Officers in several territories who first used drop-boxes were regarded almost as visionaries, but when Mrs. Brigadier John Troutt, the literary wife of the Minneapolis center manager, surveyed the country for an article on men's social service work for the Salvation Army *Year Book* in 1967, she found 3,780 drop-boxes in use in the United States, and predicted the number of these would double within the next year! Drop-boxes were clearly here to stay, but opinions about their value continued to differ. Western officers valued them in the mid-1960s primarily for their public-relations value and their convenience to the donor; they usually produced less than they cost to install and maintain, when the losses due to theft and vandalism were added against the fact that most of what was placed in the Army's drop-boxes was of little value. Colonel Paul Seiler, who became men's social service secretary in the East in 1965, took a far more optimistic view of drop-boxes; he supervised the installation of boxes at "strategic points" throughout the territory, and soon expressed his "firm belief that the salvation of this department" rested "to some extent upon the clothing collection boxes," which had more than repaid the cost of their distribution.[10]

The greatest advance of these years, however, was not in production, as important as those gains were, but in merchandising. For years officers in every territory had recognized the importance of modern and effective merchandising, but the men who made the largest contribution in the 1960s towards The Salvation Army's highly successful merchandising procedures were both from the Western Territory: Warren Johnson in Los Angeles and George Duplain in San Francisco. Both men prepared serviceable store manuals for their own centers and both used new ideas of their own and those of other successful managers to greatly increase store sales. Both men became Western Territorial Men's Social Service Secretaries, Johnson in 1965, who was succeeded by Duplain in 1967, when Johnson was transferred to the Southern Territory. As secretary, Duplain collected the new merchandising guidelines, many of which he had devised himself, into an official manual, which was then introduced by Duplain and Johnson throughout the two territories. With only slight revision by a later Western Men's Social Service Secretary, Lt.-Colonel David Riley, the manual was adopted by the Commissioners' Conference for national use in 1981.

The Salvation Army Guide to Thrift Store Operations was written for the managers and employees of the stores themselves, and left nothing to chance and little more to choice. Full of useful and profitable direction, its widespread use by store personnel for almost two decades produced the modern Salvation Army store—a service to people with "limited financial means," a place where "Neighbors May Shop with Dignity"—and the financial base upon which almost 70,000 homeless, desperate men found shelter and care every year. The manual concentrated on good customer relations, keeping clothing displays neat, well-stocked and moving out the door in the hands of happy customers. This was accomplished by means of a system of color-coded rotation of merchandise that both encouraged the sales of slow-moving items by automatically lowering the price twice after fixed periods of time on the rack, and allowed the manager of the store to exercise control over inventory, proper arrangement and pricing of furniture and a host of other details. The selling policy described in the guide was scrupulously honest: no special arrangements for dealers, relatives or employees, no lay-aways, no misleading "sales" or "discount" signs; on the other hand, store personnel were allowed to give a discount on large furniture items in order to make a sale. The sole function of the store operation was to maximize the volume of sales while treating the customer with fairness, courtesy and patience. The guide did not mention it, mostly because such marketing decisions were almost always made by the center's commanding officer, but the Army gladly cashed in on the public demand for nostalgic and bizarre clothing in the 1960s. Warren Johnson placed the oldest clothing in the Los Angeles warehouse on special manikins and gleefully sold all of it as "antique clothing."[11]

The sale of bulk rags did not cease altogether during these years. Nationwide "rags and junk" produced almost 13 percent of the total income of the department in 1965. The percentage of total income due to rags varied greatly from territory to territory. The increased attention to store sales resulted in more careful and judicious selection of materials for store sales, so that the quality of materials left for rag sales after the first sorting declined in the 1960s. On the other hand, any center that used the methods prescribed in the *Guide to Thrift Store Operations* would have generated a steady stream of items back into the rag bin by carefully gleaning from stock on hangers items that had been torn, had lost a price tag or simply had not been sold within a certain time limit—a process appropriately called "ragging." Whether directly from the sorting room or from the stores, every center produced a large quantity of rags. The market for these materials did not cease to be unreliable as a basis for long-range financial planning in any territory. Because the price per ton of these materials varied did not mean, however, that such materials were valueless. In fact, rags could be enormously valuable, if cleverly marketed: in addition to the traditional use of rags for wiper cloths in industry, filler for roofing materials and as a component in the manufacture of fine paper, a lucrative market in secondhand clothing developed in the 1960s in countries in the Middle East, Asia and Central America. What was a rag in an American suburb was a secondhand shirt in—say—Damascus or Guadalajara. The dealers who arranged such profitable transactions were anxious to obtain a steady supply of materials from The Salvation Army, whose "pack" had been the best in the industry for 50 years. The overseas used-clothing trade fluctuated directly with the value of the American dollar abroad, and with political and social conditions in important foreign market cities, and was intensely, almost hysterically competitive. Dealers were determined to have a supply, as long as foreign market conditions and a reasonably soft dollar gave them buyers. Not all dealers were perfectly straightforward in their arrangements: a few cents knocked off the price per pound at the point of supply could mean a fortune for somebody, somewhere; and bales of rags that had not been sorted for store sales were much more valuable than bales of leftovers, but the two kinds of bales were not easily distinquished by outward appearance. Rag dealers tradi- tionally used cash in their transactions. Center managers were occasion- ally presented with temptation. That so few succumbed was a trophy to the honor of the department. Men's social secretaries, fully aware of the enormous amount of good work being done daily in the centers for God, the Kingdom and for the support of many Salvation Army programs, were vigilant to preserve the reputation of their branch of the Movement. In 1969 Lt.-Colonel Ransom Gifford who had come from retirement the year before to serve as men's social service secretary, officially reminded Western officers "that each center is required to sell only to dealers of integrity and reputation who pay best prices."[12]

The flow of goods and—more importantly—services required space. By 1967 all four territories had major building programs underway. Between 1961 and 1968 total bed capacity increased from 10,388 to 11,192, an eight percent increase, in 122 centers nationwide. In October 1972, the largest men's social service center in the world, with six floors and 350,000 square feet of floor space, containing a "pleasant, livable home" for 300 men, was opened at 1627 W. Fort Street, Detroit. The new rehabilitation and merchandising programs were still carried on in old centers as well: "New York No. 1," now the Manhattan Men's Social Service Center, was still in its 1907 building; Jersey City, built in 1910, had moved only once—in 1926–1927 to make room for the Holland Tunnel—and the center was still open. The Newark Center was opened in 1929. Despite the Army's justifiable pride in new centers, much of the fiery evangelism and zeal for the lost that drove pioneer social officers lived on in embattled downtown monuments to a still-great ideal. While stationed at the Manhattan Center from 1965–1967 Brigadier Arthur Craytor roamed the Bowery in full uniform, placing on drunken or sleeping men cards that read: "God loves you, and so does The Salvation Army."[13]

Other traditional programs, however, had run their course: the era of the workingman's hotel, the Metropole, Beacon, Unity and Argonne, was over. The high cost of operating these facilities up to the standards required by public authorities, the lack of qualified personnel to administer them, and the fact that their clientele were almost entirely of two classes—transients paid for by local welfare agencies or aged pensioners, neither of which sought rehabilitation or religious instruction—meant doom for the Army's few remaining hotels. The last hotel in the South was in Nashville, which closed in 1951, and in the West, in Fresno in 1954. The Memorial Hotel in the Bowery was officially closed in 1964 and transferred from the men's social service department to the Greater New York Division for use first as a Harbor Light, then in 1972 as "Booth House II," a residential program for men with various handicaps. The last Army shelter operated under the auspices of men's social service in the Central Territory, the Minneapolis Men's Lodge, was closed on May 1, 1970. The Transient Service Bureau in New York was closed in 1963; three years later the Army declared officially that it had only "limited" resources in the metropolitan New York area for transients who simply needed overnight shelter. The men's social service centers were "not equipped for transient services" and could only occasionally "take a man overnight or for a weekend." "Transient" was defined as one whose problem would be solved the next day—a job, a trip home, an appointment with some agency—whereas the Army was now fully and officially committed to long-term residential rehabilitation. Because it interfered with the operation of just such a program in the Manhattan Center, the Lowenstein Memorial Cafeteria was closed in 1974.[14]

The 1960s was a decade of rapid social change. These changes naturally affected the men's social service program, which drew for its clientele upon a segment of the larger society. Traditionally the position of blacks within the program of the men's social service department had been ambiguous. There was never, at any time in any territory, an official departmental policy that excluded black men from the Army's centers. The cook at the New York Lighthouse in 1892 was black, and the San Francisco Lifeboat had a "colored brother" sorting corks in early 1893. The Army maintained separate hotel facilities for "colored men" in both the North and the South until World War II, but managers of social service centers were apparently free to admit blacks if they chose to do so. They did not choose to do so: in 1939 the *Kansas City Star* described the city's industrial home as "for white men only," although the same article spoke of a black employed as watchman. Arne Lekson had several black employees in the Washington, D.C. Center in the 1940s, but it is difficult to find evidence that any black men were clients or residents of centers anywhere in the country before the mid-1940s. Adjutant Agnew found in his survey of Eastern centers in 1942–1943 that every center imposed the "usual restriction" that clients would be accepted if they were white, unattached males not obviously drunk. This was the case even for centers located in racially mixed, or even mostly black, neighborhoods.

It is true that few blacks applied to Army centers, and this may be at least partially explained by the fact that the Army's program was not well understood by some blacks. While stationed in Paterson from 1938 to 1941, Major Ernest Hayes was asked by a black municipal judge to explain why there were no black men in the Army center. Hayes satisfied the official, who was at first unfriendly, by stating that few blacks came to the center and those who did thought it was a place of regular employment and left when they found that clients received no salary. It was demonstrably true that there were few blacks among the general population of homeless, transient men, the traditional casual residents of skid rows, from which The Salvation Army and other similar agencies had drawn their clientele since the late 19th century. Confusion on the part of some blacks as to the purpose of the Army's centers and the fact that a disproportionately small number of homeless transients were black cannot, however, explain the entire absence of blacks from the Army's centers across the nation. In September 1944, Lester Granger of the National Urban League wrote to the Army's national headquarters condemning the "bad interracial relationships" in "many" men's social service institutions. The next year Adjutant B. Barton McIntyre, a black officer in charge of a mostly black corps in Cleveland, read a paper at the National Conference of Social Work in which he denounced racial segregation in Salvation Army institutions, which raised "the Jim-Crow standard instead of the Blood and Fire." Both the contemporary record and the recollections of many managers explain this policy as forced on the Army by the attitudes of its regular clientele. The Army's clients would not tolerate black companions in the program. The Army's white clients, mostly men over 40, often poorly educated and hardened by the lack of happiness and success in their lives, were not malicious so much as narrowly prejudiced and happy to know of the existence of a whole class of human beings to whom even they could feel comfortably superior.

World War II was a watershed for the Army in this regard. The democratic and libertarian reasons for which the war was fought, the population migrations which it set in motion in the United States and the fact that many blacks served in the nation's armed forces and were now honored veterans, made racial exclusion nearly impossible. Despite Agnew's findings in 1942–1943, no reference to race appears in the printed edition of the 1944 *Institutes,* nor in *Standards and Practices,* the gray book of four years later. In March 1946, the Eastern regional directors called for a "definite policy" on the admission of blacks. Colonel Dowdell asked each regional director to take a single black client into the center as an experiment and to report the result to headquarters. The Southern Territory announced in December 1950, that there was "a place in The Salvation Army for the Negro," and Lt.-Colonel Decker strongly recommended in his farewell departmental brief in 1953 the "exploration of the possibility of inviting" Negroes into the Washington Center as beneficiaries in order to provide the Army's "service to all the population when it is possible." Major Lawrence Castagna accepted a black veteran as a client in Paterson just after the war, and experienced no difficulty with the other men. Other managers had similar experiences in the next few years—Captain Eugene Gesner in Miami, Sr.-Major Christian Dragsbak in Springfield, Illinois (who coolly informed headquarters in 1956 that segregation was "still practiced" in some other centers and calling upon Colonel Crawford to abolish it altogether!).

The Commissioners' Conference embraced the famous Supreme Court school desegregation case of 1954 *(Brown vs Board of Education of Topeka, Kansas)* with sincere conviction, and promptly issued an official Salvation Army position statement endorsing the decision in language that was almost uniquely enthusiastic for such documents:

> The Supreme Court's historic decision outlawing segregation in the nation's public facilities is heartily endorsed by The Salvation Army.
>
> A ruling so soundly based on Christian principles cannot but receive understanding and cooperation from all Salvationists dedicated to the ideal that in Christ all are one.
>
> We accept our full Christian responsibility to work earnestly and sympathetically to the end that a practical implementation of the decision may be successfully effected.

The process of bringing blacks into the rehabilitation program gained momentum in every territory in the 1960s. By that time the resistance of many of the white clients had broken down: many men in the Army's centers in the 1960s were veterans of the Korean War, and a few even from the contemporary Vietnam conflict, which had given them experience in integrated communal living. The key to the response of a center to integration was now the attitude of the manager, not only in admitting the man, but in encouraging the residents not merely to tolerate him but to befriend and assist him. Several key centers were integrated in this way, around 1967: Major David Mulbarger brought the first black to Tampa in 1967, for instance, as Major David Allen did in Oakland and Major Norman Nonnweiler in Milwaukee. By the end of the decade the process of integration in the department, in principle and in spirit, both in terms of employees and beneficiaries, was complete nationwide. The problems that remained were not caused by official policy.[15]

The introduction of women clients into the Army's program came later, although it is interesting to note that the Army's first social welfare institutions, in London and in New York, and its first residential program for alcoholics (in Toronto in 1887), had been designed for women. *The War Cry* described one convert in July 1888, as "the most hopeless of this infatuated class of sinners—a woman drunkard." The success of the first Army men's shelter stimulated pioneer officers to make several attempts to open similar programs for women, in 1892 and 1896, but without success. There was no effective Salvation Army program for women alcoholics anywhere in the country for another seven decades. In the long meantime the occasional woman alcoholic who came to one of the men's social service centers for help had to content herself with prayer, which was the only consolation Mrs. Captain Joseph McFee could offer to the "fashionably dressed lady" who called on the San Francisco Lifeboat for help in 1892.[16]

Seventy years later, in the same city, Major George Duplain proposed a rehabilitation program for the respectable, middle-class woman alcoholic, but resources for such a program could not be obtained. The pioneer program for women clients in a men's social service center came in Chicago in 1969. Captain William Hasney accepted women clients in the Chicago Central Center in that year, the first in any men's center in the United States. Major Norman Nonnweiler followed in Kansas City in February 1972. The fact that alcoholism was a problem among an increasing number of women and that women were admitted into the Chicago and Kansas City Centers "with no difficulty" prompted the Men's Social Service Secretaries' Conference to recommend in 1972 that centers in every territory should be encouraged to accept women alcoholics "where facilities are available."

Major George Duplain, who preferred the rigors of managing a center to those of administering the department and was thus once again in charge of the San Francisco Center, required no further encouragement to revive his earlier proposal. The Army owned a large residence in San Francisco, built originally by local philanthropists as a home for poor children, later obtained by The Salvation Army for use as an emergency lodge for servicemen's wives awaiting their husbands' return during World War II and the Korean War. The building, called Pinehurst Lodge, was ideally suited to the program envisioned by Duplain. In February 1975, the

"Pinehurst Program for the Woman Alcoholic" was formally opened. Accommodating 20 women clients, who lived under supervision, participated in the work-therapy assignments and in two chapel services at the downtown center and in several therapeutic counseling activities and an A.A. group of their own at Pinehurst, the program became a national model. Many of the clients were middle- or upper-class "closet" drinkers who had to relearn simple domestic chores. Cleaning the residence was an official part of work therapy from the beginning of the program: dusting, mopping, washing clothes—even watering the houseplants—were carefully scheduled. In 1979, however, the Army mercifully installed a hot tub to provide special therapy for ladies who were unaccustomed to the daily labor of domestic life.[17]

By 1985 there were women's programs under the auspices of the men's social services department in every territory, but nationwide results were not encouraging. The unquestionable success of Pinehurst and of promising programs in San Diego and Rochester and a few other centers to one side, there were problems in the face of the Army's earnest efforts to expand its alcoholic ministry to women. There were few applicants, few referrals from other agencies. Women alcoholics were almost always more likely to be protected by friends and relatives than were men in the same condition; women seldom became the homeless transients for whom the Army's total residential program was designed. The few women homeless transients who did apply were often in such an advanced state of physical and emotional deterioration that their needs were far beyond the limited medical and therapeutic resources of The Salvation Army. In addition, these women were almost certainly unable to perform useful work, which meant they could not participate in the Army's major form of therapy. There were difficulties even with the few women who were finally admitted. Pinehurst, San Diego, and Rochester Centers were exceptional in having separate building facilities for women clients. In other centers women clients were faced during the entire time they were in the program, with dealing not only with alcoholism but with mixed, perhaps inadequate responses from the opposite sex. Yet hasty and confusing romantic liaisons could be even more harmful than rejection to the rehabilitation of both clients.[18]

The fact remained that after 1969 the Army's men's social service centers had women in them, a fact which their official name seemed to belie. In April 1973, Major Nonnweiler wrote to headquarters for permission to drop the word "men's" from the name of his center. The same year

Major Joseph Viola in Pittsburgh proposed the wording "Adult Rehabilitation Center" in a letter to Major Raymond Howell, the men's social service secretary in the East. Lt.-Colonel Warren Johnson, now men's social service secretary in Atlanta, proposed a change for the centers even without women—something that conveyed that Army's commitment not simply to "social service" but to "rehabilitation." He and the other social secretaries agreed that women in the program made a change in designation mandatory. The Commissioners' Conference informed the secretaries at the outset that they were free to propose a name change for the centers, but that the official name of the department was fixed unalterably in the firmament of international Salvation Army Orders and Regulations. Agreement on a new name even for centers did not come easily. In 1974, the men's social service commission proposed that the centers be renamed "The Salvation Army Rehabilitation Center;" two years later—apparently with no regard for the cost of relettering—they proposed "The Salvation Army Adult Treatment and Rehabilitation Center." In January 1977, the Commissioners' Conference formally agreed to make a name change, but rejected the social service commission's suggestion. Instead, the commissioners established a committee in each territory to submit names to the territorial commander who would bring the ones he liked to the next Commissioners' Conference. The commissioners decided in May 1977, that as of June 30 the new name for the men's social service center would be "The Salvation Army Adult Rehabilitation Center." Like all members of military hierarchies, Salvationists are compulsive abbreviators: "Adult Rehabilitation Center" had only to be announced before it became "ARC," which, if it became an acronym, would conjure up the nautical imagery of the pioneer social officers: the circle was unbroken.[19]

Having finally set aside a venerated name after so much discussion, the commissioners were emboldened to make other changes in nomenclature with almost no discussion at all. In October 1977, center managers—many of whom had already become "directors"—officially became "administrators." A year later, in October 1978, the commissioners approved, on the basis of territorial discretion, an idea for a name change proposed by the innovative Major David Riley, men's social service secretary in the West since 1976: truck drivers could be "production assistants," a change which Riley, a gifted publicist, believed would convey to the drivers their important role in the operation of the center, the invaluable role of "production" in providing for the care and uplift of numbers of unfortunate men. For the same reason, Riley proposed in 1979 that the warehouse should be called a "work therapy unit." These changes in name would have the incidental benefit of helping to protect the Salvation Army Men's Social Service Department, which had for many years struggled to preserve its independence and integrity from what it regarded as unwarranted outside interference, against contemporary efforts to unionize employees in several centers.[20]

Administratively the two decades after 1960 were marked by frequent changes in top leadership in the four departments, many of which proved to be of critical importance to the development of program. In the West Lt.-Colonel Hofman served as secretary from 1958 to 1965; he encouraged and endorsed many innovations by the leading managers of the department and was succeeded in office by the two most successful of them, Warren Johnson in 1965 and George Duplain in 1967. Arthur Carl, an experienced officer, served from 1970 to 1976. His successor was Major David Riley, who had served for three years in the unique position of manager of the men's social service center and city commander for all other Army activities in Tucson. In 1982, Major David Allen became secretary after several years in staff appointments and 20 years of successful center management, 11 of them in Oakland.

Warren Johnson became men's social service secretary in the South in 1967, succeeding Lt.-Colonel William Devoto with whom Johnson worked closely for a brief period before formally taking over the department. Johnson found that Devoto had arranged for Peter Hofman, now retired, to visit every center in the territory and make suggestions to each manager about program and production. Hofman was to be an official "administrative and program consultant," an idea which Johnson eagerly confirmed. Hofman prepared comprehensive and helpful letters to every manager. He was the first, for instance, to suggest two-way radios for the trucks in the South. He also advised managers to stop using trucks to collect worthless paper, and in general supported Johnson's campaign to introduce the territory to the ideas in the new *Guide to Thrift Store Operation.* The result of the influence of these two leading officers, drawing on the best efforts of key managers in the territory who had developed similar programs on their own, was a territory-wide recognition of the fundamental importance of a treatment program for men, and a large increase in store income. Even faced with the statistical "competition" of corps-operated rehabilitation and salvage programs, within a dozen years stores in the South generated larger average income per store than those in the East or the Central. Johnson was succeeded in July 1979 by Major

David Mulbarger, who had been assistant secretary since January 1978, and a highly successful manager for over a dozen years before that, more than nine of them in the large Miami Center.

A succession of experienced managers assumed the position of department secretary in Chicago: Colonel Earl Crawford, whose experience as a manager extended back to the days of the industrial home and covered three territories, served until 1963; he was followed by Colonel Railton Genge, who had served as Crawford's assistant secretary since 1955, after 20 years in centers, 16 of them in Indianapolis. William Gant served as secretary for three years, coming to the position after relatively brief periods in charge of two of the territory's largest centers, Kansas City and Minneapolis, with one year between as assistant secretary. For two years Gant was assisted by the amiable Major William Hasney, a zealous and productive man whose career as manager of the Springfield and Chicago Central centers had been marked by such innovations as the first detox clinic and women's program in any Salvation Army center in the country. Hasney became secretary in 1976.

Colonel Frank Guldenschuh, who served as men's social service secretary in the East from 1959 to 1965, was the last of the original Service-to-Man reformers to reach high position in the Army. Thoroughly experienced and deeply committed to the ultimately evangelical purpose of the department, Guldenschuh did not have an easy administration. He came into office to find that several costly relocations had put the department so badly into debt that all spending had been frozen. He was the last social secretary to preside over the regional director system, for which he had pushed so enthusiastically 20 years before. His successor as Secretary, Colonel Paul D. Seiler, who took office in 1965, had the unpleasant duty of ending the regional directors, the last remnants of even nominal intermediate authority in any men's social service department in the country: the district officers were no more, even in shadow form. Seiler was not officially informed of the reason for this order, but it did not reflect any lack of interest on the part of territorial leadership in rehabilitation: in September 1965, Major Edwy Hinkle, who had been Metropolitan Regional Director, was appointed Territorial Service-to-Man Program Director. His duties were to travel, make suggestions to managers and reports to headquarters about every aspect of center program except production. Seiler was not an experienced men's social officer, but he accepted the appointment with the hope that he might use his considerable knowledge of property development to provide modern, comfortable housing for every client in the territory, a goal which limited financial resources prevented from being fully realized. Lt.-Colonel Giles Barrett, a former divisional officer, served from 1968 to 1970 and was succeeded by an experienced manager and staff officer, Lt.-Colonel William Charron, who had opened a new center in Pittsburgh and succeeded Hofman in the model center in Cleveland. All three secretaries were faced with a major problem, which grew worse with every passing year: many Eastern centers were in outdated facilities, in locations that discouraged even penniless transients from approaching them after dark, and in crowded urban surroundings that made it difficult to find new store locations in order to expand sales sufficiently to finance desperately needed center relocations. In 1972, Brigadier William Benton was appointed men's social service secretary for the East. His long career as a center manager in the Central Territory and for just over a year in Cincinnati before his promotion, was marked by the stories of many men whose lives had been changed because of his gentle, transparent spirit, but on his first—and only—official day in office he was promoted again—to Glory, the victim of a heart attack on the way to the office. Faced with finding an immediate replacement, headquarters happily hit upon Major Raymond E. Howell, whose five years as manager in Brooklyn had given the East its first million-dollar store. Benton's departure did not deprive the department of spiritual leadership: Howell introduced a program of religious retreats for clients and an annual holiness conference.[21]

Much of the daily work of administration in any department of a Salvation Army headquarters is necessarily taken up with recording and analyzing financial and statistical data; this is especially so for the men's social service department. A special national Salvation Army Accounting Commission met in the fall of 1959 to evaluate the accounting and statistical system introduced in 1951 to provide for the new donations-in-kind formula to reduce or eliminate center surpluses by exposing them as illusory. The Accounting Commission found that it was "quite apparent that the men's social service center, with its many programs" had "over the past 10 years run ahead of the accounting and statistical tools currently used to delineate monthly and annual results." The commission also noted that part of the problem was that there were considerable differences in the way managers filled out the forms, which some managers, to avoid this confusion, ignored altogether. The Commissioners' Conference agreed that the Army's accounting system had "lagged far behind the demands of the rapid growth of the men's social service department program," and arranged with the Burroughs Company to design new forms, which were then "field tested" in a women's residence and a men's social service center.

The new accounting system was put into effect officially on October 1, 1961, at the start of a new fiscal year. The commissioners were confident the new system would "stand up for many years." The schedules of accounts were designed to "delineate more realistically" both Service-to-Man expenses for clients and the operation of the production aspect of the center. There was a new, nationally uniform budget form, and for the convenience of center office staffs, a "write-it-once" system of entries and new, smaller cashbooks and ledgers. The new system functioned well, not only in terms of the facility it provided to managers and headquarters for quick and accurate monitoring of operations, but also in the encouraging degree of flexibility it allowed to center personnel. For instance, the entry for "Cases closed—Satisfactory" was defined as "all cases closed that are deemed satisfactory by the staff." Helpful guidelines were provided for any entry that required serious decisions, but they were not mandatory for entries reflecting the rehabilitative aspects of center operations. For "Cases closed—Satisfactory," for example, the form suggested that this figure should include men who had completed rehabilitation and left the center to take up outside employment or to go to another agency for further, more specialized help, or who remained within the center as regular employees. Not only was this accounting system much easier to operate and more accurate in terms of Army administration, but it was also refreshingly honest in what it revealed to the public and other agencies. In 1971 a major study of American philanthropy specifically referred to The Salvation Army and the Quakers as "major exceptions" to the general tendency of sectarian welfare agencies to mask their true financial structure in order to secure public support.[22]

Men's social service accounting procedures in every territory were adapted to centralized computers, slowly, over several years during the early 1980s. The final objective of this process, which differed in detail and in the rate of adoption in every territory, was to establish a national data bank into which the names of every client and every employee would be fed. This would realize at last the promise once held by the Central Registration Bureaus in the East and South, and it would do so with instant and perfect efficiency. The effectiveness of the intake interview as a diagnostic tool would be greatly improved because the complete record of the applicant in that center and in every other center in the country would be at hand. In addition, statistical and financial records could be recorded and analyzed immediately on the territorial level. The process of adopting center accounts to a central computer began in the Central Territory, whose centers went on a computerized general ledger in 1974, using the standard accounting forms. By 1982 the computer at headquarters controlled daily receipts and billing for each center, making payments on center invoices by checks printed with the individual center name and mailed from Chicago. This system provided for daily evaluation of averages and figures for each center for every aspect of production and sales. Beneficiary files were put into the central computer, center by center. Other territories adopted similar computer programs through the first half of the decade.[23]

Federal tax laws changed several times after 1960 in ways which proved advantageous to the Men's Social Service Department. The most important of these changes, from the Army's point of view, was a major revision of the tax laws in 1969 that became effective in stages over the next two years. The Salvation Army had contended for over 20 years that donations-in-kind had monetary value in the hands of their donors, a value which represented a voluntary contribution to The Salvation Army and should not figure as part of the "profit" of the operation of any particular men's social service center because this sum was not created by the productive activities of any center. Now the federal income tax laws confirmed this contention: non-cash goods donated to qualified organizations could be taken as an income tax deduction at the "fair market value," which was defined as the price a willing seller would accept from a willing buyer if both had "reasonable knowledge of the relevant facts."

This was happy news indeed. The Salvation Army's chief source of income in all four territorial departments was from the sale, in one form or another, of donated materials. The new tax laws would surely stimulate this sort of donation; according to the official federal tax guide, in fact, the changes in the law were "designed to encourage such giving." The only problem these laws raised for The Salvation Army was how to provide the donor with documentation as to the value of the gift. At first officers were instructed simply to inform the public that "donations to The Salvation Army are tax deductible" and that donors should "consult with their tax advisors in order to realize the maximum in tax savings." New official receipt forms reflected this policy. In January 1972, the commissioners authorized new pages for the *Handbook of Standards, Principles and Policies* that explained the new policy in more detail: persons whose

295

donations were valued at less than $200 by their own estimation were to be given the standard official receipt form, with the item and its "condition" listed; the donor filled in the value. This procedure was expected to cover the large majority of donations. Gifts worth more than $200 had to be accompanied by an appraisal or supporting deposition, which the center was to keep on file for three years; for gifts valued at $500 or more the Army would pay for a professional appraisal if one were needed. This proved to be a satisfactory arrangement only until other charitable agencies offered to spare their donors the inconvenience and confusion of arriving at a reasonable value of their small donations; if fair market value meant the price such goods brought in a willing and reasonable transaction, as the official definition suggested, then the average selling price for such items in a charity thrift store was their fair market value—figures which store managers could easily supply. Other agencies began to do just that almost as soon as the new tax laws went into effect. As early as September 1975, Major Howell recommended to the other men's social service secretaries that they prepare a price list for nationwide use, based on the average selling price for various kinds of standard items, which could be handed to each donor along with an official receipt. The original objections to such a plan, that the Army used to pay commissions to drivers and helpers based on the value of loads, or that too low an evaluation would alienate donors, while one too high would provoke the Internal Revenue Service, were set aside: commissions were no longer widely used, and the value of the average prices in Salvation Army stores was a matter of demonstrable fact, so no one could claim the amounts were artificial or arbitrary.

The Commissioners' Conference agreed to an official "valuation guide" in October 1978. The guide stated that it was a "list of the average prices charged in our stores if the items are in good condition," that there were many variables, and that an appraisal was "recommended" for items valued by the donor at more than $200. The Southern Territory was the first to issue the new guide to all administrators, as part of Departmental Minute 35A. Although an updated guide, issued in December 1979, was actually in use in every territory, Colonel G. Ernest Murray, the national chief secretary, had to write to the other three territories in March 1980, reminding them to issue official departmental minutes of their own, incorporating the valuation guide, so the records of the Commissioners' Conference would show "implementation" of the new policy nationwide.[24]

Not all federal legislation was equally benevolent from the Army's point of view. The Fair Labor Standards Act remained, of course, in force. The U.S. Government continued, resolutely, to claim that The Salvation Army was covered by its provisions, and should either pay every man "employed" in the centers the minimum wage or apply for a certificate of exemption as an official sheltered workshop. The Salvation Army, equally resolute, refused to do either. In 1961 the FLSA was amended again, raising the minimum wage and eliminating, over a period of four years, the distinction between "covered" and "non-covered" employees. This change caused a substantial increase in the Army's payroll expenses because hourly wages would increase along with the number of employees who were entitled to the minimum. At the same time government officials expressed continued "concern" over the Army's refusal to comply with every part of FLSA.

National Commander Commissioner Holland French, National Chief Secretary Colonel John Grace, and Mr. William Moss called on the FLSA administrator, the assistant secretary of labor and their counsel on December 9, 1963. Both sides presented their positions unchanged. The meeting was amicable. The specter of the Fair Labor Standards Act had been raised, however, and Commissioner French was not encouraged by these proceedings. He hastened to share his alarm with the territorial commanders on December 10, reminding them that compliance with FLSA would cost the Army an additional 10 million dollars annually, a sum of money the Army did not have and could not raise. Men's social service centers would be ruined. Social officers could have added that men's social service centers would be ruined even if the 10 million were available and could be paid: giving beneficiaries a regular salary would enable them to return to their former drinking patterns almost at once. Acting on French's warning, each territorial headquarters sent a seven-page memorandum to every center manager in the territory, in which each point in the Service-to-Man program and the official accounting precautions was spelled out. More memos and warnings were sent from national and territorial headquarters regularly through these years. The wording of the national commander's memo of March 2, 1964, was illustrative:

> Our basic problem is simply stated: we must maintain in
> practice as well as theory, the character of our centers as
> charitable enterprises. Our beneficiaries must be, and
> must appear to a stranger to the program, to be the

recipients of the benefits of a religious and charitable program, rather than persons employed for compensation.

Year after year, in every territory special sessions at social officers' councils, departmental instructions, warnings and letters from the secretary were devoted to reminding administrators of the importance of complying with official definitions and ratios at every point.[25]

In 1974 Moss suggested to the Men's Social Service Secretaries' Commission that when centers were surveyed for compliance, it would be proper to exclude employees engaged in rehabilitative work from the computation of the beneficiaries-to-employees ratio, a practice the Commissioners' Conference approved for questionnaires used for national surveys in 1978 and after. The status of employees was, in fact, made the object of a special committee appointed by the Commissioners' Conference in 1974. The committee, called the "Management-Employee Relations Ad Hoc Committee," had as its major responsibility the preparation of a new official national employees' manual. To draw upon a broad base of expertise, only three of the committee's members were men's social officers: Lt.-Colonel Arthur Carl, Major George Duplain and Major Ray Howell; the others were Colonel Charles Talmadge from the South and Major Mary Petroff from the Central. The new *Men's Social Service Employees Manual* was approved in October 1977 for national distribution. It carefully outlined the "principal conditions, benefits and privileges" of being an employee of the Army, and reminded them specifically that "all the industrial activities of the center" were operated only for the "express purpose of providing treatment and rehabilitation services for beneficiaries who seek help with their problems."

During the same period, the Commissioners' Conference approved a suggestion from another ad hoc committee, that the Army set a nationally uniform policy for donations-in-kind formulas: a ratio of one-third was discussed, but 30 percent was finally accepted. The committee, the commissioners and the Army's counsel all agreed that definite documentary justification for the 30 percent formula should be on hand, in case the Army was ever called upon to defend it. The Commissioners' Conference requested the national chief secretary to explore how the original 30 percent figure had been arrived at, when the donations-in-kind formula was first proposed 25 years before. Although that information was available—much of it appeared, for instance, in the published minutes of the 1956 Men's Social Conference—the Commissioners' Conference finally decided to start the appraisal process from the beginning again.[26]

The Wages and Hours Division was not indifferent to these proceedings, which from the point of view of the government were designed to fortify a legal position which the government had been challenging, with varying degrees of determination, for over 30 years. In 1975, the Wages and Hours division issued a new, more rigorous handbook of enforcement procedures and in 1977 began a series of "active investigations of complaints" raised by employees, interested citizens, and government officials, under the Fair Labor Standards Act. This boded no good for The Salvation Army. In October 1977, Mr. Moss alerted Colonel George Nelting, the national chief secretary, that centers could expect to be investigated. When an official from the U.S. Employment Standards Administration visited the Newark center in the summer of 1978, Moss advised the fullest cooperation with the official: the Army did not plan to withdraw from its long-established position, but there was nothing to gain from "premature confrontation" with government officials. To avoid "lengthy involvement" with the Wages and Hours Division, each territorial headquarters instructed its men's social service department, and all divisional staffs as well, that the Army would pay the minimum wage to all employees of men's social service centers, divisional and corps salvage programs. The Army continued to insist, of course, that beneficiaries were not covered by FLSA.[27]

The principle upon which The Salvation Army based its position in the long controversy over the Fair Labor Standards Act was one which its leaders and its general counsel considered to be so basic as to be vital. It is important to note that while the potentially ruinous financial effects of compliance were a real fear of officers and were often cited in discussions and correspondence, the fundmental ground which the Army felt itself to be defending was the integrity of the Christian religion. The Army adopted the same position in a series of disputes over the right of public authorities to license the adult rehabilitation centers, cases in which the cost of compliance was not a major consideration.

The Army's position, which was carefully formed and defended by its general counsel, was that the adult rehabilitation center was not a business, not a sheltered workshop, not even a charity: it was the pure exercise of religion. The 1960 *Handbook* stated clearly that the center program was built "on the assumption of an underlying spiritual motivation, a compulsion to help men as an expression of divine love: undergirding, inspiring, idealizing, directing;" the "final goal of all Salvation Army endeavor is not human rehabilitation but human regeneration" and for that there was "only one resource—salvation through Jesus Christ." In 1955, the Army's counsel obtained a ruling from the Internal Revenue Service that The Salvation Army was a "church, a convention or association of churches." Counsel declared that the center was a basic part of the Army's "evangelical mission," and as such was protected against unwarranted government interference by the First Amendment to the U.S. Constitution, applied to the states by the 14th Amendment. The Army was not only exempt from taxation on this basis: its counsel contended that any attempt by a state or municipal authority to "control, regulate or seriously interfere with the program of operation" of adult rehabilitation centers, beyond "limited regulations necessary for the protection of health and safety," was a violation of the U.S. Constitution. For this reason The Salvation Army refused to accept the licensing power of the New York State Department of Social Services in 1978, and resisted the attempt by the Wisconsin State Department of Health and Social Services to require the Army to obtain a license for the Milwaukee Center as a "community-based residential facility," and that of the California Department of Social Services to license the Lytton Springs ARC as a "community care facility" in 1981.[28]

The Army's objections to voluntarily accepting accreditation from professional societies for its alcoholic program were simply practical; there was no constitutional principle at stake—although Mr. Moss consistently advised the Army to consider licensing and accrediting as having similar legal implications—but such requests were difficult to accommodate for several reasons. When the Joint Commission on Accreditation of Hospitals first made overtures to selected Army centers in 1976 there was no official reaction. The Denver Men's Social Service Center was accredited by JCAH in that year, and the Men's Social Service Commission expressed congratulations to the director and his staff. Upon mature reflection, however, such accreditation was rejected as official policy. The social secretaries noted that JCAH standards were heavily oriented toward medical and psychiatric treatment, unlike those of the Army; that few Army centers could meet the minimum JCAH requirement of no more than four persons to a room; and that the JCAH requirement that each facility be controlled by a local board of trustees was impossible for The Salvation Army. The Army's own professional resources were limited, and had to be invested where they would bring the best return for the men. The Army

had, for instance, dropped its affiliation with the National Conference on
Social Work in 1970 because the emphasis in the sessions had shifted from
topics of practical interest to the Army, which now preferred to attend the
conferences of the Protestant Health and Welfare Association. In April
1977, the Men's Social Service Secretaries' Commission recommended,
and in October the Commissioners' Conference ruled, that no men's social
service center might seek or accept JCAH accreditation. Instead each
center was to develop and enforce The Salvation Army's own standards,
based on the handbook.

The fact that the Army's own standards were creditable had wide appeal
among officers. Lt.-Colonel David Riley in the West secured the cooperation of the leading social officers in the territory to produce in 1980 a full-
fledged "internal accreditation" process for officers, assistants, trainees
and centers. "Certification" of personnel was based on the acquisition of a
number of "units," by attending conferences, taking college or correspondence courses, or reading material recommended by headquarters in the
area of pastoral skills, business administration or the rehabilitation program. Centers were "certified" on the basis of program, client and facility
management. Riley devised colorful foil accreditation certificates and promoted the plan in the West with enthusiasm. The Men's Social Service
Secretaries' Commission recommended the plan for all territories; the
commissioners at their September 1981 conference declared themselves
to be "very interested and impressed" by the internal accreditation proposal, but they declined to impose the program on all four territories: each
was free to adopt the same or a similar program at its own discretion. At
the end of 1981 all 26 center administrators in the Western Territory were
certified; the West remained the only territory to employ the new system.[29]

The Army's relationship with organized labor in the United States had
been amicable. In his book *In Darkest England*, General Booth called for
trade unions to be honored and protected. The Army abandoned its first
work therapy, the "Lifeboat Workshop" in San Francisco in the 1890s,
because its feeble production was regarded by local workingmen as a
threat to their livelihood. Unions often endorsed the Army's pioneer social
welfare activities. The labor radicalism of the 1930s left the Army un-
touched; the rare beneficiary who raised the question of working conditions was gently rebuffed with the reminder that he had come voluntarily
for help. Adjutant Ernest Hayes of Youngstown suggested in 1936 that his
fellow managers remind their clients, in words that anticipated the spirit of
Service to Man, that they participated in the "benefits of the center," not

because of the Army's needs but their own. There were occasional overtures made to center employees during the years of intense union activity
after World War II, but these were rare, and came during the very years
when officers were developing and implementing the place of work
therapy in the process of rehabilitation—an idea which precluded the
interference of a union. That argument, and The Salvation Army's traditional determination to maintain the independence of its self-contained
military structure and its place as a branch of the Christian Church,
naturally led the commissioners to conclude in 1947 that there was
"hardly any place for an organized labor union in Salvation Army service." In 1948 the Commissioners' Conference decided against an official
national policy opposing the organization of center employees into unions,
leaving each territorial headquarters free to deal with individual cases.

A dispute arose in Pittsburgh in 1949–1950, when a temporary decline in
paper prices caused the manager to raise the daily minimum poundage per
truck. At that time, drivers' salaries were tied to daily weight, and the
distinction between employee and beneficiary was not as clear as current
theory and later practice required. The drivers threatened to strike. The
drivers were reminded that the Army was not a business but a religion and
a charity, and, in the end, the conflict was resolved when a new manager
restored the lower weights. The practice of tying weekly salaries to production, which meant that drivers were not guaranteed in advance the
amount of their weekly pay, continued to cause difficulties. A strike was
threatened in Jersey City in 1960, and one lasting nine months actually
took place in Brooklyn in 1969. These cases passed without fundamental
change in the Army's position.

The Salvation Army operated centers in many highly industrialized
areas of the country, places where organized labor had won the right to
represent workers only after long and sometimes bitter and dangerous
struggles. It was inevitable that labor organizers, who were not well
informed about the Army's benevolent purposes, or who were indifferent
to them, should look upon its apparently businesslike operations as likely
prospects for organization. In September 1976, the Teamsters Union attempted to organize the drivers in the Waukegan, Illinois, Center. The
danger, as far as the manager, Major Vernon Jewett, an experienced and
deeply evangelistic officer, saw it was not so much that the Army's traditional position of independence was challenged, but that a victory for the
union would eliminate the possibility of using beneficiaries as truck helpers, a position that experience taught was one of the most successful as a

means of rehabilitation. In the end there were two disputed elections which the National Labor Relations Board decided in favor of The Salvation Army.

Major William Hasney, who had been department head only a month when the Waukegan case began, quickly formed a policy response: managers should inform Hasney at once if there was any attempt to organize the men in any center, so that he could inform the chief secretary and get an official territorial response. In the meantime, Hasney reminded the managers in a lengthy department order that "the best way to keep employees from looking into the prospects of unions is to treat them right in the first place." The Salvation Army was "not anti-union," he continued, but a union was not necessary: "We feel that our employees don't need a union to obtain the things that are really important to them." And, he added, there was always the possibility that a union would make demands that were so costly that the center would have to close and everybody would lose his job.

Occasional efforts to organize the Army's drivers in other territories have so far been resolved to the Army's satisfaction in Honolulu; Springfield, Mass.; the Bronx; Philadelphia and Youngstown. A major attempt at union organization in a Salvation Army center came in San Francisco in 1981. Local 85 of the Teamsters Union sought to organize not only the drivers but the dock workers and mechanics as well. The director of the local region of the National Labor Relations Board ordered an election for April 1982, but the Army appealed the decision in January to the National Labor Relations Board. The Army's argument had two parts: the first was that the board had so far not resolved the "substantial and difficult questions of a Constitutional dimension" concerning whether or not The Salvation Army, a branch of the Christian Church, was subject to the board's jurisdiction; the second part was one of policy: assuming the Army was subject to the board's jurisdiction, the nature of the Army's relationship to its employees, and especially the role they play in the rehabilitation of the clients, by teaching them good work habits, skills, self-respect and loyalty to the principles of the Army, was unique. The purposes of the National Labor Relations Act would not be served by regulating and perhaps destroying that unique relationship. When Major David Riley sent notice on this case to the other three men's social service secretaries, he pointed out how valuable the concept of "production assistant" had been in presenting the Army's case before the Labor Board; "drivers" was a term reserved only for employees who regularly drove the center dump truck; "production assistant" referred to those who developed and supervised routes, worked with beneficiaries and handled merchandise.[30]

The Army's financial arrangements with its beneficiaries were subjected by headquarters to careful scrutiny as well during these years, and underwent change. The fact that a few beneficiaries in many centers received pensions from outside sources had been known to officers for years, but the number of these had increased by 1961 to a point at which the men's social service secretaries officially alerted all managers and ordered a survey of centers to find out the number of men involved. The secretaries discussed among themselves the fact that it was not possible to apply the full treatment program to a man with an independent income: the small gratuity as a means of control and recognition, and the promise of graduation to employee status, would have little meaning to men who were already rich by the modest financial standards of the center's population. The social secretaries suggested that managers experiment with charging the pensioners a small sum for room and board instead of giving them a gratuity. In 1973 Major Howell introduced a sliding scale of room and board charges for beneficiaries with regular income from outside the program, based on either the charges for room and board made to live-in employees or 75 percent of the beneficiary's outside income, whichever would leave the man with more money. The commissioners noted that more than just pensions were involved; many beneficiaries were now on welfare and many others were eligible. Asking the men for a part of these payments would bring in welcome funds, which could be spent on improved program. And the precedent of accepting outside financial payments for beneficiaries had already been established: by June 1976, the men's social service secretaries estimated the 60–70 percent of centers nationwide had registered at local welfare offices to receive food stamps. After this "half-step" it would be easy to go on to accepting welfare payments directly from beneficiaries. In October 1976, the Commissioners' Conference recommended that every men's social service center apply for food stamps. Accepting the arguments that charging beneficiaries with income a fee for room and board would bring in money for the expansion of the rehabilitative program, would make even more distinct and obvious the difference between beneficiary and employee, and might reduce the number of men in the centers who were over 60 (a reduction that was desirable because old age was not a treatable handicap and because custodial care for the aged was not part of the Army's official purpose), the commissioners recommended in 1977 and directed in September 1981, that beneficiaries with outside income be charged for their subsistence on a sliding scale.[31]

Changes, at least in procedure, had always been a law of life for the Men's Social Service Department, which, despite its apparently hierarchical structure, was one of the most innovative branches of the Movement of which it had, by the start of the Army's second hundred years in America, become so prominent a part. It was as well that social officers were given a reminder of their origin and their unchanging mission, even as changes swirled about them. In 1975 an Arizona developer dismantled the blocks of London Bridge, which was replaced with a new bridge over the Thames, and brought the structure to Lake Havasu as a tourist attraction. Southwest Divisional Commander Lt.-Colonel David Moulton thoughtfuly arranged a little ceremony just for the Army, and affixed a plaque on the bridge reminding passersby that it had been on that very bridge in 1887 that William Booth had conceived the men's social service work.

The acceptance of women into the program of many centers, the use of new therapeutic tools and terminology, changing tax laws, and the necessity to update bibliographical references combined to require that the green handbook, which officers had come to regard, without irreverence, as the "Bible of the Department," be revised. Lt.-Colonel David Riley made a formal proposal to that effect in 1979, and offered to supervise the work on behalf of the Men's Social Service Commission, to which the Commissioners' Conference agreed. Riley gave the project to Captain Robert Bodine, a Western social officer with a doctorate in social work from the University of Southern California, the son and grandson of social officers. Bodine produced a working copy with the updated materials correlated with material from the 1960 handbook, arranged in the same numbered sections. This material was tentatively accepted by the Men's Social Service Commission and by the Commissioners' Conference in 1981, but there was some disagreement when the commissioners requested a side-by-side comparison of the 1960 material and the revisions. The commissioners then asked Lt.-Colonel Peter Hofman, long retired, to undertake the revisions under the supervision of Colonel Murray, the national chief secretary. Hofman, however, declined with modesty, feeling too far removed from the daily activities of a center; the task then passed to Elma Phillipson Cole, a professional social-work consultant employed in the family welfare office of Colonel Hofman's son, Major Peter Hofman.

The commissioners instructed Mrs. Cole to combine professional social work standards with a distinct reemphasis on traditional spiritual values. The new handbook, *The Salvation Army Adult Rehabilitation Services Manual of Philosophy, Principles and Policies,* retained the principles and arrangement, and even much of the wording of the 1960 edition, with new terminology, sections on women, therapeutic techniques, organizations and contemporary bibliographical references.[32]

Officers had to face at least the first five years of the Army's second century in the United States without a new handbook. The old one seemed to have served well enough: in 1982 the four territorial departments generated gross income of $150,000,000, and provided perhaps 70 percent of the total budget for the four territorial headquarters. The 114 different centers that year cared for 68,000 men, of whom 7,000 made a profession of religion for the first time: one-third of the total number of converts recorded in all Salvation Army activities for the year! The bed capacity of these centers—10,270—was as great as that in all the Army's extensive nationwide network of camping facilities, and far greater than in its other permanent residences, hospitals and day care centers combined. Overall figures convey little of the variety of kinds and rates of development within each of the four territories, but the large totals suggested the importance of this branch of the Movement as it passed into The Salvation Army's second century and approached the end of its own first hundred years.[33]

The Western Territory's Men's Social Service Department enjoyed the benefits of demography and innovative leadership alike. Because the leading managers in the West had recognized 30 years before that the future of the financial side of their work lay in store sales, they had been able to develop merchandising techniques and to place their stores in strategic new locations, in areas into which the population of Western cities was expanding. The result was that by 1982, with 26 centers, the West produced within a few dollars of the same income as that produced in the East, which had 40 centers. Total store sales in the West were actually larger than in the East—$41,000,000 to $35,000,000—and the average store sales per center almost twice as large. Often located in areas that are prosperous and growing in population, the Army's Adult Rehabilitation Centers in the West are among the most beautiful and well-equipped Army facilities in the world. Commissioner Richard E. Holz, the territorial commander, arranged that the first Salvation Army building to be opened in the United States during the Centennial Year would be the San Diego ARC, which he dedicated at 12:01 a.m. on January 1, 1980. Nine of the territory's 26 programs are in new buildings constructed to the Army's specifications, and in Pasadena, San Jose and Santa Ana three additional new facilities were built in 1984–1985. The emphasis on modern and efficient merchandising had become a territorial tradition; *The War Cry* noted in 1983 that the reports it most frequently received from the Western Territory were about store openings. The West also introduced the innovation of the "Certified Collection Center"—the manned trailer placed at a location convenient for donors to bring donations for a receipt; the idea was jointly conceived by Major Duplain in San Francisco and Major Allen in Oakland. By the end of 1981 there were 92 of these in use in the territory, and when headquarters appealed to the public for more trailers, the Safeway Corporation generously donated 100 trailers, doubling the territorial capacity.

The Western Territory has officially emphasized the "adherent's" program in the centers. Men who were converted or greatly aided in their own rehabilitation in a center often wished to be associated with it in some public, formal way—as "members." The Salvation Army's official regulations have never varied in their requirement that full membership in the Army—becoming a "soldier"—requires the acceptance of a lifestyle and a range of theological beliefs that are difficult for many persons to embrace; in particular, soldiers enrolled since 1975 are required to abstain from the use of tobacco in any form. The Army does, however, have a place for "adherents," which are officially defined as "persons of good standing and character who consider The Salvation Army as their place of worship by attendance and financial support." This status was not originally conceived in terms of men's social service centers, but Commissioner Holz enthusiastically embraced the idea, put to him by several social officers, that men who wished to become "members" of a center could do so as "adherents." These would be listed on the roll of the nearest corps, but would be free to attend the services at the center. This program was advanced quickly in the West, and with great and touching success. Center adherents were given their own distinctive uniforms of maroon blazer and dark-blue trousers, and became major influences for good within their centers. In the first year of the program, 1976, there were 125 adherents; by 1981, five years later, there were 620. Some of these were among the most cheerful and zealous official delegates to the Centennial Congress of the Western Territory, held in Pasadena in June 1983, an event marked for them, and for the history of the Army, by the first official Adherents' Breakfast, honored by the presence of the General of The Salvation Army,

Jarl Wahlström, and enlivened by the music of a group of adherent musicians from San Jose, the "Back Door Minority," led by the administrator, Brigadier Robert Yardley.[34]

The Central Territorial Men's Social Service Department had 25 centers in 1984, whose managers, simply to operate a program, had to contend with shifting populations, urban renewal and regional industrial depression largely unknown in the West and South. The territory had the largest men's social service center in the world, in Detroit, relocated in 1970. A new center was opened in Romulus, Michigan, in 1970. New buildings were erected in Gary, Indiana, in 1972; Waukegan, Illinois, in 1979 and Rockford, Illinois, in 1983. The remaining centers are much older: one dates from 1960, the majority from the 1950s and 1940s, one from 1930 and the oldest from 1929. In these buildings, officers pushed a program of production, merchandising and rehabilitation that from the mid-1970s on vindicated the best hopes of those who launched the "Salvation Army Social Campaign" in long-forgotten sheds and converted rooming houses. Between 1977 and 1981 store income increased from $15,000,000 to $21,000,000 with two fewer trucks and fewer employees. The number of "cases closed satisfactorily" increased from 2,296 to almost 6,000 (or, from 16½ percent of beneficiaries served to 48 percent of them!), and those professing a new interest in religion from 518 to 637. Spiritual retreats and sobriety awards marked these years, and as if to show that centers, like churches, can have spiritual children, Major Israel Velazquez of Chicago Central ARC and Colonel Andrew S. Miller, chief secretary, dedicated the young son of Mr. George Ward in the center's chapel in 1981, where 20 years before Mr. Ward himself had been converted, during the ministry of Major Benton.

Shortly after he came into office, Lt.-Colonel Hasney set up a "center review committee" to review the problems of centers having financial troubles; the members were Major Norman Nonnweiler, Major Leonard Caldwell and Captain Israel Velazquez. Their work had clearly been profitable to the department, but in 1982 the situation changed again: the collapse of the rag market and an economic decline in the spring of 1982 in some areas served by centers caused a lull in the encouraging financial progress of the Central Territory. Hasney sent official advice to his managers in the crisis that drew on 50 years of departmental history: the dropbox—a Central Territory innovation—had proved to be a mixed blessing; some centers relied too heavily upon it, and had allowed more aggressive forms of solicitation to languish. These must be revived, and all the old techniques of telephone and door-to-door solicitation be brought back into the service. Cultivate the housewife, clean up the stores, watch for valuable bric-a-brac, but always remember to put rehabilitation of the men first, and count forever on the faithful God![35]

The Southern Territory enjoyed many of the advantages of the West; the smallest department with 24 centers in 1984, the South's gross income was almost equal to that of the much larger Central Territory, and the South's average store income per center was second only to that of the prosperous West in 1982. The Southern Territorial Men's Social Service Department enjoyed the benefit of having an exceptionally large number of its center programs in buildings constructed for that purpose: 19 centers out of 24, the highest number of any territory in 1984. The Northern Virginia center, in Alexandria, was dedicated on January 29, 1984—and to prove that the muse of the "Golden Jubilee" march has not departed from men's social circles, Salvationist composer Stephen Bulla wrote a march for the dedication called, appropriately enough, "NOVARC"—for "Northern Virginia Adult Rehabilitation Center." The South, like the West, regaled *The War Cry* in the early 1980s with stories of the territorial "Thrift Store Boom."

The Men's Social Service Department in the South had the challenge of relating its center program to that of many small "Corps Salvage and Rehabilitation Centers"—CSRCs, which were more numerous in the South than in all the other territories combined: of the 51 CSRCs in the four territories in 1982, 29 were in the South. These programs were individually tiny; all the CSRCs in the country had a total bed capacity of only 344, but for all their small size, the CSRCs generated confusion in the mind of the public, who naturally mistook them for miniature men's social service centers. And this confusion might not be confined to the general public: government officials might be unable, or unwilling, to make any distinction between the two programs. Legally any Salvation Army rehabilitation program was as entitled to full protection against the enforcement of the Fair Labor Standards Act and licensing laws as any other, and also as liable to legal attack. Many small CSRCs could not support an efficient or useful rehabilitation program. For this reason, as early as 1959, the department in the Southern Territory had arranged for the closing of all corps salvage programs with fewer than three clients, or any corps program where beneficiaries were not given room and board, since these programs could not possibly qualify as serious efforts to rehabilitate needy men. In May 1980, the Commissioners' Conference required all CSRC programs to strictly adhere to the same standards and the same program as the adult rehabilitation centers. In November 1980, the territorial commander stated that the men's social *Handbook of Standards, Principles and Policies* was the "official document" upon which all corps beneficiary programs were to be based. At the same time the men's social service department, with the full cooperation of territorial leadership, laid plans to draw the larger CSRCs into the department one by one as each reached the minimum volume of business capable of supporting a regulation ARC program. In 1984, Lt.-Colonel David Mulbarger estimated this to be $750,000 annually. By that year the department had started the process for taking over the large corps salvage program in Norfolk, and those in Baton Rouge and Sarasota were next in order for adoption.[36]

Men's social work in the United States began in the East, whether the food and shelter depot in 1891 or the first salvage brigade in 1897 was taken as the beginning of the work. The Eastern Territory was still by far the largest of the four, with 40 centers and the largest annual income. The total income in 1981, however, was only a few dollars more than that of the smaller West, and total Eastern store income was smaller—only 85 percent as much: long reliance on the vagaries of the rag and paper market, and the difficulty of finding suitable store locations, had taken their toll. The center programs are housed in buildings that include the oldest men's social building in America and one of the newest, opened in Saugus, near Boston in late 1984. Of the 40 centers in the territory in 1984, only six were built for the particular use of The Salvation Army. Among the six was the Columbus housing unit, built in 1976. The remaining five were the oldest men's social centers in the United States: the Manhattan Adult Rehabilitation Center, the venerable "New York No. 1 Industrial Home," built for the Army in 1906 and opened by Evangeline Booth in 1907; Toledo, built in 1907 for the Army; Jersey City, built in 1910 and moved in 1926/27 to make way for the Holland Tunnel; and Newark, the "closing signature" on all the beautiful industrial homes built in the 1920s, opened in 1929 with three brass bands giving accompaniment to the words, "Oh, that we had in the wilderness a lodging place for wayfaring men."

To carry on any legitimate activity in these locations, let alone to operate a profitable salvage and retail business on one hand and to rehabilitate the lives of ruined men on other, required strength and grace that seemed to defy any merely human explanation. For, incredible as it might have seemed to the "disinterested, perhaps unsympathetic stranger," these old buildings, long since deprived of even the stylish utility they formerly possessed, now chipped, patched, smeared with graffiti, still held open their doors over the blasted wastelands that were once the respectable neighborhoods that surrounded them, and their officers still extended the hand of fellowship and hope to men from whom, were this last door closed, all fellowship, all hope would be finally lost.

It would be difficult to review the statistical records of these centers, meet the officers and men, read the accounts of men whose lives were redeemed, often at nearly the last moment when even a miracle could have worked, without coming to the conclusion that if it had done nothing else in all the world that was good or worthwhile, what happened in these antique institutions in the early 1980s would have justified not just the existence of The Salvation Army, but its reputation and its undying glory.

From 1980 to 1982 Major Arthur Ferreira improved the ratio of satisfactory cases to admissions from one-in-five to one-in-two, and saw the number of religious "seekers" increase from two to 69. The Newark center, managed from 1971 to 1984 by Major William Stephens, might well have qualified by the early 1980s as the single most difficult appointment in any of the four territories. It was a battlefield. Yet from that center, the famous Newark Center Singers came in 1983 to "Men's Social Night" at the Centennial Memorial Temple in New York, and the Newark Bell Ringers, led by Herbert Foote, as well. Men in the Newark center faithfully "adopted" needy orphans on the Salvation Army mission field and supported them out of their own gratuities.

At Manhattan during the years 1980–1982, while admissions declined by 27 percent, the percentage of satisfactory cases during Major Harold Borror's last two years as manager increased from 13 percent to 90 percent. And Manhattan earned one more in a long list of distinctions in 1983: one of the center drivers, Mr. Harold Ferris Jr., completed 31 years without an accident—the best driving record of any Salvation Army driver in the history of the department. Mr. Ferris was an honest man, too. In 1984 he picked up a donated crib from a home and soon discovered that it contained an envelope containing $7,500 in cash, which he promptly returned to the grieving owners, who were dumbfounded at his action.

The overall figures for the territory at large reflect both the difficulties and the triumphs of men's social work in the urban Northeast in the early 1980s: admissions declined by 11 percent from 1980 to 1982, but the percentage of satisfactory cases rose encouragingly, from 55 percent to 70 percent, the total number of religious, therapeutic and counseling encounters between staff and clients greatly increased, and there was a 25 percent increase in "seekers."[37]

Equally encouraging was the development of the role of woman officer, which had proceeded farther in the Eastern Territory by the mid-1980s than in the other territories.

The official recognition of the place of the woman officer in the program of the center was due in large part to the influence of Mrs. Lt.-Colonel Raymond Howell, who was formally appointed Director of Women's Services, Men's Social Service Department, in May 1979—the first such position in any of the four territories. The largest part of Mrs. Howell's work has been in cooperative efforts with managers' wives to encourage them to accept and expand upon the role which Salvation Army tradition already gave to managers' wives—oversight of food services, decoration and appointments in the men's living areas, parties and entertainment for the men. In June 1984, wives of center administrators in the Eastern Territory were officially given the title "Director of Special Services," an honorific title which, like Mrs. Howell's was historic and unique to the territory.

In addition, women officers in the men's social service department were increasingly encouraged to assume the place which Army principle gave to them: complete equality with men of the same rank and ability. Again, this tendency was carried farther in the Eastern Territory than in the other three by 1985. Three women served as full administrators in that territory in the early 1980s: Major Mrs. Annie Kirby in Cincinnati and Major Mrs. Margaret Michaels in Dayton, both of whom carried on center programs after their husbands died on active duty as managers. In 1983 Major Mrs. Kirby took command of the Mount Vernon ARC, and the next year Major Marian Harttree was appointed as administrator of the Wilkes-Barre ARC. The development of Women's Auxiliaries for the Army's adult rehabilitation centers, made up of sympathetic community women, had also proceeded further in the East than in other territories. It was significant that when the General of The Salvation Army asked the wife of the national commander, Mrs. Commissioner Norman S. Marshall, to prepare a paper on the "Place of the Woman Officer" for an important meeting of Army leaders in May 1984, Mrs. Marshall officially solicited the opinion of every woman officer in the Eastern Territorial Men's Social Services Department. The trend began in the Southern Territory as well: in February 1984, Major Mrs. Lynette McConniel was placed in charge of the Memphis ARC.[38]

A thorough survey of The Salvation Army Men's Social Service Department in the mid-1980s would have revealed 115 different results. There was perhaps more diversity between units of operation in this branch of Salvation Army work than in any other. There was also remarkable continuity. Men and women responding to the same kinds of problems and experiencing the same kinds of success over many years had produced, if not typical responses, at least statistically predictable ones.

The mid-1980s were troubled times for men's social service officers. Within the structure of the Army itself, the relationship of the center's financial operation to similar kinds of corps and divisional activities, despite a steady stream of clarifying directives dating back to Victorian times, remained confused. The Army's 16 Harbor Light centers, for instance, with about one-fifth the total bed capacity of the 115 ARC's, actually provided for more clients per year because of rapid turnover. The public, even the professional public, could hardly be blamed for misunderstanding the distinction between two programs that were apparently similar, but which in fact not only did not officially overlap but which raised their support from different sources. The men's social service programs were hurt financially by the proliferation of flea markets and yard sales starting in the late 1970s; officers' opinions differ, but many felt that certain kinds of desirable items that once drew middle-class shoppers to the Army's stores were now reaching them more directly on their neighbors' lawns.

Officers were challenged by the fact that the general characteristics of the clientele in the Army program had changed in the 20 years following the turmoil and war of the 1960s. Beneficiaries tended to be younger men, less amenable to scheduling and regimentation, more prone to violence, and with fewer working skills. Many senior managers in the 1980s lamented the gradual disappearance of the client who could refinish, repair appliances, or upholster, so that his rehabilitation would combine both means and goal: using his once-valuable skill to slowly build himself back to the place where he could again use that skill in honorable self-support. Such men had always been in the minority; but in the 1980s they were all but gone.

The newer client was also much more likely to be doubly addicted, both to alcohol and drugs, making his treatment much more difficult. In some centers racial or ethnic tensions smoldered ominously. The fact that the percentage of men helped in important ways did not decline during these years is a tribute to God's grace and the development of new skills by Army personnel. In fact, the percentage of men who were "rehabilitated," or "helped in some major way," depending upon who defined the improvement and who made the estimate, seemed to have remained at roughly 20–25 percent for many years; the percentage of men who were converted and became faithful and constant in their new religion was always much smaller.

There were difficulties in maintaining desirable ratios between beneficiaries and employees. Between 1957 and 1981 the number of centers with three or more beneficiaries to one employee fell from 37 to 13, those with at least two or more beneficiaries to every employee (the essential ratio according to legal counsel) fell from 71 to 48 during the same period. In 1981 there were 64 centers with fewer than two beneficiaries to one employee, compared to 30 in 1957. The reasons for these changing ratios were two, only one of which, happily, gave cause for concern: the steady decline in admissions of men with shop skills required that more men with needed abilities had to be hired as employees in order to carry on production. An increase in "as-is" sales in stores did not entirely eliminate the need for skilled men. The second cause for the shrinking beneficiary/employee ratios was a great increase in the hiring of professional therapeutic staff. In 1957 no center had one rehabilitation employee to every five beneficiaries (even when officers were included); in 1981 there were 20 of them, and another 39 with one rehabilitation employee to 10 beneficiaries; there had been none in 1957 and only 19 in 1980. The costs of these professional additions practically eliminated the center surpluses: in 1981 only six centers out of 114 recorded income surpluses after donations-in-kind was deducted.

There were compensations, even for declining ratios, and for much more than that—compensations which continued to draw officers and staff into men's social services and to hold them there for years, decades, lifetimes of service, sometimes over generations. Brigadier Raymond Raines managed the Bronx Center—the old "New York No. 2"—during six difficult years from 1964 to 1970; yet when his son Timothy became an officer, he chose to offer himself for men's social services. Raines could not have been ignorant of the years of physical and emotional exhaustion that lay before him and his wife. He, like every other men's social service officer, also knew that for the men who come to The Salvation Army for help there is no other place to go, no other door, no other hope: the Army is a kind of net at the bottom of the social order; it catches men who fall through all the other cracks and spaces, and below that net there is—nothing. And to one who takes the plain teaching of Christ seriously, every one of these broken, hopeless men is as worthy of the love of man, and as much the recipient of the unearnable love of God, as the most radiant saint. There was a new pride among officers and staff in the department in the 1980s: no longer did officers in the other branches of the Army look down upon the men's social as a convenient refuge for the officer who could not face the rigors of a corps. The November 14, 1981, issue of *The War Cry* was the first national issue devoted exclusively to the men's social service department. As Major Clarence Kinnett, a leading divisional officer, declared in 1979, the "red shield stands in a place of honor," and this was true not just to comrade officers but to the professional community at large. In 1964, Brigadier Richard E. Baggs had been the Army's official delegate to the International Conference on Social Work. Many factors helped to raise the morale of the men's social service program: the self-accrediting program in the West; a growing number of officers who completed graduate studies; the respect accorded to the Army's professional consultants like John Judge in Chicago, or Raymond Selke, who became program consultant to the Eastern department in 1976, and in 1982 was elected to the Board of Directors of the National Commission of Credentialing of Alcoholism and Drug Abuse Counselors.

Compensations, in fact, abounded. The Men's Social Service Advisory Council, a special subcommittee of the local advisory board, brought wide community and professional support to the administrator, who no longer felt isolated from the community leadership simply because his center required no financial support beyond the donation of materials. Social officers enjoyed the experience, as challenging as it was encouraging, of explaining the Good News of the Christian faith to sizable audiences of grown men, while many field officers addressed but a handful on Sunday mornings.

The men, of course, were the best consolation of all, and, in the end, the only ones that mattered. In men's social officers' councils in every territory in the late 1970s the officers were asked, hypothetically, how they would react if legal restrictions forced The Salvation Army to abandon rehabilitation in the centers; the great majority declared that they would resign if the Army tried to find some merely commercial alternative to the beneficiary program. When a number of retired officers from every territory were asked in connection with the preparation of the present volume to relate the worst and the best thing about having served as social officers, they readily produced a colorful and sometimes surprising catalogue of complaints, but, in the course of speaking of these things, all but one or two of the veterans slowed, stopped, and began to say what had been the best thing, what had made the poverty, the disappointments, the insults, suspicion, rebuffs all worthwhile—helping the men. Every officer had a favorite story, a recollection of one man, or two, or a dozen, whose lives had not ended in the pitiful and anonymous ruin to which they had been inevitably descending until that special day in 1932 or 1948 or 1984 when they had seen at last the Light they had been so often shown before.

It was the same spirit that animated administrators in the 1980s to take a hand in the uniquely valuable work of The Salvation Army in providing a refuge and a hope for men abandoned by every other source of love and help, and often spurned even by other social agencies as beyond redemption. General Booth had given these officers their mandate in 1904, when he wrote that The Salvation Army existed to tell the worst drunkard in the world that there was hope for him "when every other light is extinguished, and every other star has gone down."

It would have been impossible to find in all this roll call of "trophies of grace" one that was most representative, most telling, or more worthy of note than any of the others, and unfair to attempt such a selection: Tom Lucas, the corps sergeant-major at the New York Temple; Dale Wolski, supervisor in the Indianapolis Adult Rehabilitation Center; Captain Romolo Giudice, saved in Chicago and now a men's social service officer in the West; Captain Jim Lane in charge of the Key West Corps, who dropped into an ARC for clean clothes on his way to commit suicide—and unnumbered others, some known by full name, many others by only a first name, nickname, or just initials—all trace of most of them lost altogether in the hurried and irregular recording that was typical of the department for half of its history.

By 1969 Frank Dyer had been arrested more times for drunkenness in Miami than anyone else in the court's history. In January 1970, the judge, believing him beyond help, kindly sent him to The Salvation Army instead of to another useless jail term. Major David Mulbarger was kind, too, and told Dyer that everything he had ever tried in his life had obviously failed him, but God was almighty, and He would help, if Dyer would let Him. Dyer was wholeheartedly converted, enrolled as a soldier in The Salvation Army in the Miami Corps in 1971, and spent the rest of his happy life as a counselor and supervisor in the Army's Miami and Houston centers.

In June 1984, the Eastern Territory held a great congress, one of those exuberant, overcrowded happy affairs, punctuated by brass bands, slide shows, stirring addresses, parades and altar services so uniquely appealing to Salvationists. One of the large public sessions, on Saturday, June 9, was called "A Celebration of Hope," and as part of that, all too appropriately, the "Center Singers," made up of men from many different adult rehabilitation centers in the East, sang twice; their first song was "O Happy Day, When Jesus Took My Sins Away," and the second was "Since Jesus Came into My Heart." When they had finished there was a thunderous, heartfelt applause, an avalanche of hallelujahs and cheers that were as much for the men as for their performance—an affirmation from every cheering, flag-waving Salvationist in the great auditorium that the Center Singers and all the men like them in all the centers in the territory, and in the country, were somebody's brothers after all.[39]

> Somebody's Brother! O who then will dare
> To throw out the lifeline, his peril to share?

Notes

Abbreviations

Acc.	Accession number
ARC	Adult Rehabilitation Center
AW	*All the World* (SA periodical, London)
Busby Coll.	Private collection, Major John Busby, Atlanta, Georgia
C	Central Territory, Territorial
Comm. Conf.	Commissioners' Conference
Conq	*The Conqueror* (SA periodical, New York, 1892–1897)
CS	Chief Secretary
DE	William Booth, *In Darkest England and The Way Out* (book, 1890)
Dispo	*The Salvation Army Disposition of Forces*
E	Eastern Territory, Territorial
FD	Field Department, Field Secretary, Field Secretary for Personnel
FLSA	Fair Labor Standards Act
Handbook	*Handbook of Standards, Principles and Policies,* SAMSS (book, 1961)
HL	*Harbor Lights* (SA periodical, New York, 1898–1900)
IH	Industrial Home
IHQ	International Headquarters
JSA	*Journal of Studies on Alcohol*
LCM	Private Collection, Laurence Castagna material, Columbus, Ohio
MSS	Men's Social Service(s)
MSSC	Men's Social Service Center
MSSD	Men's Social Service Department
MSSS	Men's Social Service Secretary
"Minutes SDOC 1923"	"Minutes, Social District Officers' Councils, Washington, D.C., February 7–10, 1923"
NCSW	National Conference on Social Work
NHQ	National Headquarters
"NOM,"	"News of the Moment," MSSDE newsletter
NYC	New York City
QJSA	*Quarterly Journal of Studies on Alcohol*
RG	Record Group
RHC	Private collection, Richard E. Holz Collection, Neptune, NJ

S	Southern Territory, Territorial
SA	The Salvation Army
SAA	Salvation Army Archives & Research Center, New York City
SDEB	Social Department of the East, Brief
SDOC	Social District Officers' Councils
Seiler Coll.	Private collection, Col. Paul Seiler Collection, Ocean Grove, NJ
SFOT	Salvation Army School for Officers' Training
SN	*Social News* (SA periodical, 1911–1922; Aug. 1917–Sept. 1919 called *War Service Herald*)
"SSS"	"Social Service Shiftings," MSSDE newsletter
THQ	Territorial Headquarters
W	Western Territory, Territorial
WC	*The War Cry,* National edition (1881–1921; 1970–present)
WCC	*The War Cry,* Central Territorial edition (1921–1970)
WCE	*The War Cry,* Eastern Territorial edition (1921–1970)
WCS	*The War Cry,* Southern Territorial edition (1927–1970)
WCW	*The War Cry,* Pacific Coast Edition (1883–1921), Western Territorial edition (1921–1970)
WSH	*War Service Herald* (SA periodical, 1917–1919)

CHAPTER I

1. Commissioner Ballington Booth, *From Ocean to Ocean, Or, The Salvation Army's March from the Atlantic to the Pacific* (New York: J. S. Ogilvie, Publisher, 1891), written in flyleaf by Ballington, in copy in Circle "M" Collection, Houston Public Library.

2. *WC* [Philadelphia], Aug. 6, 1881, p. 1; *WC* Feb. 11, 1882, p. 3; March 8, 1883, p. 1; May 3, 1883, p. 1; Aug. 2, 1883, p. 1; Aug. 21, 1884, p. 4.

3. *WC,* Nov. 30, 1882, p. 1.

4. Commissioner Frank Smith, *The Salvation War in America for 1885* (New York: Headquarters and Trade Department [1886]), 77–104; [George S. Railton], *Twenty-One Years Salvation Army* (London: Salvation Army Book Depot, 1889), 140–142; Parker quoted in Edwin D. Solenberger, *The Social Relief Work of The Salvation Army* (Minneapolis: Byron & Willard Co., 1906), pp. 27–28; *WC,* July 17, 1886, p. 3.

5. *WC,* July 24, 1884, p. 3; April 11, 1885, p. 1; October 2, 1886, p. 1; October 9, 1886, p. 1; Smith, *Salvation War,* 126–127.

6. *WC,* Dec. 25, 1886, p. 4.

7. *WC,* May 28, 1887, p. 13; Dec. 17, 1887, p. 2; March 31, 1888, p. 4; Feb. 15, 1890, p. 7; March 29, 1890, pp. 5 and 15; July 5, 1890, p. 10; July 26, 1890, p. 10. The Auxiliary League was originally formed in 1884; see *WC,* Aug. 20, 1887, p. 9, for account of its revival.

8. *WC,* March 31, 1888, p. 11.

9. [Major] Jenty Fairbank, *Booth's Boots: The Beginnings of Salvation Army Social Work* (London: SA, 1983), pp. 6–9, 84–87; Bramwell Booth, *Echoes and Memories* (London: Hodder and Stoughton, 1925), pp. 1–2; Catherine Bramwell-Booth, *Bramwell Booth* (New York: Sears Publishing Company, [1932]), pp. 283–284; St. John Ervine, *God's Soldier: General William Booth* (2 vols.; New York: The MacMillan Company, 1935) II, pp. 674–75.

10. General William Booth, *In Darkest England and The Way Out* (London: SA, 1890), preface; pp. 15, 19–20, 24, 62–63, 83, 85–87, 88, 92–155, 258.
11. *WC,* Nov. 15, 1890, p. 5, 7, 8; Nov. 22, 1890, pp. 2–3; *WCW,* Nov. 22, 1890, p. 3; Nov. 29, 1890, pp. 1–3.
12. *WC,* Nov. 29, 1890, p. 16; Dec. 6, 1890, pp. 2–3, 8; Dec. 13, 1890, p. 9; Dec. 20, 1890, p. 1, 18; Jan. 3, 1891, p. 11; Jan. 10, 1891, p. 14; Jan. 24, 1891, p. 8; Jan. 31, 1891, p. 4, 8; *WCW,* March 7, 1891, pp. 1–2; Wm. Evans to Major [R.E.] Holz, New York City, April 16, 1891, SAA: Acc. 82-75; *WC,* Sept. 12, 1891, pp. 1–3; *Conq,* Feb. 1892, p. 10; *WCW,* Jan. 3, 1891, p. 4.
13. Colonel Edward J. Parker, "The Men's Social Service Work of The Salvation Army," *WCE,* Oct. 1, 1927, p. 7; *The Salvation Army Diamond Jubilee: An Historical Interpretation of its Social Service Program* (New York: The Office of the Territorial Commander, [1940]), p. 16; Colonel Fletcher Agnew, "A Thriller of the Nineties," *WCE,* June 1, 1940, p. 3, 14; Major A. E. Agnew, *The Nineteen Hundred Forty-Four Institutes of the Men's Social Service Department* (New York: SAE [1946]), pp. 10–17; James Leiby, *A History of Social Welfare and Social Work in the United States* (New York: Columbia University Press, 1978), pp. 78–79; *WC,* March 1, 1890, pp. 1–3; March 29, 1890, pp. 1–2; Fairbank's, *Booths's Boots,* p. 131; Brigadier E. J. Parker, "Social Service in the United States," *AW,* June 1905, pp. 295–296.
14. *WC,* June 8, 1889, pp. 1–2; May 3, 1890, p. 4; Adj. W. W. Winchell, "Thanksgiving Day," *WC,* Nov. 28, 1891, p. 9; Commissioner & Mrs. Ballington Booth, *New York's Inferno Explored* (New York: SA, 1891), pp. 12 and 15.
15. Lyman Abbott, *Christianity and Social Problems* (Boston: Houghton, Mifflin and Company, 1896), p. 112, n. 1; *WC,* June 4, 1892, p. 9; Booth, *N.Y. Inferno,* vii–viii, pp. 19–30.
16. "Our New York Lighthouse," *Conq.,* February 1892, pp. 11–12; *WC,* Jan. 9, 1892, p. 8, 14; Jan. 16, 1892, pp. 7, 9; Jan. 23, 1892, pp. 3, 11; Jan. 30, 1892, p. 10; Feb. 6, 1892, pp. 1, 4–5, 8, 13; Feb. 13, 1892, p. 13; March 5, 1892, p. 2; March 28, 1892, pp. 3, 15; April 2, 1892, p. 6; April 16, 1892, p. 3; May 14, 1892, p. 4; Oct. 15, 1892, p. 2 (parade); see also Dec. 19, 1891, p. 14; Feb. 8, 1896, p. 10; *WCW,* Feb. 20, 1892, p. 6; see *Conq.,* April 1892, p. 73; *Dispo* NHQ, Nov. 1891, p. 4.
17. *WC,* Feb. 6, 1892, pp. 4–5; Feb. 27, 1892, p. 14; *WCW,* March 12, 1892, p. 8 (wood prices); *WC,* April 9, 1892, p. 2; May 21, 1892, p. 14 (statistics); Dec. 3, 1892, p. 5. Statistics in *WC* accounts varied widely in reliability; an account in May 12, 1892, p. 14, gave 5,998 occupants over 99 days, which would have been absurd; in Oct. 8, 1892, p. 3, the record for eight months gave 10,225 beds used January through August, inclusive, or 46 average per night, which was more reasonable; Ballington gave figures for 29 days that revealed an average occupancy of 32 (*WC,* Feb. 6, 1892, p. 13). All total figures were duplicated counts.
18. *WC,* Feb. 27, 1892, p. 14; March 28, 1892, p. 3; Jan. 7, 1893, p. 1; Jan. 28, 1893, p. 4; *Dispo* NHQ, Dec. 1892, p. 5; *Dispo* NHQ, Jan. 1893, p. 5.
19. *WC,* June 11, 1892, p. 7; Jan. 28, 1893, p. 10; Feb. 25, 1893, pp. 1, 4–5; *Dispo* NHQ, Feb. 1892, p. 4; SFOT, E, Mus. has several tickets made up by the Army to be sold to citizens to give to beggars; see Mus. items nos. 43, 44, 47.
20. *WC,* Dec. 10, 1892, pp. 8–9, 12.
21. *WCW,* Aug. 9, 1890, pp. 1, 4; Nov. 1, 1890, p. 2; March 21, 1891, pp. 2–3; April 11, 1891, p. 2; June 27, 1891, pp. 1–2; July 4, 1891, pp. 1, 4–5, 6; Sept. 26, 1891, pp. 1–2; Oct. 31, 1891, p. 4; Dec. 26, 1891, pp. 1–3; Jan. 2, 1892, p. 5; Feb. 6, 1892, p. 6; Feb. 20, 1892, p. 6; Feb. 27, 1892, p. 5; March 5, 1892, p. 8 ("plans"); Oct. 1, 1892, pp. 1–2; Dec. 2, 1892, p. 6 (see also Nov. 5, 1892, pp. 1–2); Dec. 10,

1892, p. 6; see also *WCW,* Dec. 25, 1891, pp. 12–14 and *WC,* Feb. 27, 1897, p. 5, on McFee; Captain [William] Day, "San Francisco," *Conq.,* October 1893, pp. 376, 377–78.

22. *WCW,* Jan. 7, 1893, pp. 1–4, 6, 9; Jan. 14, 1893, p. 6; *WC,* Feb. 11, 1893, p. 10, March 18, 1893, p. 11; *Dispo* NHQ, Feb. 1894, p. 5 (earliest listing San Francisco Food and Shelter Work); Career sheet, McFee, Joseph R., SAA.

23. *WCW,* Oct. 31, 1892, p. 5; Feb. 4 1893, pp. 1–3, 6–7.

24. *WCW,* Dec. 10, 1892, p. 10; Jan. 21, 1893, pp. 1–2, 6; Feb. 4, 1893, p. 6; March 4, 1893, pp. 1–2, 4, 7; April 22, 1893, p. 6; May 6, 1893, p. 6; May 13, 1893, pp. 2–3.

25. *WCW,* Jan. 21, 1893, p. 6; Mar. 11, 1893, p. 3; April 22, 1893, p. 6; Oct. 14, 1893, p. 6; Oct. 21, 1893, pp. 1–3, 6; Nov. 11, 1893, p. 6; Captain [Joseph] McFee, "The San Francisco Lifeboat," *Conq.,* Jan. 1894, pp. 32–34; see also "Editor's Field-Glass" section, *Conq.,* Jan. 1894, p. 44. McFee employed the staff of the "Lifeboat" during the slack summer months as the "Lifeboat cruisers." In May 1893, he rented a steam launch, the *Little Nell,* and cruised the Bay in her until late June, holding shipboard and dockside services. *Little Nell* was not entirely ship-shape, and McFee resolved to purchase a vessel for the Army's use. He soon located the gasoline launch *Theodora,* sadly fallen since her days as Captain's gig in Commodore David Farragut's ship *Hartford,* which he commanded in the Battle of Mobile Bay in 1864. McFee bought the launch for $75, refitted her, and launched her at Fisherman's Wharf on August 3, 1893. The "Lifeboat Cruisers" took her out often, holding services alongside merchant ships in port, meeting the famous "Charioteers" at river towns for joint services, and taking overjoyed children on cruises up the Sacramento River. The *Theodora* was apparently used again in the late summer or early fall of 1894. One of the Lifeboat "crew" was a Japanese convert, "Japanese Arthur," who served as cook at the sandlot soup kitchen while the "Lifeboat Cruisers" were out upon the waters. The Army had great hopes of spreading its evangelistic ministry widely among California's Japanese population, and gave "Japanese Arthur" and other Japanese converts considerable publicity. On the two vessels of the "Salvation Navy," see *WCW,* May 13, 1893, p. 6; June 3, 1893, p. 6; June 10, 1893, pp. 6, 7–8; June 17, 1893, pp. 4–5; July 1, 1893, p. 3; July 8, 1893, p. 6; Aug. 12, 1893, p. 6; Aug. 19, 1893, pp. 1–2; Aug. 26, 1893, pp. 6–7; Sept. 23, 1893, pp. 2–3; Oct. 7, 1893, pp. 2–3, 6; Nov. 11, 1893, pp. 1–2; Captain [Joseph] McFee, "The Army Cruiser 'Theodora' and her First Trip," *Conq.,* Dec. 1893, p. 468; also see *Conq,* Jan. 1895, p. 51. On the Japanese converts, see *WCW,* March 14, 1891, p. 4; June 20, 1891, p. 6; April 16, 1892, p. 6; Dec. 23, 1893, pp. 3–4; Nov. 24, 1894, p. 7.

26. *WCW,* March 24, 1894, pp. 9–10; Oct. 20, 1894, pp. 1–2; Dec. 8, 1894, pp. 8–9; Captain J. McFee, "The New California Food and Shelter Depot," *Conq,* Nov. 1894, p. 435; Captain [Joseph] McFee, "The San Francisco Lifeboat," *Conq,* Jan. 1895, pp. 28–29.

27. *Conq.,* March 1894, p. 124; Dec. 1894, p. 488; Staff-Captain [John] Milsaps, "Pacific Coast Progress," *Conq.,* Sept. 1894, pp. 348–51; Staff-Captain Blanche M. Cox, "From the Far Pacific Shore," *Conq.,* Nov. 1894, pp. 432–33; *WCW,* May 5, 1894, p. 8; Aug. 11, 1894, p. 3; Nov. 3, 1894, p. 12; *Dispo* NHQ, Feb. 1894, p. 5; Dec. 1894, p. 5.

28. Ensign Clifford Brindley, "Commissioner Richard E. Holz," *WCE,* June 22, 1929, p. 11; *WC,* March 5, 1892, p. 8; Dec. 24, 1892, p. 7; Jan. 21, 1893, p. 9; Jan. 28, 1893, p. 5 ("third"); May 27, 1893, p. 5; June 10, 1893, p. 11; Jan. 25, 1896, p. 4;

Feb. 8, 1896, p. 15 (photos); May 9, 1896, p. 15 (photos); *Conq.*, Feb. 1894, p. 83 (photos); "Our Buffalo Shelter," *Conq.*, June 1894, p. 217; "The Salvation Army Ark, Buffalo," *Conq.*, Feb. 1896, p. 81.

29. "The General's Journeys in North America," *Conq.*, April 1895, pp. 153–156, 158, 162–3; Cadet Downey, "The Army Soup Depot at Portland, Ore.," *Conq.*, June 1894, p. 236; *Conq.*, May 1894, p. 200; *Dispo* NHQ, Feb. 1894, p. 5; May 1895, p. 3; *WC*, Jan. 28, 1893, p. 5; Feb. 4, 1893, p. 2; William J. Brewer, *Lifting The Veil; Or, Acts of the Salvationists* (Boston, Frank Wood, Printer, [1895]), pp. 50, 52–53; "Our Foreign Field: United States of America," *The Officer*, Sept. 1895, p. 265.

30. *WC*, Mar. 7, 1896, pp. 8–9 (the first official notice of Ballington's troubles); Mar. 21, 1896, p. 9; May 2, 1896 (supplement), p. 2 (text of Ballington's letter of Jan. 31 to the General); Commander Ballington Booth, "The Salvation Army and the Municipality," *Conq.*, Dec. 1894, p. 456; Ballington Booth, open letter to readers, *Conq.*, March 1894, p. 102; *WC*, Feb. 1, 1896, p. 9.

CHAPTER II

1. *WC*, March 28, 1896, pp. 8–9, 16; April 11, 1896, pp. 4–5, 8; April 18, 1896, pp. 1, 4; April 25, 1896, pp. 1–4, 5, 8; May 2, 1896, p. 4; May 23, 1896, pp. 1–2, 10 ("social" issue); Harry Williams, *Booth-Tucker: William Booth's First Gentleman* (London: Hodder and Stoughton, 1980), pp. 146–158; F. A. MacKenzie, *Booth-Tucker: Sadhu and Saint* (London: Hodder and Stoughton, 1930), pp. 153–163, 164–179; *Conq.*, May 1896, p. 229 (letter from Booth-Tucker to auxiliaries); Brig. E. J. Parker, "Social Service in the United States," *AW*, June 1905, p. 196; the New York Lighthouse closed because of financial difficulties: see *WC*, Feb. 25, 1893, pp. 1, 4–5; *Dispo* NHQ, April 1894, p. 5 (New York depot no longer listed); *Dispo* NHQ, Oct. 1896, p. 3 (New York reappears); *WC*, Nov. 21, 1896, p. 12 (*Orders and Regs.* in verse) and occasionally thereafter; *WC*, July 24, 1897, p. 13 ("Dear Old Flag" song).

2. *WCW*, April 1, 1889, pp. 1–2; *WC*, July 11, 1896, p. 12; Aug. 15, 1896, p. 8; Dec. 12, 1896, p. 8; Officer's career sheet, Halpin, William, SAA; *Dispo* NHQ, July 1896, p. 2; Aug. 1896, pp. 2–3; Sept. 1896, pp. 2–3.

3. *WC*, July 11, 1896, p. 9; *Conq.*, Aug. 1896, p. 350; *WC*, June 3, 1893, p. 3; *Conq.*, July 1896, p. 316 ("Mercy Box"); *WC*, May 8, 1897, p. 3 ("Soup-Soap-Salvation"); *WC*, July 11, 1896, p. 9; July 18, 1896, p. 3; Aug. 8, 1896, pp. 1, 4–5 ("soup-soap" banner).

4. *Conq.*, Aug. 1896, pp. 364, 376, 412.

5. Commander [Frederick] Booth-Tucker, *Our Future Pauper Policy in America* (New York: SA [1897]), pp. 8–10, 24; MacKenzie, *Booth-Tucker*, pp. 164–167; Commissioner Nicol, "An Important Interview with the Commissioner," *HL*, March 1900, p. 73.

6. *WC*, June 20, 1896, p. 14; Aug. 1, 1896, p. 5.

7. Career sheet, Holland, Thomas, SAA; *WC*, Aug. 22, 1896, pp. 1–2; Oct. 10, 1896, p. 2; Oct. 24, 1896, p. 12; "Interview with Colonel Holland," *Conq.*, Jan. 1897, p. 13.

8. *WC*, Oct. 17, 1896, pp. 4, 9; Oct. 24, 1896, pp. 8, 12; Oct. 31, 1896, p. 8; Nov. 7, 1896, pp. 1, 4–5, 12; Nov. 14, 1896, pp. 4, 9; Jan. 16, 1897, p. 8; Feb. 6, 1897, p. 10; Ensign Clifford Brindley, "Commissioner Richard E. Holz," *WCE*, June 22,

1929, p. 11; [Commander Frederick Booth-Tucker], "The Housing of the Poor in the City of New York: A Serious Talk to City Gentlemen by the Commander," *WC*, Oct. 10, 1896, p. 2; *WC*, Oct. 10, 1896, p. 1 ("Hustles"); *WC*, Oct. 3, 1896, p. 12.

9. Booth-Tucker, "Housing of the Poor," *WC*, Oct. 3, 1896, p. 12; and Oct. 10, 1896, p. 2; *WC*, Oct. 24, 1896, pp. 1, 12 (illus, p. 6) and 13; Oct. 31, 1896, pp. 3, 9; Dec. 5, 1896, p. 4; Jan. 16, 1897, p. 8; *Conq.*, Nov. 1896, pp. 510–511; "By Way of the Golden Gate," *Conq.*, Jan. 1897, pp. 27–28; *Conq.*, Feb. 1897, p. 40; *Dispo* NHQ, Nov. 1896, p. 2; Dec. 1896, pp. 3–4.

10. *WC*, Oct. 31, 1896, p. 11; Nov. 28, 1896, pp. 9, 12, 16; Dec. 5, 1896, p. 16; Dec. 12, 1896, p. 9; Dec. 26, 1896 [p. 4]; Jan. 2, 1897, pp. 4–5, 9; Jan. 16, 1897, pp. 8–9; Jan. 16, 1897, p. 12.

11. Lt.-Colonel Harold R. Smith, MSSSE, "Proposal for the Observance of the Golden Jubilee (1897–1947) of The Salvation Army Men's Social Service Centers in America," June 1, 1947, under cover of letter Walter Regan to Miss Mason, NYC, MSSDE, Sept. 21, 1947, in SAA.

12. *WC*, Jan. 16, 1897, pp. 8–9, 12; May 15, 1897, pp. 10–11; Feb. 27, 1897, p. 10; Jan. 30, 1897, pp. 5, 8; Feb. 6, 1897, p. 10; Feb. 27, 1897, p. 7; March 13, 1897, pp. 6–7; May 15, 1897, p. 5; May 8, 1897, p. 10; June 12, 1897, p. 7; June 19, 1897, p. 3; *Conq.*, March 1897, p. 65; May 22, 1897, p. 2; March 13, 1897, p. 9; March 20, 1897, p. 10; May 1, 1897, pp. 2–3; Major J. N. Parker, "The Social Work in New England," *HL*, July 1898, pp. 203–204; *WC*, March 6, 1897, p. 8; March 20, 1897, p. 10; March 27, 1897, p. 14; April 3, 1897, p. 10; May 15, 1897, p. 10; May 29, 1897, p. 6; *Dispo* NHQ, Dec. 1896, pp. 2–4; Jan. 1897, p. 4; Feb. 1897, p. 4; March 1897, p. 4.

13. *WC*, Feb. 27, 1897, p. 8; Minute of the Chief of the Staff, #53, March 1, 1897, Busby Collection, Atlanta, Georgia; Brig. Gilbert S. Decker, "Rehabilitation Program Engages Efforts of Men's Social Departments," *WCS*, Nov. 1, 1947, p. 5; Nels Anderson and Sylvia R. Harris, "Report on the Men's Social Service Department of The Salvation Army in New York City," Welfare Council of New York City Research Bureau, December 1931, in MSSDE, Dept. files, notes that MSSDE in 1931 had "no definite information" on the first 17 years of its operations in NYC (pp. 9–10); also see undated letter, Alfred Jackson to Sr.-Major Ronald Irwin NYC, stating that records at MSSDE were "very meager." [1957–1959].

14. *WC*, Jan. 16, 1897, p. 12; March 13, 1897, p. 9; Feb. 20, 1897, p. 9; Feb. 27, 1897, p. 8; May 15, 1897, p. 10; May 22, 1897, p. 8; *Conq.*, April 1897, p. 89; May 1897, p. 115; Frederick Booth-Tucker to R. E. Holz "in the cars to Boston" July 22, 1898, in Richard Holz Collection, Neptune, N.J.

15. Commissioner Edward Justus Parker, *My Fifty-Eight Years: An Autobiography* (New York: [SA] National Headquarters, 1943), p. 154; William Booth, *In Darkest England and the Way Out* (London: SA, 1890), pp. 118–122, 135–137; see also pp. 107–110; *WCW*, June 13, 1891, pp. 1, 3; June 20, 1891, pp. 4–5; *WC*, July 30, 1892, p. 9; Feb. 6, 1892, p. 5; *Conq.*, April 1892, p. 94; *WC*, March 12, 1892, p. 8; May 21, 1892, p. 14; "Our New York Lighthouse," *Conq.*, April 1892, p. 75; *WC*, Jan. 28, 1893, p. 5 (duster arrives from San Francisco); *WCW*, March 4, 1893, pp. 1–2, 4, 7; *WC*, May 6, 1893, p. 3; Captain J. McFee, "The New California Food and Shelter Depot," *Conq.*, Nov. 1894, p. 435; *HL*, June 1900, p. 166. The use of woodyards to give employment to needy men was common in late 19th Century American charity. See, for example, Amos G. Warner, *American Charities* (New York: Thomas Y. Crowell & Company, 1894 [rev. 1908]), pp. 254–255.

16. *WC,* July 17, 1897, p. 3; "The Conversion of Rags, Bones and Bottles," *Conq.,* June 1897, p. 130. Career sheet, McFee, Joseph R. SAA, lists his appointment to New York as Feb. 13, 1897; *WC,* Feb. 27, 1897, p. 14, announced "plan to open" salvage work in NYC; *Dispo* NHQ first lists salvage work in April 1897, pp. 4–5, at 118 Ave. D, NYC; *Dispo* NHQ, May 1897, pp. 4–5, lists Cherry St., and the Brooklyn and Jersey City locations; [Colonel Harold R. Smith], "History of Men's Social Service Department, Eastern Territory, USA," [1947], pp. 3–4, SAA and MSSDE office files; Snellen M. Hoy and Michael C. Robinson, *Recovering the Past: A Handbook of Community Recycling Programs, 1890–1945* (Chicago: Public Works Historical Society, 1979), pp. 1–3, 17–18.

17. *WC,* June 12, 1897, p. 7; June 19, 1897, p. 3; Major J. N. Parker, "Social Work in Chicago," *HL,* Feb. 1898, p. 46; *Dispo* NHQ, June 1897, pp. 4–5; *WC,* Oct. 16, 1897, p. 14 ("two strong horses"); Feb. 27, 1897, p. 14 (Holland on land donation); *WC,* July 17, 1897, p. 3; *Conq.,* June 1897, p. 137.

18. The dates of the appointments as Divisional Social Superintendents were Parker, April 28, 1897, Winchell, Jan. 20, 1897 and McFee, Feb. 13, 1897; Career sheets for Parker, John Newton, Joseph R. McFee, William Wallace Winchell, SAA; *Dispo* NHQ, Feb. 1897, p. 4; March 1897, p. 4; April 1897, pp. 4–5; "Our National Headquarters," *Conq.,* April 1897, p. 99; *WC,* March 27, 1897, p. 7.

19. *WC,* June 1, 1889, p. 6; Aug. 15, 1891, p. 4; April 15, 1893, p. 2; Feb. 27, 1897, p. 5; May 15, 1897, p. 8; June 12, 1897, p. 6 ("old coffee pot"); *WC,* June 26, 1897, p. 3; July 10, 1897, p. 3; Adj. Fred Braun, "The Hotel as a Link in the Chain of Social Service," in "Social Department of the East: Brief, April 1911 to Jan. 1913" [prepared for Social Councils, NYC, June 1912, and included in "Brief."], p. 4. MSSDE office files, career sheet, clippings regarding Fowler, F. A., in SAA.

20. *WC,* Feb. 13, 1897, pp. 4–5; Feb. 20, 1897, pp. 1, 3, 7, 13; Feb. 27, 1897, pp. 1, 3; May 29, 1897, p. 6; June 26, 1897, p. 3; July 10, 1897, p. 3; *Dispo* NHQ, Aug. 1897, p. 4; Sept. 1897, p. 4; Oct. 1897, p. 4; Dec. 1897, pp. 4–5; March 1898, pp. 4–5; *Conq.,* Aug. 1897, p. 185; *WC,* April 24, 1897, p. 2; "One Year's Advances 'neath Stars and Stripes," *HL,* Feb. 1898, p. 45.

21. *WC,* Oct. 16, 1897, p. 4, 9; Nov. 27, 1897, p. 11; *Dispo* NHQ, Dec. 1899, p. 4; Brindley, "R. E. Holz," p. 11; *Dispo* NHQ, Nov. 1897, p. 4; Dec. 1897, pp. 4–5.

22. Edward McKinley, *Marching to Glory: The History of The Salvation Army in the United States of America, 1880–1980* (San Francisco: Harper and Row, 1980), pp. 88–93; Marie Antalek, "The Amity Colony" (unpublished Masters' thesis, Kansas State Teachers' College, Emporia, 1968); Clark Spence, "The Landless Man and the Manless Land," (paper read at [SA] Territorial Historical Commission, Asbury Park, New Jersey, June 8, 1984; courtesy SAE Literary Department files); *WC,* Jan. 16, 1897, p. 12 ("Canaan"); *WC,* Oct. 16, 1897, p. 4; "The British Farm Colony," *Conq.,* Nov. 1894, pp. 422–27; Booth-Tucker, "Housing," p. 2; *WC,* March 6, 1897, p. 7; March 13, 1897, p. 18; March 27, 1897, p. 3, 14; *Conq.,* April 1897, p. 89; *WC,* June 12, 1897, pp. 6–7; June 19, 1897, p. 3; July 24, 1897, p. 8; July 31, 1897, p. 4; Aug. 14, 1897, pp. 8, 13; *Conq.,* Aug. 1897, p. 185; [William H. Cox], "The Proposed Colonization Scheme: The Substance of an Interview with Commander Booth-Tucker," *Conq.,* Sept. 1897, pp. 201–202; see also *Conq.,* Sept. 1897, p. 208; *WC,* Oct. 16, 1897, p. 13; Dec. 18, 1897, pp. 2–4, 8–9; June 5, 1897, p. 4; June 19, 1897, p. 3; Aug. 27, 1898, p. 2; Booth-Tucker *Pauper Policy,* pp. 12–15, 22–26; "Promising Advances," *HL,* May 1900, pp. 138–39; Red morocco book marked "Chief Secretary," a report on field 1904–1913, entry for Sept. 30, 1913, Ft. Herrick listed as "miscellaneous" territorial property,

p. 80, in SAA 81-45; see also "Industrial Dept. Income and Expense," Acc. 82-46, Box 2, SAA; through 1924, Herrick was carried as a territorial debit.

23. *WC,* Jan. 1, 1898, p. 1; letter, R. E. Holz to William Booth, [NYC], April 22, 1898, in RHC; *Dispo* NHQ, March 1898, pp. 4–5; R. E. Holz to Col. [Edward] Higgins [Louisville, Ky.], May 9, 1898, and Frederick del. Booth-Tucker to R. E. Holz, "in the cars to Boston," July 22, 1898, RHC.

24. Letter, R. E. Holz to Col. Higgins, NYC, Sept. 21, 1899; Frederick Booth-Tucker to R. E. Holz, NYC, March 22, 1899; Edward Higgins to R. E. Holz, NYC, Sept. 20, 1899, in SAA 82-75; Vertical files: "Men's Social: Southern Territory," SAA; *Dispo* NHQ, July 1898, pp. 5–6; Aug. 1898, p. 5 for first listing of institutions in [later] Southern Territory; these do not appear in June or before; letter, R. E. Holz to Col. Higgins, NYC, May 9, 1898, and Higgins to Holz, NYC, May 6, 1898, in SAA 82-75; see "Addresses of Social Institutions for the Poor in the United States," in Commander [Frederick] Booth-Tucker, *The Salvation Army in the United States* (New York: SA, 1899), pages not numbered.

25. Letter, R. E. Holz to Col. Higgins, [NYC], Oct. 3, 1898 (asking for "Brief"), RHC; *WC,* July 2, 1892, p. 8 ("Chief D.O.s"); R. E. Holz to Higgins, NYC, May 11, 1899; Higgins to R. E. Holz, NYC, Jan. 7, 1898, in RHC; J. N. Parker, "Social Work in Chicago," p. 46; letter, R. E. Holz to Higgins [NYC] Oct. 23, 1898; same, May 10, 1899, and Higgins to Holz, NYC, May 10, 1899, in RHC; Staff-Capt. Jos. McFee to R. E. Holz, Chicago, April 3, 1899 in SAA 82-75; see in same collection, Adj. Wilbur Gale to R. E. Holz, NYC, May 7, 1898. All appointments to social work had to be arranged by Col. Higgins with Local Chief D.O.s; see R. E. Holz to Higgins [Buffalo], Sept. 21, 1899; E. Higgins to Holz, NYC, Sept. 20, 1899; same, May 8, 1899, in RHC.

26. Letter, R. E. Holz to Col. Higgins [NYC], Oct. 3, 1898; R. E. Holz to F. del. Booth-Tucker, NYC [report], March 3, 1899; same, May 12, 1899, all in RHC; letter of May 12, 1899 also in SAA 82-75; Minute by the Chief of the Staff, No. 59, Feb. 16, 1898; same, No. 70, Oct. 10, 1898, both in Busby Collection.

27. R. E. Holz to Col. Higgins, May 10, 1899; R. E. Holz to Staff-Capt. McFee, NYC, May 11, 1899; Frederick del. Booth-Tucker to R. E. Holz, NYC, Jan. 12, 1899, all in RHC; *WC,* Jan. 3, 1901, pp. 1–3; "One Social Officer," *HL,* July 1898, p. 226; "Our Buffalo Shelter," *Conq.,* June 1894, p. 217.

28. Emma Booth-Tucker to R. E. Holz, NYC, Oct. 10 1898; E. Higgins to R. E. Holz, NYC, May 26, 1899, RHC; Minute, by the Chief of Staff, No. 65, May 13, 1898, Busby Coll; E. J. Higgins to R. E. Holz, NYC, Dec. 28, 1898; Frederick Booth-Tucker to R. E. Holz, NYC, March 4, 1899; Emma Booth-Tucker to R. E. Holz, NYC, April 25, 1899 (quotation), RHC.

29. Career sheet, McFee, Joseph R., SAA; *HL,* Feb. 1898, p. 54; Adj. Wilbur Gale to R. E. Holz, Rochester, NY, April 6, 1898; Jos. McFee to R. E. Holz, Chicago, April 3, 1899; same, May 13, 1899; R. E. Holz to F. Booth-Tucker, March 3, 1899 (report); same, Oct. 4, 1899, RHC.

30. R. E. Holz to Booth-Tucker, March 3, 1899; F. del. Booth-Tucker to R. E. Holz, NYC, March 4, 1899, RHC; "Brief Memoranda of National and Chief Divisional Staff Councils Held in New York, May 16–19, 1899," pp. 19–20, SAA 82-75; "The Electric City," *HL,* April 1898, p. 114.

31. Booth-Tucker, "Addresses of Social Institutions," 1899; Commander [Frederick] Booth-Tucker, *The Social Relief Work of The Salvation Army in the United States* (monographs on American Social Economics, Dept. of Social Economy for the U. S. Commission to the Paris Exhibition of 1900, XX), p. 23; *Dispo,* May 1900,

p. 4; June 1900, p. 4, SAA (copy of June 1900, also in Seiler Collection); Lt.-Col. French, "Chicago and the Northwestern," *HL,* June 1900, p. 167; "Social Furniture and Fittings," in FIN 69-a/c 61, SAA; [Col. H. R. Smith] "History," p. 4 lists Jersey City as first institution to be called "Industrial Home," but this was apparently incorrect.

CHAPTER III

1. "Salvation Army Statistics for 1907 in the United States," broadside for Harvest Festival, in Seiler Coll.; *Where Shadows Lengthen: A Sketch of The Salvation Army's Work in the United States of America* (New York: The Reliance Trading Company, 1907), p. 15, SFOTE-Lib.
2. "Brief for Major [W. F.] Jenkins, [Metropolitan Province] Aug. 1, 1901," MSSDE office files; "Our Headquarters' Warriors: The Social Department," *WC,* June 7, 1902, p. 6; Career sheet, Wood, Sam; Jenkins, Walter Francis, SAA; *WCW,* May 9, 1891, pp. 1–2 (on Wood); *Dispo* NHQ, June 1900, p. 4; Jan. 1901, pp. 4–10; July 1902, pp. 4–11; June 1903, pp. 4–11; July 1903, pp. 4–12; October 1903, pp. 8–13; *WC,* Feb. 22, 1902, p. 10.
3. Brief, "Shelters," dated 1902, no author, no pages, in MSSDE office files; "The Army Shelters in Boston," *HL,* March 1900, p. 81; *WC,* Aug. 2, 1902, p. 7; March 5, 1904, p. 7; Nov. 19, 1904, p. 7; letter, Capt. C. Hendrichson to Ensign [Charles] Welte, Philadelphia, April 25, 1902, in SFOTE-Mus, item #48 ("worthy bathers"); *WC,* April 18, 1903, p. 4.
4. *WC,* Feb. 22, 1902, p. 10; Feb. 7, 1903, pp. 1, 8, 12; "Shelter" Brief, material dated March 2, 1904; *WC,* Nov. 9, 1907, p. 7.
5. Commander [Frederick] Booth-Tucker, "The Social Relief Work of The Salvation Army," *WC,* Dec. 27, 1902, p. 8; same author, *Light in Darkness: Being an Account of The Salvation Army in the United States* (New York: SA, 1902), no pages; same author, *The Social Relief Work of The Salvation Army in the United States* (monographs on American Social Economics, Dept. of Social Economy for the United States Commission to the Paris Exposition of 1900, XX), p. 23; same author, *The Salvation Army in the United States* (New York: SA, 1899), no pages.
6. *WC,* Nov. 8, 1902, p. 4; Verticle file, "Men's Social: Paterson," SAA, [Brig. Helen Purviance] Asst. Field Sec., to Maj. Ernest Hayes, NYC, Sept. 11, 1939, and Program, "Golden Jubilee: Paterson Rescue Mission, 1895–1945;" NOM, Oct. 27, 1933, p. 1; *WC,* Nov. 22, 1902, p. 5; "Brief: Jenkins," Col. T. Holland to Jenkins, NYC, Aug. 1, 1901, p. 3; Booth-Tucker, "Social Relief," p. 8.
7. Salvation Army Industrial Homes Company: Organizational Records, SAA Record Group 1.2: "Certificate of Incorporation," June 17, 1903; By-Laws, June 20, 1903 in 14-1-1; Minutes of SA Industrial Homes Co., 1st meeting, June 23, 1903 in Organizational Records, 1903; July 20, 1903 in 13-1-15; 1st regular business meeting, Sept. 8, 1903, in 13-1-1; Stock certificate sale records, in 13-1-15: "Stock Certificates, Ind. Homes Co.;" Minutes, May 25, 1905, in 13-1-3; Sept. 3, 1907, in 13-1-8; Officers for 1908 listed, in 13-1-9; letter, Commander Evangeline Booth to Comm. Howard, NYC, July 18, 1911 in Box 2, SAA Acc. 82-46, "Industrial Home Dissolution;" *WC,* Jan. 30, 1904, p. 12 (coupon to buy a share of stock); Personal book of data on institutions of Adj. Charles Welte, 1903–1904; marked "Lieut. Col. Charles Welte: Personal" on cover, in MSSDE office files, pp. 91–92; Minutes, SA Industrial Homes Co., July 19, 1906 in SAA RG 1.2 13-1-4; May 23, 1907, in

13-1-7; Aug. 9, 1907, in 13-1-7 (" 'Ginger' who died"); Edwin D. Solenberger, *The Social Relief Work of The Salvation Army* (Minneapolis: Byron and Willard, 1906), pp. 3–4, 11–12; letter, Evangeline Booth to Col. [William] Peart, NYC, May 18, 1911; Comm. T. Henry Howard to Evangeline Booth, London, Sept. 8, 1911; Frederick Booth-Tucker to Col. Jenkins, [no place: file contains only carbon copy of this letter] Sept. 11, 1911; Col. Peart to Comm. Howard, NYC, Oct. 11, 1911; Col. Peart to Evangeline Booth, NYC, Oct. 2, 1911, all in Acc. 82-46, Box 2, "Ind. Homes Dissolution," SAA; Annual meeting of stockholders, Sept. 5, 1905, in RG 1.2, 13-1-3 (on annual deficit); Porter R. Lee and Walter W. Pettit, *Social Salvage: A Study of the Central Organization and Administration of The Salvation Army* (New York: National Information Bureau, 1924), p. 39.

8. Large green album, no. 1 of four, listing information and containing photographs, on SA properties, 1903–1910, SAA; *WC,* June 6, 1903, p. 10; June 13, 1903, p. 11; MSSDC-Center files: Milwaukee; Career sheet: Parker, Edward J., SAA; E. J. Parker to Mrs. Parker, on the train en route to Racine, Wisc., March 13 [1900]; same to same, Springfield, Illinois, March 19 [1900] in Acc. 84-14, SAA; Commissioner Edward Justus Parker, *My Fifty-Eight Years: An Autiobiography* (New York: [SA] National Headquarters, 1943), pp. 153, 168–177; *WCW,* June 7, 1890, p. 5; *WC,* June 27, 1896, p. 16; *WC,* June 20, 1903, p. 5; *Dispo* NHQ, June 1903, pp. 4–11; July 1903, pp. 4–12; Aug. 1903, pp. 4–12; Oct. 1903, pp. 8–13.

9. Packet of letterheads in Acc. 80-18, SAA, includes one for "The Salvation Army National Metropole and Relief Department," which lists all its activities; "Army Shelters in Boston," pp. 82–83; Parker, *My 58 Years,* pp. 152–153; Solenberger, *Social Relief,* pp. 9–10; *WC,* Nov. 11, 1905, p. 7; Adj. Fred Braun, "The Hotel as a Link in the Chain of Social Services," in "Social Department of the East Brief, April 1911 to Jan. 1913" which includes papers delivered at Social Councils, NYC, June 1912, p. 6, MSSDE office files; "Annual Report, Central Territory, 1921," "Industrial Homes," p. 101, SAA 267-15 A615.

10. Ensign Sawyer, "Sketch of the San Francisco Industrial," *WC,* March 5, 1904, p. 10; Comm. Edward J. Parker, "The Good Old Days," papers read, "MSSDE Officers' Councils, NYC, Oct. 13, 1949," p. 1, MSSDE office files; Major A. E. Agnew, *The Nineteen Hundred Forty-Four Institutes of the Men's Social Service Department* (New York: SAE, [1946]), p. 23; FIN 69, a/c 61, "Furniture and Fittings Social Institutions," Brooklyn, Dec. 1900 ($15 horse); FIN 81, a/c 202, "Brooklyn Plant," April 8, 1905 ($85 horse), in SAA; [Col. Harold R. Smith], "History of Men's Social Service Department, Eastern Territory," [1947], p. 5.

11. *WC,* March 19, 1904, p. 5, 9; Commander [Frederick] Booth-Tucker, *The Salvation Army, Self-Denial Week, March 27–April 3, 1904: The Field Officer's Guide Book* (New York: National Headquarters, [1904]), pp. 37, 42 ("leading position"); for a statement on world-wide statistics, see William Booth, "The Open Door Before The Salvation Army," *International Congress Addresses, 1904, By The General* (London: SA Book Department, 1904), pp. 20–21.

12. Career sheet, Parker, Edward J., SAA; *Dispo* NHQ, Dec. 1904, pp. 5–9; Jan. 1905, pp. 5–12, 35, 38; Feb. 1905, pp. 5–12; FIN 81 a/e 49, Industrial Home Ledgers, inexplicably include a "Department of the West" and a "Department of the Coast" as early as 1903, SAA; Braun, "Hotel as a Link," p. 4; Career sheet, Pebbles, Ashley, Courtesy CS and FD, W.

13. Photograph 35-1789, "Welcome to Col. E. J. Parker at Braveman Hotel, NYC," SAA; Parker, *My 58 Years,* pp. 155–158.

14. Letter, E. J. Parker to Lt.-Col. Welte, Mt. Vernon, NY, Dec. 23, 1924, SAA US-20; Welte Family Papers, MS 201-1; Career sheet, Welte, Charles Christian, SAA.

15. *WC*, Dec. 3, 1904, p. 7; Dec. 9, 1905, p. 10; *SN*, May 1911, p. 8; *WC*, March 4, 1905, p. 10; Album No. 4, SA properties, on Syracuse IH, SAA; Albums No. 2 and 3, same collection, for Cleveland, Los Angeles, New Orleans; *WC*, Jan. 6, 1906, p. 14; June 16, 1906, p. 3; Nov. 19, 1904, p. 7; Minutes, Ind. Home Co., Aug. 9, 1907, RG 1.2, 13-1-7, SAA; and for Sept. 5, 1907, 13-1-8; *WC*, July 27, 1907, p. 11; April 23, 1910, p. 6; *SN*, Feb. 1911, p. 6; "Historical Data 7H" file, MSSDE office files, on Manhattan ARC.

16. Brigadier John O'Neil, "The Good Old Days," in "Report on Officers' Councils Held at Atlantic City, April 24–26, 1951," pp. 1–2; Staff-Capt. [Allan] Neill, "Beyond the City Gates: Or, the Development of Outposts," in SDEB, June 2, 1912, pp. 7–8.

17. Parker proposes uniform mailing cards, Ind. Home Co. Minutes, Dec. 14, 1905, RG 1.2, 13-1-3; SFOTE Mus. has sample cards and letters sent by IH officers to solicit funds for operation: items 70, 72a, 73 and 74; Ind. Home Co. Minutes, June 6, 1907 (General's portrait), RG 1.2, 13-1-7, SAA; same, June 27, 1907; Nicholas Vachel Lindsay, "General William Booth Enters Into Heaven," *Poetry: A Magazine of Verse,* January 1913, pp. 101–103; letter, Comm. John Allan to Major Lawrence Castagna, London, Oct. 14, 1947 in Paterson photo album, MSSDE office files; "Remarkable Testimonies to the Value of our Industrial Work," *WC,* Aug. 15, 1908, p. 9.

18. *WC,* July 18, 1903, p. 11, author is indebted to Brig. Lawrence Castagna for this reference; *WCW,* April 22, 1893, p. 6; Edward Justus Parker, *Problems of the Poor* (New York: SA Social Department, 1908) ("dissolving stereopticon"), n.p. and brochure illustrating five of Parker's lectures, both in Acc. 80/18, SAA; Ind. Home Co. Minutes, Sept. 23, 1905; Sept. 28, 1905; Oct. 12, 1905, all in RG 1.2, 13-1-3, SAA.

19. Career sheet, Parker, E. J., SAA; Career sheets, Addie, John C, FDC; Maj. Birgitta K. Nilson to author, Chicago Aug. 10, 1984; Marcussen, Emil, CS and FD, W; Holland, Thomas, SAA and see *SN,* Feb. 1911, p. 8; July 1911, p. 9; Interviews with Brig. L. Castagna.

20. Ind. Home Co. Minutes, Feb. 27, 1908, RG 1.2, 13-1-9; see also, same location, minutes of meetings on March 6, 1908; April 2, 1908; April 15, 1908; "Minutes of the Chief of the Staff," Nos. 98, 100–102, dated June 1, 1908, Wm. Peart, Chief of the Staff, Busby Coll.; "The Salvation Army Special Orders to Social Officers," Nos. 1–29, dated Dec. 1, 1910, signed E. J. Parker (Acc. 81-9, SAA) or Thomas Stanyon (Detroit ARC office files), Nos. 12, 16, 17, 20, 23; Parker, *My 58 Years,* p. 162; "Social Minute" No. 6, Jan. 1, 1911, signed W. Peart, CS, in Busby Coll.

21. *WC,* Nov. 26, 1904, p. 10; June 9, 1906, p. 8; July 11, 1908, p. 6, 8; *Where Shadows,* pp. 9–15 (quote, p. 10).

22. E. J. Parker, "The Paper Market—Memories of the Past," in "MSSDE Officers' Councils, 1949," [orig. "A Chat With The Colonel, April 22, 1921'"], p. 2; "Special Social Order" No. 21, Paper, Dec. 1, 1910; "Our Paper Out-Put During the Year 1911 & 1912," SDEB, np, *SN,* April 1920, p. 14; "To the Chief of the Staff: A Review of Salvation Army Affairs in the Eastern Territory USA for the Year, 1918" (New York: The Salvation Army [1918]), SAA 78-25 Box 3, pp. 56–57; [Captain] W[illiam] S. Greenaway, "My Observations at the Mill!" June 1912,

SDEB, pp. 2–3, 4–6; Major Emil Marcussen, "Our Industrial Homes and Their Economic Value," *WC*, Dec. 16, 1905, p. 5.

23. "An Administrative Beehive," *SN*, Feb. 1911, p. 6; *WC*, June 27, 1908, p. 12; Minutes, Ind. Home Comp., June 11, 1908; RG 1.2, 13-1-9; Mrs. Major [W. W.] Winchell, "The Industrial Home and Its Neighbors," June 1912, SDEB, p. 2; Major Wallace Winchell, "Samples of Social Methods Adopted in 'The Melting Pot,'" *The Officer*, Nov. 1915, p. 737; Commander Eva Booth, "Why a Social News," *SN*, Feb. 1911, p. 3; *SN*, Aug. 1911, p. 14; Feb. 1911, p. 13; Red morocco book, "Chief Secretary," in SAA, 81-45, contains report on all operations, USA, 1904–1913, pp. 1–9, 36, 77.

24. *Where Shadows*, pp. 13–14; *SN*, Dec. 1912, p. 6; Aug. 1913, p. 11; Major [W. W.] Winchell, "Salvation Army Carries on a Big Industry," *SN*, Jan. 1912, p. 13; Staff-Capt. [James] Simons, "The Problem of the Habitual Drunkard," June 1912, SDEB, p. 5; letterheads in SAA, MS-20-1-2, Charles Welte.

25. *WC*, Aug. 15, 1908, p. 8; Sept. 19, 1914, p. 1; Oct. 3, 1914, p. 14; Jan. 23, 1915, p. 7; for information on the first SA trucks, the author wishes to express special thanks to Brig. Lawrence Castagna, whose letters to the author, Columbus, Feb. 16, 1984 and Feb. 27, 1984 (covering: Major Norman Murray to Brig. L. Castagna, ARC, Hartford, Feb. 22, 1984) and March 24, 1984 (covering L. Castagna to Mrs. Dorothy Dimond, Columbus, March 8, 1984 and Doug Starbard to Brig. L. Castagna, E. Hartford, March 4, 1984), to Mrs. Major Edward Dimond, letter to author, Cleveland, July 5, 1984, and to Mrs. Kim M. Miller, Librarian, Antique Automobile Club of America, letters to author, Hershey, Pennsylvania, July 26, 1983 and Aug. 15, 1984, all provided invaluable assistance. In addition to factual data on the Koehler and Commerce makes, Mrs. Miller identified the vehicles in several photographs sent to her. Mr. Peter Aarsen, Librarian, Antique Truck Club of America, kindly provided information on the Koehler, Commerce and Brockway vehicles, in letter to author, Morristown, NJ, Aug. 24, 1983; *WC*, July 15, 1916, p. 6 (Parker on first truck at NY No. 1 IH); Parker, *My 58 Years*, p. 160; *SN*, June 1915, p. 16; *Waste* (New York: The SA Industrial Home, 1916), p. 5; photo, p. 2, SFOTE Lib, SA pamphlets; SAA, Fin 81 a/e 58, 63, 98, 207 on NY No. 1 IH plant and operation, contain no reference to motor vehicles of any description in the early years of operation.

26. "Industrial Homes Company, Dissolution of," SAA 82-46, Box 2, SAA RG 1.2, Stock Certificates, IH Co., No. A1182 dated Sept. 30, 1912 last issued; Capt. E. J. Bransfield, "Advertising," June 1912, SDEB, pp. 1–2, 8–9; Staff-Capt. [Allan] Neill, "Beyond City Gates," p. 4; Captain Thomas Seaver, "The Man on the Wagon," June 1912, SDEB, p. 9; *Beware of Imposters* (Brooklyn, SAIH, no date), SAA Institutional histories, Brooklyn, New York, np; SAA Broadway file No. 4, alphabetical files; Allan Whitworth Bosch, The Salvation Army in Chicago: 1885–1914 (doctoral dissertation, history University of Chicago, 1965; Chicago: University of Chicago Library microfilm duplication, 1965), pp. 231–232; Edward McKinley, *Marching to Glory: The History of The Salvation Army in the United States, 1880–1980* (San Francisco: Harper and Row, 1980), pp. 114–15.

27. *Decision of the Supreme Court of California with regard to the Municipal Charities Commission of Los Angeles and The Salvation Army* (New York: SA Printing Department, [1914]), Seiler Coll.; *WC*, Sept. 26, 1914, p. 9; Oct. 3, 1914, pp. 6, 12; Oct. 10, 1914, pp. 8, 16; Oct. 17, 1914, pp. 1, 3, 8, 12; March 11, 1916, pp. 1, 7–9, 12–13; Anita E. Phillipson, "A Study of the Columbus Salvation Army

Industrial Home," (unpubl. M.A. thesis, Ohio State University, 1930), pp. 88–98 on Los Angeles; pp. 99–111 on Buffalo.

28. *Waste,* p. 7; and solicitation card for "New Salvage Warehouse" cor. Harrison and May, Chicago, SFOTE, Museum, item No. 69, for appeal to unemployed man; Ensign Joseph Grace, "Temporal and Spiritual Welfare of the Men of Our Industrial Homes," *SN,* Jan. 1912, p. 14; Alice Willard Solenberger, *One Thousand Homeless Men: A Study of Original Records* (New York: Survey Associates, Inc., 1914 [orig. 1911]), p. 10; G[eorge] S[cott] Railton, *The Authorative Life of William Booth, Founder of The Salvation Army* (New York: The Reliance Trading Co., 1912), pp. 194–195 contains Booth's social congress address; Major George Irvings, "My Observations and Impressions of the Opportunities, Difficulties and Successes of Industrial Work," June 1912, SDEB, pp. 7–8, Agnes L. Palmer, *The Salvage of Men: Stories of Humanity Touched by Divinity* (New York: Reliance Trading Company, 1913), p. 80; *WC,* July 26, 1890, p. 1 ("Foam of Death"); May 2, 1914, pp. 1, 6; Envoy Hires, "My Experience as Manager of a Small Home," June 1912, SDEB, pp. 3–4, Mrs. Staff-Captain [John] McGee, "The Care of Our Converted Men," June 1912, SDEB, pp. 3–6; Major [Miles] Pickering, "Pressing the Claims of Salvation With Our Men," June 1912, SDEB, pp. 5–8; *SN,* Jan. 1917, p. 5; Mrs. Winchell, "Industrial Home and Neighbors," p. 1, 9; Major Wallace Winchell, "Saving the Victim of Inebriety," *The Officer,* March 1915, pp. 153–54, 156; April 1915, p. 233; *WCW,* July 14, 1894, pp. 1–2 ("Moloch of Drink"); "Special Order No. 33," Sept. 1, 1912, est. Climbers' League, SAA 81-9, E. J. Parker; "Climbers' Club" Constitution, Article I, and *The Climber: A Publication of Progress,* 8 numbers, Nov. 14, 1911 to Jan. 9, 1914, in SAA vertical file, MSSC "New York;" file also includes program for concert, Oct. 21, 1913; Major Charles C. Welte, "The Remaking of Men in Paterson," *SN,* April 1913, p. 3; "Keeps Them Sober and Tries to Give Them Jobs When They Reach Trenton 'Down and Out,' " *SN,* March 1913, pp. 13, 15; letter to author, Mrs. Brig. Fletcher Agnew [daughter Col. W. W. Winchell] on "cocktail," Asbury Park, NJ, July 16, 1982.

29. Capt. Thomas Seaver, "The Man on the Wagon," pp. 1–2, 5–9; Bransfield, "Advertising," pp. 2–4; Ensign Sawyer, "Sketch of the San Francisco Industrial," p. 10; "Three Days in an Industrial Home," *WC,* June 13, 1903, p. 4; Mrs. Staff-Captain McGee, "Care of Converted Men," pp. 5–6; Captain [John] Horgan, "A Day with an Industrial Wagon," *SN,* Dec. 1919, pp. 2–3; on difficulties of driving a wagon, accidents, etc., see letter, E. J. Parker to Brig. [Madison H.] Ferris, NYC, March 10, 1906, describing an accident at the corner of 14th St. and Sixth Ave. in which an IH wagon tipped over and injured a woman in the foot, in SAA 1-10-5; in Minutes IH Comp., June 5, 1908, about a driver who took the wrong trunk, the contents of which were disposed of before the mistake was caught; J. C. McGee to E. J. Parker, NYC [48th St. IH], May 22, 1912, announcing he could not bring converts to a planned meeting because the "reliable men" could not be spared from the production process long enough to attend; "Social orders," Nos. 17, 19, 20, dated Dec. 1, 1910, signed E. J. Parker; Brig. John O'Neil, "Good Old Days," p. 3 ("cooks are hard to get."). Sr.-Major Railton F. Sprake explained to author the difficulties of driving a wagon in city traffic, which he often did as a boy for his father John, an IH officer; interview, Los Angeles, Calif., Dec. 11, 1978.

30. *WC,* May 2, 1914, p. 6; *The Climber,* Nov. 14, 1911; Feb. 23, 1914, both in SAA; *SN,* April 1914, p. 4; March 1915, p. 13.

31. "Report to the Chief," Jan. 1918, pp. 61–63; "Special Order" No. 31, June 1,

1912 (burial fund); *Waste,* pp. 10–11; "Special Order" No. 40, Jan. 1917 (sick benefit).

32. *WC,* Oct. 11, 1913, pp. 8, 12; April 18, 1914, p. 9; May 23, 1914, p. 1; Parker, *My 58 Years,* pp. 163–64; *WC,* June 24, 1916, pp. 1, 12; *Dispo* ETHQ, June, July, Aug. 1916.

33. *WC,* March 8, 1913, p. 14; *SN,* Feb. 1916, pp. 3–4.

34. Adj. Raymond C. Starbard, "Pies and Doughnuts: A New Kind of War Munitions Furnished by The Salvation Army," *The Outlook,* June 5, 1918, pp. 220–221; also in *WC,* May 4, 1918, p. 4; Aug. 4, 1917, p. 9; March 22, 1919, p. 2; "Salvation Army—Pie and Prayers at the Front," *Literary Digest,* Oct. 19, 1918, pp. 63–67; Evangeline Booth, Grace Livingston Hill, *The War Romance of The Salvation Army* (Philadelphia: J. B. Lippincott, 1919), pp. 100–106; *WC,* Aug. 17, 1917, p. 8; July 13, 1918, p. 8; Parker, *My 58 Years,* pp. 177–179; *WCS,* Jan. 18, 1930, p. 9; scrapbook, clipping *Jersey Journal,* June 24, 1918, in SAA MS 13-1-1; material on lease of NY No. 1 IH, see SAA Acc. 82-46, Box 1; "To the Chief of the Staff: A Review," pp. 28, 35, 37, 43, 55–60; "Annual Report, Central 1921," p. 101; "Institutional History" sheets, by center, in MSSDC office files.

35. "To the Chief of the Staff: Review," pp. 32–35.

CHAPTER IV

1. Porter. R. Lee and Walter W. Pettit, *Social Salvage: A Study of the Central Organization and Administration of The Salvation Army* (New York: National Information Bureau, 1924), 40–41; *SN,* Feb. 1919, p. 3, 6; *NSH,* July 1919, p. 2; Aug. 1919, p. 10; "Minutes, District Social Officers' Councils, Washington, D.C., February 7 to 10, 1923," p. 21; Social Service Order #57, Oct. 1922, "Officer's Handbook for Men's Social Work," gray post binder, MSSDE office files.

2. *Conq.,* April 1895, p. 196; Feb., 1896, p. 76; *WCE,* Oct. 30, 1920, p. 3; *WCC,* March 26, 1921, p. 5; Dec. 3, 1921, p. 8; "The Salvation Army: Annual Report. Central Report Dec. 31, 1921," pp. 108–113, SAA; *WCS,* Nov. 25, 1950, p. 13; *SN,* March 1916, p. 10; Colonel Edward J. Parker, "Our Opportunities and Responsibilities for Prison Populations," *Social Problems in Solution: Papers Read at the International Social Council, London, Conducted by the General, 1921* (London: International Headquarters, [1923]), pp. 109–110; Colonel Richard E. Holz, "The Conduct of Prison Meetings," *The Staff Review,* III (July 1924), pp. 224–25; Brigadier [William] Hunter, "The Social Officer and Prison Work," *SDEB,* June 1912, pp. 2–5; *WC,* June 23, 1906, p. 10; Adj. J. Stanley Sheppard, "Spheres of Special Service II—Prison Work in the United States of America," *The Officers' Review,* VI (May–June 1937), pp. 228–229; same author, *The Prison Work of The Salvation Army* (New York: National Research Bureau, 1946), pp. 29–30, 77–80; on Col. Cowan, see pp. 29, 32 and 76; Sr.-Major A. Ernest Agnew, " 'Red' Sheppard, The Prisoner's Friend," The Salvation Army *Year Book,* 1957 (London: SA, n.d.), pp. 24–26; Lee and Pettit, *Social Salvage,* p. 42; Minutes, Comm. Conf. Nov. 30/Dec. 1, 1944, pp. 2–3; *WCS,* Nov. 27, 1954, p. 13; Career sheets, SAA, for Anderson, Thomas, Sheppard, Stanley; *WCE,* Nov. 17, 1923, cover, shows many aspects of prison work as part of "Men's Social Department Special Number."

3. E. J. Parker, "The Paper Market—Memories of the Past," [orig. "A Chat with the Colonel," April 22, 1921], "MSSDE, Officers' Councils, Thurs. Oct. 13, 1949 [New York City]," pp. 1–2; *WC,* July 11, 1896, p. 9; *SN,* March 1920, pp. 4, 15.

4. SAA, Institution History, MSSC, Atlanta, Washington, D.C.; MSSDS, Institution History [list of commanding officers], same insts.; MSSDS, "Brief for Men's Social Service Department, Southern Territory of The Salvation Army," Lt.-Col. Gilbert S. Decker, MSSS, August 30, 1953, pp. 30, 31–33, 64–65, 50; *WCS*, July 9, 1927, pp. 2, 10; Colonel T. W. Scott, "The Salvation Army's Housing Problems," *WCW*, Dec. 22, 1923, p. 12; Mr. H. V. Chase to Major V. R. Post, NYC, May 16, 1922; Major [V. R. Post] to Adams & Co., NYC, Oct. 27, 1922; same to Henry G. Wales, NYC, Feb. 2, 1923; same to Herbert McLean Purdy Inc., NYC, Feb. 23, 1923 (offering to sell the property on W. 48th St.); same to Brig. Arnold, NYC, Oct. 31, 1925, all this corresp. in SAA Acc. 82-46 Box 1; *WCE*, Dec. 8, 1923, pp. 7, 11; Career sheet, Dowdell, Joseph Ogden, SAA; "Program, Eastern Territorial Congress, NYC 1924, in SFOT-S-Archives.

5. *WCE*, Jan. 17, 1920, p. 4; *WCS*, June 18, 1927, pp. 4–5; July 23, 1927, p. 5; SA "Annual Report, Central 1921," pp. 102–104; Scott, "Housing Problems," p. 12; SA "Schedule 3, Income & Expenditure—Industrial & Hotel Depts., Year Ending Sept. 30, 1923," Eastern THQ, SAA 78-24; Lee and Pettit, *Social Salvage*, pp. 23, 114.

6. *The International Social Council, 1921: Official Record, Including the Principal Addresses by the General, Mrs. Booth, and the Chief of the Staff* (London: International Headquarters [1921]), pp. vii–xix; *WCE*, Aug. 6, 1921, p. 8; "Minutes SDOC 1923," p. 3; author used copy of Parker's "Special Orders" Handbook in MSSDE; *SA Orders and Regulations for Social Officers [Men's]* (London, IHQ, 1915), pp. 1–18; *SN*, Oct. 1915, p. 14; General W. Bramwell Booth, "Disciplines—II," *Int. Social Council*, p. 21; Colonel Edward J. Parker, "Fundamentals of Social Work," *The Officer*, 39 (Aug. 1924), p. 114; Anita E. Phillipson, "A Study of the Columbus Salvation Army Industrial Home" (unpublished M.A. thesis, Ohio State University, 1930), p. 16 n. 2, p. 17 n. 1, p. 18 n. 2, pp. 137–144; apparently the author confused Parker's "Handbook" with the official *O&R* [1915]: see p. 18, n. 1-c and p. 5; in 1937 Col. Dowdell, MSSSE, commended *O&R* [1915] to his officers, not for procedure but because of its "advanced" principles: see "NOM," June 4, 1937, pp. 1–2; Major Paul A. Harvey, "Soul-Saving is My Business," "Report on Officers' Councils Held at Atlantic City April 24–26, 1951," pp. 2–3, quotes 1915 *O&R* to emphasize primacy of soul-saving.

7. Social Service Order No. 41, Oct. 1922 (C.R.B.); SA-IH Cash Book, Brooklyn, Nov. 26, 1926, p. 31; Dec. 3, 1926, p. 32; Feb. 4, 1927, p. 41 (on rental of films) MSSDE office files; "SSS" Aug. 5, 1927, p. 3 on entertainments; Parker quote in "Minutes SDOC 1923," p. 12; also see p. 11; for details cited in text, see Social Service Orders Nos. 16, 38, 44, 48, 62, Oct. 1922; "Annual Report, MSSDE, October 1935 to Sept. 1936," p. 41, in SAA 78-24; *WCE*, Nov. 17, 1923, p. 5; Lee and Pettit, *Social Salvage*, pp. 24–25; Parker, "Fundamentals," p. 115; interviews with Lock and Hawley.

8. Colonel E. J. Parker, "Phases of Men's Industrial Home Work: the Utilization of Waste Materials," *The Staff Review*, IX (Nov. 1929), p. 380; Social Service Order No. 11; No. 25; *WCE*, Nov. 17, 1923, p. 12; Center files, Ft. Wayne, Ind., has photo cited in text, MSSDC; "Minutes SDOC 1923," p. 2; "Program E. Terr. Congress, 1924," lists NY No. 1 as "Social Service Center;" "SSS," April 22, 1927, pp. 1–2; also pp. 3–5; "SSS," May 20, 1927, p. 2; *The Disposition of Forces, Southern Territorial Headquarters, February 1927*, pp. 4–7; see as well, *Dispo, E*, Oct. 1930, pp. 8–14; Nov. 1931, pp. 7–11; April 1932, pp. 7–11; *Dispo, W*, May 1931, pp. 18–22; Jan. 1932, pp. 27–30; *Dispo, S*, Nov. 1931, pp. 6–8; May 1932,

pp. 5–6; but see as well *WCS,* Christmas 1936, pp. 21, 25; Col. Dowdell continued to use "IH" in orders as late as 1940: see his order No. 21, Jan. 12, 1940, in collected file in Manhattan ARC office files; for transition in Dept. name, see *Dispo, W,* Jan. 1932 and Nov. 1934, p. 4.

9. Social Minute No. 12, Jan. 1, 1911; Social Service Order No. 4, Oct. 1922; Special Order No. 32, Sept. 1, 1912; on grading, see Social Serv. Order No. 19, Oct. 1922; Brief of Appointment, Social District Officer, Eastern Pennsylvania District, Lt.-Col Chas. C. Welte, Nov. 1, 1929, pp. 18–19; Social Serv. Order 49, Oct. 1922; interview Hayes, 7-2-82 and 8-26-83; "SSS" Aug. 31, 1927, supplement pp. 1–2; Capt. E. J. Bransfield, "Advertising," SDEB, 1912, pp. 5–6; "NOM," July 26, 1929, pp. 2–3.

10. Capt. Paul Horgan, "Curiosities in Industrial Things and Persons," *SN,* Jan. 1920, p. 10; "Minutes, SDOC 1923," pp. 19–20; Social Service Order 62a, Aug. 1, 1923; "SSS," April 8, 1927, p. 2; July 22, 1927, pp. 1–3; July 15, 1927, pp. 1–2; "NOM," June 14, 1928, p. 1; Parker, "Phases," pp. 377–380; *SN,* Oct. 1914, p. 2; Edward Carey to author, Laconia NH, Jan. 20, 1984.

11. Social Service Order No. 24, Oct. 1922; Special Order No. 17, Dec. 1, 1910, SAA 81-9; *WCE,* Nov. 17, 1923, p. 5; "Minutes, SDOC, 1923," p. 25; "SSS," May 27, 1927, p. 3; "NOM," June 21, 1928, p. 2; May 17, 1929, p. 3; "SSS," May 20, 1927, p. 4; "NOM," June 29, 1928, p. 2; Sept. 27, 1928, p. 1; SA-IH Cash Book, Brooklyn, Nov. 18, 1927, p. 82; Dec. 2, 1927, p. 84; Dec. 16, 1927, p. 86; see also entry for April 1926, all related to costs of horses and motor vehicles in Brooklyn center, MSSDE office files; Hayes and Harvey interviews; also see Phillipson, "Study of Columbus SA IH," p. 11.

12. Social Service Order No. 22, Oct. 1922; No. 42, Oct. 1922; "Minutes SDOC 1923," p. 21; "SSS," Aug. 19, 1927, p. 3; Brief, D.O. Ea. PA, 1929, p. 10; Item #30 [photos, 1930] SFOTE Museum; "MSSDE, Annual Report, Jan. 1–June 1, 1931," pp. 8–9 SAA 78-24; letter to author, Pete Aarsen, Librarian, Antique Truck Club of America, Morristown, NJ, Aug. 24, 1983; interviews with Hayes, Castagna, Hillis, Craytor.

13. *WCS,* April 2, 1927, p. 2; March 26, 1927, p. 12 (photos of MSSD facilities), *Dispo,* THQS, Feb. 1927, pp. 3, 4–7; G. S. Decker, "Brief, MSSDS, 1953," pp. 1–2.

14. Career sheets, Parker, E. J.; Welte, Charles Christian; James S. Borill to C. C. Welte, Worcester, Mass., March 28, 1927 ("Elisha") in Welte correspondence, MS 20-1-3; all in SAA.

15. *SN,* Sept. 1920, p. 15; "Minutes SDOC 1923," pp. 15–16, p. 11; [Col. Edward J. Parker], "Social Employees and Officership," *The Staff Review,* III (April 1924), p. 192; W. Bramwell Booth, "The Relation of Social to the Field Work," *Soc. Problems in Solution,* pp. 33–34; Phillipson, "Study of Columbus SA IH," p. 166; Major Horace Dodd, "The Bible in Men's Industrial Homes," *The Officer,* 41 (July 1925), p. 27; "Brief D.O., Ea. Pa. 1929," pp. 17–18; Lee and Pettit, *Social Salvage,* p. 28; Col. [Richard E.] Holz, "Field and Social—Distinct, Yet One," *The Officer,* 39 (Sept. 1924), pp. 209–210; Interviews, Hayes, Genge.

16. *Local Officers' Counselor,* IV (Aug. 1923), p. 13; VII (Dec. 1925), p. 28 (These references thanks to Dr. R. W. Holz); Item #21, SFOTE, Museum, photo of Philadelphia Social Service Center Band [1925]; "NOM," June 21, 1928, p. 1; July 5, 1928, p. 1; "SSS," July 22, 1927, p. 4; *Dispo,* SA NHQ, June 1900, p. 3; Program, Eastern Terr. Congress, Nov. 1924; Program, opening of Newark MSSC, April 21, 1929, in Newark ARC office files (bookkeeper); SAA vertical file, "Newark" also has copy of program; "NOM," April 26, 1929, p. 2 (white cooks' uniforms).

17. Colonel Edward J. Parker, "The Men's Social Service Work of The Salvation Army," *WCE*, Oct. 1, 1927, p. 7; "NOM," April 26, 1929, pp. 1–3; Ensign William E. Harris, "The Remaking of Men: Being a Glimpse into the Activities of the Newark Center of the Men's Social Service Department," *WCE*, June 29, 1929, p. 13; program in SAA vertical file; *WCS*, Oct. 1, 1927, pp. 1, 6, 8–9, 10; Oct. 22, 1927, p. 2, 7; May 24, 1930, p. 5; "NOM," Aug. 23, 1928, p. 1; Commissioner Edward Justus Parker, *My Fifty-Eight Years: An Autobiography* (New York: [SA] National Headquarters, 1943), p. 163.

18. Interview with Hofman, *WCE*, June 6, 1931, p. 7; Social Band Notice, dated NYC Feb. 23, 1933, signed [George Grauger], provided to author by Brig. L. Castagna; also, interview with Castagna; letter to author, Comm. Edward Carey, Laconia, N.H., Aug. 17, 1983, and from Mrs. Comm. W. E. Chamberlain, Asbury Park, N.J. April 4, 1984; see as well *WCE*, July 6, 1940, p. 12 and SA Annual Report, MSSDE, Vol. 2, p. 8.

19. *The Salvation Army and the Present Crisis: Report of Unemployment Emergency Relief Work in Greater New York.* October 1, 1930–September 30, 1931 (New York: SA [1931]), p. 12; "NOM," March 28, 1934, p. 3; *WCW*, April 25, 1931, p. 10; Nov. 14, 1931, pp. 8–10, 16; Nov. 28, 1931, p. 16; Phillipson, "Study of Columbus SA IH," pp. 27, 29–30; "NOM," Aug. 4, 1933, p. 2; Lt.-Col. Wallace Winchell, "Migrants and Mendicants: I—The Situation as it Exists in the U.S.A.," *The Staff Review*, X (April 1930), pp. 159–163; *WCE*, Nov. 16, 1929, pp. 1, 3, 11; Commr. William A. McIntyre, "The Homeless and Transient Problem in the United States," *WCE*, July 15, 1933, p. 8.

20. *WCE*, Jan. 3, 1931, p. 9; *SA and Present Crisis*, pp. 6–8, 16–17; *WCW*, Jan. 24, 1931, p. 10; *WCE*, Feb. 21, 1931, p. 8; "MSSDE Annual Report, Jan. 1–June 1, 1931," pp. 49–51, SAA 78-24; see also *WC*, Dec. 4, 1982, "Nostalgeus" for photo of vessel.

21. "MSSDE Annual Report, July 1–Dec. 31, 1931," p. 61, SAA 78/24; Annie (Mrs. Major Andrew C.) Laurie, "Memoirs of Annie Laurie," pp. 15–25, SAA 82/3; *WCE*, Jan. 23, 1932, pp. 3, 14; April 23, 1932, p. 15; "NOM," March 2, 1934, pp. 1–2; clippings from NY *World Telegram*, Jan. 2, 1935 and from NY *Daily News*, March 4, 1935, p. 18, in Annie Laurie scrapbook loaned to author 1983; Major Andrew C. Laurie, "The Salvation Army and Mass Case Work," *WCE*, June 22, 1935, p. 10; Major A. C. Laurie, "Handling the Transient Man," "Papers Read at the Annual Councils, June 5, 6 and 7, 1934, New York, NY, SA, MSSDE," pp. 83–89, MSSDE office files; *WCE*, Aug. 7, 1936, p. 8; "NOM," July 23, 1937, p. 1–2; "MSSDE, Annual Report, Oct. 1936 to Sept. 1937," p. 44, SAA 78/24; *SA Year Book, 1933*, p. 103; *1934*, p. 104; *1935*, p. 101; *1936;* p. 109; *1937*, p. 126 (London, SA International HQ, for year indicated), all in SAA Library; Mrs. Annie Laurie to author, undated and Sept. 24, 1983, Gulfport, Fla; "MSSDE Annual Report, 1932," p. 43, SAA 78/24; same, "Annual Report, 1934", p. 4, SAA 78-24; "Statistical Reports, Wrigley Shelter, 1930–1933," and "Analysis of 856 Case Files at the SA Wrigley Shelter, Chicago, Illinois, as of August 26, 1933," in SAA MS 31-1-1; *SA and Present Crisis*, p. 12; "MSSDE Annual Report, Jan. 1–June 1, 1931," p. 2, and for July 1–Dec. 31, 1931, pp. 48–49," SAA 78-24; Nels Anderson, Sylvia R. Harris, *Report on the Men's Social Service Department of The Salvation Army in New York City,* (New York: Welfare Council of New York City, Research Bureau, December, 1931), pp. 19–20, in MSSDE office files; *SA Year Book, 1933*, p. 103; "NOM," April 20, 1934, pp. 2–3; Oct. 19 [1934], p. 3; "MSSDE Annual Report, Oct. 1936 to Sept. 1937," p. 36, SAA 78-24; "NOM," Dec. 21, 1933, p. 4; *SA and Present Crisis*, pp. 3–6; Mrs. W. E. Chamberlain, letter to

234 SOMEBODY'S BROTHER

author, Asbury Park, April 4, 1984; interviews with Guldenschuh, Hillis.
22. *WCW,* Nov. 14, 1931, p. 4; Aug. 30, 1930, p. 11; *SA in Present Crisis,*
pp. 20–21, 23; *WCW,* Feb. 14, 1931, pp. 1, 2, 4; see also in *WCW,* Jan. 3, 1931,
pp. 8–9; Jan. 17, 1931, pp. 6, 8–10; April 25, 1931, p. 10; Nov. 14, 1931, pp. 3, 6, 16
("Emergency Relief" issue); Nov. 28, 1931, p. 16; Dec. 5, 1931, p. 5; Jan. 13, 1934,
p. 9; "MSSDE Annual Report, 1932," pp. 44–46 and "July 1–Dec. 31, 1931,"
pp. 33–39, 60, 64–65, in SAA 78/24; Hillis interview; *WCS,* Feb. 8, 1930, p. 13;
Feb. 15, 1930, p. 6; Feb. 22, 1930, pp. 6, 15; Sept. 6, 1930, p. 11; Oct. 4, 1930, p. 6;
Nov. 15, 1930, p. 11; Nov. 22, 1930, p. 16; *WCE,* Nov. 28, 1931, p. 13; Anderson &
Harris, *Report,* pp. 1, 14, 21–23, 29, 32, 89–91; Capt. Birger Lindh, "The Problem
of the Transient," *WCE,* Feb. 18, 1928, p. 11; "MSSDE Annual Report, Jan–June
1931," pp. 33, 39; *SA in Present Crisis,* pp. 12–13; "MSSDE Annual Report
1932," pp. 34–36; Adj. H. W. Bevan, "Coordinating the Transient with the Industrial Program," in "Papers Read at the Annual Councils, 1934," p. 90, MSSDE
office files; "NOM," Dec. 28, 1933, p. 2.
23. "Brief, MSSDS, 1953," Col. Decker, p. 2, MSSDS office files.
24. "MSSDE Annual Report, 1932," pp. 8–9, also see pp. 3–4; Capt. Peter
Hofman, "Balancing the Budget," in "Papers Read by Officers at Spring Councils
[MSSDE] 1933," p. 117 in SAA Acc. 80-43; "NOM," Feb. 23, 1934, pp. 1–2;
Career sheet, Layman, Archibald Leigh, CSW; *Dispo, Southern,* March 1931, p. 7;
Nov. 1931, pp. 6–9, 3; Dec. 1932, pp. 5 and 7; Nov. 1933, pp. 2, 5–7 ("Districts" no
longer listed); Jan. 1935, pp. 5–7; Oct. 1935, pp. 2 and 5; Jan. 1937, pp. 3 and 6;
Oct. 1937, p. 5; July 1938, p. 6; "NOM," June 23, 1933, p. 2 (end of S.D.O.s);
"MSSDE Annual Report, 1933," p. 2; "NOM," April 29, 1938, p. 2 (Manhattan
and Bronx D.O. abolished); *Dispo, Western,* Sept. 1933, pp. 5–6; Nov. 1932,
pp. 27–30; *Dispo, Central,* Jan. 1931, Sept. 1933, Feb. 1935; interviews Briggs,
Warren Johnson, Castagna.
25. "MSSDE Annual Report, Jan.–June 1931," p. 75; "NOM," April 5, 1933,
pp. 2–3; Sept. 15, 1933, p. 2; Dec. 1, 1933, p. 4; "MSSDE Ann. Report, 1934,"
p. 7; "NOM," April 27, 1934, p. 4; July 1, 1935, p. 2; Capt. Peter Hofman, "Added
Income for My Institution," "Papers Read, 1933 Councils," p. 114, SAA.
26. Brigadier John M. O'Neill, "Is It Economy to Substitute Horses for Automobiles?" "Papers Read 1933 Councils," pp. 1–3; Captain Robert Steed, "Trucks
or Horses—Which?" same, np.; Brig. Horace Dodd, "Is It Economy to Substitute
Horses for Automobiles," pp. 1–3, same; Hofman, "Balancing," pp. 117–120; Lt.-
Col. V. R. Post, "Balancing the Budget," "Papers Read, 1934 Councils," p. 117,
MSSDE off. files; Adj. W. Harvey, "Horses vs Automobiles," in "Papers Read at
MSS Officers' Councils, Philadelphia, June 3–4, 1936," pp. 53–55, SAA 80-43;
Major Henry Newby, "Horses vs Automobiles," "Papers Read 1936 Councils,"
pp. 56–58, SAA 80-43; "MSSDE Ann. Report 1932," p. 7a, SAA 78-24; "Ann.
Report 1933," p. 12; "Ann. Report, 1935," p. 11, 14–15; "Ann. Report, Oct. 1936–
Sept. 1937," p. 2; "Ann. Report, Oct. 1939–Sept. 1940," pp. 7, 8, 19, 24, 28; in
SAA 78-24, MSS, there are 6 large ledgers, "Finance & General Statistics," 1921–
1948 [exclusive], for centers in MSSDE with horses in 1939–1940, see Ledger 5,
"Financial, 1939–1940," by center; "Syracuse, NY Social Service Center, Brief,
September, 1934, Adj. H. L. Stephan, Commanding," p. 3, MSSDE office files;
"NOM," April 28, 1933, p. 2; May 5, 1933, p. 3; May 12, 1933, p. 3; Oct. 20, 1933,
p. 2; July 5, 1934, p. 5; Oct. 26, 1934, p. 4; Nov. 17, 1934, p. 1; Nov. 22, 1935, p. 3;
Nov. 29, 1935, p. 3; Feb. 22, 1937, p. 3; Captain Christine McMillan, "80,000

Square Feet of Rehabilitation," *WCE,* April 17, 1937, p. 9; "Brief MSSDS 1953," p. 76; letter to author, Brig. E. Gesner, Maitland, Fla., March 19, 1984; clipping from Indianapolis *Star,* Jan. 15, 1933, in Indianapolis center file, MSSDC office files; interviews with Guldenschuh, Schuerholz, Hayes, Vendeville, Lock, Briggs, Castagna, Oliver, Bevan, McCormick, Hillis, Eccleston, Craytor.

27. "NOM," June 23, 1933, p. 4; April 28, 1933, p. 3; Sept. 7, 1934, p. 2; Adj. G[eorge] Granger, "Our Automobile Accident Experiences," "Papers Read 1936 Councils," p. 76; same author, "Automobile Purchase Plan," "Minutes and Papers Read at the MSSDE Officers' Councils, Oct. 26–27, 1938," p. 63, in MSSDE office files; Joseph O. Dowdell to Mgrs, NYC, June 18, 1937, in Dowdell Binder "A," MSSDE office files; Granger "Automobile," p. 64; Adj. John Phillips, "Truck Upkeep," "Papers Read 1936 Councils," p. 70, SAA 80-43; Hayes and Castagna interviews.

28. "NOM," Sept. 22, 1933, p. 3; Sept. 29, 1933, pp. 1–2; "MSSDE Ann. Report 1933," p. 38, SAA 78-24; "NOM," July 20, 1934, p. 2; Oct. 4, 1935, p. 1; May 12, 1933, p. 2; April 20, 1934, p. 4; Sept. 22, 1933, p. 5; Sept. 29, 1933, p. 4; Oct. 6, 1933, p. 5; Aug. 17, 1934, pp. 1–2; Feb. 2, 1934, p. 2; March 9, 1934, p. 1; Jan. 4, 1935, p. 2; Dec. 28, 1933, pp. 2–3; Dec. 21, 1933, p. 4; Nov. 23, 1934, p. 2; "MSSDE Ann. Report, 1934," p. 8, SAA 74-28; McIntyre, "Homeless," p. 12; Elwood Street, "The Salvation Army in Co-operative Agency Service as Seen from Without," *National Conference of Social Work, Atlantic City, New Jersey, May 24–30, 1936. Report by the National Secretary,* pp. 1–8, SAA; *SA Yearbook, 1934,* p. 104; interviews with Lock, Stephan.

29. "NOM," Oct. 4, 1935, p. 5; Oct. 11, 1935, p. 4; Nov. 22, 1935, pp. 1–2 ["NOM" did not include page numbers for several issues after Nov. 22, 1935]; McMillan, "80,000 sq. ft.," p. 9; Major H[arold] W. Bevan, "Cleanliness and Order in the Institutions," "Papers Read, 1938 Councils," p. 82, MSSDE off. files; "Brief MSSDS, 1953," pp. 75–76; "NOM," Oct. 8, 1937, p. 3; on Kansas C. center, Briggs interview; "NOM," Apr. 9, 1937, p. 1; Feb. 11, 1938, p. 1; March 25, 1938, p. 4; *WCE,* July 10, 1937, pp. 12–13; corresp. in SAA 26-10-1, Property & Legal Secretary, Correspondence: Col. George Darby to J. O. Dowdell, NYC April 29, 1940; May 9, 1940; Major T. B. Dickinson to Asst. Corporation Counsel, Borough of Brooklyn, NYC, Jan. 20, 1941; George Jackson to Col. George Darby, NYC, Dec. 17, 1940 enclosing order to vacate; on Camden center, Castagna interview; MSSDC, "Inst. History," Kansas City; MSSDS, "Inst. History," Washington, D.C.; SAA Vertical files, MSSC, Philadelphia; SAA "Center History," Camden, NJ.

30. "NOM," June 30, 1933, p. 1; July 7, 1933, pp. 1–2; Brig. L. Castagna to author, Columbus, OH, Dec. 21, 1983 covering band notices for Social Band, B/M Adj. George Granger, one no date, others Jan. 6, Feb. 23, March 3, March 16, 1933; "NOM," April 19, 1933, pp. 1–2; July 14, 1933, pp. 1–2; Aug. 4, 1933, p. 2; Sept. 22, 1933, p.1; Sept. 29, 1933, p. 2; Dec. 1, 1933, p. 2; Jan. 5, 1934, p. 4; March 28, 1934, p. 4; July 13, 1934, p. 1; Sept. 17, 1934, p.1; May 16, 1935, p. 3; June 14, 1935, p. 1; Jan. 8, 1936, p. 5; July 3, 1936, p. 3; interview with McCormick; on "Metropolitan District Social Band," see: "NOM," Nov. 27, 1936, pp. 3–5; "MSSDE Annual Report, Oct. 1935 to Sept. 1936," pp. 53, SAA 78/24; "NOM," Jan. 8, 1936, p. 6; March 6, 1936, pp. 4–5; March 27, 1936, p. 6; April 10, 1936, p. 3; May 10, 1936, p. 4; on institutional bands, see: "NOM," May 3, 1934, p. 5; Nov. 15, 1935, p. 3; interview with R. E. Holz, Sr. [NY No. 1]; "NOM," Dec. 8, 1934, p. 2; letters to author, B/M Charles Baker, NYC, Oct. 11, 1982 and Lt.-Col. Raymond

Howell, NYC, Sept. 24, 1982, the first to cover letter Lt.-Col. Wallace Conrath to B/M Baker, NYC, Sept. 13, 1982; "NOM," Feb. 15, 1935, p. 4; March 8, 1935, p. 2; March 22, 1935, p. 5; May 16, 1935, p. 4; May 15, 1936, p. 4; March 12, 1937, p. 4; Oct. 15, 1937, p. 1; July 8, 1938, p. 2; *WCE*, July 16, 1938, p. 13 [Boston]; "NOM," June 14, 1935, p. 2; Oct. 18, 1935, p. 5; Oct. 25, 1935, p. 3 [Newark]; "NOM," Oct. 4, 1935, p. 3; Oct. 25, 1935, p. 2; Nov. 29, 1935, p. 5; Oct. 23, 1936, p. 3; March 25, 1938, p. 4 [Philadelphia]; "NOM," July 10, 1936, p. 3; July 24, 1936, p. 3; Oct. 1, 1937, p. 5 [Westchester County Social Service Band]; "NOM," Jan. 8, 1937, p. 7; Jan. 3, 1936, p. 4 [Pittsburgh]; "NOM," April 10, 1936, p. 5; May 22, 1936, p. 4; May 29, 1936, p. 4; Jan. 8, 1937, p. 3 [Springfield, Mass.]; "NOM," April 5, 1933, p. 1; Oct. 5, 1934, p. 2 [Cincinnati]; "NOM," Nov. 8, 1935, p. 3 [Syracuse]; "NOM," Dec. 8, 1934, p. 3; March 9, 1934, p. 3 (minstrels) [Providence]; "NOM," May 30, 1937, p. 4 [Cleveland]; "NOM," Jan. 26, 1934, p. 4 [Dayton]; "NOM," May 3, 1935, p. 5 [MSSDE quartette].

31. "Brief MSSDS 1953," p. 2; "NOM," June 24, 1938, p. 3; *Dispo Southern,* Dec. 1938, p. 5; July 1939, p. 5.

32. "NOM," Nov. 3, 1933, p. 4; Nov. 23, 1934, p. 2; Nov. 13, 1936, p. 4; March 12, 1937, p. 3; Dowdell Binder, "S," MSSDE off. files has circular letters to mgrs on report-keeping (Feb. 1937); "NOM," July 14, 1933, pp. 2–4 [indictment of store operations]; Nov. 23, 1934, p. 2; Dec. 8, 1934, p. 3; Dec. 14, 1934, p. 1; *WCE,* Dec. 10, 1932, p. 3; "NOM," July 21, 1933, p. 2; May 12, 1935, p. 5; Jan. 18, 1935, p. 4; Feb. 15, 1935, p. 2 (and April 5, 1935, p. 4; May 12, 1935, p. 2); Nov. 13, 1936, pp. 2–3; Adj. R. Barber, "Methods of Increasing Store Sales," "Papers Read at MSSD Officers' Councils, Philadelphia, May 12–13, 1937," p. 64, SAA 80-43; same, "Increasing Store Revenue," "Papers Read 1938 Councils," p. 53 MSSDE off. files; "NOM," June 4, 1937, pp. 2–3; Major Frank J. Smith, "Balancing the Budget," "Papers Read 1938 Councils," pp. 37–39; Adj. R. E. Baggs, "Increasing Store Revenue," "Papers Read 1938 Councils," pp. 48–51; Adj. Fritz Nelson, "Salvaging Men and Materials: An Insight Into the Activities of a Typical New York Social Service Center," *WCE,* May 21, 1932, p. 12; "NOM," Jan. 14, 1938, p. 4; March 28, 1934, p. 3; July 15, 1938, p. 1.

33. "NOM," Dec. 31, 1936, p. 3; Adj. E[rnest] Hayes, "Our Method, Experience and Results of Systematic Telephone Solicitation," "Papers Read 1937 Councils," pp. 41–42; Hayes interview; "NOM," Feb. 14, 1936, p. 5; Jan. 22, 1937, pp. 1–2; "MSSDE Annual Report, 1935," pp. 37–38, SAA 78-24; "NOM," Oct. 6, 1933, p. 2; Oct. 27, 1933, p. 4; Nov. 17, 1933, pp. 2, 4; Jan. 19, 1934, p. 4; Feb. 16, 1934, p. 4; Oct. 8, 1937, p. 2; many MSSD brochures, leaflets and door cards can be found in Seiler Collection binders; Vertical file, "Scranton," SAA, has 3 SA print 1934 pamphlets cited in text. On rag sorting department, see "NOM," March 1, 1935, p. 2; March 29, 1935, p. 2; April 12, 1935, pp. 1–2, 5; April 26, 1935, p. 2; May 12, 1935, p. 4; June 7, 1935, pp. 3–4; "MSSDE Annual Report, 1935," pp. 21–22, SAA 78-24; *Dispo, Eastern,* Aug. 1938, Dec. 1938, April 1940.

34. "Men's Social Service Officer's Manual. New York No. 1, NY" [1937–1970], No. 1, Sept. 1937, No. 2, same, in Manhattan ARC office files; Brig. J. O. Dowdell to Captain Lawrence Castagna, NYC, Dec. 2, 1935, in LCM; "NOM," Jan. 29, 1937, pp. 2–3; Feb. 22, 1937, p. 2; Feb. 26, 1937, p. 2; March 25, 1937, p. 2; April 2, 1937, p. 2.

35. "NOM," Feb. 9, 1935, p. 2; Major Egon Naehring, "My Job and What it Entails," "Papers Read 1938 Councils," pp. 28–29, MSSDE off. files; Captain Clarence A. Simmons, "The Influence of the Social Officer Upon His Men," "Papers Read 1938 Councils," pp. 22–23.

36. "NOM," Dec. 13, 1935, p. 5; Jan. 24, 1936, p. 4; Oct. 9, 1936, p. 3; June 4, 1937, p. 3; May 13, 1938, p. 5; Mrs. Adj. Frank J. Smith, "The Home League in the Men's Social Service Department," "Papers Read at the MSS Officers' Councils, Philadelphia, June 3–4, 1936," pp. 12–15, SAA 80-43 (Cleveland H.L.); "NOM," Oct. 5, 1934, pp. 2–3; "MSSDE Ann. Report, Oct. 1935–Sept. 1936," pp. 12–13; "MSSDE Ann. Report, 1935," p. 3; "MSSDE Ann. Report, Oct. 1938–Sept. 1939," p. 17, SAA 78-24; *Dispo, Eastern,* re. Dayton, Ohio Corps, 1934–1940 [end fiscal year 1939], LCM; interviews with Castagna; Parker, "Phases of Men's IH work," p. 375; Laurie, "Handling the Transient," p. 894; Brig. Thomas Seaver, " 'The World for God' Campaign in the Institution," "Papers Read 1936 Councils," p. 1, SAA 80-43.

37. "MSSDE Annual Report, July–Dec. 1931," pp. 41–48, SAA 78-24; "Ann. Report 1932," pp. 28–29; "Ann. Report, 1933," p. 33; Adj. Chester Brown, "Social Case Work for the SA Social Service Officer," "Papers Read 1933 Councils," pp. 4–5, SAA Acc. 80/43; Captain A. Ernest Agnew, "Social Case Work for Salvation Army Industrial Officers," "Papers Read 1933 Councils," pp. 1–3; same author, "The Case Work Process in the Men's Social Service Center," "MSSDE Officers' Councils, Oct. 13, 1949 [NYC]," p. 1; Lt.-Comm. Edward J. Parker, "Where Are We Taking the Army," [address to SA delegates, NCSW], *WCE, Aug. 12, 1933, p. 8; Nels Anderson, "A Critical View of The Salvation Army's Social Welfare Program," "Papers Read 1934 Councils," pp. 98, 100–101; "NOM," Nov. 23, 1934, p. 3; V. R. Post, "Balancing Budget," p. 118; Laurie, "SA and Mass Casework, p. 10; Major James S. Borill, "Re-making Men," "Papers Read at the MSS Officers' Councils, Philadelphia, May 21–23, 1935," pp. 148, 150–51, SAA 80-43; "NOM," July 29, 1929, pp. 3–4; June 23, 1933, p. 1; *NCSW 1936 Report,* pp. 1–4; *The Salvation Army at the National Council of Social Work* (New York: National Research Bureau, 1948), pp. 1–4, SFOTW-Lib.; Major Charles McClements, "What Constitutes Efficient Management of Social Service Centers," "Papers Read 1936 Councils," pp. 104–105, SSA 80-43; Adj. E. A. Hayes, "Stimulating and Maintaining the Morale of Men," "Papers Read 1936 Councils," pp. 5–8; Adj. Orlo Ellison, "The Men's Social Service Department in a Cooperative Community Program," *National Conference of Social Work, Seattle, Washington, June 26–July 2, 1938: Report by the National Secretary,* p. 40; program, dedication MSSC Paterson, NJ, Dec. 3, 1939, in SFOTE-Mus., item 124; interviews with Guldenschuh, Schuerholz, Johnson, Castagna, Crayton.

38. Brig. J. O. Dowdell, "The Functioning of the Social Service Center in a Changing Society,"NCSW, Buffalo, NY, June 18–June 24, 1939: Report by the National Secretary, p. 7 ("dying embers"); *WCW,* Jan. 1, 1889, p. 5; Anderson & Harris, *Report,* p. 68; "NOM," Jan. 15, 1937, p. 3; Mrs. Captain [Loyd] Robb, "Deliverance for Drink Slaves," *The Officers' Review,* X (Oct.–Dec. 1941), pp. 210–212, 213, 215; Philadelphia MSSC "Center Bulletin," [Sept. 1955] farewell issue for Brig. and Mrs. Richard E. Baggs, loaned to author by Mrs. Patty Yellis, April 1984; Adj. A. E. Agnew, "Case Work Program in a Men's Social Service Center, April 1941," p. 23; Brig. George E. Purdum, "The Salvation Army's Approach in the Treatment of Alcoholics," dated 9/23/40, typescript in SAA 81-74, Box "E. Pa;" interviews with Schuerholz, Castagna, McCormick, Craytor.

39. "NOM," Sept. 8, 1933, pp. 3–4; Feb. 23, 1934, p. 4; May 3, 1934, pp. 1–2; "MSSDE Ann. Report Oct. 1937–Sept. 1938," p. 61, SAA 78-24; Dowdell, "Functioning of a Social Service Center," pp. 3–5; *WC,* May 23, 1896, pp. 1–2.

40. Social Service Order No. 10 (Sept. 1938) and 13 (April 1939), J. O. Dowdell, in "MS Officer's Manual" binder in Manhattan ARC office files; Comm. E. J.

Parker to Comm. E. L. Pugmire, NYC, Sept. 14, 1939; same to Col. Fletcher Agnew, NYC, Sept. 26, 1939; same to Pugmire, NYC, Jan. 3, 1940; same to Pugmire, telegram, NYC, Feb. 20, 1940; same to Pugmire, NYC, July 25, 1941; Col. A. E. Chesham to Lt.-Col. Frank Genge, Chicago, Dec. 2, 1941; Genge to Chesham, Chicago, Dec. 9, 1941, all in "FLSA storage files," MSSDC office files; Minutes of Comm. Conf., July 9–10, 1941, p. 2; April 13–14, 1942, p. 19.

    41. "NOM," Jan. 7, 1938, p. 1; *WCE,* July 6, 1940, p. 10; SAA vertical files, "Pittsburgh MSSC."

CHAPTER V

    1. A. E. Baldwin to mgrs, Atlanta, Nov. 2, 1942; Jan. 4, 1943, Baldwin letters, MSSDS off. files, copies SAA; Adj. Peter Hofman, "Answering the Challenge Through Men's Social Service," "Addresses Delivered (The Salvation Army Sessions) National Conference of Social Work, New York, 1943, St. Louis," pp. 1–4, SFOTW-Lib.; The theme of the SA sessions at the 1943 NCSW was "The Challenge of Today's Needs on the Home Front." There were no sessions in 1941 or 1942; Adjutant A. E[rnest] Agnew, "The Men's Social Service Department, Eastern Territory: A Survey Based on Social Studies of Thirteen Social Service Centers, Containing a Summary of Findings, General Recommendations, 'First Steps' for Proposed Institution of a Modernized Social Program," April 1943, p. 16. Copy annotated in J. O. Dowdell's hand, SA 78/24: hereinafter, "Survey;" Adj. A. E. Agnew, "Studies Made at the Men's Social Service Institutions by Adjutant A. E. Agnew, 1942–1943," p. 31, MSSDE office files; "Brief for Men's Social Service Department, Southern Territory of The Salvation Army," Lt.-Col. Gilbert S. Decker, MSSS, Aug. 30, 1953, p. 56, MSSDS office files; Maj. G. Granger to Maj. Chas. Shuerholz, NYC, April 25, 1945, in LCM; interviews with Guldenschuh, Briggs, Hillis, A. S. Peters; Center history, "Omaha," MSSDC; Lt.-Col. W. W. Hasney to author, Chicago, April 20, 1983; Brig. Samuel Hepburn to Col. Norman Marshall, Philadelphia, June 6, 1942, in SAA 81-74, Box 3, "E. Pa: Men's Social—Reading & Pottstown."

    2. Minutes, Comm. Conf. June 24, 1942, pp. 6–7; typical patriotic pamphlets issued by SA during the war were *The Salvation Army is Helping Uncle Sam's Defense Program, Timely Pointers in Practical Patriotism,* and *The Salvation Army and the Armed Forces;* these were found in Detroit ARC office files; a large selection of similar materials, including *The Hoarder: A Definition* from the Trenton MSSC, found in Seiler collection binders; "Omaha" Center History, p. 5–6, MSSDC office files; interview with Briggs.

    3. Hofman, "Answering the Challenge," pp. 1–4; "MSSDE Annual Report, Oct. 1936–Sept. 1937," pp. 40–42; "MSSDE Ann. Rep., Oct. 1939–Sept. 1940," p. 43, SAA 78-24.

    4. E. Gesner to author, Maitland, Fla., March 19, 1984; interview with A. S. Peters; "Finance & General Statistics," ledger 4, Oct. 6, 1944–Aug. 31, 1945; ledger 5, Oct. 5, 1945 to Oct. 26, 1945, "Horses: Renewal and Hire" replaced by "Religious Rehabilitation" [written in]; ledger 6, Jersey City MSSC, shows no further addition to the horse expense column after March 29, 1946, which indicates the horses were removed between Feb. 22 and March 29, these 6 large ledgers in SAA 78-24; Agnew, "Studies," Jersey City, pp. 85–86; Lt.-Col. Harold Smith, "A Proposal for the Observance of The Golden Jubilee (1897–1947) of The

Salvation Army Men's Social Service Centers in America," June 1, 1947, p. 6, states the last horses in the MSSDE were sold in 1946, MSSDE, SAA; Major Henry H. Newby, "Horses vs. Automobiles," "Papers Read at the Men's Social Service Officers' Councils, Philadelphia, June 3–4, 1936," p. 56 [quotation]; interview with Lt.-Col. R. Howell, who recalled that the Albany MSSC smelled of horses for 25 years after the last one was sold.

5. "Men's Social Service Department, Eastern Territory, Study of Operating Results [1939–1949], MSSDE off. files; Agnew, "Studies," pp. 4–5, 140, 77–78, 112; Hofman, "Answering the Challenge," pp. 1–4; interviews with Hofman, Briggs, Castagna.

6. "MSSDE Annual Report, Oct. 1939–Sept. 1940," pp. 25–26; Minutes, Comm. Conf. Nov. 17–18, 1943, p. 43; Sept. 13–14, 1944, p. 4; Comm. Donald McMillan to Lt.-Comm. J. J. Allen, NYC, June 6, 1945 in "FLSA Storage file," MSSDC office files; U.S. Dept. of Labor, National Advisory Committee on Sheltered Workshops, *A Statement of Elementary Standards Respecting the Policies, Organization, Operation, and Service Activities of Sheltered Workshops* (New York, National Advisory Committee on Sheltered Workshops, 1944), pp. 5–10; interview with Hofman.

7. J. O. Dowdell to mgrs., NYC, June 1, 1941, letter covering report, Adj. A. E. Agnew, "Case Work Program in a Men's Social Service Center, April 1941" [Philadelphia] in SAA 78/24; Agnew, "Case Work Program," forward and *passim*.

8. Agnew, "Survey," pp. 1–2; Agnew, "Studies," pp. 2, 117–118, 127, 128–129, 131–132; Major A. Ernest Agnew, " Service-to-Man Program," *The Officers' Review*, XVI (Jan.–Feb. 1947), p. 10; Agnew, "Studies," pp. 165–166; Alcoholics Anonymous General Service Conference, *The Twelve Traditions Illustrated* (New York: Alcoholics Anonymous World Services, 1971) [pp. 1–3]; Agnew, "Survey," pp. 27–28, 39, 123, 151 (urging utilization of AA); Major Richard E. Baggs, "Answering the Challenge Through Men's Social Service," "Addresses, NCSW, 1943," p. 7.

9. Agnew, "Studies," pp. 17–19, 20, 22–23, 39, 51, 81, 90, 96, 123, 151, 152–153, 158; Agnew, "Survey," pp. 5–7, 12, 16, 17–18, 19, 21–22, 24–25, 31, Appendix I, 5–6, 7; Baggs, "Answering the Challenge," pp. 3–5; Hofman, "Answering the Challenge," pp. 5–11; Brig. Thomas Seaver, " 'The World for God' Campaign in the Institution," "Papers Read 1936 Councils," p. 2; Philadelphia MSSC "Center Bulletin," Farewell issue [Sept. 1955] for Brig. and Mrs. Richard E. Baggs, lent to author by Mrs. Patty Yellis, April 1984.

10. Agnew, "Survey," pp. 23–24; Lt.-Col. J. O. Dowdell to Adj. L. Castagna, NYC, May 11, 1943; Castagna to Lt.-Col. Ray Howell, Nov. 18, 1980, both in "SA Historical Conf. No. 7" file, MSSDE office files; interviews with Hofman.

11. [J. O. Dowdell] to A. E. Agnew, NYC, June 4, 1943 and same to same, July 28, 1943, in SAA 78-24: [A. E. Agnew] "The Salvation Army. Social Aims, Philosophy and Program Standards of the Men's Social Service Department Eastern Territory. Issued by Authority of the Territorial Commissioner, 1943." 23 pp. typed, pp. 5–7, 8, 10–12; Dowdell to Agnew, NYC, July 26, 1943 all in 78-24; Social Order No. 30, May 1943, p. 3, "Definition and Schedule of Employees and Clients," in "Men's Social Service Officer's Manual. New York No. 1, NY" [1937–1970] in Manhattan ARC office files; Minutes Comm. Conf. Nov. 17–18, 1943, p. 23.

12. Major Albert E. Ramsdale, "Interpretation: Telling The Salvation Army's Story," *National Conference of Social Work, Seattle, Washington, June 26–July 2,*

240 SOMEBODY'S BROTHER

1938: Report by the National Secretary, pp. 29–37; Lt.-Col. Hofman, in interview
in August 1983, could still recall the very page in Booth's book upon which the
observation appeared. See William Booth, *In Darkest England and The Way Out*
(London: The Salvation Army, 1890), p. 186; Major Peter J. Hofman, "Serving the
Client and the Community through the Men's Social Service Center," *Addresses
Delivered at Salvation Army Sessions: National Conference of Social Work, San
Francisco, 1947* (New York: National Research Bureau, National Headquarters
[1947]), p. 43; interviews with Castagna, Hillis, Stephan.
13. Minutes, Comm. Conference, Nov. 17–18, 1943, pp. 6, 16; June 2–3, 1944,
p. 7; Sept 13–14, 1944, p. 4; Nov. 30–Dec. 1, 1944, p. 7; Feb. 27–28, 1945, p. 8;
Oct. 9–11, 1945, p. 5; Feb. 4–6, 1948, pp. 14–15; [Salvation Army] *Survey-Course
in Social Welfare Work for use in USA Training Colleges and Advanced Training
Systems* (new ed., no place, no publ. [1942]), chaps XIV, XVII–XXI, XXIII;
George B. Mangold (Survey, The Salvation Army, Los Angeles, California, 1939)
(Los Angeles: The Salvation Army, 1939), pp. 20–21, in SFOTW-Lib.; Gesner,
letter to author; interviews with Briggs, Johnson, A. S. Peters; letter to author
Mrs. H. Westcott, West Wickham, England, Aug. 23, 1984, and Mrs. Col. Arch
Layman, San Jose, California, Aug. 18, 1984.
14. Norman Marshall to J. O. Dowdell, NYC, Sept. 1, 1943; J. O. Dowdell to
Col. Richard E. Stretton, NYC, Sept. 7, 1943; N. Marshall to Dowdell, NYC, Nov.
4, 1943; [A. E. Agnew] "Orientation Course to Prepare for, and Introduce a
'Service-to-Man' Program to the Officer Personnel of the Men's Social Service
Department of The Salvation Army Eastern Territory. Prepared under the Direction and Authority of Commissioner Ernest I. Pugmire, Territorial Commander,
1943." 11 pp. typed; form letter, Dowdell to mgrs, NYC, Nov. 17, 1943, announcing 1st regional directors; memorandum from Chief Secretary [Norman S. Mar-
shall] to Lt.-Col. J. O. Dowdell, NYC, Dec. 11, 1943, copies to all divisional
commanders and dept. heads, all in SAA 78/24; interviews with Guldenschuh,
Hayes, Sparks, Hofman, Castagna, McCormick, Stephan.
15. Norman Marshall to J. O. Dowdell, NYC, Dec. 29, 1943; Brig. [Alfred]
Jackson to Maj. A. E. Agnew, NYC, Jan. 6, 1944; Jackson to Maj. Herbert Sparks,
Feb. 24, 1944, conveying Brief of Appt. as "Regional Director" for Pittsburgh
area; "Memorandum of Instructions issued to Major Herbert Sparks, Regional
Director, Men's Social Service Department, Eastern Territory," [Feb. 1944] signed
J. O. Dowdell; Brig. [A. Jackson] to Major F. Guldenschuh, NYC, Feb. 24, 1944,
same; Marshall to J. O. Dowdell, NYC, March 20, 1944; Dowdell to Marshall,
March 22, 1944; series of letters from mgrs in Metropolitan Region to Major F.
Guldenschuh, April 1944, in response to HQ request for reactions to "Service to
Man;" E. I. Pugmire to Dowdell, NYC, May 4, 1944; Dowdell to Pugmire, NYC,
May 12 and May 16, 1944; Pugmire to Dowdell, NYC, May 16, 1944; N. Marshall
to Dowdell, NYC, June 1, 1944; Dowdell to Marshall, NYC, June 8, 1944 (trou-
ble!); Major Frank Guldenschuh to Dowdell, NYC, June 11, 1944; Dowdell to N.
Marshall, NYC, Oct. 4, 1944; Guldenschuh to Dowdell, NYC, Oct. 5, 1944;
Dowdell to Marshall, Oct. 5, 1944; Marshall to Dowdell, NYC, Oct. 7 and Oct. 23,
1944; agenda for meeting of Dowdell and Regional Directors, Nov. 27, 1944,
entitled "General Plan for the Continuation of the Rehabilitation Program;"
Dowdell to Marshall, NYC, Dec. 29, 1944. All citations in this note in SAA 78-24.
16. Major A. E. Agnew, *The Nineteen Hundred Forty-Four Institutes of the
Men's Social Service Department* (New York: The Salvation Army Eastern Territory [1946]), pp. 44–46, 51–67, 68–78, 79–82, 114–123 and *passim;* Merrill Moore
to George Purdum, Bronxville, NY, Dec. 23, 1941 and material on the Research

Council on Problems of Alcohol, reorganized in Nov. 1943 and SA participation in SAA 81-74, Box "E. Pa. Div.—Alcoholism;" Mrs. Adj. Anita Robb, "The Yale Summer School of Alcohol Studies," *Addresses NCSW 1947,* pp. 54, 63; Adjutant Don Pitt, "Alcoholism: The Army's Role," The Salvation Army and the Alcoholic (New York: The Salvation Army National Research Bureau, 1948), p. 11; interviews with Guldenschuh, Hayes, Johnson; on Cleveland "Cedar Group" see: Agnew "Studies," p. 114; Hofman, "Serving the Client," pp. 46–47; "NOM," Dec. 10, 1954, p. 5; Jan. 6, 1956 (speaks of 11th anniversary); *WCE,* Nov. 15, 1947, p. 13; Agnew, "Service to Man," pp. 10–14; leaflet on "Suggestions for Guests" at Cleveland MSSC in Seiler Coll. binders; Minutes, Comm. Conf. Sept. 13–14, 1944, p. 4; Feb. 4–6, 1948, p. 21; June 2–3, 1948, p. 13; materials and correspondence on SA "commissions" on alcoholism in SAA 81-74 Box 3, "E. Pa.—Alcoholic Commission."

17. Brig. James S. Bovill, "Impressions and Report on 1945 Yale Summer School of Alcoholic Studies," 15 pp. single-spaced typescript, pp. 2–4, 11, 13, in SAA 81-74 Box 3; Peter Hofman to J. O. Dowdell, Cleveland, Feb. 25, 1946 in SAA 78-24; A. Robb "Yale School," pp. 59–62, 64–66; Mrs. Lt.-Col. Harold R. Smith, "Men's Social Service Work in the United States," *SA Year Book,* 1949, p. 11.

18. Major Peter Hofman, "Study and Review of Results of Orientation Course in Connection with the Service-to-Man Program Presented by Major Ernest Agnew." 8 pp. typed [early 1945], pp. 2–4, SAA 78-24.

19. Minutes, 1st Regional meeting, Columbus, Ohio, Jan. 25, 1945; Cleveland, May 7, 1945; Columbus, July 5, 1945; Major R. E. Baggs to Dowdell, Philadelphia, Feb. 19, 1946, enclosing report on program for 1945; Major F. Guldenschuh to Dowdell, NYC, Jan. 30, 1946; H. L. Stephan, Boston, Feb. 8, 1946; Major Herbert Sparks, Pittsburgh, Feb. 8, 1946 and March 11, 1946, all with same purpose [1945 report]; Minutes, Comm. Conf. Sept. 13–14, 1944, p. 5; letter, E. Gesner to author, Maitland, Fla, Mar. 14, 1984; telephone interview with Brig. Hubert Holmes, May 1984; interviews with Briggs, Johnson, Duplain, Peters.

20. Willard Waller, *The Veteran Comes Back* (New York: The Dryden Press, 1944), p. 13; Brig. Gilbert S. Decker, "Rehabilitation Program Engages Efforts of Men's Social Departments," *WCS,* Nov. 1, 1947, p. 15; Hofman, "Serving the Client," p. 45.

21. "Brief MSSDS 1953," pp. 12–13; *Dispo Southern,* Oct. 1946, pp. 8–10, 56; Nov. 1949, pp. 5–7 (April 1949, pp. 5–6); Nov. 1954, pp. 8–10, 56; Gesner letter to author; career sheets, Jobe, Wm.; Crawford, Andrew Earl; Reinking, Frederick, in FDC, and for Gesner, Harold; Lekson, Arne, in FDS; Minutes, Regional Directors' Meeting, Syracuse NY, March 13, 1946; J. O. Dowdell to Col. Bertram Rodda, NYC, March 25, 1946; Minutes, Reg. Directors' Mtg., Boston, June 19, 1946; Minutes, Reg. Directors' Mtg., Atlantic City, Feb. 14, 1947; Minutes, Reg. Directors' Mtg, NYC, Oct. 1–2, 1947, all in SAA 78-24.

22. "Brief MSSDS 1953," pp. 3–4, 7, 18–19, 35, 41–42, 43–45, 52–54, 56–57, 67–68; *WCS,* Feb. 22, 1947, p. 6, 15; June 14, 1947, p. 7; July 12, 1947, p. 5; Nov. 1, 1947, pp. 3, 5, 8–9, 9–10, 11, 16; Nov. 15, 1947, pp. 1, 8–9, 11, 15, 16; *Dispo Southern,* April 1949, p. 7; Nov. 1950, p. 6; interview with A. S. Peters, who consulted financial returns in Office of Asst. MSSS, so to provide exact information.

23. "Brief MSSDS 1953," pp. 18–19, 42; *WCS,* Nov. 11, 1950, p. 9; June 14, 1947, p. 7; *WCE,* March 8, 1947, p. 9; career sheet, Duplain, George W., in CSW; interview with Duplain.

24. Smith, "Men's Social Work," p. 9; *WCE,* Nov. 1, 1947, pp. 14, 17; Minutes,

Regional Directors' Mtg., NYC, Oct. 1–2, 1947, SAA 78-24; Program, Friday Evening at the Temple," Golden Jubilee of the Men's Social Service Department; 8:00 pm, Friday, Nov. 7, 1947," in SFOTE-Library; Program for 2nd MSSD night, Dec. 10, 1948, same collection; clippings from *Paterson Evening News,* Nov. 1, 1947, p. 14; Nov. 3, 1947, p. 16 in "Paterson" album, MSSDE office files; Brig. Alfred Jackson, "In Review," "The Men's Social Service Department, Eastern Territory, Officers' Councils, Oct. 13, 1949, Riverside Church [NYC]," pp. 2–3; career sheet, Dowdell, Joseph Ogden, SAA.

25. Ledger 6, MSSDE, SAA 78/24; Lt.-Col. Harold R. Smith to Major D. Seaver, NYC, Feb. 17, 1949 (covering 1st quarter terr. report on store sales) in MSSDE office files; Col. Holland French, "Milestones in Salvation Army Social Service," *Addresses Delivered at Salvation Army Sessions of the NCSW, Cleveland, Ohio, June 10–17, 1949,* (New York: [SA] National Research Bureau [1949]), p. 121; Smith, "MSS Work," p. 9; "Study of Annual Operating Results, Year Ending Sept. 1950," and "Study of Operating Results [1939–1948]," in MSSDE office files; SA "United Service Organizations: Operating Cash Book," fiscal year ending Sept. 30, 1947, MSSDC office files (storage); Lt.-Col. H. R. Smith, Keynote Address, "Report on Officers' Councils Held at Atlantic City, April 24–26, 1951."

26. On the 1948 handbook, see Minutes, Commissioners' Conference, Feb. 27, 28, 1945, p. 16; June 7–8, 1945, p. 18; Jan. 29–31, 1946, p. 2; Dec. 15–17, 1946, p. 20; May 14–16, 1947, p. 21; Oct. 15–17, 1947, p. 25; Feb. 4–6, 1948, p. 14; June 2–3, 1948, pp. 9–10; interview with Briggs; The Salvation Army, *The Salvation Army Social Service for Men, Standards and Practices* (New York: [S.A.] National Research Bureau, 1948) *passim.* (Citations regarding FLSA will be found in note 27.)

27. Major W. B. Jobe to Lt.-Col. F. Genge, Minneapolis, Jan. 30, 1946; John J. Allan to Comm. D. McMillan, Chicago, Jan. 18, 1946; Minutes, Sheltered Workshop Adv. Committee, NYC, June 7, 1946, pp. 4–5; D. McMillan to J. J. Allan, NYC, June 13, 194[6]; Brig. A. E. Baldwin to J. J. Allan, Chicago, June 19, 1946; all in MSSDC off. file. "FLSA" storage files; Major R. E. Baggs to J. O. Dowdell, Philadelphia, Feb. 19, 1946 in SAA 78-24; Lt.-Col. J. O. Dowdell to Brig. A. Baldwin, NYC, May 28, 1946 in MSSDC off. files, "FLSA" storage; Decker, "Rehabilitation Program," p. 15; *WCS,* Nov. 15, 1947, p. 11; Cadwallader, Wickersham and Taft to Comm. E. Pugmire, NYC, Jan. 18, 1950, 17 pp. single spaced pp. re. FLSA; MSSDC, "Manual of Instructions," Order No. 34, Jan 5, 1948 (compensation insurance); Cadwallader, Wick. & Taft to Pugmire, NYC, July 7, 1950; "Definition and Schedule of Employees and Clients (Eastern Territory—July 31, 1950)," all in MSSDC off. files, "FLSA" storage; Social Order No. 30 [MSSDE], Rev. 7-31-50, in "MSS Officer's Manual," Manhattan ARC office files; Social Order No. 43 [MSSDC] Oct. 1, 1952, "Manual of Instr." MSSDC office files, storage; "MSSDS Brief 1953," pp. 7–12; Minutes, Comm. Conf., Oct. 9–11, 1945, p. 7; Dec. 15–17, 1946, p. 11; May 14–16, 1947, p. 11; Feb. 4–6, 1948, pp. 15–16; June 2–3, 1948, pp. 9–10; Oct. 3–4, 1949, pp. 9–12; March 14–16, 1950, pp. 1–2; Sept. 19–21, 1950, pp. 7–8; Dec. 15, 1950, p. 4; Feb. 6–8, 1951, p. 5; May 22–23, 1951, pp. 4–7; Oct. 7–9, 1952, pp. 10, 12–13; William J. Moss, "The Salvation Army and the Fair Labor Standards Act," 28 pp. typed report to MSSS Conference, Oct. 3–5, 1956, NYC, *passim,* in MSSDE office files; see also by same author "Salvation Army Fair Labor Standards Act," April 25, 1951, for MSSDE officers' councils, Atlantic City, NJ, in MSSDC-"FLSA" office files under cover

Col. Edwin Clayton, Chicago, Oct. 30, 1952, to all DC and Dept. Hds; Col. L. W. Cowan, "Accounting for Donated Materials," "Report on MSSD Councils, 1951," pp. 2–4; Harold R. Smith to mgrs., NYC, Dec. 27, 1949 enclosing the "second" annual new "comprehensive" report; Lt.-Col. Guldenschuh refers to "good old days" of red or green, in "Minutes, Men's Social Councils [MSSDE], Berkeley Carteret Hotel, Asbury Park, NJ, Sept. 21–23, 1959, p. 9 in MSSDE office files. "Men's Social Service Eastern Territory: Analysis of Annual Results, 1951–1953," comparing four territories, pp. 4–5, 5C–5E, in MSSDE off. files; on Cleveland Harbor Light, interview Major Edward V. Dimond; letter to author, Arthur H. Korn, Chief, Branch of Special Employment, Employment Standards Adm., Wage and Hour Division, U.S. Dept. of Labor, Washington, DC, Aug. 30, 1984; William J. Moss to Col. Harold Shoults, NYC, June 26, 1985.

28. "MSSDE, Analysis, 1951–1953," pp. 20–21A; Major George Hulihan, "Price Stabilization Regulations," "Report MSSD Councils, 1951," p. 1; William J. Moss, "Re: The Salvation Army—Price, Wage and Material Controls," "Report MSSDE Councils 1951," pp. 1–2; Sr.-Major Herbert Sparks, "the Implications of a War Time Economy: the Effect Upon Clients and Employees," in "Report MSSDE Councils 1951," pp. 1–3.

29. Career sheets, Duplain, George; Allen, David; Johnson, Warren C.; WCS; Interviews with Allen, Johnson, Duplain; Institutional history, "Tulsa," MSSDS office files; H. R. Smith, Keynote address, 1951, p. 2; "MSSDS Brief 1953," p. 73; career sheet, Lekson, Arne, FDS; *WCS,* Oct. 31, 1953, pp. 7, 10, 11–13, 15.

30. Career sheets, Stillwell, Harry; Hofman, Peter J., in WCS; Lekson, Arne, FDS; Crawford, Earl; Reinking, Fred; Marshall, John C., FDC; Winchell, W. W.; Smith, Harold, in SAA; Minutes, Comm. Conf. March 14–16, 1950, p. 12; Nov. 13–15, 1951, p. 24.

31. Minutes, Regional Meeting, Upper NY area mgrs., Syracuse, Nov. 5, 1952; Regional Directors, NYC, June 13–15, 1953, in SAA 78-24; Brig. Frank Guldenschuh, "Assisting Clients Through Improved Facilities," "Report MSSDE Councils 1951," p. 4; Smith Keynote, p. 4; SA, *Standards and Practices,* 1948, pp. 43–47, esp. see A1, B, p. 44 and #5, p. 46; "NOM," Dec. 10, 1954, p. 5; Sr.-Major Richard E. Baggs, "Effective Help for the Problem Drinker," *The Officer,* I (Nov.–Dec. 1950), pp. 393–94; interviews with Irwin, Schuerholz.

32. "MSSDS Brief 1953," pp. 58–60; *WCS,* Nov. 6, 1954, pp. 10–11, 13; Center files, "Indianapolis," MSSDC office; Vertical files, "Scranton MSSC," SAA; details on numbers of new centers found in SAA vertical files, "MSSC files," center files in MSSDC office, and *Dispos Western* in FDW.

33. Clippings from Kansas City *Star,* May 3, 1951, May 29, 1951, Dec. 17, 1951, Feb. 2, 1952, esp. Nov. 23, 1952, in "Center History: Kansas City," MSSDC office files; Brig. C. Briggs shared undated clipping British *WC* on Youngman's clinic, which noted it was first medical clinic for alcoholics in SA world.

34. SA *Standards and Practices,* 1948, p. 5; Leonard Blumberg, et. al., *Skid Row and its Alternatives: Research and Recommendations from Philadelphia* (Philadelphia: Temple Univ. Press, 1973), pp. 148–149; Herbert W. Jones, M.D., Jean Roberts, John Brantner, "Incidence of Tuberculosis Among Homeless Men," *Journal of the American Medical Assoc.,* 155, July 31, 1954, pp. 1222–1223; interview with Briggs, who kindly loaned reprint of article.

35. Salvation Army, Standard Procedure for Rehabilitation Program in all centers (no pub. data [1952]), pp. 1–2, MSSDE off. files; Sr.-Major Roy S. Barber, "Broken Lives—Our Challenge," "MSSD Councils, 1949," p. 4; "MSSDS Brief

1953," p. 16; Brig. Peter Hofman, "The Salvation Army and Alcohol: Cooperating in Treatment," "Addresses Delivered at SA Sessions of the NCSW, Chicago, Illinois, May 9 to 16, 1958," pp. 24–26; interviews on role of wives with Irwin, Hayes, Hasney, Duplain, Bevan, McCormick, Harvey, Craytor; Lt.-Col. G. S. Decker, to Lt.-Col. L. W. Turrel, Atlanta, Sept. 3, 1953, in "MSSDS Brief 1953," p. 3; Mrs. Major Wm. Wilson, "The Wife of The Salvation Army Officer," "Minutes and Papers Read at the Men's Social Service Department Eastern Territory Officers' Councils, Oct. 26–27, 1938," p. 87; Mrs. Sr.-Major R. E. Baggs, "Helping the Client Through and During Off-Duty Hours with Volunteers," "Report MSSDE Councils 1951," pp. 1–3; "Center Bulletin," Philadelphia MSSC [Sept. 1955] farewell for Brig. & Mrs. R. E. Baggs, and "Program: Farewell Salute, Philadelphia MSSC, Sept. 12, 1955;" state Philadelphia Women's Auxiliary, founded 1950, remained only one in existence at that time [1955], these materials loaned to author by Mrs. Patty Yellis, April 1984.

36. "NOM," March 23, 1934, p. 1; Aug. 9, 1935, p. 2; Charles Saarion, "What Is It? No. 1—A Men's Social Service Center," WCE, Nov. 6, 1937, p. 3; Jackson, "In Review," 1949, p. 1 all attest to significance of rag and paper—"waste material"—to the pre-war MSS program; "MSSDS Brief 1953," pp. 41, 63; Gesner letter to author, March 19, 1984; interviews with Hofman, Hasney, Howell.

37. Captain Ray Howell, "Effective Production—Our Lifelife," "Minutes, MSSDE Councils 1959," pp. 30–31; Seiler collection binders contain number of solicitation form letters, door cards, leaflets, including those for J. D. Seaver, Utica [1945–48], J. O. Dowdell's years as MSSS [1935–46], C. Schuerholz, Schenectady [1948–51] and from San Francisco; Social Orders #28, March 20, 1942, in "MSS Officer's Manual," Manhattan ARC office files; Order No. 15, 10-1-58, "Manual of Instruction," MSSDC office storage; Sr.-Major H. Watson, "Family Service Stores," "Report Councils 1951," p. 2; Sr.-Capt. Edwy Hinkle, "Our Store Program," "Report Councils 1951," pp. 2–5; Mrs. Brigadier Frank Guldenschuh, "Bric-A-Brac," "Report Councils 1951," p. 2; "MSSDS Brief 1953," pp. 14–15; center files, "Chicago Central," MSSDC office files; Minutes, Comm. Conf., June 2–3, 1948, p. 14; "The Salvation Army, MSSDE, Financial and Statistical Report for 12 Months Ending Sept. 30, 1962," MSSDS office files; worksheet, "Financial comprehensive statement, 12 mos. ending Sept. 30, 1959," #2, MSSDC, MSSDC office files, storage; interviews with Briggs, Castagna, Duplain (who retained original hand-lettered "Good Neighbor" sign in San Francisco ARC warehouse, when author saw it in Aug. 1982).

38. Minutes, Comm. Conf. May 14–16, 1947, pp. 29–30; WCS, Nov. 15, 1947, pp. 8, 11; H. Smith to L. W. Cowan, NYC, June 8, 1954; L. W. Cowan to Lt.-Col. Ernest Marshall, NYC, Oct. 8, 1954, SAA 78-24; "MSSDS Brief 1953," pp. 22–29; Special Order No. 1, Dec. 1, 1910, citing letter to each Prov. officer by National Chief Secretary, May 23, 1906, "Special Orders to Social Officers," SAA 81-9, and Social Service Order 4, Oct. 1922, signed E. J. Parker, "Officer's Handbook for Men's Social Work," MSSDE office files; Lt.-Col. Ernest Marshall, "The Men's Social Services," report to THQE Executive Officers' Conference, May 21, 1955, pp. 18–20, MSSDE office files; Order 21, 10-1-58, "Manual of Instruction," MSSDC office files, storage; the historical and contemporary materials contain so many references to cooperation and mutual support between corps and local MSSC that it is difficult to cite even a few as representative. Minutes, Regional Meeting, upper NY area, Syracuse, Nov. 5, 1952; Alfred Jackson, report on transfer of Manchester, NH, corps salvage program to MSSD, March 31, 1953, in SAA 78-24.

39. Lt.-Col. Ernest Marshall to all mgrs., NYC, Nov. 5, 1956; Minutes, Reg. Directors, Boston, Jan. 30, 1957; Brig. Richard E. Baggs to E. Marshall, Boston, Sept. 6, 1957; E. Marshall to R. E. Baggs, NYC, Sept 10, 1957, all in SAA 78-24.

40. Brig. J. Kelly, G.S., MSSDC, to all officers, "confidential," July 26, 1954; Lt.-Col. Earl Crawford to all mgrs., Chicago, Feb. 17, 1956; Cadwallader, Wickersham & Taft to Col. P. L. DeBevoise, NYC, Sept. 21, 1955, same to same, April 19, 1956; Col. W. G. Harris to Lt.-Col. Earl Crawford, Chicago, May 8, 1956; same to same, Aug. 23, 1956; Claude Bates to Earl Crawford, Chicago, July 11, 1956, all in MSSDC office files "FLSA-storage files;" Minutes Comm. Conf. May 9–11, 1956, pp. 7–11.

41. Salvation Army, *Minutes of The Men's Social Service Secretaries' Conference, October 3–5, 1956* (New York: The Salvation Army National Headquarters, 1956), fwd., pp. 2–4, 10, 12, 26, 29–36, 37–39, 46–51, 54–55, 59, Dept. Order No. 30, dated 7-31-50 found on pp. 62–68, and *passim;* Minutes, Comm. Conf., Oct. 30–Nov. 1, 1956, p. 7.

42. Minutes, Comm. Conf. June 24, 1942, pp. 9–10; "MSS Officer's Manual, New York No. 1, NY" [1937–1970], Orders Nos. 1–3, Manhattan ARC office files; "Manual of Instruction," MSSDC, large blue binder, Oct. 29, 1946 to March 1, 1955, then, in same format, Oct. 1, 1958 to March 19, 1963, in MSSDC office files, storage; Order No. 13, 10-1-58, states that the 1948 gray book was in process of being "completely rewritten" by a committee apptd. by Natl. Commander; see again Minutes, Comm. Conference, Oct. 30–Nov. 1, 1956, p. 7.

43. Minutes, Comm. Conf., March 7, 8, 10, 1958, p. 30; Nov. 5, 7, 1958, p. 42; Feb. 4–6, 1959, p. 14; May 13–15, 1959, p. 64; Sept. 30–Oct. 2, 1959, p. 90; Feb. 3–5, 1960, p. 57; May 11–13, 1960, pp. 68–69; Oct. 5–7, 1960, pp. 49–50; March 1–3, 1961, p. 46; May 24–26, 1961, p. 84; tapes from A. E. Agnew, Wm. Jobe (1983); letter to author, Peter J. Hofman, Asbury Park, NJ, Jan. 18, 1983 and from Mrs. W. A. Browning, Williamsburg, Va., Aug. 15, 1984; interviews with Hofman, Duplain.

44. The Salvation Army Men's Social Service, *Handbook of Standards, Principles and Policies.* Approved by the Commissioners' Conference, New York, NY, October 1960 [New York: The Salvation Army, 1961], see sections 1:0–1:3, 3:7:1–3, 5:1:2, 7:5:1–4, 7:9:1–3, 9:9:4, 9;3:1–6 and Appendix II (pp. 1–5 [ed. 10–60]) 9:15:1–4, 13:5:1–2 and 13:7:1–9, and *passim.*

45. Agnew, *1944 Institutes,* p. 111; Center file, "Chicago Central," MSSDC office files; Lt.-Col. E. A. Marshall to Col. Ervin Waterston (MSSS Canada) NYC, Oct. 11, 1957; Marshall to Peter Hofman, NYC, April 15, 1957; Minutes, Comm. Conf. Feb. 3–5, 1960, p. 68; May 11–13, 1960, p. 78; March 1–3, 1961, pp. 56–58; Oct. 4–6, 1961, pp. 73–75; May 9–11, 1962, pp. 89–90; Salvation Army, *Songs for Men: The Salvation Army Official Songbook for Men's Social Service Centers and Harbor Light Centers in the United States of America* (New York: The Salvation Army Supplies and Purchasing Dept., c. 1961) fwd, p. iii, and numbers 130, 247–250, 252–261, note as well #192 by Stanley Ditmer and #210 by Sydney Cox; #251 in "Male Chorus" section of a notable and cherished arrangement of "Rock of Ages," by Wm. Bearchell; interview with Comm. R. E. Holz.

CHAPTER VI

1. Col. Paul Carlson to Col. Frank Guldenschuh, NYC, Aug. 7, 1963; Lt.-Col. John Phillips to Carlson, NYC, Aug. 9, 1963, in "Historical Data 7H" file, MSSDE

office files; "Income Statement of Income from Stores, Surplus Clothing and Rags, and Paper for Sixteen Year Period from Sept. 30, 1947 to Sept. 30, 1962," in MSSDE office files.

2. "Summary of Questionnaire"[1947], in SAA 8/79 box 3; Lawrence Katz "The Salvation Army Men's Social Service Center: I, Program," *QJSA,* 25(June, 1964) pp. 324–25, 327–28, 332 and Table I; Lawrence Katz, *The Salvation Army Alcoholic Rehabilitation Project: A Study of the increasing rehabilitation potential of the chronic alcoholic in an 'intreatment' center* ([San Francisco: The Salvation Army] 1966) pp. 15–20, 22–29, 86–88.

3. Interview with Duplain; the original "Circle of Endeavor" is on office wall, San Francisco ARC; *WC,* Nov. 14, 1981, p. 6; The Salvation Army Men's Social Service *Handbook of Standards, Principles and Policies* (New York, The Salvation Army, 1961), sect. 7:1:2–4.

4. Mrs. Lt.-Col. Harold R. Smith, "Men's Social Service Work in the United States," *SA Year Book 1949,* p. 11; Katz "SA Men's Social Center," p. 324; SA *Handbook,* 7:3:3; Mrs. Brigadier Margaret Troutt, "Men's Social Service in the United States," *SA Year Book 1967,* p. 27; David J. Pittman, C. Wayne Gordon, *Revolving Door: A Study of the Chronic Police Case Inebriate,* Yale Center of Alcohol Studies, No. 2 (Glencoe, Ill.: The Free Press, 1958), pp. 5, 16–41, 56–58, 60–63, 125–130; David J. Myerson, Joseph Mayer, "Origins, Treatment and Destiny of Skid-Row Alcoholic Men," *The New England Journal of Medicine,* 275, (Aug. 25, 1966), pp. 422–25; Major Peter J. Hofman, "Serving the Client and the Community through the Men's Social Service Center," *Addresses Delivered at Salvation Army Sessions, National Conference of Social Work, San Francisco, 1947* (New York: National Research Bureau, [SA] National Headquarters [1947]), p. 46; 2nd Lt. Chas. W. Smith, "An Alcoholic's Technique with Alcoholics," *The Officer,* V (1954), p. 89, 90–91; SA *Handbook,* 7:3:1–4, 7:5:1–4. 1:1:4; "Minutes, Counselors' Institute, Springfield, Mass., Jan. 23, 1958," in SAA 78/24.

5. William Booth, *In Darkest England and The Way Out* (London: The Salvation Army, 1890), p. 186; Mark Keller, "The Disease Concept of Alcoholism Revisited," *JSA,* 11 (Nov. 1976) pp. 1697–1701; E. M. Jellinek, "Phases of Alcohol Addiction," *QJSA,* 4 (Dec. 1952) pp. 673–76; see also, E. M. Jellinek, *The Disease Concept of Alcoholism* (Highland Park, NJ: Hillhouse Press, 1960); cases: *Easter v. District of Columbia,* 361 F. 2d50 (D.C. Cir., 1966), *Driver v. Hinnant,* 356 F. 2d761 (4th Cir., 1966); U.S. Senate, Commt. on Labor and Public Welfare, *Uniform Alcoholism and Intoxication Treatment Act* (Washington: U.S. Govt. Printing Office, 1971), pp. 3–4; "Annual Report, Natl. Commission on Alcohol," SAA 81-74 Box 3 contains "Minority Report Presented by Brigadier Albert E. Baldwin, Chairman, National Commission on Problems of Alcoholism," [1948]; Henry F. Milans, *God at the Scrap Heaps* ([New York]: The Salvation Army, 1945) pp. 64–68; Howard J. Clinebell, *Understanding and Counseling the Alcoholic Through Religion and Psychology,* rev. enlarged ed. (Nashville: Abingdon Press, 1968), pp. 93–100; Major Merle Howe, "Alcoholism: Sickness or Sin?" *The Officer,* 31(Feb. 1980) pp. 70–71,88.

6. Center files, "Springfield," MSSDC off. files; Center files, "Chicago Central," same; John J. Judge, "Alcoholism Treatment at The Salvation Army: A New Men's Social Service Center Program," *QJSA,* 32 (June, 1971) pp. 462–63, 465–67; see also, J. Siegrist, "Alcoholism Treatment Digest: New Alcoholism Treatment Methods in The Salvation Army," *Michigan Alcohol Review,* June, 1971, p. 17; "Minutes, Officers' Councils, MSSD, Western Territory USA, Nov. 16–19, 1969,"

for Nov. 17, 1969 (np); Minutes, MSSS Conference, May 12–14, 1971, pp. 2–3, in "MSS Sec. Conf., 1968–71" files, MSSDC off. files; letter to author, Lt.-Col. Wm. Hasney, Chicago, May 21, 1982; Career sheet, Hasney, William W., FDC; interviews with Hasney, Judge.

7. John J. Judge, " 'Sober House'—A Non-Penal, Non-Medical Response to Public Drunkenness Offenders," [August 1971] 8 pp. typed, in Detroit ARC office files.

8. "A Pilot Study of the Use of Antabuse in The Salvation Army Men's Social Service Center, Detroit, Michigan," no date, 4 pp. typed; Sanford L. Sillet, "The Use of Antabuse: An Approach that Minimizes Fear," no date, 2 pp. typed, both in Detroit ARC office files; J. Smilde, "Risks and Unexpected Reactions in Disulfiram Therapy of Alcoholism," *QJSA,* 24 (Sept. 1963) p. 490; "Antabuse Therapy Program," subj. file, MSSDC office files; MSSDC Dept. Order D-5, 6-27-80/10-15-80 on Antabuse liability release forms, MSSDS office files; interviews with Nonnweiler, Briggs, Hasney, Mulbarger.

9. Position Statement on Alcoholism, adopted by Comm. Conf. Nov. 1971; in "Minute Book, Southern Territory," MSSDS office file.

10. Katz, "SA Men's Social Center," p. 326; Lloyd Smith to Lt.-Col. Frank Guldenschuh, Columbus, Aug. 1, 1961 in SAA 78/24; photo of 1st drop-box in Detroit ARC office files; "Minutes, MSSDW Officers' Councils, 1969," Col. Paul Seiler to all Mgrs., NYC, Dec. 29, 1966, filed with "Financial and Statistical Report for 12 mos. ending Sept. 30, 1966," MSSDE offices files; Captain George Duplain, "Drop Boxes," "Men's Social Service Department, Western Territory Officers' Councils, Feb. 10–12, 1964," p. 23, in MSSDS office files; Troutt, "Men's Social in U.S.," pp. 30–31; Brig. Andrew Telfer, "Sorting, Packing and Disposing of Rags," "MSSDW Councils 1964," pp. 29–30; interview with Johnson, who gave list of 1st million dollar center in each territory.

11. Salvation Army Men's Social Service Department USA *Guide to Thrift Store Operation* ([np]: The Salvation Army, 1981) pp. 11(esp. 11a)–14, 18–19, 20–28, 30; Brig. Warren C. Johnson, "Brief—Los Angeles Men's Social Service Center, Jan. 31, 1965," p. 2, MSSDS office files; interview with Johnson, Duplain.

12. SA, *Guide to Store Op.,* p. 27; Gifford quote, "Minutes MSSDW Councils 1969," p. 6.

13. Troutt, "Men's Social in U.S.," p. 26; Donald W. Barton to Lt.-Col. W. Burroughs, Detroit, nd., with info. on dedication of Detroit MSSC Oct. 15, 1972, calling it largest in world; also, Program, dedication of Detroit MSSC, Oct. 15, 1972, in Detroit ARC office files; "Center Histories," Manhattan, Jersey City, Newark, in SAA; interview with Craytor.

14. Harris, Kerr, Forster & Company, "The Salvation Army Men's Social Service Centers: Feasibility Study of Facilities New York Metropolitan Area, June 1969," p. 111, in MSSDE off. files; "Center History: Minneapolis," MSSDC off. files; "Center History: Manhattan," SAA; Salvation Army, *Salvation Army Guide to Social Welfare Services* (New York City: The Salvation Army, 1966) pp. 3, 5; Major John Edeen to author, NYC, March 12, 1984; interviews with Howell, Hasney, Raines, Peters.

15. *WC,* Feb. 6, 1892, p. 4; *WCW,* March 4, 1893, pp. 1–2; Kansas City *Star,* Nov. 5, 1937, clipping in Center File: Kansas City, MSSDC office files; "Salvation Army Annual Reports, Men's Social Service Department, Eastern Territory, USA," October 1938–Sept. 1939, pp. 39–40, SAA 78-24; Adj. Burpee McIntyre, "Experience in Lessening Racial Tension," *Addresses Delivered at Salvation*

Army Sessions: NCSW, Chicago, Illinois, 1945 ([New York]: National Research Bureau, 1948) p. 60, in SFOTW Library; Minutes, Regional Director's Meeting, Syracuse, March 13, 1946, SAA 78/24; Hofman, "Serving the Client," p. 48; *WCS,* Dec. 9, 1950, p. 7; Lt.-Col. Gilbert S. Decker, "Brief for Men's Social Service Department, Southern Territory of The Salvation Army, August 30, 1953," p. 80, MSSDS office files; Position statement, against segregation, Comm. Conf. Nov. 1954, in "Minute Book Southern Territory," MSSDS office files; Sr.-Major C. H. Dragshak to Col. Earl Crawford, Springfield, Ill., Sept. 15, 1956, in "FLSA storage files," MSSDC off. files; position statement, "The Salvation Army and Inter-Group Relations," app. Comm. Conf. May, 1964; rev. May 1973, in "Minute Book," MSSDS; Adj. A. E. Agnew, "Studies Made at the Men's Social Service Institutions by Adjutant A. E. Agnew, 1942–1943," pp. 16, 33, 48, 62, 89, 107, 163, in MSSDE off. files; Comm. Conference Minutes, Sept. 13–14, 1944, p. 25; Nov. 30–Dec. 1, 1954, pp. 3–4; interviews with Hayes, Nonnweiler, Velazquez, Allen, Johnson, Anson, Castagna, Mulbarger, Peters; letter, E. Gesner to author, Maitland, Fla, March 19, 1984; Leonard Blumberg et. al., *Skid Row and its Alternatives: Research and Recommendations from Philadelphia* (Philadelphia: Temple University Press, 1973) p. 147; Myerson & Mayer, "Origins, Treatment, Skid Row Alcoholic Men," p. 420.

    16. *WC* July 21, 1888, p. 3; Sept. 10, 1892, p. 9; May 23, 1896, pp. 14, 16, see also p. 11; *Conqueror,* April 1892, p. 88; *WC,* June 25, 1892, p. 7; Feb. 6, 1892, p. 9; G. S. Railton, *The Authoritative Life of General William Booth: Founder of The Salvation Army* (New York: The Reliance Trading Company, 1912), p. 190.

    17. Letter to author, Lt. Col. W. Hasney, Chicago, May 21, 1982; MSSS Commission Minutes, May 25–27, 1972, pp. 1–2, MSSDC, "MS Sec. Comm. 1972" file; Vertical file, "Rochester MSSC," SAA, contains letter, Col. John Waldron to Maj. Ray Howell, NYC, Nov. 13, 1973 on potential for women's program in Rochester MSSC; Col. James Osborne to Lt. Col. David Riley, Rancho Palos Verdes, Calif., July 29, 1981, on the possibility of extending Pinehurst program for its graduates, in "General files, A–D Center files, 9F–ARC: Pinehurst," MSSDW office files; "Pinehurst Program for the Woman Alcoholic [1981]," "Salvation Army Men's Social Service Center, San Francisco, California: Intern Manual: Revised, July 2, 1982," "Pinehurst Post," newsletter, began Vol. 1, 1979, complete files, along with file of letters from successful graduates, all in SF ARC office files; interviews with Nonnweiler, Hasney, Duplain, Ksanda.

    18. Interviews with Howell, Hasney, Allen, Mulbarger and many active and retired managers of MSSCs; MSSDC Dept. Order, D-7, 2-11-75/10-15-80, "Guidelines for Residential Service for Alcoholic Women," and Subject file: "Women Alcoholics," MSSDC office files.

    19. Subject File: "Proposed Change of Designation of Men's Social Service Centers," contains extensive correspondence; Minutes MSSS Conf., May 24–25, 1973, p. 3; May 16–17, 1974, pp. 2–3; June 2–3, 1976, p. 4; April 4–5, 1977, p. 4; see also Comm. Conf. Minutes, Oct. 1976, pp. 153–54 and Jan. 1977, p. 138, MSSDC off. files; Memo, Col. Orval Taylor to all THQ officers, Atlanta, July 21, 1977 announcing Comm. Conf. decision of May 1977, in "Directives," MSSDS office files; Dept. Order Index A-8, effective 7-18-77, updated 10-15-80, in MSSDC "Dept. Orders," office files; "Men's Social Program Helps" in 1980 at MSSDE, interview with Howell and MSSDE office files; letters to author, Major Joseph Viola, Los Angeles, Feb. 13, 1984 and Col. G. Ernest Murray, Verona, Sept. 1, 1983 (conveying copies of Minutes, Comm. Conference).

20. Minutes, Comm. Conf. Oct. 1977, p. 163; Oct. 1978, p. 250; letter to author, Lt.-Col. David Riley, Portland Oregon, Feb. 23, 1984.

21. Extensive correspondence in Lt.-Col. Hofman's advisory tour of MSSDS centers in 1966 in "Lt.-Col. Peter Hofman Administrative and Program Consultant" file, MSSDS office file; *WCS,* Jan. 17, 1970, pp. 12–13; Keynote address, Lt.-Col. Frank Guldenschuh, "Minutes, Men's Social Councils [The Salvation Army Eastern Territory], Asbury Park, NJ, Sept. 21–23, 1959," p. 8, MSSDE office files; "NOM," Jan. 23, 1963, pp. 1, 11; March, 1966, p. 3 (see also Sept. 1965, p. 1 and Feb. 1966, p. 4); Lt.-Col. David Baxendale to author, NYC, July 6, 1982; Career sheets: Crawford, Geuge, Gaut, Hasney, in FDC; Devoto, Johnson, Mulbarger, in FDS; Duplain, Gitford, Carl, Riley, Allen, from ESW; "Center Histories:" Chicago Central, MSSDC office files, Brooklyn, Manhattan, SAA; *Dispos,* all territories since 1960; interviews with Howell, Seiler, Guldenschuh, Charron, Hofman, Briggs, Hasney, Allen, Johnson, Duplain, Castagna, Oliver, Mulbarger, Peters, with Col. Giles Barrett (7-10-78).

22. Minutes, Comm. Conference, Sept. 30–Oct. 2, 1959, pp. 5–6; Feb. 3–5, 1960, p. 4; May 11–13, 1960, pp. 6–8; Oct. 5–7, 1960, pp. 5–7, 49; March 1–3, 1961, pp. 4–6, 9–10; May 24–26, 1961, pp. 2–3; Oct. 4–6, 1961, pp. 2–3; Philip Klein, *From Philanthropy to Social Welfare: An American Cultural Perspective* (San Francisco: Jossey-Bass, Inc., 1971) p. 276; "Definitions: National Statistical Form NSS-19: Adult Rehabilitation Centers" for "Cases Closed-satisfactorily," p. 92, in MSSDC office files.

23. Interviews with Captain Norman R. Nonnweiler, Caldwell, Edelman, Mulbarger.

24. Carol Grigsby to Brig. C. C. Briggs [Piggins, Balmer, Grigsby, Skillman & Erickson] Detroit, May 21, 1969 enclosing copy of new U.S. Treasury regulation 1.170-1.(c) in Detroit ARC file; U.S. Dept. of the Treasury, Internal Revenue Service, Publ. 561 (10-70), *Valuation of Donated Property* (Washington: U.S. Govt. Printing Office, 1970) pp. 3, 7, 10; SA *Handbook,* new pp. 207a–207d [secs. 13:7:3] dated January 1972; Minutes MSSS Commission June 2–3, 1976, pp. 16–18, 19; Minutes Comm. Conf. Oct. 1976, 175–177; William Moss to Col. George Nelting, NYC, April 8, 1976, all in file "MSS Sec. Commission 1976," MSSDC office files; Col. G. Ernest Murray to Cols. Miller, Patru, Pratt and Scott, NYC, March 26, 1980 and "Valuation Guide to Items Donated to The Salvation Army," 12/79, both courtesy Lt.-Col. David Riley at MSSS Conference, 1982; Salvation Army, *Men's Social Service Department Western Territory Accounting Manual,* revised October 1980 (np. SAWTHQ, 1980); printed in W, in national use; see pp. 1–4, 57–58, 35; Salvation Army, Eastern Territory, "Accounting Procedure Guide for use by The Men's Social Service Department in Adult Rehabilitation Centers and other Centers of Operation, compiled Major Donald E. Tolhurst, 1977; approved for national use, Comm. Conf. May 22–23, 1980; revised Oct. 21, 1980," pp. 4–7, MSSDE office files; Major Harold E. Shoults to all Directors, MSSDC, Chicago, Nov. 23, 1977, in Detroit ARC files; interview with Howell, who kindly explained D.I.K. and percentage remittance.

25. Comm. Holland French to Comm. S. Hepburn, NYC, Dec. 10, 1963; memo, 7 pp. typed, same to all officers MSSD, NYC, Mar. 2, 1964; Wm. J. Moss to Lt. Comm. John Grace, NYC, Jan. 26, 1965, 9 pp.; Cadwalader, Wickersham & Taft to Lt.-Col. Earl Crawford, NYC, Jan. 21, 1967; Wm. J. Moss to Lt.-Comm. Grace, NYC, Feb. 7, 1968; quotation from National Commander's memo of March 2, 1964, pp. 2–3; see entire memo in detail, all these materials in "FLSA: storage

files," MSSDC office files; Col. Paul Seiler to all mgrs, NYC, June 26, 1968, in Newark ARC office files; Lt. Col. Peter J. Hofman, "The Fair Labor Standards Act," "MSSDW Councils, 1964," p. 13; "Minutes, MSSDW Councils 1969," p. 9; Major George Baker, to all adms., Rancho Palos Verdes, Sept. 14, 1979, in "Directives file: 79-80," MSSDW office files; series of Dept. Directives confirming official adherence to *Handbook* standards: Brig. Warren Johnson Oct. 1, 1967, Lt.-Col. Warren Johnson, Aug. 26, 1976, Major David Mulbarger, Dec. 15, 1980, all directed to all mgrs., Atlanta, w/date; all in MSSD "Directives" file, MSSDS office files.

26. Minutes, MSSS Commission, May 24–25, 1973, pp. 2–3; May 16–17, 1974, p. 1 (includes ref. to Minutes Comm. Conf. Feb. 1974, pp. 146–148); W. J. Moss to Col. W. R. H. Goodier, NYC, Feb. 18, 1975; Minutes, MSSS Comm., June 2–3, 1976, p. 25 (includes Comm. Conf. Minutes Oct. 1976, pp. 190–213); see also Minutes Comm. Conf. Oct. 1976, pp. 145–147; Jan. 1977, p. 136 and Oct. 1977, p. 172, all these materials in "MSSS Commission" files, 1973–1977, in MSSDC office files; Salvation Army, *Men's Social Service Employees Manual*, approved by Commissioner's Conference, NYC, October, 1976 (no publ. data), pp. 8, 13–15, 18–21; Moss to Shoults, letter, NYC, June 26, 1985. See SA Minutes of the Men's Social Service Secretaries' Conference, October 3–5, 1956 (New York: SA NHQ, 1956), pp. 37–39.

27. Moss to Col. George Nelting, NYC, Oct. 13, 1977 in Minutes, MSSS Comm. 1977; Moss to Orval Taylor, NYC, Aug. 16, 1978, in Minutes MSSS Comm. 1978, in "MSSS Comm. Minutes," files, 1977–1978; Col. Gordon A. Foubister to MSSS, Chicago, March 28, 1977, in "MSSD Directives" files, all in MSSDC office files.

28. SA *Handbook,* 7:9:1–2; Moss to Orval Taylor, NYC, Oct. 13, 1978, in "Accreditation/Licensing ARC" file; Moss to Albert Scott, NYC, Dec. 14, 1978, in "Licensing Centers (USA)" file; Minutes, Comm. Conf. Feb. 1979, p. 134 in "MSSS Comm. Minutes 1979" file; Moss to G. Ernest Murray, NYC, July 25, 1980 and to Ms. Barbara Voltz, NYC, same date, in "MSSS Comm. Minutes, 1980," all in MSSDC office files; [George] Baker to James Osborne, Rancho Palos Verdes, Aug. 26, 1981; Jack Brown to Brobeck, Phleger & Harrison, Rancho Pl. Verd., Aug. 26, 1981; Wm. C. Anderson (Brobeck firm) to Brown, Los Angeles, Aug. 4, 1981, 7 pp. typed; W. J. Moss to G. E. Murray, NYC, Aug. 5, 1981, 3 pp. typed, all in General Files, "A-D Center Files," Lytton Springs case, MSSDW office files.

29. Minutes, MSSS Comm. June 2–3, 1976, pp. 4, 20–21; April 4–5, 1977, pp. 1–3; Comm. Conf. Oct. 1977, pp. 155–157, in "MSSS Commission" file, 1976–1977; Minutes, Comm. Conf. Sept. 1981, pp. 266–68; see also Jan. 1977, p. 148, Oct. 1976, pp. 182–83; letter to author, Lt.-Col. David Riley, Portland, Ore., Feb. 23, 1984; Lt. Col. David Riley, "Internal Accreditation Process for The Salvation Army Adult Rehabilitation Center, USA," copy of paper presented at Protestant Health and Welfare Assembly, Louisville, March 15, 1982, and guidelines on Program Staff and Officer "certification" programs, in MSSDW office files; interviews with Baker, Johnson.

30. *WC,* Sept. 25, 1886, p. 3, extolled "The Salvation Trades' Union," made up of saved workingmen; William Booth, *In Darkest England,* p. 112; *WCW,* June 6, 1891, p. 4; Adj. E. A. Hayes, "Stimulating and Maintaining the Morale of Men," "Papers Read at the Men's Social Service Officers' Councils, Philadelphia, June 3–4, 1936," p. 6, SAA 80/43; Minutes Comm. Conf. Sept. 13–14, 1944, pp. 17–19; May 14–16, 1947, p. 26 (quote); June 2–3, 1948, p. 5; file in "Pittsburgh No. 1

Chauffeurs (strike)" 1948–1950; "Minutes Personnel Board" (Sept. 14) and "Truck Drivers' Meeting" (Sept. 15) under cover F. Guldenschuh to Brig. Edward Howells, NYC, Sept. 28, 1960, these materials in SAA 78/24; brief reference to Brooklyn strike in Lt. Col. Ray Howell to Maj. Dorothy Breen, NYC, Jan. 15, 1985; "Teamsters' Union—Waukegan" [2 folders], MSSDC office files; Departmental Order, Index A-17, eff. 03-31-76, updated 10-15-80, 8 pp., in MSSDC "Department Orders," MSSDC office files; Jean C. Gaskill [Brobeck firm] to George Duplain, San Francisco, Jan. 14, 1982, 8 pp. enclosure; Lt.-Col. David Riley to all members, MSSS Comm., Rancho Palos Verdes, Jan. 11, 1982, 50 pp. enclosure, both in "MSSS Comm. 1982" file, MSSDC office files; Gaskill to Duplain, SF, Jan. 12, 1982 enclosing briefs NLRB No. 20-RC-15445, 228 NLRB 1134 1977, 225 NLRB 406 1976, 247 NLRB No. 62 (1979), all in San Francisco ARC office files; interviews with Hasney, Caldwell, Duplain; Moss letter to Shoults, NYC, June 26, 1985.

31. Minutes, Comm. Conf. May 24–26, 1961, pp. 83–84; Oct. 4–6, 1961, p. 64; Feb. 7–9, 1962, pp. 77–78; May 9–11, 1962, p. 87; Col Gordon Eplett to Maj. Hasney, Chicago, May 5, 1977, "Directives" file, MSSDC office files; Minutes, MSSS Comm. June 2–3, 1976, pp. 23–25 and p. 11; Minutes Comm. Conference, Oct. 1976, p. 169; Oct. 1977, pp. 160–161, all in "MSSS Comm." files, 1976–1977, MSSDC office; Comm. Conf. Minutes, Feb. 1981, pp. 178–180; May, 1981, pp. 375–77; Sept. 1981, pp. 271–272, in "MSSS Comm." 1981 file, MSSDC office; Minute No. 205, rev. 15 Dec. 1981 and No. 201, rev. July 27, 1982, both in "Minute Book Southern Territory," MSSDS office.

32. Letter to author, Lt.-Col. Ray Howell, NYC, Aug. 8, 1983; "Working Document: The Salvation Army Men's Social Service Handbook of Standards, Principles, and Policies," approved by Comm. Conf. 1981, courtesy of Maj. George Baker, MSSDW; letters to author, Captain (Dr.) Robert Bodine, Fresno, Calif., July 21, 1983, and April 26, 1984 covering abstract of Robert James Bodine, "A Study of Crisis in a Residential Treatment Center for Alcoholics" (dissertation, Doctor of Social Work, Univ. of Southern California, 1974); program for dedication of Lake Havasu plaque, Feb. 4, 1975, courtesy Lt.-Col. David Moulton; interviews with Howell, Baker, Hofman.

33. And without being included in a major, if short-lived project. *The Second Century Advance: Recommended Action Plans for The Salvation Army as Prepared by the National Committee of Task Force Chairmen, Oct. 26, 1981,* unaccountably made almost no reference to the Men's Social Service Department: even the pages given to "social service work" (21–22) were phrased in general terms and seem to refer to corps and divisional operations. This official report represented the work of territorial "task forces" appointed by the Commissioners to make long range planning recommendations for the Army's second hundred years in the USA. Interviews with Fleming, McCabe. Factual data in the text from MSSDW, "Annual Review, Jan. 12, 1982," "Financial Report Comparison 12 Months Ending Sept. 30, 1981," p. 58 (four territories), from territorial and national statistics published in latest issues of territorial *Dispos* (Nov. 1983) and discussions with Howell, Hasney, Allen, Mulbarger.

34. *WC* Nov. 14, 1981, pp. 20–21; Jan. 8, 1983, pp. 4–5; Jan. 16, 1983, p. 1, 3; July 23, 1983, pp. 12–13; Jan. 14, 1984, p. 21; MSSDW, "Annual Report 1982," adherents, pp. 3–4, 6, 80; letters to author, Brig. Robt. Yardley, San Jose, California, March 26, 1984; Lt. Col. David Riley, Portland, Ore. Feb. 23, 1984; The Salvation Army, *Definitive Statement of The Salvation Army Services and Ac-*

tivities in the United States of America approved by the Comm. Conf., NYC, March 1957; revised 1969, 1979, p. 19 ("adherent"); letter to author, Major Robert Tobin, Rancho Palos Verdes, March 23, 1984; interviews with Howell, R. E. Holz, Hasney, Caldwell, Allen, Johnson, Duplain.

35. Institution histories for all 25 ARCs; "MSSDC Program Review, April 1982;" Lt.-Col. Wm. Hasney [to all mgrs.], Chicago, June 16, 1982, 11 pp.; same to all directors, Chicago, March 28, 1977 in "MSSD Directives" file, all these materials in MSSDC office files; interview with Caldwell; *WC* Nov. 14, 1981, pp. 17, 22.

36. Letter to author, Major A. S. Peters, Atlanta, March 30, 1984; *The Southern Spirit* (terr. newsletter), March 5, 1984, pp. 1, 3; "Departmental Orders," April 2, 1959 in "Departmental Orders, MSSD [1950–1959]," Territorial "Minute" No. 35B, Nov. 25, 1980, p. 3, in "Minute Book, THQS;" *Corps Salvage and Rehabilitation Center Manual* (Atlanta: Southern Territorial Finance Council, Nov. 1980), these materials in MSSDS office files; interviews with Ditmer, Mulbarger, Peters; *WC* Nov. 14, 1981, p. 19.

37. MSSDE, "Financial and Statistical Report for 12 Months Ending Sept. 30, 1982," MSSDE office files; "Center Histories," Newark, Jersey City, Manhattan/ New York No. 1, SAA; letters to author, Capt. Timothy Raines, NYC, Feb. 21, 1984; Lt. Col. Paul Seiler, NYC, April 12, July 9, 1984; Program dedication "our new Social Service Institution for Men," Newark, April 21, 1929, courtesy Castagna; *WC* Feb. 5, 1983, p. 15; March 17, 1984, p. 14; "NOM" Summer 1979, p. 3.

38. Mrs. Lt. Col. Ray Howell to author, NYC, Feb. 7, 1984 and Oct. 3, 1984; Lt.-Col. Charles Southwood to Mrs. Major R. Howell, NYC, May 16, 1979 in MSSDE office files; "NOM," Sept. 1979, p. 1; book of letters, "What is The Place of the Woman Officer in The Salvation Army," MSSDE, covered by letter, Mrs. Lt.-Col. Raymond Howell to Mrs. Comm. Orval Taylor, NYC, July 19, 1983; Mrs. Lt.-Col. Howell, "The Role of Women Officers in the Men's Social Service Department," Cadets' Seminar, Jan. 20, 1984, all in MSSDE office files; Mrs. Lt.-Col. Ray Howell to author, covering copies of two "Farewell Brief for Center (Women Officer)," for Mrs. Capt. T. Raines [Trenton], NYC, Sept. 2, 1982; *WC*, July 16, 1983, p. 15; interviews with Irwin, Bevan, Harvey, Craytor, Mrs. Howell.

39. "National Composite Analysis of Adult Rehabilitation Center Questionnaires Fair Labor Standards Act for Years Ending Dec. 31, 1957, 1979, 1980, 1981," MSSS Conference, Chicago, May 17, 1982; interviews with Raines, Lane, Castagna, Caldwell, Baker, Hofman, Howell, Hasney, Allen, Mulbarger (visits to various centers in all territories); "Center History: the Bronx," SAA; *WC*, Nov. 14, 1981 the 1st issue (national) devoted to MSSD in USA (Gariepy interview); Major Clarence Kinnett, "Keeping a Balance," *The Officer*, (May 1979), p. 226; "NOM," Sept. 20, 1963, p. 4; Sept. 1982, p. 2 (see also March 1976, p. 1); Warren Johnson address Feb. 25, 1975, pp. 14–20, in "MSSS Conf. April 1975 FLSA" file, MSSDC office files; "Lt.-Col. Peter Hofman, Adm. & Program Consultant," file, MSSDS office files; William Booth, "The Open Door Before The Salvation Army," *International Staff Council Addresses, 1904, by the General Together with Various Papers by Commissioners and Others* (London: The Salvation Army Book Department, 1904), p. 26; Clinebell, *Understanding*, p. 100; letter to author, Major Ronald Larsen, Indianapolis, Aug. 2, 1983; *WC*, Nov. 14, 1981, p. 24 and interview with Dyer; program, "The Salvation Army Eastern Territory: Camp Meeting Congress, June 8–11, 1984, Ocean Grove, NJ."

Bibliographical Essay

The present volume is the first comprehensive history of the Salvation Army Men's Social Service Department over the whole period of its operation in the United States. Scholarly professional interest in the rehabilitation program for men in The Salvation Army has not been extensive. The endnotes for the present volume, particularly those for Chapter VI, contain a thorough sampling of materials available at the time research on the volume was conducted. There are several causes for this poverty of scholarly references to the work of the Army, which are discussed in the relevant parts of the text itself. Whatever they are, the result has been that the present history of the Salvation Army Men's Social Service Department rests largely upon documentary materials generated by The Salvation Army itself. To the extent that this is a weakness, it is an unavoidable one.

There is certainly no shortage of internal materials, in terms of sheer volume, but these vary widely in quality and in both chronological and geographical distribution. Published materials such as *The War Cry* are useful—in fact, indispensable, as there are often no other materials available, particularly for the early years—in providing details about the development of programs, but far less valuable in evaluating the results. The recollections of retired, and the reflections of active, officers are more useful in this evaluation, and in filling in much that the printed record omits. Most useful of all in understanding the development of programs and whether or not these programs were regarded by officers and clients as successful, and why, are surviving correspondence, evaluations and reports which were prepared only for private, official use. There is a large amount of such material, preserved in the Salvation Army Archives and Research Center, in the offices of the four territorial men's social service departments and in private hands, but what has survived is only a small part of what was generated, and for earlier periods follows no chronological or topical pattern.

The Salvation Army Archives and Research Center, 145 W. 15th St.,
New York City, New York (10011), contains the largest collection in the
country of materials illustrating the history of The Salvation Army. The
library contains a large collection of books, pamphlets and printed materials, printed and mimeographed collections of minutes and papers read at
territorial, national and international social officers' councils and other
materials relating to the history of the Men's Social Service Department in
the United States. For the period up until 1920, when three territories were
created, and 1927, when the Southern Territory was created, the archives
houses the best available collection of materials on the nationwide development of the Army. For material on the period since 1927 the archives
collections center disproportionately on the Eastern Territory, although
there are many items from other territories as well. The archives also
contains originals of many, and microfilm of all, surviving issues of Salvation Army serial publications produced in the United States since 1881;
most importantly these include *The War Cry* (USA National edition, 1881–
1921, 1970–present; Pacific Coast edition, 1883–1900, Eastern Territorial
edition, 1921–1970, Western Territorial edition, 1921–1970; Central Territorial edition, 1921–1970; Southern Territorial edition 1927–1970), *The
Conqueror* (1892–1897), *Harbor Lights* (1898–1900), *Social News* (1911–
1922, called *War Service Herald,* 1917–1919); and of many important
international publications as well, including the valuable *Officer* (*The
Officer* began publishing in January 1893 [the first editor was Frederick
Booth-Tucker]; from January 1900 to June 1913, it was called *The Field
Officer;* in July 1913, it resumed the title *The Officer* and continued as such
until January 1932; from 1922 to January 1932, there was an additional
journal, *The Staff Review;* these two were amalgamated in the January–
February 1932 issue of a new journal, *The Officer's Review,* which con-
tinued until the January–February 1950, issue, when it became, as it had
begun, *The Officer,* which continues to the present [1985]), and the annual
Salvation Army Year Book.

The archives' vertical files, arranged by individual men's social service
centers, contain items from the entire period of the operation of each
center, often including dedication programs, newspaper clippings, Service-to-Man questionnaires and pamphlets. There is much of interest in
the alphabetical files listed as "Broadway files" [1982]. The archives has a
large collection of historic photographs related to the history of the
department, many of them cataloged, including four large green photo
albums of Army properties nationwide 1903–1910.

During the period 1982–1985 during which research on the present volume was conducted, the archives housed a number of record groups containing materials from, or related to, the Men's Social Service Department. These are briefly summarized in the following list:

Accession Number 78-24: "Chaplain's Brief, Men's Social Service Department, Eastern Territory, USA, Oct. 1, 1929;" six large ledgers, "Finance and General Statistics," 1: 1921–1923, 2: 1930–1932, 3: 1932–1934, 4: 1939–1943, 5: 1934–1941, 6: 1945–1948; annual reports and audits, 1935–1970; two blue bound typescript volumes, "Salvation Army Annual Reports, Men's Social Service Department, Eastern Territory, USA," Vol. I, Jan. 1, 1931–Dec. 31, 1935, Vol. II, Oct. 1935–Sept. 30, 1940, inclusive; correspondence, minutes of meetings, reports on the development of Service to Man in the Eastern Territory, 1941–1959, including surveys prepared by Adjutant A. E. Agnew for the 1944 "Institutes;" "1957–1960: Brief for Incoming Officer, Jersey City, NJ;" Harris, Kerr & Forster, audits for proposed MSSD consolidation project, for Eastern Territory for year ending Sept. 30, 1970 and for each center, Eastern and Central Territories, 1969–1971; "Men's Social Program Helps for Men," beginning 1973.

Acc. 78-25: [Box 3]: "Report to the Chief of the Staff from Commander Evangeline Booth, Jan. 1918, regarding status of Salvation Army operations in the USA in 1917 in comparison with 1905 when separation was made;" "To the Chief of the Staff: A Review of Salvation Army Affairs in the Eastern Territory USA for the year 1918" [two reports].

Acc. 78-27: material related to MSSDE [unprocessed].

Acc. 80-3: "Farewell Brief, McKeesport, Pa., Jan. 9, 1953;" "Brief: Administration Dayton Ohio Sr.-Major Clarence A. Simmons, 1957–1960" [June 26, 1960]."

Acc. 80-18: brochures by E. J. Parker.

Acc. 80-43: Minutes, MSSDE Officers' Councils, 1933–37, 1947–48.

Acc. 80-44: bound in binders, photocopies of correspondence, Commissioner Edward J. Parker, 1899–1920.

Acc. 81-9: bound volume of separate orders, "Special Orders to Social District Officer," originals from Philadelphia No. 1 Industrial Home.

Acc. 81-45: red morocco book stamped "Chief Secretary," contains report and statistics on all Army operations in the U.S., 1904–1913.

Acc. 81-56: material from Commissioner E. J. Parker.

Acc. 81-74: [box 3]: "Annual Report, National Commission on Problems of Alcoholism, Salvation Army Section, National Conference on

Social Work, April 16, 1948;" "Proceedings Chicago Institute on Problems of Alcoholism, Chicago, Ill., April 7, 1948."

Acc. 82-3: "Memoirs of Annie Laurie: Fifty Years of Service in The Salvation Army," St. Petersburg, Fla., 42 pp. typescript.

Acc. 82-25: Diary of Frederick Booth-Tucker, microfilm.

Acc. 82-26: scrapbook, prepared by E. J. Parker in 1905 for visit of Commissioner Randolph J. Sturgiss in 1906, contains material on Industrial Homes in Newark and Jersey City and on Braveman Hotel.

Acc. 82-46: [Boxes 1–5], "Finance Department," has material on MSSD operations, esp. Box 2, income and expense data, and Box 4, "Adjustments of Industrial Rents."

Acc. 82-75: "Brief Memoranda of National and Chief Divisional Staff Councils Held in New York, May 16–19, 1899," 26 pp. typed; material from Commissioner Richard E. Holz [Sr.].

Acc. 82-80: material from Lt.-Colonel Peter J. Hofman.

Record Group 1-10-5: Madison J. H. Ferris.

Record Group 1.2: Industrial Home Company Records.

Record Group 2.10.1: Finance Department Series 12 account books, esp. Vol. 2, corps and institutions listed alphabetically by capital account, 1937–1946.

Record Group 26.10.1: Correspondence, Property and Legal Secretaries.

MS 13:1–5: material from Lt.-Colonel Wallace Winchell.

MS 15: Diary, [Richard E.] Holz, 1892.

MS 16: material from Frederick Booth-Tucker.

MS 20: Charles C. Welte Family Papers.

MS 31:1:1: "Analysis of 856 Case Files at The Salvation Army Wrigley Shelter, Chicago, Illinois, as of August 26, 1933."

FIN 33–38, 40–41, 69, 81–83, 93–94: microfilm rolls of ledger pages; 34–35 are MSS cash ledgers, 40 is General Social, 41 is Family Welfare, 69, acct. 38 is "Industrial Homes," 69 acct. 261 begins "Hotel and Shelter Accounts."

Men's Social Service Department offices, Eastern Territory, 120 West 14th Street, New York City, house the oldest and largest of the four territorial departments which, in addition, was the center of national administration of men's social activities until the territorial subdivisions of 1920 and 1927. Although it does not cover every aspect of operations for any period except the most recent and in addition has chronological gaps from which no records remain, this is by far the largest and most useful of all departmental collections. It includes: "Brief for Major Jenkins, Re: Metropolitan Province, Aug. 1, 1901;" "Personal Minute Book, Lt.-Colonel Chas. Welte" [1903–1904]; "Brief, Re: The Shelters, March 2, 1904;" another "Shelter Brief" [1902]; "Social Department of the East, Brief, April 1911–Jan. 1913," large bound volume, lettered in gold, containing correspondence, memos and papers read at the Social Department Officers' Councils, June 1912; "Special Orders for Social Officers," bound volume of minutes, 1910–1911; *Officers' Handbook for Men's Social Work,* gray canvas covers, signed E. J. Parker, 1922–1923, includes later "Minutes," 1928–1936; Shipping Book, Industrial Home [Erie Pa], 1922–1933; Cash Book, Industrial Home, Brooklyn, 1926–1928; Cash Book, Industrial Home, Erie Pa., 1930–1932; Anita Phillipson, "Study of the Columbus Salvation Army Industrial Home," (MA Thesis, Ohio State University, 1930), 2 vols.; "Brief, Syracuse Social Service Center, Sept. 1934;" collections of papers read at MSSDE Officers' Councils held in 1934, 1938, 1949, 1951, 1954, 1956, 1959, 1969; Nels Anderson and Sylvia R. Harris, "Report on the Men's Social Service Department of The Salvation Army in New York City," (Welfare Council, New York City, Research Bureau, 1931); personal Minute Book, Brigadier J. O. Dowdell; MSSDE Annual Reports, 1931–1940; large ledger sheets, MSSDE Income, 1942–1947; "Studies Made at the Men's Social Service Institutions by Adjutant A. E. Agnew, 1942–1943;" comparative income and statistical studies of institutions in territory, 1947–1962; Hotel Register (Manhattan), 1944–1946; binder marked "Lt.-Colonel J. Phillips," financial returns, men's social service centers, 1946–1965; program for Paterson Golden Jubilee, 1947; programs from MSSDE Officers' Councils held in 1948, 1949, 1951, 1959, 1960, 1965, 1968, 1974; Minutes, Executive Officers' Conference, Atlantic City, April 20–22, 1955; leather bound volume, minutes and correspondence, men's social service secretary, 1949–1953; leather binders marked "Lt.-Colonel H. R. Smith" and "Colonel Paul Seiler;" Harris, Kerr & Forster analyses of Metropolitan New York area and Boston Centers, 1969; three large wire-bound green volumes of mimeographed newsletters: "Social Service Siftings," [April 1927, to Aug. 1927], which became "News of the Week" [April 24, 1928] and finally "News of the Moment" [May 3, 1928] in Vol. 1 (1926 [1927]–1929), Vol. 2 (1932–1935) and Vol. 3 (1935–1938); files, "Historical Data 7a;" "SA Historical Conference 7;" and "Newspaper Clippings;" materials in the office of Mrs. Lt.-Colonel

Howell on the role of women in the department, program helps, etc. Career sheets on officers in this department provided by Salvation Army Archives and Field Secretary for Personnel.

Men's Social Service Department offices, Central Territory, 860 North Dearborn Ave., Chicago, contain the most complete and best prepared set of "Center Histories" of any in the four departments; the center files have many historical items, and are complete for the past dozen years; current departmental files include department orders since 1974. There are a large number of valuable historical files listed as in "Storage;" these include many files on Fair Labor Standards Act developments [sometimes filed under "FLSA"], and on the activities of the Men's Social Service Secretaries' Conference [or Commission]. There are center and departmental analyses, 1954–1962, and statistical worksheets, 1954–1959, and much besides. Career sheets for officers in this department provided by the Assistant Field Secretary for Personnel.

Men's Social Service Department offices, Southern Territory, 1424 NE Expressway, Atlanta, Georgia, contain many subject files of great historical value, a good collection of uncataloged photographs of centers and operations since 1927, a set of "Monday Morning Letters," 1942–1947, from A. E. Baldwin [copies in SAA]; "Brief for Men's Social Service Department, Southern Territory of The Salvation Army, Lt.-Colonel Gilbert S. Decker, Aug. 30, 1953," a valuable historical description of the entire department; "Minutes, District Social Officers' Councils, Washington, D.C. Feb. 7–10, 1923;" "Brief, Los Angeles Men's Social Service Center, Warren Johnson, Jan. 31, 1965;" "Departmental Orders, Men's Social Service Department" [1950–1959]. Career sheets for officers in this department provided by the Assistant Field Secretary for Personnel.

Men's Social Service Department offices, Western Territory, 30840 Hawthorne Blvd., Rancho Palos Verdes, California, have extensive and well-arranged files on current activities, but have retained the least amount of material relating to activities before 1976, of any of the four departments. There are a number of excellent photographs in the office of the administrative assistant to the MSSS [1982]. Career sheets for officers in this department provided by the Chief Secretary and the Field Secretary for Personnel. In addition the Chief Secretary, Colonel James Osborne, kindly made a complete set of the minutes of the Commissioners' Conference available to the author in 1982.

Several *Adult Rehabilitation Centers* have files that contain much of historical interest, although the press of current business activities allows for little long-term storage in most centers. Among centers with historical files of value are Manhattan, Detroit and Columbus (where Brigadier Lawrence Castagna (R), has collected a large amount of photocopied material); Mr. Ron Carr, public relations officer at the Santa Ana ARC, has collected a number of excellent photographs showing the development of men's social operations over time.

The Libraries and Museums of the four Territorial Schools for Officers' Training contain much of value relating to the development of the men's social service department in each territory. The library and museum of the East, in Suffern, NY, is particularly valuable in this respect; it contains a large number of historic items, both in the museum and library (lock case and pamphlet files). The museum at the Western school has a large collection of well-cataloged historic photographs, and the library has, among many useful items, a collection of the minutes and papers, Salvation Army sessions, National Conference on Social Work, 1936–1954, 1956, 1958, 1959, 1963, 1964, 1967. The SFOT Museum's collection in Atlanta was not cataloged when the author visited in 1984; there are many items of interest housed there, including posters, photographs, many programs, a set of cadets' notes [1912] covered by letter, Captain Phil Needham to Major Fred Ruth, St. Petersburg, Fla., June 29, 1978, and "Farewell Brief for Major Glen Winters by Major David Mulbarger [Miami, Fla.] Jan. 25, 1978." The school library and museum in Chicago likewise has several interesting items, but the holdings related to men's social operations are not extensive. All four SFOT Libraries contain complete runs of the national serial publications and those of the particular territory, either in original or on microfilm, or both, and the standard SA historical and biographical works. The Field Departments of each territory contain the most complete run of territorial *Disposition of Forces* as can be obtained.

Private Collections. The collection of Colonel Paul Seiler (R), Ocean Grove, NJ, is the largest and most valuable private collection of Army historical material in the United States; it is not fully cataloged, but contains a large number of interesting and useful items, including correspondence, posters, photographs, pamphlets, the brief on "The Decision of the Supreme Court of California [1916]," and "Brief of Appointment, Social District Officer, Eastern Pennsylvania District, Lt.-Colonel Chas. Welte, Nov. 1, 1929." Commissioner Richard E. Holz and his brother, Commissioner Ernest W. Holz, formerly the national commander, possess a large collection of valuable materials, much of it from the hand of

their grandfather, the first Commissioner Richard E. Holz. Of special
value for this study was a collection of letters sent and received by then
Colonel R. E. Holz as national social secretary, 1898–1899, kindly lent to
the author by Commissioner Richard Holz in 1982, who also provided
useful information on the development of the adherents' program in the
Western Territory and on the social service bands of the 1930s in the East.
Brigadier Lawrence Castagna (R) has made a long and careful study of the
history of the Army, particularly of all aspects of the work in Columbus,
Ohio, and of men's social operations in general. He has a large collection
of correspondence and photocopied materials which he kindly made available to the author, and which proved of great value. Major John Busby,
Atlanta, also has a considerable private collection of Army memorabilia
and historic documents, including a complete series of "Minutes from the
Chief of the Staff," 1889–1908.

THE RANKS OF THE SALVATION ARMY, 1878–1985

RANK	ADOPTED	CURRENT STATUS
General	gradually assumed from 1878	active
Chief of the Staff*	1880	active
Commissioner	1880	active
Lieutenant-Commissioner	1920	discontinued 1973
Colonel	1880	active
Lieutenant-Colonel	1896	active
Brigadier	1889	discontinued 1973
Senior-Major	1948	discontinued 1959
Major	1879	active
Staff-Captain	1881	discontinued 1931
Field-Major	1923	discontinued 1931
Commandant	1916	discontinued 1931
Adjutant	1888	discontinued 1948
Ensign	1888	discontinued 1931
Senior-Captain	1948	discontinued 1959
Captain	gradually assumed from 1877	active
Lieutenant	1879	active
Second Lieutenant	1948	discontinued 1959
Probationary Lieutenant	as early as 1917	discontinued 1973
Cadet	1880	active

*Not formally a rank, but a position held by a Commissioner.

From 1887 to 1934 the National Commander of The Salvation Army in the United States, although holding a rank equivalent to Commissioner, was given the title of, and addressed as, "Commander," and is still entitled to that form as a courtesy.

RANKS OF THE SALVATION ARMY, continued

Ranks in use for various years:

1890	1920	1940	1950	1985
General	General	General	General	General
Chief of the Staff	Chief of the Staff	Chief of the Staff	Chief of the Staff	Chief of the Staff
Commissioner	Commissioner	Commissioner	Commissioner	Commissioner
Colonel	Lieut.-Commissioner	Lieut.-Commissioner	Lieut.-Commissioner	Colonel
Brigadier	Colonel	Colonel	Colonel	Lieut.-Colonel
Major	Lieut.-Colonel	Lieut.-Colonel	Lieut.-Colonel	Major
Staff-Captain	Brigadier	Brigadier	Brigadier	Captain
Adjutant	Major	Major	Senior-Major	Lieutenant
Ensign	Staff-Captain	Adjutant	Major	Cadet
Captain	Commandant	Captain	Senior-Captain	
Lieutenant	Adjutant	Lieutenant	Captain	
Cadet	Ensign	Probationary Lieut.	Lieutenant	
	Captain	Cadet	Second Lieutenant	
	Lieutenant		Cadet	
	Probationary Lieutenant			
	Cadet			

MEN'S SOCIAL SERVICE SECRETARIES, 1896–1985

NATIONAL HEADQUARTERS, 1896–1905
William Halpin, June 1896, National Social Secretary
Thomas Holland, September 1896, National Secretary for Social Work
    February 1897—"Men's Social Wing"
Jan.–April 1897—Divisional Social Superintendents
    Pacific Coast—William Wallace Winchell
    Northwestern—John Newton Parker
    Greater New York—Joseph McFee
July 1897
    Northern Pacific—F. H. Fowler
Richard E. Holz, October 1897, National Secretary for City Colonies
[The first appointment of an officer to the sole responsibility of supervising men's social operations in the United States]

From October 1899 until October 1903 supervision of men's social activities was divided among several offices; in October 1903 all men's social operations were divided into two branches:

> Thomas W. Scott, October 1903, Secretary, National Industrial Department
>
> Edward J. Parker, October 1903, Secretary, National Metropole & Relief Department

DEPARTMENT OF THE EAST, 1905–1920
Edward J. Parker, Private Secretary to the Chief Secretary for Social Work, then Secretary, Department of the Metropolis [both 1905]

Thomas W. Scott, Secretary, Midwestern Social Province

Edward J. Parker, Men's Social Service Secretary, 1908 [until 1927; separate Eastern Territory created 1920]

DEPARTMENT OF THE WEST, 1905–1920
Ashley Pebbles, 1905
Emil Marcussen, 1908
    The Department of the West was divided into three parts from 1909–1913:

> Western Social Department—John C. Addie
> Pacific Coast Social Dept.—Emil Marcussen
> Central Social Department [1910–1911]—Thomas Holland

Emil Marcussen, 1913

MEN'S SOCIAL SERVICE SECRETARIES

EASTERN TERRITORY, 1920–1985

Edward J. Parker	1908
Charles C. Welte	1927
(Edward Underwood, interim	1932)
Vernon Post	1933
Joseph O. Dowdell	1935
Harold Smith	1945
Ernest A. Marshall	1954
Frank Guldenschuh	1959
Paul Seiler	1965
Giles Barrett	1968
William Charron	1970
(William Benton*	1972)
Raymond Howell	1972

WESTERN TERRITORY, 1920–1985

Emil Marcussen	1920
Arthur E. Smeeton	1923
Christian Christopherson	1924
Arthur E. Smeeton	1925
Archibald Layman	1931
Sydney Cooke	1945
Harry B. Stillwell	1951
Peter J. Hofman	1958
Warren C. Johnson	1965
George Duplain	1967
Ranson D. Gifford (R)**	1968
Arthur Carl	1970
David Riley	1976
David Allen	1982

CENTRAL TERRITORY, 1920–1985

David Miller	1920
Fletcher Agnew	1928
Harper Crawford	1931
Albert W. Baillie	1932
Frank Genge	1938
Albert E. Baldwin	1946
John C. Marshall	1948
Earl Crawford	1955
Railton Genge	1963
William Gant	1973
William Hasney	1976

SOUTHERN TERRITORY, 1927–1985

Albert W. Baillie	1927
John McGee	1928
Albert W. Baillie	1929
Albert E. Baldwin, Asst. Secretary, 1932–1935; no Secretary listed	
William H. Range	1935
Albert E. Baldwin, Acting Secretary	1938
Albert E. Baldwin	1939
Gilbert S. Decker	1946
Lawrence W. Turrel	1953
William L. Devoto	1960
Warren C. Johnson	1967
David Mulbarger	1979

*died after one day in office
**retired officer who returned to active service

Index

265

STUDIES IN AMERICAN RELIGION